SOUTHERN EMANCIPATOR

SOUTHERN EMANCIPATOR

MONCURE CONWAY,
The American Years
1832–1865

John d'Entremont

New York   Oxford
OXFORD UNIVERSITY PRESS
1987

Oxford University Press

Oxford   New York   Toronto
Delhi   Bombay   Calcutta   Madras   Karachi
Petaling Jaya   Singapore   Hong Kong   Tokyo
Nairobi   Dar es Salaam   Cape Town
Melbourne   Auckland
and associated companies in
Beirut   Berlin   Ibadan   Nicosia

Copyright © 1987 by John d'Entremont

Published by Oxford University Press, Inc.,
200 Madison Avenue, New York, New York 10016

Oxford is a registered trademark of Oxford University Press

Library of Congress Cataloging-in-Publication Data
d'Entremont, John, 1950–
   Southern emancipator.
   Bibliography: p.   Includes index.
   1. Conway, Moncure Daniel, 1832–1907.
2. Abolitionists—United States—Biography.
3. Unitarians—United States—Biography.
4. Slavery—United States—Anti-slavery movements. I. Title.
E449.C768D46   1987   973.6'092'4[B]   86-23756
ISBN 0-19-504264-6 (alk. paper)

10 9 8 7 6 5 4 3 2 1
Printed in the United States of America

For my mother

PREFACE

Little boxes are the sinful temptation of biographers and the bane of historical figures. Biographers build boxes; their subjects are stuffed inside. Too often the exercise has the look of any packaging process: the outside shines, but obscures the thing within.

I have tried not to do this to Moncure Conway, whose own life was especially defiant of little boxes. I have resisted formally subdividing this study of what I call his "American years" into more precise categories. His life, like many others and probably more than most, was constantly redefining itself, even at times of greatest surface calm.

Some readers, however, may still want a more precise map through the vast landscape that follows. They may, with the above caveat, proceed as follows: The first three chapters describe Conway's aristocratic Virginia background and analyze the process by which he gradually came to question and reject it. The middle three consider the evolution of his career as social reformer and religious radical, focusing successively on his education at Harvard Divinity School (with his simultaneous public commitment to abolitionism) and his controversial ministries in Washington and Cincinnati. The final three recount his Civil War experience, culminating in his unhappy decision to remove himself physically from a conflict that was killing his spirit. The postscript briefly summarizes his later career and his ongoing intellectual and moral pilgrimage, though those years really constitute the second and last major portion of his life, what I choose to call his transatlantic years.

Boxes again. American. Transatlantic. This time, though, they make sense. Conway's American years ended, in a real way, in 1865, with the close of the Civil War. Although he had been in England for two years by then, the war had continued to haunt him and consume his energies. Once it ended, he was free—thanks largely to his providential new job at London's South Place Chapel—to begin a new life.

For the rest of his days Conway would be a transatlantic man, sailing the ocean so many times that the crew of the *New York* would call him their mascot. He would live mainly in London until 1885, mainly in New York from 1885 to 1893, mainly in London from 1893 to 1897, mainly in Paris from 1898 to his death in 1907. Always, he would travel widely. Throughout, he would consider himself a citizen of the world. It was no accident that his best scholarly work was a life of another such citizen, Thomas Paine.

So to that extent the boxes fit, if not entirely. This book on the American years, though the first of a projected two-volume work, appropriately stands alone and self-contained.

Authors, however, seldom stand alone; and this work has depended on the inspiration, criticism, and kindness of many. Willie Lee Rose first suggested the idea to me, and nurtured it into a healthy obsession. She gave me intellectual sustenance and personal support; and when disaster rendered her unable to help the project further, she boosted my fortitude and faith through her own example of determination and courage. I know of no other professor who elicited such loyalty and love from his or her students. There is not one of hers who is not grateful, and proud.

I was lucky to have the considerable help of William Freehling and Ronald Walters in the project's later stages. Their careful, frank, and cogent comments on the manuscript improved the final product immensely. I am grateful for both their criticism and their friendship.

Special thanks are also due to Walter Beach, Lori and Randall Bishop, Anna Bryan, Peter Cadogan, Bill Harris, Katherine Conway Haymes, Terry and Tom Jacklin, David and Naomi Lamoreaux, Terry Rockefeller, Charles Coleman Sellers, Martha Slotten, Danna Spitzform, Sam Tanenhaus, Rachel Toor, Dennis Welland, the staff at the manuscripts room of the Butler Library at Columbia University, and the members and friends of the South Place Ethical Society, London.

Eleanor Conway Sawyer, Moncure Conway's granddaughter and last direct descendant, did not live to see this book in print. She did, however, live to read the manuscript in dissertation form and for more than eight years offered help, encouragement, good cheer, and acid wit. She was a joy to know.

J.D'E.

Boston
June 1986

CONTENTS

INTRODUCTION

Frances Garrison Villard was almost sixty-three in 1907, though that seemed, she thought, "incredible." Her famous abolitionist father was nearly thirty years dead, her dashing industrialist husband over seven. The big house on Madison Avenue was getting lonely, and steadily there were fewer and fewer who understood. They were dying now, one by one, those grand old antislavery warriors who remembered the antebellum past, who *were* that past, national treasures a country in a hurry seemed no longer to cherish. Another was moving to the grave on this fittingly terrible mid-December day—gray, vicious, a torrential rain mixing with wet snow, a gale turning umbrellas inside out or breaking them. It was not a day to be outside when one felt old. But she had to go. She wanted to go. So she pulled on her gloves and her boots and the armor of her warmest coat, and walked out to face the world.[1]

The one hundred fifty mourners assembled in the basement, the only space big enough in Eustace Conway's house to hold them. Eustace was a shy man, few people really knew him, but today he carried himself well. He sat at the front in an armchair, flanked by a bust of his father and a small table, resplendent with roses, on which sat a simple square wooden box containing the ashes of Moncure Conway.

Fanny Garrison took her seat. Unitarian minister Robert Collyer spoke first, in his picturesque Yorkshire brogue, touching the audience with stories of a fifty-one-year friendship now broken. Then Eustace read a tribute by Ralph Waldo Emerson's son Edward, and a young man from London's South Place Chapel movingly sang Moncure's favorite hymn, "Sweet day, so cool, so calm, so bright." Bronson Howard of the Authors Club followed, then Harriot Stanton Blatch, who made closing remarks and read the burial service used by Conway during his South Place ministry. Fanny Garrison knew what a painful labor of love this was for Blatch, whose mother, feminist leader Elizabeth Cady

Stanton, had so prized the man now leaving them. Five years earlier Conway had been the chief eulogist and one of the few males at Stanton's private funeral, and his talk on that occasion had been one of his most eloquent.

It was over. It had been short, simple, very moving, and altogether unchurchlike. "Nothing was said of immortality," noted one guest, "of his continued living excepting in the hearts of those *who loved him*."[2]

And many did. Anyone scanning the room could see that, and could not help being struck by their variety. There were conventional Christians, Unitarians, freethinkers, atheists; Americans and Europeans; writers, reformers, businessmen, lawyers, artists, housewives; rich (Andrew Carnegie was there, remembering Conway's recent visit to his Scotland castle, when Conway had danced a reel with the servants) and not so rich; famous and unknown; and, appropriately for this man, an equal dash of men and women.[3]

There were many more who could not be there. In Paris, young photographer Edward Steichen remembered this "big man" who had so enriched his life and those of other young writers and artists. In London, members and supporters of South Place moved to endow a yearly lecture in Conway's name. (The subscription list included William Michael Rossetti, J. A. Hobson, and Havelock Ellis.) Later they would build Conway Hall, which still remains a haven in the heart of London for truth seekers and unpopular causes. And in Washington, D.C., a black man remembered Conway's service to his slave parents during the Civil War, when Conway personally had taken them to Ohio and settled them as free people. "I have often heard them speak of the noble deeds of this grand man," wrote Peter McGwinn. "I rejoice to know that my ancestors and my people as a whole had the protecting influence of so great a man."[4]

Moncure Conway, to borrow a phrase from Walt Whitman, contained multitudes. He was successively Methodist minister, Unitarian minister, Theistic minister, freethought minister, no minister at all. He was a Southerner who left the South, an American who left America, a citizen of the world who belonged everywhere and nowhere. He seemed equally at home—and detached—on the Australian frontier (which he visited in 1883) and in a London drawing room. He was both a platform polemicist and a serious scholar whose biography of Thomas Paine is in many ways still the best. He was respectable and Bohemian, gentleman and radical. He had a genius for friendship and a talent for provocation. "I never yet have heard him speak that he did not have something . . . worth saying," said Thomas Wentworth Higginson, "nor did I ever hear him speak, I may add, that he did not say something worth differing from."[5]

Therein lies the fascination, the importance, and the elusiveness of this man. "Little wonder he rarely appears in our histories," writes one historian; and indeed Conway has been neglected far more than many lesser lights. "One really does not know what to make of him, or to do with him. He does not fit."[6]

Or does he? Sometimes those who do not fit in conventional ways, fit best in the ways that reveal most. The traveler tells us more than the native. Uprooted but craving to belong, detached but always engaged, Conway threw himself into the thick of things while retaining a sense of distance found only in the pilgrim (his favorite word), the visitor, the exile. His powers of observation were keen, and the mirror he consciously held up to others was often sharp and clear and vivid with reflected meaning. The Emersonian metaphor of the "transparent eyeball," seeing so much more than ordinary eyes, seems specifically meant for Conway.

But Conway's life reveals more than what we gain merely by watching his own daily actions, reactions, and interactions, or from his own shrewd observations and subsequent recollections. By *being*, he reveals. To know a religion, know its heretics; a movement, its schismatics; a country, its exiles. Precisely by not fitting, Conway tells us something about those worlds he could not enter or remain in for long. We must only truly understand him and why he did not fit. Understanding him, we better understand the imperatives of the antebellum Southern aristocracy, the boundaries of nineteenth-century organized Christianity, the nature of the abolitionist movement, the broader moral and political implications of the American Civil War. And by realizing the extent to which he *did* fit, we better understand what was possible in the settings in which he moved.

Fanny Villard went home, touched and haunted by memories. One stood out above all. On the night of December 31, 1862, she and Conway had gone to the black church on Boston's Beacon Hill. There the eighteen-year-old daughter of America's leading abolitionist and the thirty-year-old renegade son of the Southern slavocracy (they were the only whites present) joined with Boston's blacks to usher in the year of jubilee. At midnight the Emancipation Proclamation took effect. Fanny and Moncure joined hands, stood with the others, sang themselves hoarse, and wept. Though they lived far apart in later years, that experience bound them as soul mates for life.[7]

But Fanny Garrison could not have known—perhaps never knew—the mix of emotions in her companion that night. For her the event was an apotheosis, a joyous climax; for him it was but a brief, happy interlude in a chain of psychically devastating events now reaching its denouement. The Civil War was the culmination of turbulent crosscurrents that had been swirling across Conway's life almost from the beginning. It made him confront fully his feelings about bloodshed, domination, arbitrary power. It made him fully appraise his own position as a man without a home, or with two homes colliding in mortal combat.

Ultimately, it was more than he could bear. Less than four months after leaving the Joy Street Church with Fanny Garrison, Conway would leave the country. Fanny's life in a glorious new America was just beginning. Moncure's American years were coming to an end.

This is the story of those years.

PART ONE / THE MAKING OF A SOUTHERN ABOLITIONIST

CHAPTER 1

"Why?" the little boy whined, flailing his arms and stomping the floor, harrowing his hapless mother with his own special blend of precocity and obnoxiousness. The woman was used to it from this moody and inscrutable second son, his curiosity boundless, his questions unending, his frustration excruciating when comprehension eluded him. This time, as at others, she could not follow his frantic gesticulations. "Moncure," she pleaded, "I do not understand you." The boy started back, his face contorted in childish consternation. "Don't understand me!" he cried, "Well, what a woman! What a woman!" And he stormed from the house "with his cogitations," recalled his mother, "to wait till he would ferret out his conclusions."[1]

The boy walked the fifty yards from his house to the banks of the muddy Rappahannock and sat there in the rich brown Virginia soil to do his customary pondering. There was so much to learn, so much to know, and he had to get it all straight. He saw the deference everyone showed his father, his uncles, his cousins, deference that would be shown him someday if he did not fail, if he upheld his birthright, if he learned quickly, if he got it all straight. He was important, he was special, and he knew it because everyone told him so. As an uncle once said to him, "You have us all in your power—all our names are represented in yours. . . ."[2]

The names were Moncure, Daniel, Conway; and from the moment he entered the world during the blizzard of March 17, 1832, Moncure Daniel Conway was a person surrounded by the perquisites and pressures of privilege. The Conways had been in Virginia since 1640, the Daniels since 1634, the Moncures—French Huguenots (the name derived from *mon coeur*)—since 1733. They had clustered in Stafford County, an overwhelmingly rural and agricultural expanse lying thirty to fifty miles south of Alexandria. There, numerous progeny had acquired so much land and had so thoroughly intermarried that by the

3

early nineteenth century the county almost literally belonged to them.[3]

Stafford was an old county, created in 1664, but its development had come through the expansion of agricultural holdings by leading planters rather than through urbanization or rapidly constructed links to the outside world. In the mid-nineteenth century Stafford still lacked a major town. Falmouth, a village on the Rappahannock at the southern end of the county, made a bid for that status in the eighteenth century, when it stood at the head of navigation and seemed likely to become a river port of some significance. But the Rappahannock did not cooperate; by 1800 the river had become so cluttered with silt and sand at Falmouth that commercial traffic had to stop at Fredericksburg, one mile downstream on the opposite bank. So Falmouth lost its chance and never transcended small-town status, its population never reaching one thousand.[4]

From Falmouth north to the border of Prince William County stretched twenty miles of dense hardwood forest, peppered with farms and plantations (growing mostly food grains) and an occasional crossroads hamlet. At Stafford Court House, roughly in the center of the county, planters met on Court Mondays to spar and plot politically, catch up on local gossip, plan social events, buy and sell land, livestock, and people. Although a rail line was built in the early 1850s from Fredericksburg to Aquia Landing on the Potomac, midway up the eastern edge of the county, not until after the Civil War could a traveler cross all of Stafford by rail on a journey between Richmond and Washington. Stafford was in many ways an isolated corner of the world, steeped in its own traditions and ruled by its own inbred elite. This was the rural South, where everyone (or so it was hoped) had a place and the worst thing possible was to lose it.

The place occupied by Moncure Conway's family in Stafford and in Virginia was large. The privilege of the Moncures, Daniels, and Conways was a reflection of their power, and by the second third of the nineteenth century that power was substantial. Moncure's mother was a Daniel, whose maternal grandfather (Thomas Stone of Maryland) had signed the Declaration of Independence, and whose father, John Moncure Daniel, had been a prominent United States Army surgeon. Her uncle, Peter Vivian Daniel, was from 1841 to 1860 an associate justice of the United States Supreme Court. Her brother, Travers Daniel, was lieutenant governor and then attorney general of Virginia. And her mercurial nephew John Moncure Daniel became in 1847 the editor of the Richmond *Examiner*, a major force in Southern journalism.[5]

Moncure's father's side had its worthies too. His father's brother-in-law, Richard C. L. Moncure, was a prominent lawyer who became a Virginia Supreme Court justice in 1851, rising to chief justice in 1867. His paternal grandfather, John Moncure Conway, was clerk of the County and Superior Courts of Stafford from 1804 to 1851, when he was succeeded by his own son Henry. Moncure's uncle Eustace Conway

(b. 1820) was elected to the Virginia legislature at the age of twenty-six, became a power there before resigning in 1849, and in 1850 was elected judge of the eighth circuit, becoming the youngest circuit judge ever elected in Virginia. Eustace Conway was a rapidly rising star in the national Democratic party. Chosen to nominate Franklin Pierce at the 1852 presidential convention, he himself seemed unalterably destined for high national office.[6]

But for young Moncure Conway, his father overshadowed them all. Walker Peyton Conway was a man of firm will, fierce integrity, and fixed opinions. Known as a roustabout in his youth, in young adulthood he had been converted at a Methodist camp meeting and had stunned his Episcopalian family by becoming the first person of high birth in Stafford to embrace the more somber and rigorous demands of that evangelical faith. Walker Conway instilled in his children a powerful, almost frightening sense of duty—to God, to family, to community. Such adherence to duty could bring rewards: he had become simultaneously a large landowner and slaveholder, a successful businessman, and presiding justice of the county court, a post he held for over thirty years. Frequently Walker Conway would take his sons to the courthouse, where they might learn the same lessons his own father had taught him. In the courtroom Moncure would gaze in awe at his father, who sat at the high bench and pronounced judgment on their neighbors. This man was perhaps the most powerful individual in Stafford. Having won that power by his own sweat and piety, he expected his sons to know how to keep it when it passed down to them. His first son, Walker Peyton, Jr. (b. 1830), bore the brunt of this pressure. But Moncure, the second son, was made to know well enough what was expected also of him.[7]

Walker Conway was born in Stafford County in 1805, the year after his father, John Moncure Conway, began his half-century tenure as clerk of the county court. John Conway, an 1800 graduate of William and Mary, was a man who exuded rectitude and dignity; never abandoning his eighteenth-century blue dress coat with plain brass buttons, white cravat, and ruffled shirt, he early established himself as a revered Stafford institution. And so Walker Conway grew up against the backdrop of the county courthouse, watching the trials inside and the auctions outside, listening to stump speeches, absorbing all the legal, political, and mercenary maneuverings which were the little community's reasons for being. It was a perfect education for the life he would lead. When it became clear that his older, less ambitious brother, Valentine, was headed toward the medical profession, it became equally clear that it was Walker—ten years older than any of his other brothers—who would become the steady, reliable patriarch of his generation of Conways and assume a place with his father as a pillar of Stafford society.

He was to play the role expected of him with exquisite skill and considerable grace. In many ways Walker Conway epitomized the antebellum Southern aristocracy at its best. He was proud of his family traditions and family ties and regarded the maintenance of family honor as a sacred obligation. He never shrank from the onerous duties which his class and station demanded of him. He was known widely as a man of absolute personal honor and integrity, becoming, for example, what seemed "the factotum of all the widows and spinsters [in the area] who wish their property taken care of." "The last thing I remember just before leaving home [in 1853]," recalled his son Moncure, "was a widow in the hall asking for Mr. Conway."[8] Not only was he a dependable and supportive neighbor, he was also steadfast in the performance of his broader civic responsibilities. Not ambitious for far-reaching political fame, he declined to run for re-election after one term (1832–33) in the state legislature. But he regarded disinterested service to his own locality as mandatory, and won a reputation as a trustworthy county judge who combined sternness with impartiality. Whenever circumstances required more of him, as after the Civil War when he was elected to the Fredericksburg city council, he did not think of shirking the call to duty. Fully absorbing the principles of a patriarchal and paternalistic society, he took power and honor seriously, seeking both while abusing neither by the standards of his time and place. So completely did he represent the Southern power structure that any rebellion against his values inevitably entailed a rebellion against that structure itself. True to the needs of his society and his class, Conway could afford to be nothing but ruthless in the face of such a rebellion, even if—especially if—the rebel should be his own son.

By the time of his marriage in 1829, Walker Conway was a lawyer of some repute and a farmer of steadily growing wealth. When their second child, Moncure, was born, the Conways were living on a 500-acre estate with a taxable value of $2,430, some twelve miles west of Stafford Court House. But this was not their only holding: tax records from the 1830s and 1840s show Conway to have been one of the most active buyers and sellers of land in the county, always diligently adding to his personal domain. In 1834 the family moved to another farm and homestead, "Inglewood," two miles from Falmouth. The following year came acquisitions at Aquia Creek (325 acres) and Crow's Nest (196½ acres), in 1836 at Horse Pen (401 acres), in 1839 at Deep Run (1,076 acres) along with 333 choice acres at Stafford Court House. In 1838, when the family moved into the largest house in Falmouth, a thousand-dollar two-story brick dwelling destined to be their home until the Civil War, Walker Conway was not only one of the most prestigious of the county's residents, but also one of its wealthiest.[9]

Falmouth provided Conway with yet another outlet for his energy and ambition. Cotton prices were falling to their lowest levels in American history in the economic slump of the 1840s, and Conway was quick to see the opportunity offered by the combination of low cotton prices and the water power generated by the nearby falls of the

Rappahannock. By 1840 he and J. W. Slaughter of Fredericksburg had founded the Falmouth Cotton Factory, valued at over $23,000, importing cotton from the lower South and turning it into cotton yarns, heavy osnaburgs, and heavy brown shirtings, advertised as "all of superior quality." The factory continued through the decade, but Northern competition, the rapid rise in raw cotton prices after 1850, plus booming grain prices which made further investment in food crops more lucrative, evidently killed the venture; it disappears from the tax rolls after 1851. By this time, however, the energetic Conway had plenty of other things to keep himself occupied. He continued to buy and cultivate more land, continued to preside at the county court. By the 1850s he had added banking to his repertoire, serving on the board of directors of the Bank of Virginia—Fredericksburg's richest bank—and becoming its president in 1857.[10]

Although born into the gentry, wealth and prestige had not come automatically to Walker Conway, as if by divine ordination. With high birth had come the responsibility of upholding the family name, of aspiring toward the high place which awaited if only one worked for it. Walker Conway was a worker, with an almost compulsive fervor. Duty, honor, and sheer hard work were watchwords for this tall, strong, impressive man, whose seriousness was made even sterner by his harsh personal asceticism and all-consuming religiosity.

When Conway converted to Methodism, evidently in the late 1820s, his father—an Episcopalian by birth who attended no church—was so appalled that he refused for a time to speak to him. The feud was short-lived, however; the elder Conway must have seen that evangelicalism was sweeping this region where the staid old Anglican faith had fallen into sterile decrepitude, and that he was powerless to change it. Eventually Walker was reinforced by the conversions of three of his sisters and of his brothers Valentine and Eustace. For young Walker, the change wrought by Methodism was abrupt and dramatic. Formerly a card player and dancer who was known to sip a toddy from time to time, he at once forsook games and amusements, condemned dancing as sinful sensuality, and became an ardent enthusiast for prohibitionist legislation. Throughout the rest of his life he was one of the mainstays of the Methodist church in Fredericksburg. Perhaps this new set of values and commitments, which he found at the threshold of adulthood, was necessary as an aid to coping with the sobering and formidable responsibilities ahead of him. Whatever the case, he embraced the values totally, and measured by his terms they served him well.[11]

Walker's wife, Margaret Daniel (b. 1807), was a Methodist convert too: but her journey into Methodism had been of a very different sort. An orphan in 1813, she was placed in the care of an uncle and aunt. It was ostensibly an Episcopalian household, but her aunt's background was Presbyterian, and she was by conviction a brooding, sin-obsessed, tyrannical Calvinist. Kept spinning and gasping in a whirlpool of moral and religious pressure, Margaret broke and went under: she became hysterical and very ill, and was bled until she almost died. After this sort of upbringing, Methodism was a breath of spring air. It carried the message that salvation was hers for the asking, that destiny was not foreordained but was whatever she would make it. It was a religion which found scope for sociability, hope, and happiness. If it had brought order to her husband's life, it brought freedom to hers. If it had given him a system through which he could deal with the seriousness and responsibilities of life, it gave her a means of tasting its joys. Here was one crucial reason for the difference between the overbearing asceticism of Moncure Conway's father and the genial indulgence of his mother.[12]

Walker Conway's was not the only work the Conway children witnessed; their mother, too, had a profession. Their father was a magistrate who judged and sometimes punished people; their mother was a self-taught homeopathic doctor who comforted and sometimes healed them. Homeopathy was a system which seriously challenged orthodox medicine in the second third of the nineteenth century. Its central premise was that an irritation which upset the body's "vital principle" was the usual cause of disease. The irritation could be removed and the "vital principle" restored by small doses of drugs (usually diluted) which produced effects similar to symptoms of the disease. By the 1830s there were homeopathic schools throughout America, offering more rigorous scientific training than most orthodox medical schools, and in 1849 a national professional organization was created. The system de-emphasized strong drugs and eschewed purgatives and bleedings. It probably did no more harm than regular medicine, and may have done more good, during the few decades of its popularity. Homeopathy was also much more receptive than orthodox medicine to female practitioners. Margaret Conway, who had suffered from bleedings as a child and despised the "*drugging* ordeal that always *reduces* the vital powers," described herself in the 1850s as "the only person in this vicinity who has read this system carefully." Although she attended no homeopathic school, her practice seems to have been sizable. From the 1830s until her death in 1891, her services were much in demand, and in the 1870s Moncure claimed her practice was "larger than that of any physician in the neighborhood." "I have such constant demand on me for care for the sick in this town," she wrote in 1874 in a lament which could have been made with equal justification thirty years earlier. "It is a hard life to look into medical matters and write prescriptions all day, and be exhausted sitting by bedsides."[13]

Moncure's mother was no decorative appendage of her husband; she was an important, active, even overworked figure in the household and in the community, providing her son with proof that a person could combine tenderness with strength and effectiveness. If she mirrored her husband's piety, hers was tempered by tolerance. If she shared her husband's sternness, hers was softened by compassion. She was also a widely read, thoughtful, and strikingly intelligent woman. With her indulgence, Moncure clandestinely devoured novels and plays, forbidden by his father. Since his father paid more attention to the eldest son, Peyton, Moncure naturally fell under the wing of his mother, who stressed to him the importance of carving out his own sense of self. His "maternal inheritance," Conway later recalled, consisted of "a passion for beauty, ruddy-hearted love of life, and a personality not to be conventionalized."[14]

Indeed, Moncure gravitated generally toward the women in his family. "I was not popular among my comrades," he remembered many years later. "I was homely, was not spirited, and was a poor creature beside my handsome and dashing brother Peyton, always ready to wrestle or fight,—things I hated." "Too shy to mingle freely with other boys," Moncure opted for the company of "the beautiful ladies of Falmouth, and numerous aunts and [female] cousins from the country, of whom some were always visiting us." Chief among these were his aunts Jane and Margaret Conway, who were his lifelong champions, and his cousin Elizabeth Daniel, daughter of the Supreme Court justice. The latter, who visited occasionally to discuss Dickens or Scott or Shakespeare with his mother, struck up a correspondence with ten-year-old Moncure—"not condescending nor patronizing, but written as to a friend"—which instilled "some faith in my homely and shy self."[15]

It was not that Moncure actually repudiated activity categorized as male—he swam in the Rappahannock, threw wood on political bonfires, and shot robins and ate them for snacks. Most importantly, he grew up accepting the terms of his birth, preparing himself to fill a role like those of his male relatives. But a side of life which most boys disdained seemed to provide him with the highest degree of pleasure, stimulation, and satisfaction. Taught by his mother and other female relatives to love books and music and to shun violence, he found women to be good company. He loved both parents but also felt something like fear toward his father. He preferred his sister, Mildred (b. 1837), to his brother Peyton, while his younger brothers (Richard, b. 1840, and Peter, b. 1842) were too young to play major roles in his boyhood. Walker Conway bought a piano for Mildred, but she and Moncure learned to play it together, getting all the Methodist hymns by heart. "I set my mother, sister, aunts, to singing them," Moncure recalled, "joining in myself with a fervent second."[16]

At times events occurred which offered Moncure an insight into the special burdens which women carried. On April 16, 1839, his eight-day-old sister Catherine died. It was the first time that Moncure had to confront the death of a person, and it was combined with the ineradicable image of his mother, pale and ill and exhausted, calling him to her bedside and trying to explain.[17]

Not long after this, an old woman who lived on the outskirts of Falmouth began to be singled out by the townspeople as a witch. Nancy

Calamese's real crimes seem to have been reclusiveness and unattractiveness, but ghastly rumors were spread about her and she "hardly dared pass through the streets for fear of being hooted [at] by boys." Margaret Conway sympathized with her and visited her, telling Moncure that she was intelligent and kept a neat house and garden. But the strain of persecuted isolation proved too much. One morning Nancy Calamese walked into the Rappahannock and did not walk out.[18]

The women in young Moncure's life represented particular things to him: culture, refinement, sensitivity, gentleness, peace. They taught him to treasure these things as they did, and because he learned his lesson well, he grew up cherishing both the values and the women who held them. His most comforting boyhood memories were those involving women: singing together in the parlor, reading aloud underneath a tree, or sailing at twilight on the Rappahannock,[19] where he would nestle against a pretty cousin's breast and listen to the rippling water and the sweet soprano voices raised in a ballad or folk song, as the darkness deepened and the moon rose, and the rich colors of the day faded hauntingly to black and white.

All the slaves had names, though only a few of them survive. There was Moncure's nurse, Maria (d. 1845), whom he remembered as good-natured and indulgent, meeting his mischief with a laugh and a teasing cry of "Come, Monc, 'fess your faults." There was Maria's son, Peter Humstead, who at age twenty swapped a necktie for reading lessons from his young "Mars Monc," even though teaching a slave to read was a violation of the spirit of Virginia law. There were Dunmore and Eliza Gwinn, intelligent, shrewd, and somehow literate, the de facto leaders of the Conway slaves. And there was James Parker, Walker Conway's valet, who was permitted periodically to visit his wife in a lunatic asylum in Baltimore, always returning and yielding any unused spending money to his master, to whom he seemed unswervingly devoted.[20]

But mostly they are check marks in the census. Walker Conway is listed as owning twenty-three slaves in 1850 and twenty-nine in 1860, the only time that separate slave schedules were tabulated. Yet there were probably more: the census was explicitly designed to count the slave population, not to pinpoint slave ownership, and it is possible, even likely, that Conway owned slaves not listed under his name. Moncure resettled thirty-three ex-Conway slaves in Ohio in 1862, and this was less than the current total. Moncure's 1864 statement that his father had owned "fifty or sixty" slaves in 1832 is certainly exaggerated, but the figure is not impossible for the later 1840s or 1850s. In any case, when John Moncure Conway drew up his will in 1853 he excluded his sons Eustace and Walker from the division of his slaves, since the two men were already so "amply supplied with domestic labor."[21]

Moncure Conway was born only four months after the authorities of Southampton County hanged Nat Turner, whose slave revolt the preceding August had killed sixty whites and sent a shudder through the entire South. The bloodiest of nineteenth-century North American slave rebellions had been followed quickly by Virginia's—and the South's—last public debate on the wisdom of slavery. Early in 1832 the Virginia legislature debated the advisability of gradual emancipation, a program supported largely by delegates from the western part of the state, where slaves were scarce. On January 25, 1832, legislators from the counties along the Rappahannock helped defeat convincingly all antislavery motions. Later that year, a William and Mary professor, Thomas R. Dew, published the most systematic and unflinching defense yet produced of slavery as a positive good. By this time, William Lloyd Garrison's abolitionist Boston newspaper, *The Liberator*, was more than a year old. The lines were hardening; by the mid-1830s, the years of widespread public soul-searching on the slavery question were over in Virginia.[22]

Moncure Conway grew up amid slavery, and among human beings who were slaves. Slave children were his earliest and most constant playmates. In fact, he recalled, "parents were more particular about the white playmates of their children than about colored associates." Together they fished for shad and perch, raised pigeons, and cultivated melons, having contests to see who could grow the biggest and the best. When they got older their paths diverged, the blacks trudging to the fields as Moncure pranced to the academy. But even then he did not consciously question the system, any more than did other white Virginia boys. "I had no means of knowing that there was any thing peculiar in the condition of the blacks," he wrote in 1864, "or that the recurring sufferings of both whites and blacks were any more to be questioned than the hot skies and low fevers of our summer."[23]

Moncure's father, who had diverged from his own father's more conciliatory and nationalistic Whig politics to join the Democratic party, was a "warm advocate of the [slave] system," even though he once startled his son by observing that slavery was "a doomed institution." Walker's younger brother Eustace, the golden boy of the tidewater Virginia Democrats, was a firebrand on both slavery and "Southern rights" in general; like George Fitzhugh, the eloquent proslavery ideologue who was his personal friend, Eustace regarded slavery as a blessing for black people and a system far superior to the Northern wage system. It was Eustace who authored the "Conway Resolutions" which went through the Virginia legislature after the Mexican War, warning Congress that if it barred slavery from all land acquired during the conflict, Virginia would be forced to consider secession. If these men were role models for Moncure Conway—and they were—then Moncure Conway was destined to be no enemy of slavery. But they were not his only models.[24]

In Conway's 1887 first novel, *Pine and Palm*, a New Englander and a Virginian befriend each other at Harvard Law School and decide to exchange places for one year after graduation. Walter Wentworth, the New Englander, travels to South Carolina and eventually makes his way north to "The Palms," the plantation of his friend's father on the Rappahannock. One evening he is having dinner with Judge Stirling, master of "The Palms." At the table are several visiting planters and the judge's daughter, Gisela. Mellowed by a steady diet of upper-class Southern hospitality, Wentworth now begins to gush about the benevolence he has witnessed under slavery. "I have seen enough kindness toward that [black] race," he tells the planters, "and comfort among them, and enough justice among their masters, to modify my—"[25]

At that point Gisela Stirling abruptly excuses herself and leaves the table in anger and distress. Late that night, she comes to Wentworth's room and leads him to another part of the house. There she shows him a slave woman, Alice Ross, whom she had taught to read. Ross and her new husband are to be sold separately the next day. Gisela: "I only brought you to see one of the victims you are deserting. I could only weep for your weakness, but God has rebuked it. I lay sleepless with sorrow that a man should bend from his cause. . . . Now that you have seen her you can return to your repose." Wentworth leaves the room meekly, while Gisela packs a bundle of clothing for the slave. "The day was faintly breaking when, with a last kiss, she parted with her humble friend at the kitchen door, and watched till, with a despairing wave of the hand, she blended with shadows." It is unclear to what extent this episode is taken from Conway's own experience, but whether it describes an actual event or merely illustrates a more general condition, it struck a nerve with one Conway when he read it. Moncure's ex-Confederate brother Richard, reading the novel at his Virginia farm, scribbled testily in the margin: "*Quo ad hoc*, it is a lie, pure and simple."[26]

But it was not a lie. Gisela Stirling was modeled after Fanny Tomlin Moncure, daughter-in-law of Richard C. L. Moncure and the younger sister of Eustace Conway's wife. This was one of those lady relatives in whose company young Moncure delighted, and if specifics concerning her hostility to slavery are lost to us, there is evidence enough to indicate that it was part of a broader pattern of antislavery feeling among that group of people who most affected Moncure Conway during his formative years.[27]

In her memoirs, the English traveler and essayist Harriet Martineau recalled that she had "never met with a lady of southern origin who did not speak of slavery as a sin and a curse—the burden which oppressed their lives." One need not take Martineau's comment literally to take it seriously. Having discovered belatedly that women are figures of historical significance, historians have only recently begun investigating the attitudes of Southern women toward slavery, and much more needs to be done before firm conclusions can be drawn. Yet recent work, especially that of Anne Firor Scott, has shown that the hostility expressed in the famous diary of South Carolina's Mary Boykin Chesnut, rather than being the unique attitude of an unusual person, was widely shared among women of the slaveholding classes. Mary Minor Blackford, an upper-class woman who lived in Fredericksburg from her birth in 1802 until she moved to Lynchburg in 1846, was unequivocal in her moral hatred of slavery. "How the practice of injustice hardens the feelings is perfectly wonderful," she wrote in 1832. "The time will come when we shall look back and wonder how Christians could sanction slavery." She freed her own house servants in 1827, tried to persuade two of her sons to move to the North, and approved of *Uncle Tom's Cabin*. Even in the very heart of proslavery Southern particularism, the South Carolina sea islands, antislavery women could be found without difficulty. Visiting the cotton plantations of Edisto Island in 1855, Bostonian Charles Eliot Norton wrote home that all the men he had met, however refined and intelligent, were quick to uphold the "monstrous principles" underlying slavery. But, he noticed, "It is very different with the women—there are many who are as clear-sighted in regard to the wrong . . . as truly Christian women should be;—but they are bewildered often, and their efforts are limited by weakness, inexperience, and opposition. Their eyes fill with tears when you talk with them about it, while the men often look at you with a certain scornful pity for having yielded to the prevailing sentimentality of the day so far as to believe slavery anything but a blessing."[28]

The reasons why some Southern women harbored antislavery sentiments were varied, but among the most important was the extreme burden of work the peculiar institution placed on the mistress of a farm or plantation. Such a woman was in a double bind. Expected to play a starkly subservient role in a patriarchal society, having almost no legal personality apart from her connection to her husband, she was nevertheless saddled with enormously onerous supervisory responsibilities that played havoc with the literary image of the pampered, genteel Southern belle. She was expected not only to bear and raise a steady stream of children of her own, but also to oversee the health and welfare of the slaves. It was generally the mistress who was in charge of slave clothing, food, and health care, and who was forced to mediate an unceasing flow of personal and interpersonal problems. Dealing with many slaves more closely and constantly than did most men, women grew to know them better as human beings. Often berating their black charges and complaining bitterly of the burden of caring for so many dependent beings, Southern white women simultaneously developed close personal attachments to the very people who so vexed them, and felt more keenly than could their men the effects of the personal indignities to which the slaves were subjected.[29]

There were darker, more psychologically charged reasons for a white woman to hate slavery. One need not accept the twentieth-century cinematic image of the Old South as a nonstop multiracial orgy to know that sexual exploitation of black women by white men was a common occurrence. "It is one of the most dreadful circumstances of this traffic," wrote Fredericksburg's Mary Blackford in 1833, "that the women frequently become the prey of the brutal lust of their oppressors." Such exploitation of a subservient class by the dominant one has not, of course, been limited to slave societies or to the antebellum South. But there it seemed especially repugnant due to its racial dimension, the absoluteness and extremity of the exploited woman's position, the degrading proximity of the offended wives to their men's black partners and mulatto offspring, and the extent to which forced interracial sex mocked the patriarchal ideal and mangled the white woman's respect for herself and her men. "[E]very lady tells you who is the father of all the mulatto children in everybody's household," Mary Chesnut complained, "but those in her own she seems to think drop from the clouds. . . . My disgust sometimes is boiling over." In Virginia, miscegenation was one of the most common offenses cited by women who petitioned for divorce. The offense was not hidden from young Moncure Conway: the family slaves included a few mulattos, one of whom, the son of Moncure's nurse Maria, was his favorite slave companion. When an abolitionized Conway later attacked slavery as an institution calling forth "the terrors of devoted parents . . . and the inception of nameless vices among their sons," he could have had specific people in mind.[30]

It had dawned on Moncure slowly and gradually, but, as he recalled in 1864, during the 1850s he had come to the full realization "that my mother had in her heart cherished for many years a fervent hatred of Slavery. Every Southern woman has, God knows, enough reason to hate it."[31] Margaret Conway was in charge of tens of slaves in and about the household, while her medical reputation placed demands on her for the care of other people's slaves as well as her own. Her duties to the slaves—which she complained were more exhausting than their duties to her—were carried on while bearing six children in twelve years. The strain taxed her to the breaking point. "You know that, saving the black visages, *I* am the greatest slave here," she lamented to Moncure in 1856, after he had embarked on his abolitionist career.

> . . . The servants of our household . . . are raised in a state of dependence of thought and action, so they will not even make an effort to make their own clothing. . . . I often think if someone would arouse me some morning from my sleep with the intelligence they had every one left the premises I should feel such a sense of freedom and relief from responsibility. . . . If any abolitionist could exactly know what I have endured from overpressure of work for thirty negroes for the last month, and the worry I have had to get them to do any of it for themselves, they would look upon me with the greater pity than on them, for besides so much of our means is consumed that we can hardly have any thing [left] over to use on our own enjoyment and culture of our minds or making our homes pleasant— such exertion has brought on me premature decay of all my powers.[32]

Dissatisfaction with slavery did not make Margaret an immediate emancipationist before the Civil War, any more than it did most antebellum Southern women who expressed misgivings about the institution. Neither did it cause her to break with many of the racial and class assumptions of her time and place. Abolition was something she thought about, however, and a major reason why she could not support it was that, if freed, the blacks she knew "would be in a state of extreme suffering and their numerous babies would perish." There is no reason to doubt her sincerity on this matter. Poignant letters written by the Conway freedmen for some thirty years after the war provide evidence that Margaret had developed close and caring personal relationships with some of her slaves, as had her daughter Mildred and her son Moncure. "Not only was she your mother but she was a mother to all— both white and colored," Dunmore Gwinn reminisced to Moncure about his former mistress. Mildred and Moncure seemed included in the freedmen's affection, remembered for the way they had treated the slaves as fellow human beings. Gwinn fondly remembered sitting by the river eating fried perch with Moncure and his sister; Gwinn's wife, Eliza, wrote to Moncure "as though you were my own dear boy," and Churchill Taylor, an illiterate field hand, named a son after Moncure. About the other white males in the family the freedmen's letters are icily silent. Walker Conway was not physically inhumane, but he was a true believer in the institution of slavery, as were his other sons, and this difference was not lost on the slaves. It would be hard to imagine a slave approaching Walker or Peyton or Richard or Peter, and asking to be taught how to read.[33]

During the Civil War, Margaret took her antislavery feelings to a dramatic extreme: she joined the Yankees. Early in the war, having "taken up such strong opinions against secession that her continuance in Fredericksburg [*sic*] had become imprudent," she traveled to Easton, Pennsylvania, to live with Mildred, who had spoken derisively of slavery and secession during the 1850s and had in 1860 married a professor at Lafayette College, Francis Andrew March. During the war Margaret corresponded with her ravenously pro-Confederate husband, whom she continued to love as thoroughly as she hated his cause. But she was through compromising with slavery, now regarding abolition as "a *godsend* to the Nation, North and South." The division in the Conway family during the war was almost completely along sexual lines: Walker Conway was in Richmond, his sons in the Confederate army, while his wife and daughter were in the North supporting emancipation and the Union. The one exception was Moncure, on the side of the women.[34]

It was not just members of the immediate family who provided young Moncure with examples of people who disagreed with their region's conventional moral and political wisdom. When paternal grandfather John Moncure Conway wrote his will in 1853, distributing his slaves among his children, he left each daughter a "maid servant" and divided the rest among his sons (except Walker and Eustace, who already had enough, and George, whose peculiarity is described below). But on October 19, 1856, he found it necessary to add a codicil: "Having recently become fully confirmed in my opinion as to the sentiments entertained by my single daughters, Jane and Margaret in regard to slavery, and thereupon unwilling that any portion of my servants shall be subject after my death to their free disposal, I do therefore most reluctantly revoke that part of the clause in my Will leaving my said daughters a maid each with an unfettered disposition of them at their death, in stead thereof, I do hereby bequeath the same, as in the first devise, to my sons Henry R. and Eustace Conway in trust, for their use and benefit and with pleasure giving my said daughters the privilege of giving the property aforesaid to either of their brothers and sisters that they may elect and prefer so to do."[35]

Moncure's aunts Margaret and Jane were frequent visitors while he was growing up, and may actually have been part of the household for a time. As is evident from John Conway's will, their loyalty to the slave system had long been suspect, and it is very likely that their nephew was aware of this. In any case, it was their nephew who almost certainly was the cause of their father's action against them. In a much-publicized episode, Moncure Conway's Unitarian congregation in Washington had fired him on October 5, 1856, because of his antislavery sermons. Two weeks later John Conway wrote the codicil which prevented any slave from coming under his two daughters' control. The conclusion is irresistible that Margaret and Jane had spoken unequivocally in support of the abolitionism of the nephew they had helped to nurture.[36]

We cannot gauge with precision the influence of his female relations in shaping young Moncure's moral and political outlook, and indeed it seems clear that by the time he left Virginia permanently in 1853 his views had become more radical than those of anyone else in his family up to that point. In addition, certain male relatives had a strong, though fleeting, impact on him during his adolescence. But the women surely left their mark. In 1855, shortly after Conway had entered the Unitarian ministry and had committed himself to radical abolitionism, his mother complained that "your father has assigned me the encourager, if not the originator, of your heresies." Margaret was unhappy at the degree of her son's religious liberalism, and he had gone beyond her, at this stage, in his advocacy of immediate emancipation. In a real sense, then, Walker Conway's accusation was unfair. But it also was true.[37]

Conway's unusual closeness during the years of his youth to a group of women whose values and convictions often did not mesh well with the publicly inviolable worldview of the antebellum Southern establishment must help explain the gradual emergence of a radical abolitionist out of a privileged son of the Virginia aristocracy. And it helps explain not only the fact of Conway's abolitionism, but also the style and form his abolitionism took. As one historian has written, "Southern opponents of slavery and their arguments were generally conservative and cautious. They did not rest upon a very strong belief in the potentiality of the Negro; on the whole the antislavery argument in the South was dominated by a concern for white men and their prosperity." Unlike most other white Southern abolitionist males, notably Cassius Marcellus Clay, Daniel Reaves Goodloe, and the virulently anti-black Hinton Rowan Helper, Conway's antislavery stance was grounded not in politics or economics but in morality. From 1852 through the end of the Civil War, Conway's antislavery comments, speeches, and writings consistently downplayed (without omitting) arguments dealing with the retardation of the Southern economy or the interests of non-slaveholding whites, and revolved instead around moral arguments likely to have been of greater concern to women: the offensiveness of arbitrary violence and domination, the moral myopia with which slavery cursed its white supporters, and the threat which slavery posed to marriage and the family.[38]

With his greater similarity to South Carolina abolitionists Angelina and Sarah Grimké than to other Southern white males, Moncure Conway is unique in Southern history. Among white male antislavery Southerners, probably only Princeton-educated James Birney of Kentucky and Alabama, and Lane Seminary–educated John Fee of Kentucky, come close to him in their concern for the moral question involved in slaveholding.[39] Birney, however, who converted to abolitionism in the year of Conway's birth, never questioned the basic racial and social assumptions that consigned blacks and women to generally inferior places in society. Fee, whose Quaker mother may have had something to do with his conversion to antislavery in 1844, was more advanced than Birney in his commitment to genuine black equality (Cassius Clay refused to be a trustee of Berea College, which Fee helped to found in 1858, because it admitted blacks),[40] but Fee was never so active or nationally prominent as Conway became, nor was he nearly so much a child of the Southern power structure. Thus Conway stands alone as a man who, though raised within that power structure and expected to occupy a place in it, utterly rejected its authoritarian, hierarchical, patriarchal, male-oriented values and sought to smash them with an explicit frontal assault. Moncure Conway knew what he was doing when he repudiated his father and challenged his father's world, just as Walker Conway knew what he was doing when he defended his world and repudiated his son. Moncure Conway was the most thoroughgoing white male radical produced by the antebellum South, and the threat his values of equality and individual autonomy posed to the Southern social system was as real and as fundamental as a threat could be. It is for this reason that Conway stands as one of the most important and illuminating antebellum Southern deviants, and as a major figure in American history.

* * *

On some level of consciousness Moncure's experience with and affinity for women was slowly leading him not only toward antislavery, but also toward an incipient feminism. Margaret Conway's lament, "*I* am the greatest slave here," was deeper in meaning than a simple complaint about overwork. Although it would be absurd to contend that Margaret's physical situation was comparable to that of her slaves, it is nonetheless true that the disparity between the amount and intensity of her responsibilities, on the one hand, and the recognition and reward she received on the other, was stark. And it is also true that what caused Margaret her frustration and relative powerlessness were the mechanisms of social control erected by the same white patriarchal system that kept its blacks enslaved. When George Fitzhugh spoke contentedly of society's "weak and dependent" beings, the "wife, children, or slaves" whose role in life was to obey their natural masters—adult white men— in exchange for "the right to protection," he was describing an ideal society which many in the South were working hard at making a reality.[41]

Radical feminists were not oblivious to the similarities between the subjugation of blacks by whites and the domination of women by men. Many antebellum comments can be found to support John Stuart Mill's assertion in his classic, *The Subjection of Women* (1869), that "the wife is the actual bond-servant of her husband, no less so . . . than slaves commonly so called," and many extended the argument from wives to all women. Feminist leader Elizabeth Cady Stanton, later Conway's personal friend, warned in 1856 that the position of women was "very much like Sambo's on the plantation." Given the opportunity, "they will take to their rights as naturally as the negro to his heels when he is sure of escape." But the explicit connection was not limited to those in the feminist movement. Mary Chesnut, wife of a leading South Carolina politician and slaveholder, watched a woman sold on the auction block in 1861 and reflected upon the link between black slavery and the slavery of all women to their husbands. "You know what the Bible says about slavery—and marriage. Poor women. Poor slaves."[42]

The connection made between women and blacks was facilitated and strengthened by the common nineteenth-century perception that both groups possessed (as both compensation and explanation for their powerlessness) a more finely developed affectional and emotional sense than white males. The idea was often used for conservative ends, to justify the submission of blacks and women to a supposedly more aggressive and effective race of beings. But it could also be used to gather sympathy for them; and in any event the perceived link between blacks and women often served to call attention to their shared oppression, whose common source was the untempered aggressiveness, arrogance, and avarice of white males. Northern abolitionist writer Lydia Maria Child believed that both groups had been unjustly overpowered because "both are characterized by affection more than by intellect; both have a strong development of the religious sentiment; both are exceedingly adhesive in their attachments; both, comparatively speaking, have a tendency to submission. . . ." Conway, who shared this perception (if not deterministically or entirely consistently), was willing in his abolitionist days to take it to what for him was its logical extreme. If, as Northern editor Theodore Tilton wrote, the "negro race is the feminine race of the world," and if the more spiritual, intuitive, "feminine" virtues were (as Conway believed) more vital and precious than the more grasping values held by white males, then both blacks and women should be brought immediately into the mainstream of society. Conway knew from his own experience that caring and nurturing qualities did not have to be merely decorative. Rather, they could be driving forces in a more humane social order. The removal of disabilities from women and blacks would help civilize society. "Strike out the word *white* and the word *male* from our laws," he wrote in 1865, "and we shall reach the noblest transformation." In 1864 he even took the bold step of advocating interracial marriage, to temper the selfish aggressiveness of Anglo-Saxons and to reconcile blacks and whites, women and men, feminine and masculine impulses, all at the same time.[43]

Behind Conway's championship of racial intermarriage—unusual even among abolitionists—lay a biographical detail which few of his readers could have known. By the time Moncure was in his teens, it had become clear that one of his uncles was different. During the 1840s George Washington Conway (b. 1818) fell in love with a young mulatto woman owned by a neighbor. This was not a casual, forced sexual liaison; had it been, it could have been overlooked and overcome. This was a real love affair, and as such it transcended the remotely permissible and cost George Conway his place in society. Lacking slaves of his own, George worked hard enough to be able to buy his lover; by 1852 they were living as de facto husband and wife on a small farm in the Stafford woods, supporting their two children and one elderly black woman, all of whom were technically George's slaves. If George had ever entertained the ambitions held by his brothers, he had learned to live without them, contenting himself with a simple life in which love took precedence over material advancement. "Even my father declares that he is the best-hearted of the family," Moncure wrote after a visit to the couple in 1875, when time had slightly mellowed the bitter feelings and fierce prejudice which George's behavior had evidently elicited. Alone among the Conway males of his generation, George had flouted convention and defied his family's expectations, and his moving, solitary life in the Stafford interior, an undigestible bone in the county's throat, raised a number of questions and offered a variety of lessons for anyone sensitive enough to confront them. George was and is a shadowy figure, having no professional or public career, leaving no papers. We do not know how much contact Moncure had with his uncle George, but he knew he was there. And if George set an example for his nephew of how boldly a man could transcend convention for an ideal, he also showed him how devastating a price he would have to pay. While remaining in Stafford County, George had deserted the world of the upper-class white man and had opted literally for the world of women and blacks. The price was that, contrasted with what he might have been, George was as peripheral as the women and the slaves. One of the few things that separates him from them is that the census permits him his name.[44]

Occasionally an event occurred in Moncure's boyhood which perfectly symbolized the connection between male domination of women and white domination of blacks. The constable in Falmouth was a certain Captain Pickett, who made his living in part by whipping slaves. Owners unable or unwilling to do the job themselves would send their recalcitrant slaves to Pickett for the required discipline. The captain's "small, prison-like building" was predictably a favorite gathering spot for the white boys of the village; when a whipping occurred there was a scramble for position at the windows by boys eager to watch the transaction. Moncure, like the others, passed some time at Captain Pickett's, though with a mixture of curiosity and revulsion. "A glimpse I once had of the old man," he later wrote melodramatically but revealingly, "with lash lifted over the tender form of a young girl, abided in my memory." In the later 1850s Pickett hanged himself, "simply because," Conway chose to believe, "the shame of being an official negro-whipper became intolerable."[45]

A neighbor who had no such scruples was Captain Brown, a well-to-do planter who twice defeated Richard Moncure in legislative elections and who subsequently became an officer in the Confederate army. Brown had won some notoriety in Stafford in the late 1830s by beating one of his slaves to death: Walker Conway had been infuriated by the act but could do nothing as magistrate since only other blacks—without rights in a courtroom under such circumstances—had witnessed the murder. Not many years later, Moncure was outside the courthouse when Brown emerged with three of his female slaves, whom a jury had just acquitted of trying to poison their master. Brown was in a disagreeable mood: "I remember well," Conway recalled, "how the man's face was flushed with a sense of his power over these women." Brown tied the women to the rear of his wagon and tore their dresses from their backs. Ordering the driver to proceed, he walked along behind, whipping the women with a rawhide strap. "The crowd stood witnessing all this with a mere curiosity," standing about as the wagon passed over the horizon, the blows of the whip lingering in earshot for a few moments longer. "The horror made an ineffaceable impression on me," Conway later wrote, "though I was too young to generalize on it."[46]

An example of the precarious position of someone who was a slave was provided by the fate of Charles Humstead, whom Conway always remembered with guilt and regret. Charles was evidently the son of

Moncure's nurse, Maria, but he was "nearly white, besides being embarrassingly like a pious [white] gentleman who now and then visited us." Moncure clung to Charles, some nine or ten years his senior, more than to any other slave, for Charles had been appointed his protector. When their house at the Inglewood farm burned and the Conways moved to Falmouth in 1838, they continued to send Moncure and Peyton to the small school they had established near Inglewood. Charles's assignment was to accompany the boys (and later Moncure alone) on their two-mile walk between home and school. Moncure recalled Charles as a young man of "vivacity, wit, and amiability; and at his sixteenth year I remember him as one of the handsomest and noblest specimens of Humanity." Charles was a master of mimicries and impersonations, a weaver of fascinating stories and romances, and an entertaining singer of songs. Moncure concluded in 1866 that "he had more gifts than any other boy I ever knew in Virginia."[47]

But Charles's gifts were not given room to flourish productively. In 1841 Moncure was sent to join Peyton at the century-old Fredericksburg Classical and Mathematical Academy and began to see less of Charles and other blacks on anything approaching equal terms. "It is doubtful whether either my brother or myself had natural gifts equal to the slaveboy Charles; nevertheless we were carried past him, and abandoned him. His knowledge, which once seemed to us unlimited, we gradually discovered to be inferior to our own. We gained new (white) companions, and should have been ashamed to be seen playing at any game with Charles." Charles, who after his separation from the white boys had been assigned more conventional menial work, grew inwardly frustrated and outwardly misanthropic. "The whole family was kept in perpetual panic. Punishment only made him defiant." Charles's problems in dealing with Walker Conway grew acute; he could not speak to his white master without stuttering and looking away. "I always heard of him as a rascal," Moncure's younger sister Mildred said in 1897. "He had a white father and I never heard of him as brilliant, but as a liar and thief and a stammerer." Before long, Charles had burned down a deserted building, which prompted Walker Conway to sell him to a trader who took him to the lower South. Despite extended efforts to locate him in later years, Moncure never heard of him again.[48]

The protective service performed for Moncure by this unfortunate slave had a special significance. From little Moncure's viewpoint, Charles's primary function was to guard him from the many snakes, including water moccasins, which lurked in the swamps between Falmouth and Inglewood. Charles, who both entertained and frightened his young charge with stories of serpent lore (a blacksnake could suck a cow and pollute its milk; a horsehair left in rainwater would turn into a snake), was good at his work. "Advancing ahead of us, stick in hand, . . . his eye could not be cheated by the reptile's mimicry of clay, nor did he fail to strike the point on its back that left it helpless." This was central to Moncure's attachment to Charles, for the former's terror of snakes was pervasive and intense.[49]

"My horror of snakes was indiscriminate," Conway remembered. "The first duty of man on seeing that crawling devil was to kill it." The horror lingered for years. In his early teens, Moncure was permitted to visit a traveling circus—the only organized entertainment he saw during his youth. His pleasure was marred, however, when he entered a tent and was confronted by the chilling sight of a voluptuous young woman enveloped in the coils of a huge snake. After the experience, "I knew what was meant by my father's dislike of 'sinful amusements;' my conscience took his side, and I never petitioned to go to another circus." At age sixteen, on a visit home from college, the old fear showed itself again. Moncure, with his father and a neighboring couple, went for a Fourth of July drive to the ruins of old Potomac Church. "Walked about," Conway wrote in his diary, "very Beautiful and romantic— however its romance was interrupted by a serpent's protruding its body in loop fashion from the wall couldn't kill him."[50]

The threat posed by the serpent to the "Beautiful and romantic" was of penetrating importance to Conway as he grew up, for he perceived the threat on more than one level. Doubtless his early fear of snakes developed partly because of an objective situation. There were, in fact, a lot of snakes in the region and in the swamp he had to cross on his way to school; some of these were water moccasins, and it can be genuinely unpleasant to step on a water moccasin. But the intensity and persistence of the phobia was out of proportion to objective conditions. Even later in life, long after he had left Virginia and his terror had been at least outwardly shed, Conway retained a deep fascination with snakes, and serpent imagery pervades his adult prose. Usually the imagery is employed to dramatize instances of arbitrary power arrayed against the weak or innocent or beautiful. As a war correspondent in France in 1870 he saw a brigade of soldiers sent into battle, which reminded him of a "huge serpent gliding out on the field." In one of his novels a sweet, pretty girl of fourteen is driven to the altar at a revival after being terrified by the "pythonic rage" of the minister. And he regarded resistance to physical or mental enslavement as resistance to reptilian forces, be they in the form of the "political python, Slavery," or the "vaster dragon—Superstition."[51]

It was no accident that Conway should have employed this imagery in such a way. Snakes represented evil, both tangible and abstract. And evil, as Moncure came to define it, was all but monopolized by insensitive, violent, power-hungry white males, who either ignored or violated the "Beautiful and romantic." The snake was a masculine image, whose sexual connotations are obvious to twentieth-century minds. And the evils it stood for were masculine. This was all especially compelling for a sensitive boy brought up on biblical literalism. "The serpent lore impressed me," Conway remembered, "because of my firm faith that the Devil was a serpent." Only when this is considered does the overpowering fear which Moncure felt on seeing the woman at the circus become fully explicable. Here was the struggle between good and evil, the feminine principle which attracted him versus the masculine principle which repelled him, Eve versus the Devil. "I think the first thing that impressed me in the Bible," he recalled, "was the snake in Eden."[52]

Very early in his life Moncure Conway learned the Bible, memorizing long sections in return for small prizes (usually religious books) at Sunday school. Although his parents "held very pronounced views against Calvinism," Conway recalled, "we were under a rather rigid regime. . . . It was constitutionally natural for my father to live by rules, and to order everything about his house with precision. We must be ready when the bell rang for family prayers, morning and evening." While his mother was "less precise about regulations," she was nevertheless equally concerned that Moncure receive strict Methodist training, and that he understand the awesome importance of making his commitment to Christ. The religious emphasis in Moncure's upbringing was epitomized by his Sundays, the stifling sobriety of which contrasted painfully with the day of play enjoyed by his nonevangelical peers. He remembered Sunday as a "treadmill of services"—a church service in the morning, Sunday school in the afternoon, a prayer meeting at night, no worldly recreation permitted. In 1884 Conway confessed that after this childhood, "to this day it gives me a keen delight to see anybody breaking the Sabbath, especially if it is with games and amusements."[53]

Since Falmouth was too small to sustain a denominational church, the Conways belonged to the Methodist church in Fredericksburg. The town had not always been friendly to evangelism. George Whitefield was treated rudely on a visit in 1765, while Methodist leader Francis Asbury, complaining of "AWFUL Fredericksburg," was unable to make serious inroads in the 1780s and 1790s. In 1801 the first Methodist meetinghouse was built in the town, but by 1810 its membership was probably no more than seventy. By the 1820s, however, change was sweeping Virginia, and Fredericksburg was not immune. Methodism, with its message of the equality of all believers before God, was making headway among lower- and middle-class whites, to whom Anglicanism seemed passionless and overly hierarchical. Moreover, by this time Methodism in the South had effectively made its peace with slavery, making the creed a possible option for upper-class whites as well. For a brief time after the founding of the church in America, Methodists had been forbidden to hold slaves; and although this was quickly changed, the church's antislavery image persisted for some years—in fact, the slave conspirators in an abortive 1800 uprising in Richmond reportedly excluded Methodists from whites targeted for destruction.

But in 1808 each annual conference was permitted to make its own rules on the institution, and in practice this gradually came to mean that a well-to-do slaveholder could be a Methodist without incongruity. Thus by 1830 the stage was set for the entrance into Methodism of a man like Walker Conway, who needed a framework of order and discipline in his own life, who wanted to be a leader in the white community, and who needed a religion which was compatible with, even potentially supportive of, slavery.[54]

As a boy, Moncure Conway felt the tension inherent in being a person of privilege who was simultaneously taught to do honor to his high station in life while ascetically repudiating worldliness or show. Especially in his early boyhood the Methodist congregation in Fredericksburg consisted of poor and unlettered people, who gathered in a dilapidated building without organ or choir, their hymns "led by a good man with a cracked voice and a tuning-fork." "It was pleasant to drive over in our big round coach and back," Conway recalled. "But I saw my cousins and playmates on their way to the fine churches, and in my tenth year going to the meeting-house began to be a half-conscious martyrdom. I have a vague remembrance of humiliation by some boys' jesting references to Methodists." In 1841 the Methodists moved into a new building, but still it lacked an organ, and at the end of the service Moncure would exit hurriedly and run down Princess Anne Street to St. George's Episcopal Church, which he would reach in time to sit in a cushioned pew and listen to a fine choir sing the final hymn. "I was indeed allowed now and then to attend the whole service," he remembered, "and was trained by that choir . . . to a passionate love of sacred music."[55]

Moncure's reaction to the local Methodist church and to the Methodist rank and file was not, however, simply that of a disdainful young patrician. If he sometimes felt restricted by the material starkness of his religion, he was also deeply moved and impressed by its ability to unite socially diverse individuals in a common act of devotion. Moreover, Methodism showed him a side of his father he could discern in no other context. On Sunday afternoons an adult Bible class met at Walker Conway's house, with Moncure sitting in. Sometimes his father would lead the class; at other times he and his wife would be among the students, and the town tailor, James Petty, would lead. And although most of the Methodist classes were segregated by sex, church records from 1846 show the class at Conway House to have been the only one composed of both sexes. Its thirteen women and six men reflected the sexual composition of the congregation as a whole. Here Moncure saw his father shed all arrogance and fearsomeness and take on simple grace and humility, as one of a group of sharing and devoted men and women. "I find the scene engraved in my memory," Conway later wrote, "this fine intellectual father of mine, accustomed to preside over courts, . . . surrounded by poor, dusty, patched people, of whom some could hardly read. . . . They looked up to him with reverence, but in humility he surpassed them all. Somehow I . . . think of my handsome father's appearance as noblest when seated among those dingy and illiterate people." Here, too, as at the camp meetings where Walker frequently pitched his family's tent, Moncure saw a strong, gifted, powerful man exercise a positive moral influence over a group of less privileged men and women, without resorting to the usual weapons of intimidation. Here was the sort of leadership which Moncure could see himself exercising, a model he could emulate. It was one of the few items in his paternal inheritance—perhaps the most important—that he consciously embraced.[56]

Moncure's uncle Eustace was also a power among local Methodists, having been converted at age fourteen at a camp meeting in Prince William County. "He loved to remember the hour of his conversion," his obituary noted. "He spoke of it often while in health, and it was almost the last thing he spoke about on earth." Like his brother a trustee of the Fredericksburg church, Eustace's enthusiasm for Methodism was exhibited as militantly as his enthusiasm for Southern rights: he once expelled three men "for immorality" from his sixteen-member all-male Bible class. It was only a matter of time before his two enthusiasms would merge.[57]

By the 1840s slavery extension had become a live issue in the national Methodist church, causing renewed intradenominational warfare over slavery itself. In 1844 Southern delegates stormed out of the General Conference in New York City after it voted to ask Bishop James Andrew of Georgia to "desist from the exercise of his office" until he ceased to be a slaveholder. The following year Southerners met to organize the Methodist Episcopal Church, South. When ripples of the schism reached Fredericksburg, it found Eustace leading the insurgents, and his brother Walker on the opposite side.[58]

The split came late to Fredericksburg, for that town was on the southern edge of the Northern-aligned Baltimore Conference, which extended into Pennsylvania. Some leaders in the local church had personal ties to Northern Methodists, and Norval Wilson, the local minister, opposed rebellion. Walker Conway, though a strong supporter of slavery, objected to agitation of the issue. Moreover, he felt committed to the Baltimore Conference through his position as a trustee of Dickinson College, a Methodist institution in Carlisle, Pennsylvania. Thus when the issue was forced in Fredericksburg, it was Eustace Conway who took up the burden of rebel leadership. Meeting in August 1848, the Fredericksburg Southern Methodists voted to censure their minister and withdraw support from any clergyman "who is connected to a church, the leading characteristic of which is the deep rooted hostility to the institution of slavery." Eustace provided over twelve hundred dollars to put up a new church building for the insurgents. At first the Southerners were in a minority—89 members in 1848 compared to the Northern wing's 140. But despite Eustace Conway's death in 1857, the Southern faction eventually overtook its more established rival. In 1861 it had 290 members, its rival 164.[59]

What the slaves thought of this internecine religious warfare among their white neighbors and masters is not recorded, but the pattern of their own religious lives did not change. Whites had noted the uses to which the Bible could be put in strengthening the institution of slavery (St. Paul, after all, exhorted servants to obey their masters), and once evangelicalism ceased to be associated with antislavery they were more than happy to see their slaves imbibing Christianity—whether out of a sincere desire to save black souls or the more self-interested motive of reconciling slaves to their fate. Although a few of the Conway slaves seem to have shared the valet James Parker's "quiet contempt" of religious emotionalism, most embraced evangelical Christianity with enthusiasm. Here again, Moncure saw the immense unifying potential of religion. But as he grew to young manhood he began to see more and more clearly that that unity did not lie in the universal acceptance of the same social assumptions or sectarian dogmas, but rather in the ability of religion to provide each participant with strength and self-esteem. During the Civil War, Conway remembered watching the slaves at their nightly prayer and hymn sessions, held in an outbuilding in the yard. Not only the forms but also the emphases of their religion were so different from those of the whites as to make it something new. "These humble and ignorant souls . . . had conceived a symbolism of their own, and burdens of prophecy. . . . The cant phrases of white preachers whom they listened to had become alive to them, and mingled strangely in their [own] speech and hymns. . . ." As he later wrote, "The negroes are almost the only literal and primitive Christians left among us. . . . Their faith has cheered this race through the long night of oppression, and that faith is as different from anything taught in 'white' churches as Buddhism is." Far from inculcating them with a sense of the justice of slavery, the Bible—especially the story of Moses, and the Apocalyptic prophecies—gave the slaves a means of enduring their captivity with dignity while simultaneously looking forward to their own vindication and the overthrow of their oppressors. If Conway learned lessons from the devotion of the poor whites who met in his father's basement, he found those lessons strengthened and extended as he watched the slaves being immersed in the Rappahannock, shouting and clapping at a revival, or singing haunting hymns of suffering and redemption. It was no accident that when Conway parted from religious dogma, he clung all the more tightly to the fundamental, sustaining value of religion.[60]

But that was in the future. In his boyhood what he was taught most explicitly and constantly was the need to come to Christ, the need to be saved from damnation. This pressure Moncure shared with his older brother Peyton, who was sent to Dickinson College in 1846 partly to strengthen his religious convictions in an all-encompassing Methodist environment. Walker Conway was a friend of the college's president, Robert Emory, to whom he wrote more than once requesting that Emory pay attention to Peyton's soul. Whether an illness which necessitated Peyton's temporary withdrawal in early 1847 was induced by religious pressure is not clear, but it is certain that his religious anguish was painful and unrelenting. "It would give me unalloyed pleasure to hear that Peyton *enjoyed* religion," Walker wrote in early March 1847, after Peyton's return to school. "I have long known that he was influenced greatly by the precepts of our Holy Christianity," even though he was only "partially enlightened . . . by the Divine Spirit, without the enjoyment of God's pardoning love." Peyton had "been for some time serious and occasionally somewhat morbid, and subject to irregular fits of high spirits and of depression," but everything would fall into place— his health restored, his studies improved—if he found Christ. In the meantime the pressure should not cease.[61]

Soon he would have company. As an afterthought, Walker Conway informed Emory that he intended to send Peyton's "Brother now 15 years of age with him at the commencement of the next Collegiate year."

CHAPTER 2

The founders had not planned it that way, but in 1833 Dickinson College went Methodist. Launched in the quiet southern Pennsylvania town of Carlisle through the efforts of prominent physician Benjamin Rush and conservative Revolutionary politician and pamphleteer John Dickinson, the college's 1783 charter had expressly forbidden religious favoritism. Its faculty had at one point included the distinguished Deist Thomas Cooper as professor of chemistry and natural philosophy, and its graduates—among them future United States Chief Justice Roger B. Taney, a Roman Catholic—had come from a variety of religious faiths. But the school was beset by habitual feuding between the trustees and the faculty, and its financial problems were chronic and severe. Unable to stay afloat any longer, the trustees finally transferred ownership to the Methodist Episcopal church, which agreed to assume the college's financial obligations. The new board of trustees would have a Methodist majority, and the students' new regimen would revolve around strict religious training.[1]

Academic respectability was not to be forsaken at Dickinson, however, for the Methodist church was anxious to show it had come of age as a religion both acceptable and attractive to the American mainstream. The church had founded its first college, Randolph-Macon, in southern Virginia in 1832, but the acquisition of Dickinson represented a significant advance. Dickinson brought with it a reputation, a tradition, and an attractive ready-made campus dominated by a Benjamin Latrobe masterpiece. To oversee the new regime the trustees chose former Senate chaplain and *Christian Advocate* editor John Price Durbin. Buoyed by a generous flow of Methodist money, Durbin worked diligently during his nine-year presidency to assemble a faculty that was both strongly religious and intellectually superior. Only slightly jolted by the church schism of 1844, which trimmed somewhat the percentage of Southern students, the school by 1847 was the finest Methodist educa-

28

tional institution in the country, and in a position to hold its own against any college of comparable size in America.[2]

Moncure Conway joined his brother at Dickinson in May 1847, his preparation at the Fredericksburg Academy placing him immediately in the sophomore class and enabling him to become the youngest member of the junior class in September.[3] The Dickinson experience was to be significant for Moncure, for it exposed him to a wider circle of acquaintances and opinions and forced on him a severe religious crisis.

The faculty was young and effective. One of Moncure's favorites was Natural History teacher Spencer Fullerton Baird, future director of the Smithsonian Institution, who managed to awaken in him a lifelong interest in science. Baird, the faculty's only non-Methodist, had an infectious enthusiasm for his subject. This was never more evident than on his weekly field trips into the countryside, during which he introduced his students to his animal and floral associates. Conway remembered in particular Baird capturing harmless snakes and explaining their physiology to the boys, demonstrating how they differed from their poisonous cousins. "He even persuaded the bolder among us to handle them," Conway recalled, without revealing whether or not he had been one of the bold.[4]

Conway had other able teachers. There was Chemistry and Natural Philosophy professor William Henry Allen (known to the boys as "Bully" because his corpulent build resembled John Bull's), future president of Girard College, an excitable and popular classroom teacher despite his tendency to intimidate. There was Merritt Caldwell, a gentle and tubercular teacher of English composition who died before Conway graduated, but who bequeathed his student an understanding of "the importance of weighed words, exact statement, and tones sympathetic with the sense." And there was John McClintock, a Methodist minister and teacher of Latin and Greek, who would go on to become editor of the *Methodist Quarterly Review*, pastor of the American church in Paris, and president of Drew University. McClintock, at thirty-four a slender, scholarly, serious, and ambitious man, was to have perhaps the most significant effect on Conway. This effect, however, derived less from McClintock's role as a Classics teacher than from his more unpredictable and incongruous activity as a political agitator.[5]

Many people accused John McClintock of being an abolitionist, and the articles he had been writing for the *Christian Advocate* had done nothing to dissuade them. From February to April 1847 a series of four articles by McClintock had appeared, all aiming to prove slavery incompatible with Christianity. The series was inflammatory enough to cause the journal's editor to defer to an angry readership and cancel a fifth article scheduled for May. Throughout this series McClintock had attempted to put space between himself and the organized abolitionist movement, criticizing abolitionist tactics and rhetoric and refusing to condemn all individual slaveholders as sinners. But his simultaneous praise of abolitionists for "stimulating public opinion in the North, and improving the condition of slaves in the South," and his satisfaction that "the anti-slavery feeling of the North is a hundred-fold what it was when they [abolitionists] began, in point of power, activity and boldness," tended to narrow that space in the eyes of critics. The outcry against his articles showed how little consensus there was even among Northern Methodists in the wake of the 1844 split. But slavery was an issue which would not die. The institution's possible expansion into territories being won in the Mexican War was making it more urgent and unavoidable than ever. Early in June 1847, the issue came to Carlisle.[6]

It came in the form of three fugitive slaves owned by James Kennedy and Howard Hollingsworth of Hagerstown, Maryland—a man, his ten-year-old daughter, and the wife of a free black living in Carlisle. The trio had been captured in nearby Shippensburg. On June 2 they were in Carlisle, the Cumberland County seat, where an owner had come to claim them. Kennedy had reason to hope for cooperation from local officials. An inbred community of some 4,500 residents, the town was hardly a hotbed of radicalism. In 1835 the short-lived Carlisle Anti-Slavery Society had dissolved after J. Miller McKim, probably its only white member, departed for Philadelphia and a high place in the abolitionist movement. Since then its black population (349 in 1850) had lived on in demoralized isolation in a county which still contained 24 slaves as late as 1840. Authorities of such a place were unlikely to obstruct the wishes of a slaveowner recovering his property, despite a recently passed Pennsylvania personal liberty law which made partial obstruction possible if not compulsory. On the morning of June 2 a friendly justice of the peace gave Kennedy a custody certificate, while agreeing to keep the runaways in jail until a hearing on a writ of habeas corpus could be held that afternoon.[7]

McClintock later claimed he was picking up his afternoon mail at the post office, saw the animated crowd outside the nearby courthouse, and only then went over to see what was causing such commotion. Whether or not this was really when he first learned about the fugitives, McClintock lost no time before involving himself in the proceedings. Entering the courtroom to grumblings of "Put the abolitionist out," and "There goes McClintock—the damned abolitionist," the professor strode to the bench and asked the judge if he was aware of the new personal liberty law. When the judge grunted a negative response, the aroused scholar scurried home to get a copy of the law. Quickly returning with it, McClintock found the judge unimpressed. Within minutes the slaves were being marched down the courthouse steps to a waiting carriage, their would-be champion following close behind, a crowd of furious Carlisle blacks closing in. Then came the riot.[8]

"A general rush was made on the slave-owners and constables by the negro men and women," the Carlisle *Herald* reported, "and a frightful melee ensued in the street, in which for some minutes paving stones were hurled in showers and clubs and canes used with terrible energy." By the time the chaos subsided, two of the fugitives (the woman and the girl) had been rescued, a number of blacks had been arrested, McClintock had made himself conspicuous by intervening on behalf of an old black woman being harassed by two white men, and the slaveowner Kennedy had been trampled, sustaining injuries from which he would die three weeks later. Within hours a writ was issued for McClintock's arrest on the grounds of inciting to riot.[9]

News of the event spread quickly through the town and was soon the talk of the Dickinson campus, a five-minute walk from the courthouse. Southern students were especially aroused. At 7 P.M. they held an impromptu meeting on the steps of the college chapel. The rumor that one of their professors had led an attack against slaveholders lawfully attempting to regain their property had sent many tempers to the boiling point. There was much talk among the Southerners, including Peyton and Moncure Conway, of withdrawing from the school. President Emory appeared and tried to calm the students, but they were not appeased until McClintock himself arrived and gave the crowd his own account of what had happened. He explained that he had only tried to acquaint the judge with a new Pennsylvania law and had taken no part in fomenting violence. McClintock then told the students, as he noted in his diary, "to go down and ask any *decent* person they chose and they would find it confirmed. They [the students] behaved very well." McClintock then went off to let the students decide on a course of action, joining his family at Emory's house, where it was thought prudent he should spend the night. The following day Emory posted three hundred dollars bail for McClintock, whose trial was scheduled for August.[10]

Their professor's dignified account of his conduct had impressed the Southern students, who within a few days had drafted resolutions friendly to McClintock, sending them to the local press for publication. Of the ninety-four Southerners enrolled, ninety (including the Conways) signed. "The story did indeed come to us at first so perverted and exaggerated," the students wrote, "that with the natural warmth of Southerners, many of us were excited against him. But after several meetings, we have become convinced of the falsity of the accusation." "The boys have shown me a degree of confidence and affection," wrote McClintock, "which I could not have dreamed of."[11]

McClintock went to his trial, held during the college's summer vacation, well prepared. His lawyers were William Biddle, a college trustee, and William M. Meredith, a prominent Whig attorney soon to be Zachary Taylor's treasury secretary. During the four-day trial the lawyers convinced the jury that their client had been a victim of a vindictive conspiracy, and along with twenty-one of his black codefendants, he was found not guilty. The acquittal angered the judge, who sharply rebuked the jury and said that had the case been a civil one he would have set such a verdict aside. All was not lost, however, for the jury found thirteen blacks guilty of rioting, and Judge Hepburn was able to sentence eleven of them to three years of solitary confinement in a state penitentiary.[12]

The "McClintock riot," as it came to be called, did not make Moncure Conway an abolitionist, but it was the first time he had seen an antislavery man acting fearlessly on his principles, and the impression lingered. In fact, McClintock, who was the only teacher with whom Moncure carried on a sustained correspondence in later years, may have been the first white male Conway had ever heard make an unequivocal attack on slavery. The professor, moreover, was quite willing and eager to discuss his views with his students on any appropriate occasion. After the riot, when McClintock's father asked him if he ever preached antislavery sentiments in class, the annoyed teacher responded: "If you mean to ask whether I have ever taught *abolitionism* (properly so called) before my classes, I say simply that I have never taught it there or any where else. But when the subject properly comes up I have never failed to impress upon my pupils that slavery is contrary to the spirit of Christianity. Surely no *Christian* would find fault with this."[13]

John McClintock, who took his Christianity seriously, was at home at Dickinson College. There, he reported, the students' souls were meticulously nurtured. Awakened daily at 5:30 A.M., the boys assembled at 6:00 for prayers, a meeting repeated each evening at 5:00. On Sundays, Bible classes met at 8:00, followed by preaching at 11:00, more Bible studies at 3:00, more preaching at 6:30. This methodical, structured life, McClintock hoped, would gently condition the boys to a steady life of godliness.[14]

In this hope McClintock specifically opposed a common evangelical notion about the requirements for salvation. To be saved, many felt, one had to suffer through a painful process of doubt, guilt, and despair followed by an awareness of sin and an embrace of God's grace, often climaxing in a mix of anguish and ecstasy at a revival. Echoing the sentiments of Congregationalist minister Horace Bushnell, whose influential *Christian Nurture* had been published a year earlier, McClintock in 1848 denounced the habit of "baptizing infants and then treating them as if they were heathen, until the breath of a revival comes over to convert them, instead of holding them as initiated into the church . . . and training them up for her service, and God's." In his view, creation of an environment for gradual spiritual growth was preferable to prolonged pressure for sudden, immediate regeneration.[15]

But whatever the views of such scattered critics, the conversion experience had become commonplace, an expected event for young people in all conservative Protestant sects. Moncure Conway, whose parents had had conversion experiences, grew up hearing that such an event was indispensable. "I felt that it was something that had to be gone through with," he recalled, "like vaccination." The pressure did not abate when he went to college and found himself surrounded by other adolescents feeling similar pressures, equally anxious about heavenly and earthly futures. The prayerful Dickinson environment, whatever McClintock may have hoped, was less conducive to gradual spiritual evolution than to periodic explosions of youthful religious emotion.[16]

The intensity of the explosion sometimes reflected the strain involved in a student's trying to extract emotions from himself which would not surface naturally. This effort might go on for months or even years. At Dickinson nearly every student was trying to achieve conversion, under the impression that it would halt his adolescent doubts about himself and his future, signal his passage into adulthood, and exhibit to others his own moral and spiritual rectitude. In July 1847 a letter in the *Christian Advocate* ascribed the relative lack of student disorder at Dickinson to the "large number of students of sincere religion, and possessing decided habits of piety." But the potential for student resentment against religious pressures was revealed in a satirical sketch which a fifteen-year-old, still unconverted Moncure Conway delivered in the college chapel in the fall of 1847. After an uninspired and rather silly assault on various academic annoyances which make for "bored students," Conway alluded to the spiritual demands being made on himself and his friends. Evidently defending the self-proclaimed class "infidel," Conway denounced a state of affairs in which a student, "though he be an Infidel . . . is forced . . . to give utterance to the clearest and most conclusive arguments in favor of Christianity—and—though unwilling—is forced to become either a convert or Hypocrite." Only a few months later, Moncure willed himself into conversion.[17]

"We rejoice to learn that a powerful revival of religion is now in progress, in the M[ethodist] E[piscopal] Church in this borough," the Carlisle *Herald* reported on January 12, 1848. "The meetings, held every evening, are attended by immense crowds, and a large number of both sexes, chiefly young persons, have been awakened to deep concern for their eternal interests." The church, on High Street midway between the campus and the courthouse, had been for some days the meeting place for young women from the Carlisle Female Seminary, young men from Dickinson, and an odd assortment of townspeople, all fervently reinforcing each other in an effort to come to Christ. Word of the revival had reached Moncure on January seventh, and his journal for that day indicates a sudden departure: "Made a nine in Mac's [McClintock's class]—went to Bully's lecture—dry—all at once determined to be a Christian went to church—and to the altar."[18]

It did not work. Moncure knelt, prayed, stiffened, grimaced, concentrated—and prayed some more. Others knelt and prayed for him. Nothing helped. He still felt too much pride. The Holy Spirit did not descend. He left. The next evening, after listening to declamations all day at the college, he made his way through falling snow to the church. "Went to the mourners bench again," he wrote. Again he prayed. Again others prayed. "Too much self-righteousness." Another failure. He left again. The next day, Sunday, January 9, he "was strengthened in my determination to become a Christian—went to church in the morning." The service was bracing; he would have the will and the stamina to try again that night. In the afternoon he talked it all over with a schoolmate. "Did me good—got ready to go to church." Before he left he got on his knees and prayed for this to be the time. He wanted it to happen now, to be put off no longer. As darkness fell he walked through the snow and the bitter cold to the church. He knelt. He prayed. Others prayed. He felt ashamed. He felt sinful. He felt sick. He swooned. Friends sang. Girls wept. The preacher exulted. The Holy Spirit embraced him and he was in rapture. "Was converted—felt happy that night." It had happened.[19]

"Had doubts as to the genuineness of my conversion," he wrote the next day, "—silenced them by prayer." Perhaps it had not happened after all. The situation called for encouragement, reinforcement. Three days later he heard his friend and classmate George De Bonneville Keim (a future railroad president in Pennsylvania) had been converted. "Thought I should go crazy—went to see him—heard him tell his experience five times in five minutes—didn't do much in the way of studying." The next day Moncure presented his friend with a personalized red morocco Bible. He and Keim had buoyed each other. Their experiences seemed genuine. They were children of the Lord. On the fifteenth, Moncure sat alone in the school chapel and spoke aloud his love for Christ. "Fine time at church that night." The next day he went to Bible class and exuberantly told the story of his conversion. "Never enjoyed myself so much." Later in the day he, Peyton, and some forty others were received into communion at the town church. "Went to two prayer meetings in the afternoon and church at night." It was real after all.[20]

Or was it? Conway's nagging doubts about the sincerity of his conversion, the reality of his oneness with God, the definitiveness of his salvation, would not depart. Conversion, which was supposed to solve everything, had solved nothing. For the next two months he struggled with doubts harder to bear than the earlier pressures to convert. The undigestible infusion of piety began to affect both his mental balance and his health; by March he was missing classes because of illness. On the fifth he recorded himself as "not feeling very well in my mind." At Bible class that day he told of his latest experience but regarded it as "not very flattering—determined to do better—was not at church during the day—unwell."[21]

Before long, Walker Conway was in Carlisle investigating reports of his son's bad health. Arriving on March 19, the elder Conway promptly gave Moncure a hymnbook as a present and congratulated him on his conversion. The next day Moncure had a "violent chill" and his father decided to take him back to Virginia to recover. Peyton packed his brother's trunk. The three prayed and read the Bible together, and then retired for the evening. At 3:00 A.M. Walker and his younger son arose to catch the train for the South. "Felt remarkably well," Moncure noted.[22]*

Although Moncure's illness was virtually gone by the time he returned to Virginia, he was permitted to remain away from school until the start of the fall term. During the more than five months he was home, Moncure fell under the influence, more than ever before, of male relatives. Having now lived away from home and professed his seriousness by going through conversion, this sixteen-year-old could be considered a boy no longer. Moreover, with his older brother away during much of this period, and with his younger brothers (ages six and eight) still in short pants, Moncure was in a position to receive a large share of his father's attention. Walker Conway was determined to educate his son in Virginia politics in this heated election year, and began the lessons by sending him to his uncle, Richard Moncure, a candidate for the state legislature.

It was a pleasant beginning for young Conway, for his uncle Richard was generous and genial, a detached Episcopalian who indulged his nephew's love of reading by giving him the run of his library, and who took his legal work more seriously than he took himself. This uncle, who in 1851 would be given a seat on the Virginia Supreme Court, seemed personally less intimidating than most of the Conway or Daniel men. (When Conway wrote *Pine and Palm* nearly forty years later, the character of Judge Stirling, father of a character modeled loosely on the novelist, was based not on Walker Conway but on Richard Moncure.) When his young apprentice came to him in early April Richard shook his hand warmly, grinned, and asked, "Have you seen any voters?" Together, candidate and nephew went in search of them, Conway trading political gossip with the country people and listening admiringly as his uncle gave them "first rate" stump speeches. On election day, April 27, Conway earned two dollars by serving as clerk at the Falmouth

* Although he takes some literary license, Conway's account of a revival experience in his pamphlet *Revivalism* (London, 1875), 12–14, seems to derive from the episode at Dickinson. Prompted, by the exploits in England of American revivalist Dwight L. Moody, to explain the psychology of the revival to British agnostics, Conway wrote in this pamphlet: "When I got far enough in time away from that proceeding to reflect on it, I began to perceive that its explanation was to be found in physiology, not in religion. And in the hundreds of conversions which I subsequently witnessed, I observed that they generally took place when the body was reduced to the point of exhaustion. . . . delirium sets in, beginning with a sense of depression which results in a reaction. This reaction is nature's relief to the overstrained system, and it is sometimes pleasant enough to be called conversion, or finding Jesus."

polling place, and gloated as the returns came in showing his uncle the winner over his Whig opponent, Charles Francis Suttle. It had been fun, and it whetted his appetite for more.[23]

On May 10, Moncure went with his father to a Democratic gathering at King George Courthouse, where the latter was elected a delegate to the upcoming national convention in Baltimore. Walker Conway went to the Baltimore meeting that summer in no mood to humor the growing element in the Northern wing of his party which wanted to forbid the expansion of slavery, and he was disgusted by the behavior of the New York Free-Soilers (termed "barnburners") who left the convention rather than share the floor with the "hunkers" in a more conservative rival delegation. When these New Yorkers met subsequently with other Free-Soilers and nominated ex-President Martin Van Buren as their third-party presidential candidate, Moncure Conway's contempt mirrored his father's. "M Van Buren has accepted the nomination of the Barnburners," he wrote in his journal, "—a scoundrel and traitor."[24]

Moncure wrote a letter about the King George meeting to his cousin, editor John Moncure Daniel, who printed extracts in his Richmond *Examiner*. Moncure read the *Examiner* regularly during these months—. "my favorite paper," he called it—and through it became infatuated with his capricious and conspicuous cousin. Daniel, whom one historian has called "half genius, half misanthrope," was barely twenty-two upon assuming his editorship in 1847, but with undeniable ability made the *Examiner* the most talked-about newspaper in the state. Mixing an omnivorous mind with a carnivorous disposition, he peppered his paper with verses by Poe, reviews of Emerson and Hawthorne as well as Southern writers, extracts from abolitionists (whom he excoriated but whose vitality he adored) and proslavery ideologues (whom he applauded but whose narrowness he despised)—along with the wildest and most irresponsible personal attacks on public figures printable in an age of partisan journalism. He was a sensitive aesthete who lamented the lack of appreciation for art and music in the South, and a swaggering hothead who fought several duels. His insatiable curiosity, lacerating wit, mystifying moodiness, and seeming disregard of consequences prompted some people to judge him brilliant. Later Conway would realize that Daniel's bitter extremism was a function of his spiritual estrangement from a milieu he both loved and loathed. But in 1848 Moncure was drawn to him. Here was a young man who was an activist, a spirited Democratic partisan, and a powerful figure in Virginia society, but who was also a reader, a thinker, a writer, even in some ways, perhaps, an artist. It was exciting for Moncure to discover that one could combine those things, and for a time he took John Daniel as a man to be emulated.[25]

Eustace Conway also entered Moncure's life more boldly this summer. Moncure was attracted by the magnetic personality of this ambitious uncle, at twenty-eight a rising legislator, and was impressed by the size and tenacity of his personal following. Regarding his uncle as a man of "untiring energy and perseverance together with a strict sense of justice," Moncure resented it when Reverend Wilson preached a sermon on the Methodist schism over slavery which, though "mild," gave some offense "to the members of the [local] Southern Church, [of] which Uncle E. is chief." In August, Eustace took his enthusiastic nephew on a political tour of northern Virginia, stopping at the courthouses in Stafford, Prince William, and Fairfax Counties.[26]

It was for this uncle that Moncure wrote his first piece for publication, an obituary of Eustace's four-year-old son which the Fredericksburg *Democratic Recorder* printed in April. Although Moncure confided to his journal that he "felt ashamed" of the little article, the sight of his work in print propelled him toward more ambitious journalistic forays. His second piece, an anonymous satire of Charles Suttle just after his electoral defeat by Richard Moncure, raised local Whig hackles and brought a rebuke from his father, who disliked its crudeness and intemperateness. But Moncure pushed his pen onward, apparently encouraged by John Daniel, who had pleased him by publishing his account of the Democratic meeting at King George. Soon he was trying his hand at literature, writing poetry and short stories, signing them "Cleofas II" and "Alphonso III," nervously dropping them through the *Recorder*'s mail slot and skedaddling before anyone could see him. The fiction and verse were kept anonymous with special care, for Conway lacked confidence (justifiably, no doubt) in his talent, and he knew his father would never approve. The only person in whom he confided about these efforts was his eleven-year-old sister, who pronounced them all excellent.[27]

Conway's most elaborate literary project during these months was a novel which was never published, *The Flute Player*. The plot involves a Venetian pianist who rises to fame, falls in love with one woman, leaves her, and falls in love with another, becoming engaged to her. On a successful concert tour in America he scorns a young musician who seeks his help. On the ship back to Europe, he meets a flute player who tells him he is in love with the same woman to whom the pianist is engaged. The pianist haughtily tells the flutist of his betrothal, and the flutist staggers off and commits suicide. Soon after this, the protagonist discovers that his fiancée and the woman whom he had loved previously are his two long-lost sisters. The sordid news impels him to follow the flutist's lead; he, too, kills himself.[28]

Unfortunately, the text of *The Flute Player* does not survive, but enough is known about its plot to invite speculation. The novel was written at a time when Moncure was consciously viewing himself (and being viewed) as entering adulthood, a milestone ratified by the un-precedentedly close attention being paid him by his father and other male relatives. He was taking an active part in the world of party politics, an all-male, kinsman-infested domain; and he was moving away, in his outward life, from the women who had clutched him so close in his boyhood. In the midst of these developments, he chose to write a novel about a man of artistic temperament who is destroyed partly because he refuses fellowship with other men, partly because of his fondness for women; about two different men both driven to suicide by their love for women; and about the subterranean subject of incest. Perhaps this private literary endeavor was a reflection of Moncure's felt need to enter a man's world and an expression of his own anxiety about having belonged—perhaps still belonging—to a woman's world, complete with fears about his closeness to specific female relatives and about his own sexual inclinations. Perhaps it indicated the intensity of the pressure he was feeling to throw over one world for the other.

Moncure returned to Dickinson in September 1848 energized by his experiences in Virginia politics and journalism and eager to continue them from a distance. Filled, as he wrote later, with "an engendered anti-northern feeling," he set about gathering material for articles intended for John Daniel's paper. The first of these, published in December, was a philippic directed against the hypocrisy of Yankees who preached to the South about its racial policies while treating their own black population with contempt. "The most common phrase here is, 'D——n a nigger, I hate 'em like h—ll!' This seems to be a sort of formula for universal usage. *Northern benevolence*—faugh!" There was, of course, a large kernel of truth in this, but Conway's aim was not so much to attack Northern racial injustice as to criticize abolitionists and defend Southern slavery. Northern blacks, he wrote, "are taken from protection, and thrust into the depth of degradation, and then are mocked by being called *free*." If blacks were not deluded by a false picture of slavery, "there would be found *many* who would *run away* from the North into voluntary slavery. . . . I'd most certainly prefer the existence of a dog, than that of a negro at the North."[29]

Moncure's second and last article written from Carlisle appeared in the *Examiner* in January 1849, a denunciation of the town's customs and climate ("the place where nature blows its nose") and a priggish assault on the habits of Northern students, alternately too stilted and too raucous. One could not even meet a girl, he complained, without a formal introduction; "the social principle—so sedulously cherished in Virginia—is apparently extinct." And the students' revelries at Christmas were disgusting to any young man of taste. "Peep into one of their rooms in the morning and see the washbasins filled with egg-nog. . . . Peep in again at midnight and see the buckets full of vomit, and the beds full of young human hogs." It was all a very sad spectacle. "A Southerner, especially a Virginian, can never overcome his repugnance to northern conventionalities, inasmuch as they are so totally disconsonant with his own."[30]

But these articles, written obviously to please his cousin and in primitive imitation of John Daniel's own style, only imperfectly expressed Moncure's thinking. His attraction to journalism encouraged him in March 1849 to found and edit a new college literary magazine, *The Collegian*, and its pages revealed an approach both more moderate and more uncertain. An article on slavery, in the first issue, written unmistakably by Conway, indicated his views were more complex than he had been willing to say in the *Examiner*. Reviewing an article on William Ellery Channing published in a recent issue of the *Methodist Quarterly Review*, Conway vowed that the late Unitarian pioneer's opposition to slavery would not "prevent me, though a son of the south, from according to him the merit due to upright and honest purpose." He went on to defend the general benevolence of slavery in practice, despite "the possible or actual abuses" of the institution, and rebuked Northern detractors of the system, but in relatively mild terms: "If, instead of indulging in indiscriminate and often unjust reproaches, northern men would devote their energies to devising some practicable plan of emancipation; if, forbearing to provoke by harshness, they would strive to win by kindness, we think much more could be effected towards gaining their object." And then came an interesting admission: "Southerners feel that slavery is an evil, but an evil which the present generation had no part in originating. They would gladly be rid of it, but know that this cannot be done in a day, and consider themselves better judges of the time, means, and manner of effecting it, consistently with the interests of both races, than those who are far removed from the difficulties which any plan of emancipation must involve." Moncure's infatuation with Eustace Conway and John Daniel had not led him to embrace their outright proslavery opinions.[31]

Conway's college life was not limited to study, religion, and politics. Not completely the pious prude he sometimes appeared, he found time for occasional healthy flirtations with frivolousness and moral inconsistency. This was especially true in his senior year, when he was gaining in confidence and was more on his own, Peyton having left school before the start of the fall term in 1848. During the Christmas holidays that year Conway traveled with a friend to the latter's home in Harford County, Maryland, stopping overnight at a country inn. There he massacred the logic of his anti-liquor diatribe in the *Examiner* by settling back with a supply of whisky punch (his first taste of alcohol), and smoked his first cigar. If the whisky was pleasing, the cigar was a revelation. He soon began to indulge freely his newfound passion for tobacco, a passion which would continue until the moment he died, a filled ashtray by his side.[32]

During his senior year Conway was the star player in a practical joke forever enshrined in Dickinson folklore. President Emory had recently died and been replaced by Jesse Peck, a rotund, pretentious, condescending minister, who later became a bishop. Hearing that the much-loathed Peck was about to attend a Methodist conference in Staunton,

Virginia, Conway wrote pseudonymously to the superintendent of the Staunton lunatic asylum, warning him that a maniac who imagined himself president of Dickinson College was on his way, in his derangement determined to make a speech at the conference. The letter had an effect beyond Conway's wildest dreams. Officials of the mental institution met Peck upon his arrival at Staunton, and the Dickinson president, thinking this was part of his official welcome, quietly accompanied them to the asylum before the joke was perceived. Peck suspected Conway of the prank but could not prove it. Not until 1892, when he received an honorary doctorate from the school, did the guilt-burdened prankster confess.[33]

Nearing his seventeenth birthday, Conway fell in love. In *The Collegian* that spring he wrote lightheartedly that for "pious students" love was "the only species of dissipation in which they can consistently engage," that "their affections naturally enough come as nigh to worldliness as possible, and there rest—and the resting-place is invariably some pretty girl." For Conway the pretty girl was Kate Emory, young sister of the departed Dickinson president, born on exactly the same day as Moncure. Kate's letters show her to have been straightforward, articulate, sensitive, serious, religious, and unswervingly conventional. Moncure, utterly bewitched, felt sure she would be his wife one day, despite his plentiful competition and their properly chaperoned relationship. Kate was the first woman outside his family whom Moncure loved, and the experience was in every way enlarging. "This love was the second of my births," he later wrote. When Kate agreed to correspond after his graduation, Moncure's hopes soared. He spent the night before commencement day hovering about Kate's house, pining and dreaming, until sunup.[34]

The temperature on that commencement day, July 12, 1849, reached ninety-six degrees, but the crowd packing the Methodist church bravely withstood sweat and smell as twenty graduates delivered self-conscious orations before receiving their diplomas. Conway, graduating in the middle of his class, chose for his topic "Old Age," which at least one wilted auditor thought "unfortunate." "Apparently very young himself," the observer commented, "his performance failed to make the impression of certainty which results from experience. It was only a guess, tolerably shrewd, and clothed in the garb of fancy, at what the feelings, joys and sorrows of old age might be." Although his speech was "prettily written," Conway's "delivery was marred by an over-strained energy."[35]

Over-strained, also, were Conway's apprehensions about the future. He was only seventeen, the youngest in his graduating class, but the pressure of choosing a vocation was upon him. It was time to go back to Virginia and begin in earnest the business of being a Conway, if possible in a way consistent with his own aptitudes and desires. The enormity of the task was unsettling. "It is a critical period in our lives," read his farewell editorial in *The Collegian*, "when we are compelled to decide what part in the machinery of society we shall fill. . . . It will be important to discover what pursuit, from the peculiar character of our minds, best suits us, and to that, to direct our energies. Mistakes here, though often made, are fatal."[36]

Initially, Moncure coped with this "critical period" in his life by making no decisions at all. His brother Peyton was studying law, but Moncure's inclination was toward literature, and Virginia offered little scope for such a person. And so he lapsed into a period of housebound stagnation in Falmouth, writing occasional literary pieces for the Fredericksburg paper, annoying his father, who thought them frivolous and a waste of time. Also, like any recent graduate, Moncure lived in the past, musing over old experiences, missing old friendships, longing for the wholeness and excitement and satisfaction (romanticized in memory) of his college days. In September 1849 he revisited Carlisle, talking to acquaintances who remained, looking askance at new faces, and visiting Kate Emory, who was as sweet, pretty, and frustrating as ever.[37]

Back in Virginia, his malaise deepened. His father was, to him, a smotheringly respectable man. Now Moncure lived in the same house with him and his dutiful lawbook-toting older son, worrying about his approval and resenting him for withholding it. Moncure wanted things his father could not understand or appreciate, and so he continued his gravitation toward other men, like Eustace Conway and John Daniel and various Southern extremists in Fredericksburg.

Pressure came from these men too, but it was more indirect, more subtle, less constant. And there was vitality in them: they rocked boats and rattled sabers, talked inspiringly of causes and of fighting to defend the sacred institutions of Virginia. While their basic values and beliefs were little different from Walker Conway's, their politics were aggressive, combative, disruptive. In contrast to Walker's dislike of agitation, they thrived on it and scorned any (national) status quo. It was this energized iconoclasm, more than their defense of the Southern position, that drew Moncure Conway toward these men.

Late in 1849 Moncure attended a meeting of a Southern Rights Association in Fredericksburg, peopled by influential men receptive to secession in defense of slavery. But his father was no more pleased by this than by his literary efforts, and told him so. "Don't be the fool of those people!" Walker chided him, telling him that however defensible and proper, slavery was "doomed," and that secession would ruin the South. Life in his father's house was becoming unbearable for Moncure. Hurt by his failure to please a man whom he seemed constitutionally unable to please, early in 1850 he abruptly and clandestinely left.[38]

He turned up in Richmond, sending his father a note saying he had left secretly lest his departure be forbidden. Soon he was in the *Examiner* office, looking for work. His editor-cousin was willing to find something for him to do, but John Daniel was wary of Moncure's apparently sudden rebellion and did not encourage him to proceed under strained circumstances. Within a few days Moncure's uncle Eustace, serving in the legislature, took him under his wing and persuaded him to return to Falmouth. There, his angry and concerned father told him that this period of drift had reached its end, and that Moncure would find himself and his niche by the study of law. Confused and exhausted, his son submitted. In early March, Moncure was packed off to the town of Warrenton, some forty miles northwest, where he was to begin studies with a family acquaintance, Colonel William Fowke Phillips. On the stagecoach he did not think about law. Pulling out a copy of the Richmond *Examiner*, he read a story, "The Great Stone Face." "The writer of it, Nathaniel Hawthorne, is a striking writer," he noted. "Man of great reflection."[39]

Colonel Phillips was an unreflective, stylized man of impeccable manners and dress, and, like most of Conway's relatives, a Democrat of conviction. In his home Moncure heard Daniel Webster's famous "seventh of March" speech read aloud, an anti-abolitionist and pro–Fugitive Slave Law address made in defense of the compromise bill then consuming the attention of the Senate and the country. While antislavery Northerners regarded Webster's speech as a cowardly sellout to Southern interests, Conway thought it showed Webster a "Titan" whose dust should be "subjected to chemical analysis after he's dead." With Phillips, Moncure attended court sessions and got to know the leading lawyers of Fauquier County. One of these, prominent Whig Robert Eden Scott, had led the opposition to the Conway Resolutions in the Virginia legislature, and partly because of this had lost his seat. Scott was now trying to regain his place in Richmond, and Moncure listened to his speeches in order to abuse him in the pages of the *Examiner*. Conway denounced as "puerile in the extreme" a "cloggy speech" on March 25 in which Scott denounced the notion of a Southern confederacy. Much later Conway would lament that Scott had been "a real nobleman, representative of the best traditions of Virginia, and I knew it not." At the time, however, Moncure was happy to see Scott go down to defeat once more. Eustace Conway's old adversary was destined to be an increasingly ignored figure in Virginia, fated ultimately to sit out the Civil War until he was murdered by Northern soldiers who had invaded his farm.[40]

Moncure tried to apply himself conscientiously to his legal studies, but it was not easy. Phillips was "exact in his office, and my work there was an instruction in precision." Not fond of precision and possessing a spirit which craved a less prosaic outlet than a law library, Moncure lunged at every opportunity for a momentary artistic escape. Occasionally he rode to Fauquier Springs to visit a young woman who played the piano and introduced him to Mozart and Beethoven. On Sunday afternoons in the Episcopal church where he taught Sunday school (the local Methodist church was hostile to the Baltimore Conference, to which Moncure still adhered) he sat at the organ and played to his heart's content as a black sexton blew the bellows. And he found time to write a review of the first two volumes of Griswold's *Works of Poe*, praising the "highly-wrought and finished" language of the tales—his favorites were "The Fall of the House of Usher" and "Marie Roget"— and proclaiming Poe's poetry "unrivalled in our land."[41]

The problem was that he loved these expeditions into music and literature far more than anything he did in Phillips's library or at the courthouse, despite his continued efforts to conform. The strain was not easily contained, especially as he came to realize that every day spent studying law brought him another step closer to becoming a conventionalized country lawyer, and another step away from devoting himself to things that made him happy. Conway later described himself at this stage as a soul "aimless, morbid, passionately longing for it knew not what." As had happened two years earlier in Carlisle, he became nervous and ill, and was forced to retreat to Falmouth for a temporary respite. There, in April 1850, came a turning point in his life.[42]

He later described it as one would describe a religious conversion, and so it was. He was bereft of hope, feeling desperately inadequate and purposeless. And then, at the darkest moment of physical exhaustion and moral despair, grace descended and he embraced it, and his life was revolutionized. It was a steady and gradual revolution, for like any conversion it required long meditation and study to make the initial rapture meaningful. But it would be no less dramatic for that. What mattered was that "thenceforth the world was for me changed." In April 1850 Moncure Conway discovered Ralph Waldo Emerson.[43]

The discovery was made in the December 1847 issue of *Blackwood's Edinburgh Magazine*, the lead article of which was an unsigned summary and analysis of Emerson's work. One warm and sunny April morning, while trying to recuperate at home from his Warrenton depression, Conway went for a walk down the Stafford side of the Rappahannock. In his hand was the magazine, casually purchased in Fredericksburg. Stopping by a secluded spring atop the first hill downriver from Falmouth, he sat beneath a tree and began to read. The title of the article—"Emerson"—was hardly gripping, for Conway had barely heard of the man, despite John Daniel's occasional notice of him in the *Examiner*. "The genius of America," the article opened, "seems hitherto disposed to manifest itself rather in works of reason and reflection than in those displays of poetic fervour which are usually looked for in a nascent literature." Moncure, with his own minor efforts at poetic fervor, may have winced at this, but the thought was provocative and he read on. On the first column of the second page the article's protagonist was introduced, presented as the American whose work showed, more than any of his countrymen's, "the undoubted marks of original genius." His curiosity aroused, Conway proceeded. "For what is the prevailing spirit of his writings? Self-reliance, and the determination to see in the man of today, in his own, and in his neighbour's mind, the elements of all greatness. . . . The germ of all lies within yourself. This is his frequent text." Conway felt a rush of excitement; spring, river, hillside, everything around him faded utterly, and he was lost in the intensity of the words, which sprang from the printed page and penetrated him "like an arrow." He moved quickly to the next column, where an extract from Emerson's essay on history struck something primal and brought him to a halt.[44]

It is remarkable that involuntarily we always read as superior beings. Universal history, the poets, the romancers, do not, in their stateliest pictures, in the sacerdotal, the imperial palaces, in the triumphs of will or of genius, anywhere make us feel that we intrude, that this is for our betters, but rather is it true that in their grandest strokes, there we feel most at home. *All that Shakespeare says of the king, yonder slip of a boy that reads in the corner, feels to be true of himself.*

Reading the last sentence, italicized in the article, Conway sat trans-fixed. He was just a boy in a corner, who had a life marked out for him, one he did not want but felt powerless to change. And yet here was a man—a man—telling him, as if speaking to him personally, that life was full of possibilities, and that his life was as important as that of any king. "A sentence only!" he wrote years later. ". . . Its searching subtle revelation defies any analysis I can make of its words. All I know is that it was the touch of flame I needed." He sat there for a long time, musing about the meaning of that phrase "true of himself." His pondering set in motion a mood which was to build and gather strength in the months and years ahead, a mood which told him he had needs that were important and special and that the world must respect and not trample. What was set in motion would take a lifetime to work through, but the catalyst, Conway always believed, had been "one sentence, quoted from Emerson, which changed my world and me."[45]

At Chester White's bookstore in Fredericksburg they had never heard of Emerson, although they did have an arithmetic book by someone of that name. Conway did not want an arithmetic book. He wanted *Essays, First Series*, by the Concord transcendentalist, and before long the bookstore's order was met and the book was in his hands. The treasured volume made the rounds of the household, Moncure's parents and sister eager to understand what the excitement was about. To thirteen-year-old Mildred, Emerson was simply "a Chinese puzzle," but his parents had definite opinions. The implications of his son's fondness for Emerson were not lost on Walker Conway. "I remember when I introduced him at home," Moncure wrote a few years later, "that on reading his writings Pa was severe on him because he had made me discontented (as he thought) with everything. . . . But my mother, who has a most deeply religious soul, read him, and did not wonder that I loved him." Margaret Conway seemed to understand and appreciate, as her husband did not, what attracted her son to Emerson. "What I love him for," Moncure wrote, "is . . . that he is heroic, truthful,—and because I never read his words . . . without feeling ennobled. He helps me to scorn dapperness and hypocrisy, and to live and be myself."[46]

It was some time before Conway's new sense of excitement and energy was to find direction and focus. Emerson's words had given him a dynamic feeling of largeness and possibility, but had not provided him with specific signposts pointing away from his present predicament and toward something higher and better. So for a time his life went on in the same pattern. Late in May he spent a week in Washington, listening to the Senate debates on the compromise bill and making some extra money by writing about it for the *Examiner*. By the end of the month he was back with Colonel Phillips in Warrenton, going to court and studying his lawbooks. But he was now reading other, potentially subversive things. In Washington he had picked up a collection of essays by Horace Greeley, whose New York *Tribune* he was also beginning to read. Greeley acquainted him with communitarian ideas and a vast array of reformist notions, which he began to discuss with his increasingly puzzled acquaintances. He was reading Horace Mann, too, on the public school system of Massachusetts, which made him wonder why Virginia had no such system. Then came Emerson's *Essays, Second Series*. On August 11 he "thought much, and took the idea of writing an Allegory on the subject of a mind voyaging the unsafe boundless ocean of speculations." People were starting to look askance at him; he began to feel that he "was an object of misgivings." Somehow, now, it mattered less. In late August came a letter from Kate Emory, to whom he had been bemoaning his fate, which boosted his ego and lifted his spirits. "I can scarcely believe that with your religious sentiments, your education, and the talents God has given you," she wrote, "you can be sincere in saying you are living with no end in view. . . . You will be very useful—a shining light in the church and in the world.—You must excuse my writing in this way, but really I could not help it, for I feel interested in your welfare and should regret it very much if I could think you were wasting your talents—as you *say*." By the end of the summer, Conway's mood was of anticipation. His spiritual logjam was loosening. Confusion there still was, but now it was the confusion of movement rather than paralysis. Things were about to happen, and the initiative was his.[47]

CHAPTER 3

Conway's quickened energies in the summer and fall of 1850 first focused on the cause of compulsory public education. A convention was about to meet in Richmond to revise the Virginia constitution, and Conway hoped to persuade the delegates to establish a statewide network of public schools. His medium was a pamphlet, his first independent publication, written during August and September and printed, at a cost to the author of fifty dollars, in October.[1]

The pamphlet relied heavily on Horace Mann's report on Massachusetts. "A contrast between Virginia and Massachusetts is painful," wrote Conway, appealing to Virginia pride. "It would be crushing were we not hopeful of better things." While Massachusetts settlers had stressed very early the education of their children, Virginia pioneers had been so busy eradicating Indians and accumulating wealth that "they gloried in the absence of education." The result was that in Virginia 1 out of every 13 free adults was illiterate, compared to 1 in every 189 in Massachusetts.[2]

The situation was even more galling because many Yankees blamed the general demoralization of Virginia nonslaveholding whites on slavery. In fact, Conway insisted, every thinking Virginian knew that lack of education, not the peculiar institution, was the culprit. Though only eighteen years old and unknown, he had just been arguing that very point by letter with Horace Greeley. But Greeley had scoffed at his arguments, and in September had said editorially that he was making "a distinction without a difference. Free-schools, or Common Schools of any kind, cannot flourish with Slavery." Slavery kept poor whites so demoralized, Greeley contended, that they lacked the required interest in schooling. "Never will Virginia's White children be generally schooled until her Black ones shall cease to be sold. Our friend may be sure of this."[3]

"Men of Virginia!" Conway exhorted. "Are you dumb to such words

46

as these? . . . We *can* have Common Schools, and that too, co-existent with slavery." The leading politicians of the state should come to his assistance in exposing Northern slander. They should show the world that slavery was not at the root of Virginia's problems. They should demonstrate that the slave system did not discourage responsible leaders from meeting the social needs of all free citizens. Full of anticipation, Conway sent copies of his pamphlet (five hundred in all) to every member of the convention and every other prominent Virginian he could think of. But nothing happened. Eustace Conway, a member of the convention, opposed free schools. John Daniel lent no approval in the *Examiner*. Walker Conway, although proud of his son's industry, did not agree with him. Already, at Colonel Phillips's house in September, Moncure had mentioned the free school issue to the visiting senator from Virginia, James M. Mason, author of the new Fugitive Slave Law; and Mason had snarled "that such education would be surely followed by the introduction into the South of the entire swarm of Northern 'isms.' " Ultimately the convention refused to act. It was all disillusioning, and more than a little irritating. Conway had stood at the barricade against the New York *Tribune*, and the Virginia ruling class had left him to man it alone. The Virginia establishment seemed to have no taste for a crusade that was not reactionary. It made him wonder whether Greeley might be right.[4]

"Conservatism is a mean, at least a suspicious thing," Conway had written in his pamphlet, "a coverlet under which Ignorance and Hypocrisy may always be found." For a long time he had felt his father to be the epitome of complacent, immovable, unchangeable conservatism, a man who told him to be content with his predestined place in a preordained order. In reaction he had moved toward other relatives and other men who seemed unafraid of change. But now they had betrayed him: nothing must be done, no matter how noble or needed, which would possibly interfere with slavery, the linchpin of the status quo. It made him wonder more coherently than before about slavery, about the stultifying impact of the system. This pattern of authority appeared to him like a water moccasin blocking the path to the schoolhouse door, paralyzing the free will of whites as well as blacks. He, a son of the Virginia slavocracy, was in danger of thinking the unthinkable.[5]

A new racial theory helped momentarily to preserve his waning loyalties. The theory was polygenesis, the notion that the black and white races had been created separately and hence were still separate, unequal species. Although polygenesis had had proponents throughout the 1840s, it acquired considerably more prestige in July 1850 when Louis Agassiz, the renowned Swiss naturalist who had taken a post at Harvard in 1848, supported it in an article in the Unitarian *Christian Examiner*. John Daniel embraced the theory and talked with his young cousin about it. Despite its heretical implications—it did not mesh well with the first book of the Bible—polygenesis appealed to Conway in two ways. First, it was shocking, provocative, a blow to complacency. Second, it provided him with an increasingly required justification for slavery. "We hold that negroes are not *men* in the sense in which the term is used by the Declaration of Independence," John Daniel wrote. "Were the slaves men we should be unable to disagree with Wendell Phillips."[6]

Sometime in the late summer or fall of 1850 Conway defended polygenesis in a talk at the Warrenton lyceum, much to the discomfort of many religiously orthodox listeners. In December, reeling from his inability to interest Virginia in free schools, his loyalties fraying, he sat down to write an article on the subject. He began with another assault on timorousness: "The great Evil Spirit of the Earth is Conservatism. . . . We feel as if some one had introduced a viper into our chambers, if a new star comes—no matter if it be a Star of Bethlehem or not. . . ." He proceeded to attack the "vile abolitional press," which *"feared to report"* the "conclusive arguments" of Agassiz, and arrived finally at the central point of his essay: "The general Proposition . . . that we anticipate making good is this, *that the Races of Man are not of one pair, that the Caucasian race is the highest species of animal and has the same right of dominion (in kind) over the lower species of his own genus that he has over quadrupeds.*" Anyone who disagreed had to produce evidence of accomplishment by black people. No evidence existed. "Why has the Ethiop never invented anything, never conquered other nations in war, never produced one erudite man?" Runaway slaves who find employment and education in the North rise to no distinction, even though, by contrast, "we find instances of self-education and subsequent greatness against fearful oppression amongst our Race," since "it is impossible to enslave or imprison the Caucasian's mind." True, blacks sometimes become known. "They have . . . lifted up from them a [Joseph Jenkins] Roberts to be President of a colony [Liberia, which had become an independent republic in 1847] or a [Frederick] Douglass to edit a paper and make speeches; and to these they point with enthusiasm. Very well: but has the reader ever read one of President Roberts' messages to his sable subjects; has he ever bored himself over the columns of the *North Star* of Fred. Douglass? If he has, he will agree with us who have also, that their situation is only analagous to that of 'an ape among cats.' Their greatest efforts would be ridiculed from a white man."[7]

Conway pondered what he had written, and was disappointed in it and in himself. He had set out to prove something and had proved nothing; his piece was no more than a wild polemic whose violence mirrored the tension in the soul of the writer. Fifty years later Conway discovered the essay in a pile of old papers and it recalled to him "the moral crisis in my life. . . . I had [in 1850] caught a vision of my superficiality, casuistry, perhaps also of the ease with which I could consign a whole race to degradation." He who dreaded and detested any absolute authority applied against himself, now defended the arbitrary "right of dominion" of himself and his white compatriots over a vast group of prostrated people. An "overwhelming sense of my own inferiority came upon me," he later wrote. He sensed how slavery had been working its will upon him, making him no less than the others its tool. The viper was conservatism itself, the forced or unthinking submission to an established pattern; and polygenesis, far from being a new star, was only a new way of bowing to the old pattern. Emerson had written of the sacredness of what was "true of himself." No slave had the privilege of attending to such things, and his article made him feel like a slave. John Daniel would have printed it and paid him for it. But Conway put it away forever. He would write no more for the *Examiner*. And he would be no lawyer.[8]

Within days of abandoning his article on polygenesis, Conway wrote his father that he was leaving the law and was applying to the Baltimore Conference for admission as a Methodist minister. This decision surprised his parents, but as good Methodists, both Walker and Margaret approved. Moncure had not given much thought to the ministry before, and his decision to apply was sudden. "It was long a mystery to me," he later reminisced, "but Emerson was at the bottom of it." Emerson's emphasis on self-reliance had given Moncure the courage to tend to his own needs. The Methodist ministry meant turning away from law and politics toward a life dedicated to spiritual pursuits, in a way consistent with his own background and his parents' good will.[9]

In substance, of course, there was a chasm between Methodist orthodoxy and Emerson, who had been unable to live within the confines of Unitarianism. That Emerson's inspiration could propel a young man into so orthodox a role was at best peculiar. And yet there were similarities between Emersonianism and Methodism, and not wholly superficial ones. If they differed on the means (and the meaning) of salvation, both at least stressed the responsibility of each individual for his or her own soul. Both personalized spiritual life and stressed immediate communion between man or woman and God. Both transcendentalism and evangelicalism had a profoundly romantic streak in their legitimization of faith and feeling. Moreover, although Conway knew from the *Blackwood's* article that Emerson was not an orthodox Christian and had abandoned the Unitarian ministry, he had not read the Divinity School Address or any of Emerson's specific critiques of conventional religion. What he had read (the *Essays*, first and second series) had tended to sanctify the ordinary rather than undermine the sacred. The mystically religious side of Emerson had impressed Conway deeply and would continue to do so even after he better understood his unorthodoxy, thus smoothing Conway's path both into and out of the Methodist ministry. "I don't for an instant admit or dream that he has not the highest, most religious soul in the country," he wrote in

January 1854, a year after leaving the ministry. "I don't understand what persons mean when they think him irreverent."[10]

The ministry attracted Conway also because it would give him an opportunity to teach the less fortunate. It would permit him to emulate his father in the one way still possible, the father he saw communing with the common people at Sunday Bible classes in the basement of the family home. Conway's pamphlet on free schools had not reached these people, but with the spoken word he could inspire them. A visit of several days to a Loudoun County camp meeting in August 1850 had demonstrated to him anew "the effect on large assemblies [produced] by sermons."[11]

Having moved purposefully toward a vocation, Moncure was welcomed back to Falmouth to await his assignment by the church. (He was accepted as a junior minister, on trial, without formal ordination.) His sense of direction and self-confidence could not even be destroyed by a letter from Kate Emory terminating their correspondence and their relationship. He did go to Carlisle in January to talk things over with her, meeting with her "in good faith and heart" and suffering through a series of "very free-spoken" conversations. But his attitude toward his rejection was philosophical. "Man was never made, I believe, to go or look backward."[12]

On his way back to Falmouth from Carlisle, Conway spent some time in Washington. On February 18, 1851, he heard the Senate debate a fugitive slave episode that had occurred three days earlier. An escaped slave named Shadrach had been spirited out of a Boston courtroom, without violence, by a large group of blacks who had taken the proceedings by surprise. The rescue was not agreeable to most senators, who had spent the bulk of the preceding year concocting a compromise package of which a toughened fugitive slave law was a central component. Henry Clay, in particular, stormed against the "outrage" and warned blacks not to meddle with the workings of a government not their own. Conway, who only two months earlier had been writing that blacks were subhuman, was still no abolitionist. But now Clay's attitude jarred him.[13]

On his nineteenth birthday Moncure was appointed an itinerant junior minister for the Rockville circuit in Montgomery County, Maryland. The night before his departure Dunmore and Eliza Gwinn called him to their cabin and told him how pleased they were that their master's son had decided to work for the Lord. Dunmore told him of a vision he had beheld of a multitude assembling from all directions to listen to Moncure preach God's word. Filled with this inspiration, Moncure departed on April 1, 1851, to take up his duties in Maryland. He was riding a beautiful chestnut horse with a new saddle and saddlebags, all gifts from his father. He had pleased him, it seemed, at last.[14]

* * *

The Rockville circuit stretched for twenty-five miles up the Potomac from Washington D.C., and consisted of about ten appointments to be visited each week. Conway's senior in the circuit was Reverend William Prettyman of Rockville, father of Barrett Prettyman, a Dickinson class-mate. As a bachelor and junior minister, Conway had no fixed residence, living on horseback and sleeping in the homes of the hospitable.

His first sermons delivered from a pulpit came on April 7 at Goshen and Brookville. The congregations were full, as people were eager to take the measure of this new young preacher. At Brookville, in partic-ular, he found a relatively well-to-do group of listeners. "Found a large concourse of the finest looking people I ever saw before. The church—people—everything looked neat and refined." Soon, however, he would discover that his job was not always so exhilarating, his congregations not always so enjoyable, his churches not always so full. On April 16 he complained, "Never had such a cold time everyway. 3 people there: I the only male." Two days later he encountered the "coldest affair yet which I've seen in the Church way. There were many fat girls there who didn't behave remarkably well." Still later he preached to a congregation of "1 white woman—1 black boy—1 dog—1 cat."[15]

Despite these occasional irritations, Conway was a dedicated exhorter, and for some months maintained an enthusiasm high to the point of shrillness, often expressed in insufferably self-righteous and judgmental tones. After staying overnight with one family he noted in his journal that "they have a bad little boy that asked me for tobacco down at the gate." He condemned two young women so severely for dancing that their family joined another church. As late as April 1852 he railed, after a satisfying conversation with a friend, "friends by cards and wine, ye know not what this is!" In May 1851 he preached a funeral sermon with the text "The night cometh," and then went away to record spleenfully what he really thought of the deceased and his demise: "Wicked man—died suddenly. 'He that being often reproved and hardeneth his heart shall suddenly be destroyed.' "[16]

The eruption of this tone at the beginning of his ministry was due partly to Conway's initial conviction that he had found his resting place and with it the Truth. After a time of terrible soul-searching and drift he had come, with Emerson's help, to dedicate himself to things of the spirit; in the only tradition he knew, that meant bringing people to Christ. During the first month of his ministry he noted that Barrett Prettyman "reminds me of myself a year or so ago, in his skepticisms." Skepticism, for himself, was a thing of the past. This newfound confidence was bracing, and never more in evidence than in the summer of 1851 when the weather was warm enough for outdoor camp meetings. At one such meeting he quaked before "a descent that was allied to what I would imagine of Pentecost." At another he had "a charming Love Feast. I felt full of the Spirit. I spoke under the Spirit." At still another he was delighted at seeing Barrett Prettyman and his own brother Peyton, who was visiting, approach the mourner's bench. The last camp meeting of the season was an extravaganza, the biggest soul-saving splash of all. On the second day there was one mourner, that night six, the next day several. On the fourth day Conway "got quite warmed up" but the throng was impassive. The breakthrough came on the sixth day. "Not much good done until about 10 at night. When there wasn't one mourner, T. Morgan exhorted and asked the Christians to rise: the others rushed: in one moment the Altar was crowded. The work of God!" Conway worked feverishly into the night leading ecstatic or exhausted seekers into the arms of the Lord. The body count was proof of success. "We had a fine meeting: by 3 or 4 almost every mourner was converted."[17]

Conway was not the unrelieved prig such journal entries would indicate, however; nor was he so much in the world of the spirit that he lacked interest in more earthly (and earthy) activities. He was smoking cigars regularly, despite his shock at the bad boy by the gate. And though he still had twinges when he thought of Kate Emory, he was eager to meet young ladies in his circuit and seldom more happy than when in their company. "Went to Mr. Porter's: fine and pretty ladies," was a typical notation. Occasionally he would be linked to one or another young woman in particular. May 7, 1851: "Saw a very pretty girl Miss Laura Brady—quite quiet." May 8: "Walked 4 miles with Miss B. home!! Had some quaint times.—Know I shall never hear the end of that walk." May 11: "Dined at Mr. Gaither's: plagued me about Laura Brady—I knew it!"[18]

Conway's inner life, too, was neither as simple nor as settled as his camp-meeting persona projected. He was reading constantly and de-votedly. Since his circuit bordered Washington, he was able to make frequent raids on the capital's bookstores, taking away everything he could find by Emerson (adding at least *Nature; Addresses and Lectures* and *Poems* to the two volumes of *Essays* which he continued to read and re-read) and Carlyle (notably *Latter-Day Pamphlets*, *Life of Sterling*, and *The French Revolution*), along with Greeley's *Hints Toward Reforms*, Quaker Samuel Janney's *Conversations on Religious Subjects between a Father and his two Sons*, Coleridge's *Aids to Reflection*, and Hawthorne's *The Scarlet Letter* (followed in 1852 by *The Blithedale Romance*). A valued acquisition was *The Soul; her Sorrows and her Aspirations*, by the English Theist Francis William Newman, which defined the spiritual nature as feminine and was overlaid by such piety in language and tone that Conway was only gradually aware of its unorthodox implications. These books vied for space in his crowded saddlebags with the Bible and the Methodist Discipline. Surely few Methodist itinerants have toted such libraries.[19]

His chief fascination continued to be with Emerson, forever new, and a constant warning against stagnation. "I remember that in reading Emerson repeatedly," Conway wrote years later, "I seemed never to read the same essay as before. . . . There was always something I had not previously entered into." Rising early to give himself extra time, Conway would ride slowly through the Maryland countryside, twisting the reins around his saddle horn or resting them gently across his horse's mane, his head bowed over the open book, his thoughts lost in the moving evocations of his faraway teacher. He was becoming more and more aware of Emerson's own unorthodoxy now, but the awareness did not repel him. Rather, he took increasingly to heart the exhortations to be true to his own spirit, and began, slowly at first, to question whether his own spirit and Methodism were compatible.[20]

If he had already begun wondering whether he could make a good Methodist, the reaction to his only sermon in Falmouth, June 22, 1851, must have done nothing to quiet his doubts. Speaking by exchange with a Virginia minister, Conway entered the pulpit of the little "union" church on the hill behind his parents' house and looked down upon his family, friends, and neighbors. Taking as his text "Thou wilt show me the path of life," he preached about the need for every person to fulfill his or her own special purpose on earth. It was the speech of someone who wanted to improve this world, without a word on how to prepare properly for the next. Moncure was not entirely amused when his father half-jestingly commented, "One thing is certain, Monc: should the devil ever aim at a Methodist preacher, you'll be safe!"[21]

Conway's most sophisticated congregation was in the village of Brookville, where the Methodist church was attended by members of other denominations, including John Hall, an Episcopalian at whose home Conway sometimes stayed. Hall's wife was a Quaker who attended no church, showed no interest in organized religion, and was raising her daughters accordingly. But she and the eccentric itinerant quickly developed a warm relationship, conversing openly on a wide range of subjects. Before long Mrs. Hall had concluded that this young Methodist had more than a touch of the Quaker in him, and decided that he might profit by exposure to her family. She was, it turned out, the daughter of Roger Brooke, unofficial leader of a thriving community of Hicksite Quakers at nearby Sandy Spring.[22]

"Went down with Mrs. H. to Roger Brooke," Conway wrote on July 31, "was disappointed to find him absent. Was very much pleased with the Quaker folk." By August 11 he had met Brooke, and was "perfectly fascinated with him." Brooke, a tall, grandfatherly man who looked the part of a sage, was ready to converse with Conway on any subject, in an unpolemical spirit and with no desire to convert the young man to a system. But his questions sometimes hit their mark. When Conway told him that the Quaker doctrine of the "inner light" reminded him of Methodists "called by the Spirit" to preach, Brooke asked, "Suppose tomorrow . . . you should find that the Spirit didn't meet you in your pulpit?—What a fix!" Not believing that the Spirit would fail to come at the strong desire of the truly saved, Moncure quickly answered, "I should think God's arm wasn't shortened that he could not save, nor his ear heavy that he couldn't hear, but that my iniquities had separated between [sic] Him and me—so I should pray until he came." Brooke made no more reply than a smile and a puff on his long, old-fashioned pipe, but something about his own answer dissatisfied Conway: what "iniquities" did he have that were really so serious? It was subsequent solitary reflection upon such questions and answers that further unraveled his faith.[23]

The Hicksites whom Roger Brooke represented were spiritually descended from those who had followed a Long Island farmer named Elias Hicks (1748–1830) out of the yearly meeting in 1827, disgruntled by compromises orthodox Quakers had been making with the secular world. Hicks himself had been both a religious zealot and a hardened reactionary, as opposed to public schools and improvements in transportation as he was to using the products of slave labor. Those who bore his name by no means always shared his opposition to education, science, and technology. But they did share with him a fiery commitment to behavior as the sole criterion of a person's worthiness. Dogma, passages from the Bible, adherence to a formal creed—all meant next to nothing. What mattered was the way one lived. For Hicksites this meant a life of conscientious self-culture within a framework of ascetic simplicity and a strict moral code.[24]

At their asceticism, especially the absence of music, Conway demurred. At their efforts at self-culture, he marveled. He was especially impressed by the Fairhill Female Academy and its instructor, an energetic and congenial young Hicksite, William Henry Farquhar. "The house, room and all seemed as if some Minerva had arranged it for the study of Philosophy," Conway thought. "Had I a daughter she should be there." Farquhar delighted him during his first visit by delivering a thrilling lecture on the French Revolution, taken largely from Carlyle. Later the two young men chatted, discovered numerous shared enthusiasms, and became fast friends. "I owe more than words could express," Farquhar told Conway years later, "to the impressions made on me by your conversation in the days of our early intimacy . . . and by the books procured through you." Conway took special joy in introducing Farquhar, and through him the whole Sandy Spring community, to Emerson.[25]

These were extraordinary people. Making their living from the land, images of unadorned rusticity, Sandy Spring Quakers spent leisure hours immersed in literature, science, and comparative theology. Reading the letters of William Farquhar, who corresponded with Conway for decades thereafter, one feels one is reading the words of a sophisticated scholar rather than a simple farmer. Conway's youthful letters to Sarah Farquhar, daughter of Roger Brooke and sister-in-law of William Farquhar, show her to have been equally well-read and intelligent, and equally dear to Conway. Even in disagreement—he thought for a time that William Farquhar was "too much a Rationalist to be a great man"—Conway found this community to be a pleasant oasis on an unexciting circuit. Here he could talk freely about books, ideas, religion, anything that really mattered. The Quakers' emphasis on the "inner light" spoke directly to a young man searching for a sense of self, while the caring stability and attractiveness of their community provided a setting in which individuality could be nurtured. The Quakers, moreover, challenged Conway's thinking on other subjects besides religion. Their opposition to slavery and their agricultural success without slave labor furthered his growing inward rebellion against the institution. For a time he even thought of joining them, of "donning broadbrim and drab, and there await[ing] the period when the Earth should flower into a large Quaker settlement." Quakers seemed to say everything that Methodists said about individual responsibility, while laying greater stress, like Emerson, on what Conway longed for most of all: autonomy.[26]

However liberating it was to think new thoughts and consider new ideas, the questions raised by the Hicksites were not always compatible with a Methodist minister's peace of mind. For all the time Conway spent with the Quakers or with other friendly families, he was usually alone now, with plenty of time for pondering, a solitary itinerant with only horse, books, and thoughts for companions. The warm and exciting fellowship of a college revival, coupled with wholehearted encouragement of parents, neighbors, and peers, had facilitated his public commitment to Methodism. Now the silent dialogue he held with himself as he traveled unaccompanied along rural roads and trails was killing that commitment.

He examined Christian dogmas from an intellectual standpoint and found them riddled with inconsistency and confusion. Say, for example, someone died, decayed in the ground, blended with grass which was eaten by an animal which was then eaten by a man who suddenly died, his body containing part of the essence of the first man. How could both men be resurrected as before? More compelling than intellectual doubts were moral qualms. The most happy, stimulating, and confident homes he had seen were those without anxiety over salvation or terror of hell. Increasingly the dogmas "were not believed because they were not beloved." Less than a year after he thought he had found the answer, he found that answer inundated by new questions. Rebelling against a legal career lest it cripple his individuality, he had entered another profession which was doing precisely that. Early in November 1851, his anxiety and suspicions of hypocrisy mounting, he turned to one who might fully understand. He opened a correspondence with Emerson.[27]

Conway's letter was the scribbling of a young man in pain: brief, obscure, and not entirely coherent, part accolade and part reproach, half statement, half scream. "I am a minister of the Christian Religion,—the only way for the world to reenter Paradise, in my earnest belief. I have just commenced that office at the call of the Holy Ghost, now in my twentieth year." The rest was a cry of hurt, blaming the hurt on Emerson and his writings, which Conway said he had "studied . . . sentence by sentence. . . . I have shed many burning tears over them; because you gain my assent to Laws which, when I see how they would act on the affairs of life, I have not the courage to practice." It was as if he were asking Emerson to do something about it, to say something, to stop the hurt. "I sometimes feel as if you made for me a second Fall from which there is no redemption by any atonement."[28]

Emerson's reply was full, compassionate, and clear. "I believe what interests both you and me most of all things, and whether we know it or not, is the morals of intellect; in other words, that no man is worth his room in the world who is not commanded by a legitimate object of thought." Having flattered Conway by linking him with himself, Emerson proceeded to provide the personalized inspiration his young admirer craved. "The earth is full of frivolous people, who are bending their whole force and the force of nations on trifles, and these are baptized with every grand and holy name, remaining, of course, totally inadequate to occupy any mind; and so sceptics are made. A true soul will disdain to be moved except by what natively commands it, though it should go sad and solitary in search of its master a thousand years." If Emerson was reinforcing Conway's sense of isolation, he was also bolstering his feeling of individual responsibility and kindly reminding him that he must solve his own problems. In what may have been a gentle bid to end the correspondence, he concluded by hastening to thank Conway "for your frank and friendly letter, and to wish you the best deliverance in that contest to which every soul must go alone."[29]

Conway wrote again in December. His tone was different: calmer, clearer in pinpointing his distress. "I have always thought it the meanest thing to have one's habit of thought molded by conventionalities; but that's just my fate. I feel as if I would come to a time soon when I shall be a slave, and unable to speak the truth at all and so will have to be dumb. My Island is getting smaller every day. . . . What is any man but a skeptic?"

> . . . Just think now of one being made a Natural Radical—to whose soul Radicalism is as air to a bird,—and having his lot and earthly converse amongst talented conservative Virginians, such as my father's family and all my early friends are. The details would be worse, but I will not trouble you with them. I suppose you think it strange that I should trouble you at all. But I have no sympathy on Earth. If I were to tell the people to whom I minister what my real troubles were—there is not one in the circuit who would not laugh at them.

If Conway wrote with an exaggerated sense of self-pity, the pain he had been feeling was real. But Emerson's words—especially about "that contest to which every soul must go alone"—had renewed his strength and had boosted his resistance to a future spent, as he put it in this letter, "dragging the dead corpse of the community along." "I have many correspondents," Conway wrote, "but I might almost say yours is the only Letter that was ever written to me."[30]

Increasingly, he was thinking his own thoughts, or at least thoughts at variance with those expected of him. His reading continued, and his boldness in discussing what he derived from it intensified, earning him a reputation for eccentricity among the orthodox to whom he preached. And the eccentricity was not limited to religion. When he traveled to Philadelphia in the fall of 1851 to consult a doctor about his eyes, he noticed that the "Bloomer" costume worn by some unconventional women was neither ugly nor offensive. "It is decidedly pretty," he remarked, "and just as becoming and decent as the other. People say 'how would you like to see your sister dressed thus'—ans. 'Just as well as I would like to see them put on a longer dress if this [bloomers] had been the fashion a century [ago].' "[31]

By late February 1852, at the end of Conway's term on the Rockville circuit, it was clear that another time of decision was impending. At the Quarterly Conference early in March, Conway squirmed in discomfort through a series of "very illiberal speeches" made against a departed minister who had opted for Unitarianism. While still at the conference he received a letter telling him of news which would precipitate the final break with Methodism, with the South, with his father. His brother Peyton was dying.[32]

"Sunday morning Mar. 14. We are around the family altar but one is not there! O God help us my dear brother Peyt. is no more. Wherever I look I seem to read—'Died March 13—10 o'clock W.P.C.' I feel as if a half of my Soul was paralyzed." The agony Moncure felt at the death of his older brother (who had lapsed into a coma by the time of his arrival) was deep and complex. Home while awaiting his next ministerial assignment, he now had much more to think about than his loyalty to the Methodist religion. Not only did he mourn the loss of his brother, he also felt new and heightened pressure on himself. He was now the oldest son. His father would look to him for the leadership of the next generation of Conways, leadership Moncure would not and could not provide. Moreover, the death of his brother intensified his religious rebellion, in such a way that his religious rebellion and his familial rebellion blended and became one.[33]

It was hard to believe, with Peyton's corpse in the parlor. Death had never been easy for Moncure to accept: it was so violent and arbitrary and cruel. He had never had another pet after his duckling died when he was a small boy. His baby sister's death had left a lasting impression. He had told his sister Mildred never to write to him about "horrible accidents and deaths of near friends &c"; it made him queasy. And corpses were appalling. "As yet I have never seen one die," he wrote in September 1852, "and have never but in one or two awful unforgotten times seen one dead. I could not bear the sight." His mother had taught him the sanctity of life, and Emerson wrote of the inviolable worth of each person. But God slaughtered them all. He set the rules and weighted them all in His favor. His authority was all that mattered, the beauty and the aspirations of His creatures counted not a jot. "Lord I believe, help Thou mine unbelief. My dear brother!" It was hard to believe, with Peyton's corpse in the parlor.[34]

The day of the funeral, March 15, was mockingly sunny and warm. In the morning Moncure and his father took a walk along the river, saying little. Later they followed the "immense" procession across the bridge to the cemetery in Fredericksburg, the Sons of Temperance marching as a unit, the band sending the strains of a dirge up and down the Rappahannock. Moncure strained for wholeness. He would find comfort in family and in God. "We who remain will nestle closer and ask for strength. Our God will give it. Is all this a dark wild dream that is on me?"[35]

On March 25, the day before leaving for his new assignment on the Frederick circuit in western Maryland, Conway went to church in Fredericksburg. The service made him wonder more about Peyton. The minister's voice faded and things blurred, and Peyton whispered "Weep not, I am happy now." But did he, was he—really? "Que tout notre raisonnement se reduit à ceder au sentiment—says Pascal. How often have I felt the force of it. Sweet consolation of impossible fancies never leave me to the coldness of sense!"[36]

On April 28, his earliest opportunity, Moncure was at Sandy Spring, sitting in the long silence of the Quaker meeting. "I had much spiritual exercise. . . . The spirit searched into the 'hidden things.' . . . The great Question was, am I truthful? Am I living in full faith up to the Inward Voice?" What follows in his journal is a soliloquy of anguish, the thrashing of a person deeply and genuinely tormented. The word "father" is repeatedly used, and it is not always clear whether the being meant is Walker Conway or God. "Thou God seest me; Thou knowest that no excommunication that could come from Earth would affright me; but O my Father,[*]—hath he not grief enough already? When I hear him cry 'One son in an untimely tomb another in the grave of disbelief!' my heart recoils I cannot—O I cannot. God help me! . . . O my Father bear with—take not Thy Holy Spirit from me—may I not

---

* Conway used this journal when preparing his memoirs some fifty years later, and here penciled in a lowercase "f" over the capital "F" which had begun the word as written in 1852. Very little of the journal—and nothing concerning Peyton's death or its aftermath— actually made its way into the memoirs.

one day yet be Thy Child." The fathers have blurred and melted together. Conway craves the love of both, even as he resents the arbitrary authority and the impossible demands of each. His rebellion against one constitutes rebellion against the other. This rebellion is far advanced now, and Conway's pain lies in his inability to stop it.[37]

His Quaker friends knew that something was about to break. Roger Brooke took him home to dinner and treated him kindly. Then followed two days with William Farquhar and his family, now diligently embarked upon the study of Emerson. And finally came a visit to Sarah Farquhar, who echoed the Concord sage in reminding Moncure that he should "learn to lean for help in none—but within." If only the Frederick circuit had such an oasis! But it did not.[38]

The old systems were collapsing. Methodism was nearly dead in his heart, its interment postponed until an alternative other than chaos could be found. And a quarrel Moncure had had on the Potomac boat during his journey from home in March indicated how far he had cut his ties also to Southern political orthodoxy. His opponent on that occasion was Reverend William Smith, president of Randolph-Macon College, who was arguing the positive merits of slavery. Showing some impatience and condescension toward his youthful adversary, Smith got Conway to admit that slavery was simply "the submission of one will to another." Then, argued Smith, it was not really so terrible, as submission of some to others was essential in any government, in any society. "Then," answered Conway, "government is inconceivably wrong. And I stuck to it that there could and should be a social existence without slavery and if government meant slavery it should be 'reformed altogether'—I'd prefer anarchy." Nobody should work his will on another, and that principle transcended all others. Smith's unilluminating response was to tell Conway to go marry woman's rights pioneer Fanny Wright. Later Conway could only sigh with relief that his own "star didn't carry" him to Randolph-Macon.[39]

At the moment, the place where his star had carried him was not much more uplifting. He had a pleasant base of operations in the village of Jefferson at the home of a Mrs. Rice and her black servant, Becky, with a room of his own that opened into a beautiful garden. But the Frederick circuit was a string of conventional congregations composed of people who could not understand him. Argument soon became a way of life for him. His reading of Margaret Fuller's memoirs, in particular, was now raising eyebrows. "It was not," some of his charges warned, "a Book for me." On May 1 he left the breakfast table in consternation after his "usual controversy with the 'ower righteous' as Burns would style the Orthodoxy." Retreating to the garden, he sat down and began to register his complaints in his journal. "I do think the literal orthodox should send up a petition to God to put out men's eyes. If a man does but think it casts a shade on him as on 'lean and hungry' Cassius:- 'He thinks too much; such men are dangerous.' "

Suddenly a little red and green blur streaked past him and arrested his attention. He watched it dart about the garden until it hovered over a flower and he saw it clearly: a hummingbird, always beloved to him for its grace, its beauty, its delicate fragility. Soothed by the sight, he returned to his journal. "Sweet wee thing," he chirped to the hummingbird, "I would I were as free to clap my wings and draw sweets from all flowers! I would not be afraid of poisons nor vipers!—not I."[40]

In July Moncure was in Carlisle to see old friends and receive a Dickinson master's degree, a perfunctory honor granted to every alumnus of three years or more who maintained good moral character and paid five dollars. Walker Conway, at the commencement as a trustee, was vexed at the selection of George Burnap, Unitarian minister in Baltimore, to address the college's Union Philosophical Society during the same week. After that address, father and son had tea with Burnap and the venerable John Price Durbin, Dickinson's first Methodist president. Burnap and Durbin launched into a debate on the direction of American religion, Durbin contending that it was becoming more conservative, Burnap that it was heading toward liberality and diversity. "I think B. was ahead," Moncure noted.[41]

Later that month Conway sat in a tent on a campground, "whereon I don't anticipate enjoyment," and scribbled in his journal that the Rubicon had been crossed. "I have opened a correspondence with my Parents on my scruples concerning the Church and my remaining in it. It will every way be sad for them and me. . . . O God do Thou help me to the Right and give my dear dear Parents Thy support! How much wilt Thou require of me this early?" His father responded quickly. "Pa is evidently agitated," wrote Moncure in early August. But at least it was out in the open between them. Now the issue was whether he could complete his term on the Frederick circuit. "I never say anything that is untrue," he reassured himself, since his sermons were now limited to general subjects like love and charity. "And if I thought that my remaining a Methodist would make any one more Orthodox I wouldn't remain a day." But strain there was. "It is an awful thought but true that I am now representing a Faith I know to be untrue!"[42]

In October Conway attended simultaneous Quaker and Unitarian conventions in Baltimore. Here he renewed his acquaintance with George Burnap, who introduced him to Orville Dewey, an eminent conservative Unitarian whom Conway found "interesting, but in politics too conservative for my young unsophisticated taste." Aware of this bright and serious young man's spiritual meandering, Burnap and Dewey took him aside and spent long hours conversing with him on "the highest problems of theology." Returning to his circuit, Moncure sensed that "there must have been signal change in my manners and appearance: for my friends ask me in a whisper whats on my mind? O if they only knew what [is] starting!" What was starting, though momentarily a secret, was a new career as a Unitarian. Conway had concluded "by advice of Drs. Burnap and Dewey" to attend Harvard Divinity School in preparation for the Unitarian ministry. His father would be the first to know. "I have written to Pa telling him of my Cambridge plans! O my Father support him in all things."[43]

Conway still wanted to finish his term on the circuit and then leave the Methodist ministry quietly. But his heresy was so far advanced that even remarks which he regarded as innocuous were making his listeners angry. In November the young black servant who worked at the house in Jefferson died and Conway preached the funeral sermon. He spoke of Becky's natural innocence and goodness, and was startled when some people hotly objected to his incidental comment that death was not the outgrowth of sin. "I had not dreamed of the unusualness of the thought with them," he wrote. "I maintained my point albeit they 'were astonished at my doctrine.' I think immense evil has been done by making men think that death is the constant obvious punishment for sins they've never committed: it makes them discontented with Laws that are good: The idea that it came from Adam's sin I have long seen to be nonsense." Shortly after this a pious woman approached him after a sermon and whispered, "Brother, you seemed to be speaking to us from the moon."[44]

Even before the sermon at Becky's funeral, two leading Methodists on the circuit had written to Walker Conway asking him to call his son home; in mid-November the letter from the elder Conway came. The pretext was health: Moncure had been plagued by a bronchial infection. But he clearly could no longer function effectively on the circuit even when in the best of health, for his opinions were no longer welcome. His last sermon as a Methodist was on December 4. In February he wrote to the ministers of the Baltimore Conference, telling them that because of a "change in many of my theological tenets, and a consciousness of immaturity in others," he would decline to apply for further orders. "May I not trust," he continued, "that your Creed, however dear, may not end, like that of the Nicene Fathers, with an Anathema against all who dissent,—but rather with a prayer that those whom you think in error may become Children of the Light."[45]

By December 15, 1852, after a stopover in Sandy Spring, where the Quakers urged him not to permit his opinions to be *"made-up"* by others, Conway was back in Falmouth, where he would spend two months before leaving for Cambridge. At first it was a relief to be home: "Forgot all my sorrows, all my cares, in the comforts of dear dear home. O my Father may my love and fond memory of home never cease." Christmas was idyllic, with Peter and Richard rejoicing in "the riches which Christ Cringle has heaped into their stockings," and Moncure setting off fireworks in the back yard "for the benefit of white and black." But discussion of his changing opinions and upcoming plans could not be deferred for long. Even before Christmas there were some tense moments between him and his father. Only four days after his arrival he was fearing "that these two months are the last I shall ever spend peacefully at home."[46]

The tension created by his religious views was exacerbated now by Conway's open opposition to slavery, which quickly became the talk of Falmouth and Fredericksburg. This public reputation was earned at a time when townspeople were growing increasingly edgy about the subject of race relations. In September the Fredericksburg *Herald* had complained that "a greater degree of insubordination has been manifested by the negro population within the last few months, than at any previous period of our history as a State." The paper expressed its horror that it was "now a debatable point, *as to which color shall use the sidewalk, and which give way*—a point which we think had better be settled at once." The neighborhood was not, in short, in any mood to indulge the dangerous deviations of an incipient abolitionist, and if Conway thought otherwise he was rapidly disabused of the illusion. His uncle Eustace, whom he had so admired only three years earlier, threatened to have him "drummed out of town." Jack Marye, one of Fredericksburg's elite, met him on the street and gave him a "lecture" on the issue. An innocent visit to the Fredericksburg chess club disintegrated, "as is *my fate*," into an argument on slavery. Some townspeople complained to Walker Conway, who was livid that his son was "divulging 'peculiar views' " in public. But Moncure was oblivious to reprimand or pressure. "As I saw the Slave-hiring today," he wrote on New Year's Day, "I found out how much *hatred* I had of the Institution—and how much contempt for the persons engaged in it."[47]

" 'You look,' said a friend, 'as if you were not in the World.' I am not. My dear relations and friends cannot sympathize with and encourage the deepest chords of Faith and Reverence in my Soul. Courage my Soul! Your Infinite Father hath not forgotten thee! . . . O My Father do Thou love me in this time of fire." The time of fire was not one of utter isolation, however, for some people stood by him. His sister was a comforting and constant companion. His cousin Fanny Moncure (the model for his 1887 fictional character, Gisela Stirling) leaped enthusiastically to his defense when some relations "laughed at and persecuted" him for his "radicalisms and skepticisms." And his mother, although hurt by the developing family schism and grieving at her son's departure from what she considered religious truth, refused to say a word against him. "Whilst my father was stricken with grief at my evident determination to avow and advocate the abolition of slavery," Conway recalled, "my mother indicated less anxiety concerning the fate of the institution than that of myself." Margaret Conway (who was now reading Margaret Fuller, at Moncure's urging) and her rebellious son seemed to draw even closer during these strained interim weeks, often standing as one in debates with argumentative visitors. Moncure was especially pleased by an argument they had with his father and a male neighbor concerning "the Intuitions" versus "Reason." Contending for the superiority of feelings over intellect, upholding "the sentiments as truth," Margaret and Moncure noted that boys had to construct *"rules"* for their games, but girls—intuitively appreciating other people's feelings—did not require such devices. With this line of argument, Moncure was certain that he and his mother had put their opposition to flight.[48]

Walker Conway found an excuse to be absent on February 14, 1853, when his son took his leave. Early that morning Moncure saddled his horse and rode up and down the Rappahannock, savoring a last moment of communion with the woods and the river and the hills which he had always known as home. Returning to the house, he tied his horse to a poplar in the yard, went to his room, and brought down his saddlebags— empty now, as all his books had been sent north to a warmer climate. In the yard he said his good-byes to the slaves, to his sister, mother, and younger brothers. Then he approached the horse, that beautiful reminder of his father, whose gift it had been only two years before. Moncure stood silently as the puzzled animal eyed him and nervously pawed the earth. With one motion Conway draped the saddlebags across the saddle. Then he turned and walked alone to the railroad station in Fredericksburg to begin his new life in the North.[49]

Moncure Conway always thought of himself as a pilgrim. He applied no word to himself more often. It was more apt than wanderer, which ignored purposefulness, and more precise than seeker, which might imply vagueness or drift. A pilgrimage connotes both movement and a particular purpose. And yet the movement in Conway's life is so startlingly chronic and wide-ranging that it threatens at times to overwhelm the purpose; threatens, like the hummingbird Conway envied, to spin one's head and blur one's vision. Because he sampled so many flowers and never ceased to clap his wings, Conway has long defied cohesive explanation or even close examination. But his life had coherence, the source of which is the source of its tragedy and power. For him, the need to avoid slavish obedience to convention or external authority was supreme. The movement and the purpose were one.

Conway left Virginia because he was unable and unwilling to fill the roles expected of him. He was most obviously repudiating his father, who played those roles with enthusiasm and expertise. Walker Conway was an autocratic, upright, unrelievedly responsible man, icily intolerant from the point of view of one who did not share his allegiances. To him, self-reliance meant fortitude to carry out inherited responsibilities. He would be generous to his charges as long as they showed they knew their place. But citizens who broke the law would be sentenced to jail. Slaves who acted defiantly would be sold. And sons who revolted would be cast adrift from family money, prestige, and power. Walker's authority was unbending and all-consuming. He lay like a serpent in his son's path, scorning his more idiosyncratic predilections and aspirations, upholding with quiet violence his culture's absolute set of values. Young Moncure looked with fear on the prisoners in the jail at Stafford Court House, "a whited sepulchre to my eyes," he recalled, "from whose small grated apertures looked murderous phantoms." The manacled prisoners were frightening in their own right, but they were frightening also because they reminded him of his father's omnipotence. Moncure attended their trials feeling "awe" as he watched "a fellow man dragged prematurely before the bar of God."[50] He would not let his father do that to him. Against the threat of imprisonment in a life which knew no freedom or self-expression, he rebelled.

And yet the rebellion was never total, for Conway took a great deal from his father, more than he may have consciously realized. His fear of his father cannot be fully appreciated, in fact, without an appreciation of his respect for him, his admiration, even his love. We may fear those we hate or disrespect, or those who wish us harm; but how much more pervasive, more searing, more psychically chilling, is our fear of those who threaten our identity as well as challenge our behavior, of those whom we care about, whose approval matters, and who grip us tightly with their love and threaten to overwhelm us, drowning us in our inability to establish our own separate space. Moncure's problems with his father were acute only because he respected him so much. The space which Moncure created was separate, but within it his father's legacy was large.

Central to the legacy was confidence. To be sure, his confidence lacked his father's constant certainty of his own rightness and of the wrongness of those who deviated from his standards. But confidence does not imply certainty so much as strength. From his earliest boyhood Moncure knew he need feel inferior to no human being. Leading citizens of Virginia were guests in his house; they treated his father with respect, and they treated Moncure with respect because he was his father's son. He was brought up to regard himself, his problems, his ideas as important. This sense of family worth, of place and of roots, provided him with much of the confidence which characterized his life. When at eighteen he lobbied the state constitutional convention, when at nineteen he shared his burdens with Emerson, when at twenty he vociferously argued politics with a college president, he was engaging in no impertinence. He was merely exercising the prerogative of a well-educated upper-class man. Some people, after reading his luminary-ridden autobiography, have labeled him a "tuft-hunter" or "name-dropper."[51] But these epithets, applicable to a middle-class social climber, have no connection to the reality of his life. He always moved with ease in high social and intellectual circles, both because he was welcome there and because he had always done so, by habit and by right.

Walker Conway also instilled in his son his obligation to be a leader. Leadership was part of being a Conway man, and if Moncure could not emulate his father in detail he could do so in general aim. Without resorting to his father's weapons of coercion and control, Moncure aspired to a similarly central place in the community, where he would be respected for wisdom and moral uprightness and consulted for advice in times of trouble. He would attempt to bring to this role quieter and gentler qualities than his father possessed: tolerance, affection, appreciation for aesthetics, and legitimization of the emotional life—all gained from his mother and other female relatives. But, like his father, he would seek to lead a community of men and women because it was his responsibility.

And he would always long for a community—a place of order, cohesion, and comfort, wherein everyone worked harmoniously, sharing the same basic sensibilities, values, and goals. He was giving this up when he repudiated the dominant beliefs of antebellum Virginia and moved forever from the state, and the sense of loss was traumatic and lasting. The only house he ever built—in a new community of artists and intellectuals on the outskirts of London—he named "Inglewood," after his early boyhood home in Virginia.

But no community could be allowed to rob him of his free identity, and this fear of psychic obliteration, of going "through this life dragging the dead corpse of the community along,"[52] caused him several times to undermine his own personal situation when it threatened to become too comfortable. Perhaps the only thing stronger than his longing for a stable community was his fear of the inner lifelessness that seemed so often to go with it. There was always the threat of submission to societal expectations and conventionalities, submission to a spirit not one's own. "Destiny had lavished on my lot everything but freedom," he wrote in 1875, recalling his departure from Virginia. "At last I went forth into the world, a homeless wanderer but a free man."[53]

Conway viewed his battle of wills with his father as a titanic effort to avoid and then escape enslavement, and from it he came to regard personal freedom as the most important thing in life. The battle was with everything he most loathed and feared: violence, imprisonment, death. "To be chained to a false position is death!" he cried late in 1852, just before returning to Falmouth for those last uncomfortable weeks. And during those last weeks his behavior in the presence of his father actually mirrored that of a slave. He was ill at ease with him; he tried to avoid conflict, but when confronted he stammered and stuttered and was rebuked, he wrote, for "half laughing after everything I say." He was like Charles Humstead, the gifted slave who killed the serpents but who stammered before his master and was sold away when he stepped out of line.[54]

"I feel that the sorrows of life have entwined new chords in my soul with all who mourn," Moncure wrote on January 1, 1853. He had long been friendly toward his father's slaves, but the crisis precipitated by the necessity of choosing a career had opened his eyes to the full magnitude of their predicament. His own effort to resist the pressure to "set down and be a slave without more struggle" had opened a new line of empathy between himself and those whose slavery was fixed and final. He noticed too how a habit of violence and arbitrary domination, overt and implied, permeated a slave society and infected even its nobler supporters. Slavery, he wrote in 1864, seemed "to have been so worshipped as at length to have been invested with the awful power of creating a generation of human beings in its own image and likeness"; one which was "willing to sacrifice . . . all that is human or generous." He was determined to be different. When the struggle for his own emancipation became conscious and concentrated, he found himself committed likewise to the emancipation of the slaves.[55]

That women whom he loved also hated slavery must have contributed to and reinforced his commitment to abolition, and must have struck him as both fitting and logical. Those women, it seemed, did not seek to manipulate, coerce, or control, but were tolerant of individual foibles and solicitous of individual needs. There was more than a touch of romanticism in Conway's developing attitudes toward women, but it was romanticism based in reality. The women he knew *were* less violent, domineering, and threatening; *were* more tolerant and gentle, more interested in art, literature, music, and in cultivating the emotional life. "You know," Moncure told Sarah Farquhar, "that I have met many valuable female friends in my life who have confirmed my reverence for the sex as I received it from my mother." The reverence, however, was not for pretty decorations but for gentle, nurturing beings who were also thinking, functional members of society. When Conway went to Cambridge he was initially disappointed in the young women he met precisely because they seemed more pampered and innocent than those he had known in Virginia. "They seem to have no experiences; they [experiences] have been kept off as they have fallen as rain by an umbrella." Conway's special affinity for women, especially those who combined sensitivity with conviction and purpose, proved lifelong.[56]

Conway's pronounced fondness for women did not, however, imply an inability to deal with men and did not reflect sexual dysfunction or neurosis, any more than it derived from an allegiance to sentimental stereotypes. Surely part of Conway's special enthusiasm for women was sexual. Remarks on the physical attractiveness of women he meets are common in his diaries and letters. His adult approach to sexuality was open and positive, and once married he enjoyed a sex life that was fulfilling and free. But women, to him, were neither sexual objects nor sentimentalized angels. They were people whom he found particularly attractive, who often shared values he most cherished, and who had potential as unlimited as men's. The majority of Conway's friendships were with women, who in later life included a variety of artists, professionals, and homemakers, along with Helen Hunt Jackson, Elizabeth Cady Stanton, and Annie Besant. Many of those friendships were to show how dynamic, productive, unaffected, and mutually fulfilling a male-female friendship could be. Far from reflecting a life of paralyzed, "feminized" triviality, Moncure Conway's association with women in an essentially patriarchal world, and his conscious commitment to sexual reconciliation and cooperation, gave his life much of its consistency and power and stood as a driving force behind much of his life's achievement.[57]

To say all this does not solve the man. There are inner resources, fortunately, which defy dissection and preserve the ultimate mystery of every human being. In his first two decades lurk abundant clues to Moncure Conway's unusual life, but the pattern they form is shifting and uncertain. To understand a person, moreover, is not to explain him. Other similarly situated boys in the antebellum South may have had authority problems with their fathers, others may have been close to women in their families, others may have had difficulty coping with the demands of their culture. But hardly any of them—by some standards, none—joined Conway in so dramatic or far-reaching a rebellion. There was nothing inevitable about the course Conway took, and knowledge of what forces helped to prompt it should not obscure the fact that his self-assertion was, among other things, an act of high courage. Those inner resources exist, and Conway knew it, for he kept reaching until he touched them.

PART TWO / THE EDUCATION OF A RADICAL

CHAPTER 4

On February 25, 1853, Moncure Conway smashed into Boston. His train careened at forty miles per hour into a wayward freight train, derailing cars and injuring several people. Conway dusted himself off, looked over the wreckage, recovered his bags, and ambled into town. "That was my first experience," he laconically informed a friend, "in the 'fast' state of Massachusetts."[1]

Conway reveled in the cultural and intellectual atmosphere of Boston and Cambridge. His life was a crowded series of lectures, plays, concerts, operas, readings, discussions. Moving with the self-assured ease of a young aristocrat and having a certain exotic attractiveness as a liberalized castaway Virginian, Conway quickly gained entrance to the homes of many of the most distinguished literary and religious figures in the region. He found himself moving in a society that was socially cosmopolitan and significantly free in thought. He was amazed and delighted.

Armed with letters of introduction from George Burnap and the advanced Unitarian, William Henry Furness (whom he had met in Philadelphia on his way north), Conway quickly became acquainted with Ephraim Peabody, the Unitarian pastor of Boston's venerable King's Chapel. Peabody possessed a theological moderation soothing to a young man in transition, and a personal tolerance and openness refreshing to one in rebellion against cultural deprivation. With the Peabodys, Conway heard his first oratorio, "The Messiah," which he found "grand and transporting." The deliciousness of the event was intensified by its happening on a Sunday evening. This, Conway had previously been taught, was a somber time unsuited for pageantry or anything smacking of entertainment. Now he was going out on the Sabbath, and a minister was going with him.[2]

Other acquaintances followed quickly: John Gorham Palfrey, Bronson Alcott (whom Conway found "dry," a man who "lived and moved in a waking dream"), James Russell Lowell, Henry Wadsworth Longfellow,

Jared Sparks. Lowell and Conway immediately developed a mutual dislike which was destined to persist. Lowell's thick Boston accent and precocious long beard unnerved the young Virginian. Further, Conway was annoyed by the poet's apparent apathy toward Emerson and by his derision of Robert Browning. In all, Conway recalled, "there was a certain provincialism about him which I suppose irritated my own Southern provincialism. . . . His look, accent, shrewdness, all recalled the 'Yankee' conventionalized in Southern prejudice."[3]

Longfellow and Sparks, however, rapidly developed a parental fondness for Moncure, opening their Cambridge homes to him and listening with genuine interest to his tales of life among the Virginia gentry. Longfellow, in whose Harvard poetry class Conway subsequently enrolled (as he also did in the classes of Bernard Roelker in German and Louis Agassiz in science), introduced him to Dante and Goethe and deepened his appreciation (if not his aptitude) for verse. Sparks, pioneer historian and recently retired Harvard president, opened his library to Conway, bolstered his knowledge of American history, and became the first person to tell him "that Thomas Paine was to be respected." Both the Longfellow and Sparks families introduced him to the opera, which became one of his life's joys. Even *Don Giovanni*, which offended Mrs. Sparks by the suggestiveness of certain scenes, captivated him. "I anticipate the greatest gratification of my passion for music in Boston," he wrote in March. Falmouth, Carlisle, and Montgomery County had been nothing like this.[4]

Conway's "passion for music" also found an outlet at the Divinity School, for he was given fifty dollars to play the organ at weekday prayers. The money was needed. Having lost the financial support of his father, Conway came to Harvard with approximately one hundred dollars in savings and another hundred and sixty raised by his dedicated sponsor, Burnap. Prohibited by school regulations from preaching for pay until his senior year, Moncure was not affluent. To save money he walked between Cambridge and Boston rather than ride the omnibus, and joined a group of students who pooled their resources and shared inexpensive vegetarian meals. But what he saved on food and transportation he spent on books and entertainment. His bankroll shrank perilously, replenished only by the timely arrival of his senior year and the opportunity to give occasional sermons in pulpits throughout the region. Luckily senior year came quickly for Moncure, since his Methodist experience was deemed sufficient to cut in half the three years normally required for the B.D. degree. Thus in March 1853 he enrolled in the middle class, only three semesters of work ahead of him.[5]

Conway's religious pilgrimage had proceeded far by the time he got to Harvard. Gone was his faith in biblical literalism, gone his belief in hell and in Satan, gone any certainty about the nature of Jesus. But perhaps the most important thing he had shed was the notion that some things were not to be questioned, the fear of comprehensive inquiry. He came to Cambridge intending to study theology thoroughly, "that I may come at last to a firm belief or else a truthful disbelief of Historic Christianity."[6]

Some things, however, died harder than others. Conway still found much personal comfort in certain aspects of Christian doctrine. On March 27, 1853, Easter Sunday, he went to King's Chapel and heard Peabody preach on "Life and Immortality brought to light by Christ." "O how glorious is the Christian hope," Moncure exulted that day. "It burst on me fully this Sunday as I partook the Communion. O I know I love my dear Redeemer." But the Bible he was using in his studies evidenced another side of his religious profile, one which reflected the Unitarian emphasis on dispassionate study rather than blind faith. "Christ never refers to two consciousnesses," he wrote in the margin of the Gospel of John (ch. 1, v. 34–35). "He never tells of any past heavenly experience. He speaks only from his experience as a Jew and God's spirit." Two of Conway's deepest needs were trying uneasily to co-exist. He needed to cultivate what his world knew as religious sentiments, those which transcended the selfish and commonplace, accenting morality and man's altruistic, spiritual side. But he also needed to reject imprisonment by irrational dogma whose primary weapon was the arbitrary weight of tradition. As yet he was attempting to do both within the context of a specific creed, no matter how liberalized his Christianity had become. As long as that context remained, his religious thinking would be marbled by tensions, paradoxes, and contradictions.[7]

But Unitarians had been living with such tensions for a long time— so long, some felt, that they had complacently forgotten their existence. New England Unitarianism had developed during the eighteenth and early nineteenth centuries in reaction both to Calvinism and to the harsher aspects of evangelicalism. It rejected the doctrine of total depravity and insisted upon the supremacy of ethics over dogma. "It is the doctrine of a portion of the Christian church," wrote Burnap, "that human nature is essentially evil. It is my purpose to maintain the *rectitude of human nature*." In keeping with this spirit of civility and reason, the Unitarian church had spawned a generation of scholars who investigated the Bible, discredited its unreasonable passages, but left its basic message intact. There was a personal God. Christ was not God, but he was God's agent and man's redeemer. The Bible was divinely inspired, even though much of it could not be taken literally and many of its details were inaccurate. People were essentially good, and if they led good lives their salvation was assured. It was a religion of confident and comfortable people, content that they stood as harbingers of a more sensible and humane faith for mankind. "Boston," wrote Henry Adams, "had solved the Universe."[8]

But things were not as serene as they sometimes appeared; tensions and paradoxes could not be smothered. If men and women were essentially good, then why did they require Christ as their redeemer?

If rational investigation of Scripture was right and proper, then why should not scholars analyze the plausibility of Christ's divinity? The problem seemed epitomized in Conway's professor of ecclesiastical history, Convers Francis. Francis, "a florid old gentleman, good-natured, tolerant, mystical," was less conservative than his principal colleague, George R. Noyes. He was the brother of abolitionist Lydia Maria Child, was sympathetic to a variety of reforms, thought highly of each person's intuitive sense, and had incorporated much Emersonian transcendentalism into his thinking. He admitted to Theodore Parker that a long list of specified miracles could not have happened. But he stubbornly stood firm on the divinity of Christ, the Resurrection, and the "supernatural element" at work in the New Testament. It was such thinking that prompted Parker's description of life at the Divinity School: "One professor is milking the barren heifer and the other is holding the sieve."[9]

The heifer had not always been so barren. At its founding in 1819, the Harvard Divinity School (always Unitarian in fact if not in explicit design) had been the home of some of the finest minds in American religion. Chief among them was Andrews Norton, who served as Dexter Professor of Sacred Literature from 1819 to 1830 and continued his literary and theological pursuits in Cambridge until his death in September 1853. Norton devoted his life to showing that piety and Christian belief were not incompatible with theological liberalism and bold intellectual rigor. His three-volume opus, *The Evidences of the Genuineness of the Gospels* (1837, 1844) stood as the classic statement of nineteenth-century mainstream Unitarianism. Dealing in learned and candid detail with numerous biblical discrepancies, Norton nevertheless concluded that "The Gospels are the history of a miraculous communication from God to men." But what was bold and liberal during Norton's professorship seemed increasingly stale and conservative by the 1850s. Critics abounded within the ranks, wielding weapons placed in their hands by the mainstream Unitarians themselves. Unitarianism was approaching an internal crisis, brought about by those who took the principles of the "rectitude of human nature" and the importance of rational investigation to their logical extremes.[10]

The first line of criticism had been pioneered by Ralph Waldo Emerson, who shocked the Divinity School commencement audience in 1838 by assaulting Unitarianism for its meek submission to a secondhand creed and its neglect of the intuitive inspiration at the heart of true religion. "To aim to convert a man by miracles is a profanation of the soul," Emerson had proclaimed. "A true conversion, a true Christ, is now, as always, to be made by the reception of beautiful sentiments." Decrying the "noxious exaggeration about the *person* of Jesus," Emerson avowed that divinity lay inside, not outside, people. "The sublime is excited in me by the great stoical doctrine, Obey Thyself." Such thoughts were more than what Unitarian ideologues had bargained for in affirming the goodness of men and women—and more than they had expected to hear even from Emerson, who had left the ministry because of his unwillingness to administer the Lord's Supper. There were inevitable rebuttals, notably Norton's *On the Latest Form of Heresy* (1839); but transcendentalism, with its confident assertion of human beings' dignity and power, its blend of person and nature in a mystical union needing no assistance from the supernatural, could not be banished from the air.[11]

The second line of attack followed the scholarly approach which Norton had done so much to foster. Biblical scholarship had blossomed in the German universities, and it was this milieu that produced in 1837 the most serious challenge yet to Unitarian Christianity, David Friedrich Strauss's *Das Leben Jesu*. Strauss approached the Gospels with a Hegelian appreciation for historical change. The early Christians, he argued, did not share the same forms of thought as modern scientific researchers. To be understood they had to be studied on their own terms. Their era had upheld the validity of myths and legends as legitimate modes of conceptualization and expression, and their writings were mythological in form and content. The central purpose of the Gospels had been to demonstrate the incarnation of the divine spirit in people, and this did not demand our belief in events that had no objective foundation in fact. There was something to be gained from the Bible, as a means of understanding another culture and as a general work of inspiration. But it was not a work of history, and it was not a safe or logical guide to any religion compatible with the scientific spirit of the nineteenth century. *The Life of Jesus* was published in America in the mid-1840s. Predictably, it received far more attention from Unitarians than from other sects. Just as predictably, it was the target of substantial Unitarian hostility. But like Emerson's Divinity School Address, it marked the mature arrival of a line of attack on orthodox Unitarianism which gathered adherents within the ranks and could not be turned aside.[12]

By 1853, a number of Divinity School graduates, influenced in varying degrees by transcendentalism and by scriptural criticism not based in Christian self-justification, held pulpits from which they tweaked the Unitarian establishment. They were not exactly a school, but together they came to be identified as the radical left wing of their church. They included men who would make significant contributions to reform, both lay and religious, and to the study of comparative religion: O. B. Frothingham, Thomas Wentworth Higginson, Samuel Johnson, David Wasson, John Weiss. And overshadowing them all was the *bête noire* who carried the standard of the 28th Congregational Society, which met weekly at Boston's Music Hall. Unlike Emerson, he always remained within the Unitarian church; also unlike Emerson, he attracted the continual and genuine detestation of the church's mainstream leadership. It was a habit of Andrews Norton to include a petition against his influence as part of the family's daily prayers. To be a Unitarian in the 1850s meant coming to terms with Theodore Parker.[13]

Parker had been one of the first Americans to read *Das Leben Jesu,* and had reviewed it sympathetically (while disagreeing that the Gospels were exclusively mythic) for the *Christian Examiner* in 1840. In 1846 he assumed command of the 28th Congregational Society and quickly developed his reputation for uncompromising radicalism. Much of this reputation was due to his association with reform, especially with radical antislavery. More overtly and consistently than any of his clerical colleagues, Parker believed the pulpit should be used as an instrument of social change, and more than any of them he was treated by reformers as one of their own.

His style, too, made conservatives shudder. Self-consciously the grandson of a man who had led the minutemen on Lexington Green, Parker was unrestrained in his rhetoric and in extreme cases was not above sanctioning violent action on behalf of a noble cause. Theologically, however, he was less radical than his detractors often perceived. No materialist or rationalist, his religion remained essentially theistic, and he always believed in a divine benevolent order to the universe which could aptly be termed God. But this was enough to brand him a heretic in the eyes of conventional Unitarians, who were further alienated by his seemingly irreverent use of sarcasm and humor and by his holding services in a theater rather than a church.[14]

Moncure Conway went to the Music Hall his first Sunday in Massachusetts, and Parker did not please him. "I don't like him at all," Conway noted in his journal, "and wish I had worshipped at King's Chapel with dear Mr. Peabody who with his whole family I love in truth." To Sarah Farquhar he explained his consternation. Parker's sermon, a simple talk on the importance of love and good temper, "was a good practical lecture. But I was very sorry I went to hear it. It kept me and every one else in a constant titter of laughter, by its odd and comical words [and] anecdotes. It was hard to divest myself of the idea that I was hearing a Comedy, for he doesn't preach in a church. I have then to report that a nearer sight has not given me an exalted impression of Theodore Parker."

Conway, fresh from a wrenching break with Methodism and his family, was not ready to take his religion in so secularized a package as that offered by Parker at the Music Hall. The contrast with what he had known all his life was too abrupt, too stark. Religion was a serious matter; Parker made people laugh too much. And the people who flocked to hear him, men and women with dress and hairstyles as unorthodox as their opinions, struck the young man from Virginia as a singularly unpious lot. They were, in fact, "the roughest people I ever saw—the mustachoed men and *rouged* females." In this transitional moment Moncure found more comfort in Ephraim Peabody's old stone church on Tremont Street, where he could kneel with good Unitarian conformists, listen to traditional platitudes and verities, and feel that no matter how far he had wandered, he had never left home at all.[15]

Further experience made Conway think again. Shortly before leaving Falmouth in February 1853, Moncure had been approached by Nancy Williams, one of his father's slaves. Nancy's husband Benjamin, owned by a neighboring farmer, had run away with the intention of seeking refuge in Boston. But Nancy had not heard from him. Now she wanted her master's son to help her find him, so that she and her husband could devise a means of corresponding. Conway could not do it alone, of course, for as an unknown Virginian he would be decidedly suspect in Boston's black community. It was this errand on behalf of a slave woman which brought Conway and Parker together.[16]

Having heard that Parker likely could locate a fugitive slave, Conway appeared before the fiery minister less than two weeks after the irksome occasion at the Music Hall. Parker readily agreed to help in the search for Williams, but something in his manner still vexed Conway. "Met with Theo. Parker," he wrote that night. "I shall not ever like him." A few days later the famous preacher and the obscure divinity student tramped through the streets of Boston's "Negro quarter" together, going from door to door among the tenements clustered on the back side of Beacon Hill. This was a different Parker, who mixed gentleness and sensitivity with his ever-present streetwise shrewdness. He needed no introduction to these people, the most scorned residents of Boston, who met him on a plane of obvious and genuine mutual respect. There was neither presumptuousness nor condescension in Parker's attitude, and no feigned humility in the blacks with whom he conversed. "He spoke sweetly and graciously to young and old," Conway remembered, "and I was ashamed that I had disliked him." Eventually they found someone who had had contact with Williams, and ascertained that the runaway had proceeded to Canada. Soon afterward Conway obtained his address and sent it to a free black in Falmouth, who forwarded it to Walker Conway's slave.[17]

This episode marked the beginning of Conway's admiration for Parker. Increasingly as the months wore on, his Sunday morning treks from Harvard to Boston took him not to King's Chapel but to the Music Hall, where he listened with deepening fascination to this new guide, and where he felt a growing kinship with an audience he had previously regarded as bizarre. And as he came to know the man better, he realized that Parker was far more than a strident, irreverent agitator. Rather, this preacher possessed in one personality the combination of traits Conway prized most. He was a man of action, a man of thought, and a man of sensibility. "Parker is chiefly known to the world . . . as a religious iconoclast," Conway wrote later. "[But] there was a deep, sensitive, personal piety in this hard-striker, a sweet feminine devoutness, which were the habitual breath of his spirit."

The Virginian was destined to be no carbon copy of the Bostonian.

Conway would go beyond Parker in religious radicalism, while staying in some ways more conservative politically, being less inclined to direct action in the name of a cause and never appreciating Parker's insights into the economic basis for social injustice. But if anyone provided a model for the sort of ministry to which Conway aspired, it was Theodore Parker. His was a ministry which paid attention to the times, faced moral issues, and made people think. Parker was not simply comforting but creative, not simply soothing but life-giving and catalytic. "His thoughts were mother-thoughts," Conway said in 1889, when he spoke at the dissolution of the 28th Congregational Society. "They were not only maternal, but bore other thoughts."[18]

Conway did not lack company on his Sunday trips to Boston. Parker was a sort of folk hero to many Harvard students, including enough at the Divinity School to make the faculty nervous. Conway and other Divinity students held weekly discussion sessions in the school chapel, and frequently Parker's sermons provided fuel for their debates. The class unanimously asked Parker to speak at its graduation, and only his prudent refusal avoided a major clash with school authorities. There was probably no non-establishment figure better liked at the Divinity School, not even Emerson, with whom he was frequently and inevitably compared. "I think he has the better of Emerson—who *seems* a little cold, though he too has a great heart," wrote Frank Sanborn, a Harvard student and kindred spirit whom Conway met in 1853 or 1854. "But Mr. Parker overflows with warmth of sympathy."[19]

Fear of a cold reception kept Conway from making an Emerson pilgrimage to Concord during his first weeks in Massachusetts, as did the distressing thought that he would "not find him as majestic as his Essays." For two weeks he kept a letter of introduction from John Gorham Palfrey to Emerson tucked away in a drawer. But a meeting was inevitable, for in a real sense it was Emerson who had brought him where he was. Finally, before dawn on the morning of May 3, 1853, Conway rose and stole noiselessly from Divinity Hall, having told nobody of his plans. By six-thirty he was riding the Fitchburg Railroad to Concord.[20]

While mustering the courage to knock on his hero's door, Conway spent part of the morning wandering about the town. After breakfasting at an inn he strolled to the Old Manse, "where Hawthorne gathered so many fresh and beautiful 'mosses.'" Then he proceeded the short distance to the Old North Bridge, "the spot where [began] the Revolutionary War which gave us all (negroes excepted) freedom." The arched wooden bridge over the slowly moving river, the simple granite obelisk marking the historic spot, and the general stillness of the secluded setting affected Conway deeply. He stood there alone for a long time. Finally he whispered with self-conscious conviction "a vow that I would love freedom forever, as they [the minutemen] did; that freedom was worth my blood if theirs."[21]

Whether he had been fortified by his visit to the bridge or had simply run out of ways to procrastinate, Conway was soon walking down the Lexington Road toward Emerson's simple white frame house. Before long he was in the presence of his idol. Conway stood nervously as Emerson sat behind his desk and spent what seemed an eternity perusing Palfrey's letter. Only when the sage looked up, smiled, and asked him to sit down did his nerves begin to settle. Emerson remembered Conway's letters to him and wanted to know all about his young enthusiast's life during the time since they were written. "He straightway entered on an examination of my attainments. He knew in about a half hour everything I had ever read and what I was ignorant of. He then found out what kind of people I had met with." Emerson heard the young man's story with interest, and played down his own role in Conway's evolution, remarking that "when the mind has reached a certain stage it may be sometimes crystallized by a slight touch." But Conway would have none of this self-effacement. Emerson was his guiding star, his "spiritual father," as he would often call him—and that day he saw that his own fear of disappointment in the man had been groundless. "[H]e let the full blaze of his volcanic light on me," Conway wrote two days later. "Such electric words never touched me before. Eloquent, wonderful, grand and simple, his speech flowed constantly, bearing the wealth of ages on it. . . . That day was an Era with me. I saw a *great* man." The philosopher and the student discussed their mutual fondness for Quakerism and their mutual fascination with Margaret Fuller. Emerson thrilled his visitor by giving him a copy of *Woman in the Nineteenth Century* bearing Fuller's autograph. Finally, moved by the young man's unspoiled enthusiasm, Emerson took him on a literary tour of Concord.[22]

The highlight was a visit to Henry David Thoreau, who was known to Conway even though his masterpiece, *Walden*, would not be published for another year. When Thoreau politely asked his unexpected guest what he was studying at Harvard, Conway answered, "The Scriptures." " 'The Hindu, Arabic or Jewish?' he asked with great naïveté. I burst out into a loud laugh. Emerson sat across the room and also commenced laughing,—remarking that it was rather dangerous to bring me near such a scoffer as Thoreau." This man was always a puzzle to Conway, whose strain of gregariousness and need for causes blocked his comprehension of one so distant and self-contained. Thoreau's love of nature was also too strong for Conway, whose interest was more in people's constructive manipulation and control of their environment. "I could not enter deeply into wild nature," he wrote revealingly, "but dearly loved a garden." Accordingly, he exaggerated Thoreau's real eccentricities and never seemed willing to consider the man on his own terms. When in 1854 he read *Walden*, he objected to it on three grounds:

"1. That it hasn't optimism enough . . . 2. That one couldn't pursue *his* Art of Living and get married. 3. That one hasn't time to spend or strength to spare from what is his work to take care of such universal rebellion." To Conway, Thoreau would remain a disconcerting oddity, a "naturalist [who] can't live unless snakes are coiling around his leg or lizards perching on his shoulder."[23]

But Emerson was a different story. Conway's love for him soared. If Parker gave Conway a model for a socially useful and theologically fearless ministry, Emerson's constructive tolerance and gentle zest for exploration influenced him in possibly deeper, certainly more all-encompassing ways. Conway would never be a vulgar Emersonian mimic. He would, in fact, move significantly far from him. But Emerson's inspiration would always run deep. Conway's mature commitment to the life of thought in itself, to life as a constant voyage of discovery, was Emersonian in spirit if not always in detail.

The relationship of these two men, moreover, was personal as well as philosophical or professional, and probably fulfilled psychic needs in both. Cut adrift by and from a father whose habit of dominance repelled him, Conway looked to Emerson for the sort of father Walker Conway (only two years younger than his transcendental substitute) could never be: one who set standards while also permitting him his freedom. Emerson provided the perfect blend of tolerance and authoritativeness. He not only encouraged Moncure to be himself, he ordered it. And for Emerson's part, Conway probably represented the sort of son he wished to have. Emerson's beloved first son had died in 1842, and his second, only eight years old in May 1853, showed little intellectual promise. Conway was probably not the only person who profited emotionally when Emerson extended a hand to him, an earnest young pilgrim on a journey far from home.

At Emerson's urging Conway spent the summer of 1853 in Concord, boarding in a house on Ponkatasset Hill on the outskirts of town. Here he strengthened his acquaintance with the Concord circle. He expanded his reading, which included Montaigne and Boccaccio, more of Browning and Shakespeare, and Froude's *Nemesis of Faith*. He went for walks with the ever-inscrutable Thoreau. And with Emerson he spent many hours talking about books and ideas. Emerson introduced his charge to Eastern religion and Oriental literature, notably the Hindu *Bhagavad Gita*, the Persian *Desatir*, and Sadi's *Gulistan*. "He used to give me advice about my health," Conway remembered. "He took care that I should know the best women—the Ripleys, Elizabeth Hoar, and others,—and I was invited to all the picnics. He and his wife gave me, indeed, a home, and the delight I found in comradeship with their children healed the hurts suffered by past alienations."[24]

Conway's increasingly visible connection with Emerson gave rise to severe misgivings among Divinity School authorities during his last academic year, reaching a climax of sorts in April 1854 when Emerson offered to read a paper in his young friend's room at Divinity Hall. Conway, making the most of the occasion, sent out a number of invitations. Those present included Henry Wadsworth Longfellow and his wife, James Russell Lowell, Charles Eliot Norton, Frank Sanborn, and a visiting Arthur Hugh Clough. The paper, "Poetry," was innocuous enough, but when word of Emerson's unauthorized invasion of Divinity Hall reached the faculty, there was considerable alarm. Frederick Dan Huntington, Professor of Christian Morals (who in 1860 would move to Episcopalianism), angrily told Conway that the incident reflected a "decline of moral earnestness" at the Divinity School. Professors Francis and Noyes visited Conway in his room, under the impression "that Emerson had now become a regular teacher in Divinity Hall, the students having organized a school within the school for the 'Emersonian' cult." The teachers seemed mollified by their student's assurance that this was not the case, but the incident annoyed Conway and loosened his allegiance to the Unitarian establishment.[25]

There was more to be upset about in 1854, however, than the defensiveness and pettiness of Unitarian conservatives. It was a year when the sectional crisis reached an unprecedentedly ugly and dangerous stage. The milestone event was the Kansas-Nebraska bill, introduced in January and passed in May. Repealing the Missouri Compromise and opening territories above the old compromise line to slavery if enough proslavery voters settled there, the law gave a new urgency to the festering issue of slavery in the territories. It paved the way for a civil war in Kansas and markedly quickened the breakup of the old political party system. Conway was not immune from the passions it aroused. In March he told Emerson that he could not "see any other result from this Nebraska bill than the making of that beautiful country a slave-breeding sink and the perpetuation of the Institution for a hundred years by making it rich."[26]

Although he had come to Cambridge with considerable hatred for slavery, Conway had thus far attempted to distance himself from organized radical abolitionism. He believed above all that abolitionists were self-righteously uncharitable toward the white Southerners whom they glibly stereotyped. His first acquaintances in Boston were mostly politically oriented Free-Soilers like Palfrey. When he first saw William Lloyd Garrison—at a banquet on May 5, 1853, for retiring Free-Soil senator John Hale of New Hampshire—his attitude toward the abolitionist was sympathetic but skeptical. His status as a renegade Virginia blue blood made conversations on slavery inevitable, but during his first months at Harvard he attempted to maintain a moderate position when confronted by the polemics of true New England radicals. "I had not so pleasant a controversy on Slavery with [fellow students] Fowler and Stone," he wrote during his first month at school, "who are fanatics and who I fear, will make me an old Hunker." But if some sort of moderate course was possible for Moncure in 1853, Kansas-Nebraska made it both more difficult and less desirable. Finally, in May 1854, an extraordinary twist of fate made it impossible.[27]

On the night of May 24, 1854 (the day the Kansas-Nebraska bill was passed in the House of Representatives), a young black man was walking home through the streets of Boston from the secondhand clothing store which had employed him for two months. Suddenly he was accosted by three official-looking white men, backed up by toughs from a local saloon, who accused him of breaking into a nearby jewelry store. Barely given time to protest, he was grabbed by several of the men, dragged through the streets to the courthouse, pushed and pulled up several flights of stairs to the offices of the federal district court. There United States Marshall Watson Freeman confronted him. No more needed to be said about a jewelry store burglary. Anthony Burns now knew for certain what was happening. The warrant Freeman flashed before his face signaled the end of his brief life in freedom. His master had come all the way from Virginia to get him.[28]

Charles Francis Suttle, shopkeeper, Alexandria militia colonel, and politician, was not a man to take betrayal lightly. And he felt betrayed by Anthony Burns. He had given this slave considerable freedom. He had let him hire himself out in Richmond and thus live apart from his master's supervision, demanding only that he report periodically to an associate, William Brent. Burns had taken full advantage of Suttle's confidence. He had gained experience in a wide variety of occupations, taught himself to read and write, acquired enough knowledge of religion to become a part-time preacher. But in the end he had proved ungrateful, taking a job on the Richmond docks and stowing away on a northbound vessel. A letter he subsequently wrote to his brother, also owned by Suttle, was intercepted by their indignant owner. Within days Suttle and Brent were on their way to Boston to recover the recalcitrant property.

Word of the arrest spread rapidly on May 25. At Harvard there was talk of little else. Southern students assembled to pass a resolution of sympathy for the slaveowner. A contingent of them went to Suttle's lodgings at the Revere House in Bowdoin Square to offer their services as bodyguards. The offer was happily, perhaps wisely, accepted. For Conway it was a time of unavoidable decision. To join with the other Southerners was preposterous. But how far should he go in expressing support for Burns? The details of the case left no room for evasion, for the principal actors were people he knew. Burns had apparently been born in Falmouth, and Conway later claimed he had known him personally. Undoubtedly he knew Brent, who was a distant relative of the Conways, and Suttle, who had lost a legislative election to Richard Moncure in 1848 and soon afterward been lampooned by Conway in the Fredericksburg paper. Conway's presence was known to the slavecatchers, who would certainly spread the word of his action (or inaction) when they returned to Virginia. On the other hand, people determined that Burns be rescued were looking to Conway for signs that his repudiation of Virginia was genuine, and for the sort of unique service that only he could render their cause. It seems a few even suggested he use his credentials as an old Virginia neighbor to lure Suttle into an ambush.[29]

Fifty years later, his septuagenarian memory playing down much of his earlier militance, Conway remembered himself as primarily a "studious observer" and "silent listener" who sympathized with Burns but remained detached from the passions of the enraged Bostonians around him. The reality was something different. Although repulsed by the suggestion of violent treachery, he was no bystander. The details of his actions during the nine days of tension following Burns's arrest cannot be pieced together, but one thing is clear: this event brought Conway into personal contact with abolitionist leaders, and made him a committed adherent of their movement.[30]

Events moved swiftly. On the night of May 26 an emotional crowd packed Faneuil Hall to hear incendiary speeches from Samuel Gridley Howe, Wendell Phillips, and Theodore Parker, who ominously reminded his audience that "there is a means, and there is an end; liberty is the end, and sometimes peace is not the means toward it." At the same time, Boston black leader Lewis Hayden and Unitarian minister Thomas Wentworth Higginson led an assault on the courthouse, killing a guard (and demonstrating, if anyone was interested, the moral ambiguity of such militance) but failing to rescue Burns. The violence raised tensions to the breaking point and turned Boston into an armed camp. As Burns went before Fugitive Slave Commissioner Edward G. Loring for a hearing on May 29, the area around Court Square was patrolled by troops from Fort Independence and marines from the Boston Navy Yard, along with a menacing-looking civilian posse of one hundred armed men. Inside, even Suttle's lawyers were armed with pistols and bowie knives. An angry crowd, estimated at as many as seven thousand, milled about the area throughout the day. The scene was repeated during the next two days of the hearing, and again on June 2, when Loring announced his decision.[31]

"Since the Revolution there has been no such excitement in Boston," wrote Charles Eliot Norton on May 30. He overstated the case very little. The city was in an ugly mood, and it was more than just the usual hard-core abolitionists who were upset. To many moderates and conservatives the Kansas-Nebraska Act (passed by the Senate and sent to President Pierce on May 30) seemed a cruel betrayal of the spirit of compromise, a message to the North that it must not only respect the rights of Southern states within their own borders, but also serve Southern interests in distant regions. The Act seemed a major step toward making slavery a national institution; and now this fugitive slave case was offering vivid evidence of just how far the process had gone.

A city that obviously had no stomach for sending people back into slavery was being compelled to do so even if it required a display of military force. "We went to bed one night old-fashioned, conservative, Compromise Union Whigs," wrote industrialist Amos A. Lawrence, "and waked up stark mad Abolitionists."[32]

Despite the alienation of unprecedented numbers of people, the authorities would not compromise. Franklin Pierce sent a telegram to Federal Marshall Freeman personally approving his action in calling out federal troops. On May 27 Charles Suttle concluded that Burns might be more trouble than he was worth and considered an offer by Boston merchants to buy the slave. But U.S. District Attorney Benjamin Hallett intervened, produced legal arguments against the sale, and finally threatened Suttle with a bill for the expenses already incurred by the government in keeping the peace. The determination had been made: Boston, the home of the American Anti-Slavery Society and *The Liberator*, of Garrison and Wendell Phillips and Senator Charles Sumner, would be taught a lesson. It had defied the law too much already. In 1850 William and Ellen Craft, slavehunters hot on their trail, had found refuge with Theodore Parker and then had been bundled off to safety in England. In 1851 Shadrach had been snatched from a Boston courtroom by a bold group of local blacks. Later that year another fugitive, Thomas Sims of Georgia, had been successfully returned, but had to be marched aboard ship in the middle of the night to avoid incident. Burns was the first fugitive arrested in Boston since Sims, and this time the law would be enforced in the broad light of day.[33]

On the morning of June 2, Commissioner Loring ruled that he had no authority to judge the constitutionality of the Fugitive Slave Law, on which Burns's lawyers had concentrated their arguments. He then ruled that Burns was manifestly Suttle's slave and ordered him returned immediately. Early that afternoon, martial law having been declared in Boston, Burns was marched out of Court Square and down State Street to the harbor where Suttle and Brent awaited him aboard a revenue cutter. Police and militia lined the streets, keeping back a crowd of many thousands as Burns proceeded with his escort: three companies of marines, a company of infantry, sixty volunteer guards, a detachment of cavalry from the National Boston Lancers, and a loaded six-pound cannon. Occasionally missiles flew at the soldiers from out of the crowd. Somewhere within it Burns's chief attorney, Richard Henry Dana, was knocked senseless by a hooligan's blackjack. A cartman who apparently tried to block the path of the march saw his horse skewered by bayonets. William Lloyd Garrison watched the procession from a window in the law office of radical attorney John Andrew, at the corner of State, Court, and Washington streets. With him were several associates and a new ally from Virginia, Moncure Conway.[34]

* * *

On July 4, 1854, abolitionists and their friends gathered for their annual picnic at Framingham grove, their numbers swollen to an unprecedented level by recent developments. The platform was carefully decorated for the occasion, bearing a portrait of Garrison, an American flag hung upside down and draped in black, the mottoes "Virginia" decorated with triumphal ribbons and "Redeem Massachusetts" dressed in servile crepe, and two white flags bordered with black, labeled "Kansas" and "Nebraska." In the morning session Garrison was the featured speaker. He was determined to make the most of the occasion.[35]

Events had been making him both more respected and less necessary as more and more people declared themselves unwilling to surrender to slavery's advance. Boston's fury at the return of a fugitive slave showed how much progress had been made since a mob had dragged Garrison through its streets in 1835. Moreover, for all its limitations, there was more genuine antislavery in the Republican party then forming than anyone would have thought possible in a major party when the American Anti-Slavery Society launched its lonely crusade more than two decades earlier. And if Garrison remained firm in his rejection of the conventional political process, its sensitizing to antislavery aspirations was due in no small measure to his efforts. But on this day at Framingham, the abolitionist pioneer was determined to press his advantage rather than rest on his laurels, exhort his followers to tackle the work ahead rather than congratulate himself on work already done—and show the movement and the country that he had lost none of the old fire. Today, in fact, the fire would be visible—hissing, smoking, crackling, in one of the most rousing pieces of political theater ever staged.

"Alas!" he roared, "our greed is insatiable, our rapacity boundless, our disregard of justice profligate to the last degree. . . . Theoretically the government is of the people, and for their good, but in fact, it is in the hands of party demagogues . . . who are themselves the tools and vassals of the Slave Power, ready to do its bidding, no matter what the crime or the peril may be. The forms of a republic are yet left to us, but corruption is general." With that, Garrison announced he would offer "the testimony of his own soul to all present, of the estimation in which he held the pro-slavery laws and deeds of the nation." He held high a copy of the Fugitive Slave Law. He set a match to it. He chanted "And let all the people say, *Amen.*" Amens swept through the crowd. He held out a copy of Edward Loring's decision in the Burns case. He burned it too. Still more amens. He held aloft the United States Constitution. He branded it, with its accommodation of slavery, "a covenant with death, and an agreement with hell." He committed it to flames. "So perish all compromises with tyranny! And let all the people say, Amen!" There were scattered hisses and boos. But they were doused by a final hypnotic, thunderous *Amen.* "That day," wrote Conway many years later, "I distinctly recognized that the antislavery cause was a religion."[36]

In the afternoon Wendell Phillips led Conway to the lectern and, *The Liberator* reported, told the crowd that "when a Virginian ruled the Court-House, the Vigilance Committee was not without a Virginian also; and that was the friend who now stood before them." When the cheers subsided the young Southerner—his words "evidently from the depths of a soul very strongly stirred"—began his first antislavery speech.[37]

He started by recounting his attendance at the Burns hearing, made possible only because someone told a guard he was a Virginian. And then he talked about the South and about himself. "It was a characteristic of the Southern people [so *The Liberator* reported his speech] to become insane on some subjects, and he believed that they were very nearly insane on the subject of slavery. People of delicacy and tenderness in other respects, who have generally only kind feelings towards other people, as soon as anyone mentioned that subject, no matter if he were their own brother or even their child, they denounced him for it, if he could not feel it in his heart to support that institution." Finally he had asserted his own dignity and had embarked on a path which led to an abolitionist platform, "because he felt that there was something in being free, for once in his life, to speak his thoughts freely on the subject of slavery, for hitherto he had had his lips padlocked, because, in Virginia, they not only had slaves, but every man with a conscience, or even the first throbbings of a conscience, is a slave."[38]

Finally Conway told Northerners something about themselves. They could be slaves too. "The great evil was that the Northern people had no faith. When the South pushed slavery against the North, they always found there was nothing but mush—that there was nothing to stand against them." Northerners needed to withstand the pressure of those who placed the status quo above liberty, for to do otherwise was to sacrifice one's own liberty. "The only remedy for slavery was, that those who hate the institution should be revolutionists, all of them." Each person needed "to abolish slavery in his heart," to decide that he would assert himself as an autonomous being and permit slavery no more conquests. Then, "the work would be done." When the cheers died down, Phillips followed with a speech. He applauded "my friend, Mr. Conway," who had "described us rightly as just as much slaves as the parties in whose behalf we move."[39]

Conway had drawn on a central theme in his own life, and with it had touched a responsive nerve in these people. In the past he had fought his own self-perceived servility alone. Now he found a small army of good, decent men and women willing and eager to share the burden of that struggle. He was moving in uncharted places now. His rebellion had taken on a new dimension of public commitment and irrevocability. It was not with the greatest of ease. He disagreed with the Garrisonians' view of politics and the Union. He was still sensitive to blanket attacks on Southerners when made by Northerners. But from the time he stepped from the platform at Framingham grove, Moncure Conway was an abolitionist. More, he was an increasingly well-known antislavery celebrity, prized by the movement for his intelligence, his polemical ability, and especially his origins. He had cut his ties to home. If he had not found a new home, he at least had found a network of people who shared his sense of morality, valued him for the person he wished to be, and offered him an outlet for the fulfillment of his deepest personal needs.

Conway was more reticent at his graduation on July 20, 1854, than he had been three weeks earlier at Framingham. Of the seven recipients of the B.D. degree, only two agreed to deliver the usual commencement speeches on subjects assigned by the faculty. The rebellion of the others had been sparked by the faculty's refusal to approve graduate James Hackett Fowler's speech on "The use of liturgies in public worship," which Fowler had made a vehicle for his spiritualist enthusiasms. Feeling that free speech was being throttled, Conway and the other insurgents petitioned the authorities to let Fowler be heard and to permit all students to speak on topics of their own choosing. The faculty's response was an uncompromising reassertion of its own prerogatives. Thus Conway sat in stony silence at his graduation, filled with a sense of martyrdom in the cause of free expression.

He was not placated by the Harvard alumni meeting that same day. There Theodore Parker and John Weiss inquired about the graduates' silence, found the issue not worth agitating, and stood aside as the alumni passed a unanimous resolution of support for the faculty. Leaving the meeting, Conway met Emerson in Harvard Yard and lamented, "I am misunderstood." "To be great is to be misunderstood," was the soothing response of his spiritual father.[40]

Far less soothing was the treatment recently accorded another would-be graduate. The trouble involving William Leaman began in June, when Conway and two companions, H. G. Denny and Loammi Ware, decided to celebrate the end of school by smuggling three bottles of wine into Divinity Hall, where alcoholic beverages were prohibited. The three bottles were placed in Ware's room, but two days later only two could be found, filled with water. The students' investigation led them to Leaman, a graduating senior due to enter the ministry in a few weeks. Conway was proctor of Divinity Hall (a job paying thirty dollars), and was obliged to report dishonest behavior to the authorities. He had of course committed an offense himself in bringing the wine into the building. But Leaman's transgression seemed of a different order of magnitude, a violation not of a bureaucratic regulation but of the rights of another person. It did not seem to matter to Conway that if he had not illegally brought the wine into the building, Leaman could not have illegally made off with it. Thus, in one of his more ambiguous acts of conscience, Conway told the whole story to Professor Noyes. Noyes was so impressed with his student's self-incriminating honesty that he forgave the wine smugglers completely. Leaman's fate was less happy. On June 20, report the faculty minutes, he was "dismissed from the school for immoral conduct, with the injunction not to preach under penalty of having his misconduct publicly exposed."[41]

Leaman's movements during the next two years are unknown. But by June 1856 he had drifted to Kansas and met John Brown. In Brown's cause he may have seen an opportunity to cleanse himself of the past disgrace he evidently kept carefully hidden from his new companions. According to biographical information given by Brown associates to Richard J. Hinton in the 1890s (and repeated by historians ever since) Leaman's birth date was 1839 (which would make him the youngest of Brown's followers), he "received a moderate degree of education in the common schools of Saco and Hallowell [Maine], and at the age of fourteen went to Haverhill, Mass., to work in a shoe factory." But the Harvard catalogue for the year 1852–53 lists William Leaman of Hallowell, Maine, as already in the middle class at the Divinity School. Probably Leaman tried to cover his tracks by lying about his age as well as about his past. In any case, Brown was his means of recovering his good name, and in 1859 he went to Harper's Ferry full of hope that vindication was at hand. "Mother it will bring me a *Name & Fortune*," he wrote on the eve of the raid, in a statement that has been wrongly interpreted as revealing a mere desire for plunder. Leaman's hopes were partly met. He would thereafter be known as a simple young man who went to the limit for the oppressed. But it was not all as he had wished. He was one of the first men killed in the raid. His body lay exposed for hours, used for target practice by passing Virginians until it was hardly identifiable.[42]

Moncure Conway was gaining steadily in recognition, and his first job after Harvard promised to accelerate that trend. Shortly before graduation he had been asked to give a series of sermons in the fall at the Unitarian church in Washington, D.C., with the promise of a permanent appointment if his words were well received. The congregation, divided on slavery and not suspecting the extent of his radicalization, had chosen him partly because of his Virginia origins. Evidently conservatives thought he could be trusted to avoid agitation of the issue.[43] Thus, at the age of twenty-two, Conway assumed one of the most sensitive and closely watched ministerial posts in the nation.

"I shall be glad to hear that you have received a call to Washington," wrote Frank Sanborn in September. "But will the Society hear what you wish to tell them? That is the question."[44] It was indeed.

CHAPTER 5

"I don't see how it is possible you should remain *very* long in Washington," admonished William Henry Furness, who, as his seventy-one-year affiliation with Philadelphia's First Unitarian Church implies, knew how to get along with a congregation. Furness also knew the Washington church's reputation for running through ministers—it had had ten of them since its founding in 1821. With its many political transients from various parts of the country bringing an inordinate number of large egos and a disproportionate array of viewpoints into the pews, any minister there had to be a master of diplomacy, and Furness knew Conway was short of that. Moreover, with the sectional crisis reaching a dangerous pitch, agitation on the slavery issue was not likely to be accepted in good grace. An occasional nod in that direction could be tolerated, for to some extent ministers had to be indulged. But it was unlikely that a congregation united only by religious liberalism, whose founders had included personalities as diverse as John Quincy Adams and John C. Calhoun, would sit calmly while its minister embraced straight-out abolitionism. "If you adopt that course at Washington," warned conservative Orville Dewey, who had served at the church, "you will not be able to sustain yourself there."[1]

As he would be quick to remind them two years later, Conway told his prospective parishioners very early that he was antislavery. In his first sermon, on September 10, 1854, he spoke of the evils facing the world: "[S]ee man's hand lifted against man in war; see trade polluted by dishonesty, so that what we eat and wear is poisoned and stained with crime; see man enslaved by man, until we scarce know in their degradation those brothers of Christ, to whom we are anything but brothers. . . ." And on October 29, the day of his election, he exhorted: "The Church must . . . hold itself ready to give free utterance in relation to our special national sin—the greatest of all sins—Human Slavery." But in neither case had the antislavery passage been the focal point of the sermon—perhaps purposely, since Conway knew too much plain speaking would lose him the job. The congregation's political conservatives were willing to overlook the statements as the sort of moralistic mouthings a young minister was prone to make on occasion. The congregation was also tired of searching. The church had had trouble finding a permanent minister—it had been without one for three years— and William Henry Channing, who craved the job, had just been rejected as unsafe on slavery. At least this new man was young and just beginning his career, and thus would be anxious to please and susceptible to control. Moreover, it seemed inconceivable that an upper-class Virginian could turn into a radical abolitionist. "I told them that I had conversed with Channing and agreed with him on the Slavery question," Conway wrote to Emerson. "But my being a Virginian made the difference."[2]

Some conservative parishioners may have had second thoughts when Conway invited a trio of advanced antislavery Unitarians to speak at his ordination on February 28, 1855. Participating in the ceremony were Samuel Longfellow of Brooklyn (who had preached on a trial basis in Washington in the 1840s before being rejected), John Weiss of New Bedford, and William Henry Furness. Feathers were sufficiently ruffled that Conway had to reassure some members privately that his guests had been invited only out of friendship and deference, and that in particular he did not agree with the political views expressed by Furness. Even though Conway said later that he had been referring only to Furness's Garrisonian disunion principles, a number of the disaffected either believed or chose to believe that he was disavowing abolitionism in general. The trouble passed. But doubts lingered. Conway's old mentor, George Burnap, the only other clerical participant in the ordination, took his young protégé aside after the service and expressed his own misgivings. He was bothered by what he called "the abolition complexion" of the ceremony, and warned Conway that "one ism is enough at a time."[3]

If his Washington congregation was initially unaware of Conway's growing antislavery radicalism, his father was only too well acquainted with it. The triumphant return of Charles Suttle and William Brent to Virginia had brought in its wake a new round of rumors about the young heretic from Falmouth. Stories about Conway's behavior during the Burns affair circulated rapidly through Fredericksburg and Stafford County. One had Conway testifying against Suttle in court. Another had him conspiring in a rescue plot.[4] But even without embellishment the truth was bad enough. Walker Conway's son had consorted with William Lloyd Garrison and Wendell Phillips while a countryman was in town trying to recover his rightful property. Afterward he had appeared on an abolitionist platform and seen his speech featured in *The Liberator*. Whether or not the elder Conway knew about the Framingham meeting, he had heard enough to know that he did not wish to see his son.

"It is my sincere advice to you not to come here, until there is reason to believe your opinions have undergone material changes on the subject of slavery," wrote Walker on September 18, 1854, in one of his rare letters to this son. He was fearful that Moncure, newly settled in Washington, might decide to cross the Potomac to visit old friends and relations. His own distaste for that possibility merged with concern for its consequences in leading him to warn against it. "If you are willing to expose your own person recklessly, I am not willing to subject myself and family to the hazards of such a visit. Those opinions give me more uneasiness just now than your horrible views on the subject of religion." The father then moved to a personal attack on the son, rebuking him for a charge Moncure had made earlier that "it is strange that you meet with intolerance no where but at home." "If you had but a small amount of that best of all senses,—'common sense'," Walker stormed, "it would not seem at all strange that such should be the fact." Many people might, out of politeness, indulge eccentric young men far from home. But a man's family and early friends had a duty to deal with him honestly and directly, unpleasant though the truth might be. "A single moment's reflection would teach any common sense person the reason and propriety of our course." Finally, despairing of changing him, Walker consigned Moncure "to the mercy of God, through our Lord and Savior Jesus Christ." There was no visit to Falmouth that month.[5]

But in January 1855 Moncure decided to make the test, decided to see for himself just how much an exile he was. The trip was occasioned by an unexpected invitation (from Patrick Henry Aylett, a friend of John Moncure Daniel) to preach one Sunday in the long-unused Universalist church in Richmond. This strictly theological sermon, on January 21, 1855, was received coolly but politely. Conway's stay in the Virginia capital, where he was the guest of his uncle Travers Daniel, was pleasant. Nothing was said by anyone about slavery.[6]

In Falmouth it was different, as it was bound to be. Conway was perhaps brash in stopping at his hometown on his way back to Washington, but to bypass it seemed unthinkable. He was not quite so enamored of martyrdom that he was willing to embrace it if he could avoid it, and he genuinely wished to see his family. But his old home was no home for him now. Although he was welcomed with affection by his mother and with civility by his father, a number of townspeople were disinclined to tolerate his presence.

On the morning after his arrival he was walking through Falmouth's main street toward the Rappahannock bridge when he noticed a crowd gathering. Within moments he was surrounded. Among those confronting him were aggressive types who spoke menacingly of tar and feathers. But the spokesmen, old acquaintances of Conway's, were more respectful of amenities. The Conways were powerful in the region, and Moncure's relatives, no matter how much they loathed his opinions, were certain to resent any harm done him. So Conway's interceptors conveyed their message with methodical restraint, telling him he would be spared pulverization if he left town at once. Charles Suttle had passed the word that Moncure was an abolitionist who had done all he could to keep him from recovering his slave. No such person could be trusted in proximity to local blacks. (The accusers actually had a point. Unknown to them, slaves had twice approached a startled Conway the previous night under the impression he was there to help them escape.) With no alternative that salvaged his dignity and only one that allowed him his hide, Conway told his fellow townsmen he would cut short his visit by two days and leave the following morning.

He departed as promised, without telling his parents the real reason for his sudden change of plans. His father's personal slave, James Parker, drove him to the railroad station. On the train to Aquia Creek he chanced upon Walker's brother Valentine, who lashed out at him scathingly. Aboard the Potomac boat Moncure sat alone on the cold and windy deck, humiliation tearing through him, and wept.[7]

With pathetic stubbornness, Conway was still not prepared to give up on Virginia. In April he went back. But this time he went to a part of the state where he had never been, where he was far less well known and less notorious. He visited Harper's Ferry, proceeded south through the Shenandoah Valley to Natural Bridge, then turned northeast to Charlottesville. Until now he had been a tourist, but a visit to the University of Virginia spurred him to a more official action. He still dreamed of returning to his native state, finding a home there, preaching to tolerant and sympathetic listeners. The atmosphere of the university stirred his enthusiasm and made him think that here, perhaps, was that home. So he hurried into Charlottesville and rented a hall, plastering makeshift signs around the university announcing that he would speak and answer questions the next day on liberal religion. The lecture was well attended, but Conway was deeply disappointed by the unanimity of disapproval it encountered. He kept slavery out of the discussion entirely. But even on strictly religious subjects these students, supposedly the cream of Virginia's youth, clutched their Bibles close to them and shrank from all traces of heresy. On the same visit Conway watched students roast an effigy of Harriet Beecher Stowe. "My experiences at Richmond and Charlottesville," he recalled later, "convinced me that the mission of an apostle *in partibus orthodoxorum* was not mine." Remembering his Charlottesville experience a few years later, he concluded bitterly that Virginia "is a great place for live fossils."[8]

At this same time he learned that it did not help much to send entrenched Virginians north in the hope of enlightening them. That opportunity had come early in 1855 when a group in New Haven wrote to Conway requesting him to find a proslavery spokesman to speak at Yale in conjunction with a speech by Wendell Phillips. Enthusiastically he set about getting George Fitzhugh, a friend of Eustace Conway whose articles in the *Richmond Examiner* had just been refined into a widely noticed book, *Sociology for the South* (1854). Regarding Northern industrial workers as more oppressed than Southern slaves, Fitzhugh believed that enslavement of all workers was the most humane and proper solution to society's problems. A country lawyer who seldom ventured far from home in eastern Virginia, Fitzhugh at forty-nine had never been to the North. Conway regarded it as a major coup when, through the efforts of his uncle Eustace, the reactionary theoretician accepted the New Haven invitation.

Smarting from the rebuff he had suffered in Virginia in January, Conway was anxious to prove to himself that sober intersectional communication was still possible. He also hoped that exposure to the facts of Northern life would broaden Fitzhugh's thinking. But while the Yale speech came off uneventfully in mid-March and no ugly incident marred Fitzhugh's Northern visit, he returned home unchanged. Samuel Foote, an uncle of Harriet Beecher Stowe, had given him a tour of New Haven and had pointed out the living and working conditions of the masses, apparently less deplorable than portrayed in Fitzhugh's writings. But he was not convinced. "Truly one half of them [his listeners] are atheists seeking to discover a 'New Social Science,' " he wrote to a friend, asking that the letter be forwarded to Moncure Conway; "the other half Millennial anti-church, anti-law, and anti-marriage Christians. . . . I do not believe there is a Liberty man in the North who is not a Socialist." As for Phillips's speech, "It was flat treason and blasphemy—nothing else."[9]

After his experience in the first few months of 1855, it seemed Conway would have to put aside any immediate prospects of reconciling himself to Virginia, or of Virginia being reconciled to him. His home would be wherever he happened to find himself, and at the moment that was really not so bad. Not a cultural mecca, Washington was nonetheless an exciting city for an interested observer of public affairs. In his congregation, a group of four to five hundred "educated and refined" people containing "none of the so-called working class and no negroes," Conway found a sizable cadre of sympathizers and a contingent of thoughtful and likable people his own age. And for all its squabbling, the congregation was impressive: intelligent, tolerant of religious differences, cultured, sophisticated, powerful. Among the prominent in its ranks were William Cranch, long-lived chief judge of the Circuit Court of the District of Columbia; Joseph Gales, Jr., and William W. Seaton, both former mayors of Washington and current co-editors of the sober and prestigious *National Intelligencer*; noted meteorologist James Pollard

Espy; prominent local booksellers Hudson and Franck Taylor; Charles W. Upham, congressman and able historian of the Salem witchcraft upheaval; and, occasionally, Senator Charles Sumner.[10]

Shortly after his return to Washington after the incident in Falmouth, Conway moved out of a boardinghouse and into the home of Hudson Taylor and his wife, both of whom shared his beliefs and stood by him through all the tribulations he was to endure as their minister. He also became close to Hudson's brother Franck, recalling that he and his wife "were almost parental in their kindness to me." With two booksellers among his closest friends, he was able to gratify his passion for reading. After only two months in Washington he had purchased the works of Carlyle, Comte, Tennyson, Longfellow, Matthew Arnold, Osgood's *Studies in Christian Biography*, and a homeopathic textbook.[11]

With Franck Taylor's bright, attractive daughters, Emily and Charlotte, Moncure developed close and lasting friendships. He was always a little in danger of falling in love with one or the other, and probably would have done so with Charlotte, the more sensitive and spiritually restless of the two, had she not already been attached to eighteen-year-old Gerald Fitzgerald, who also became Conway's good friend. Fitzgerald's own sensibilities had joined with Charlotte Taylor's charms in leading him to repudiate his conservative Irish Catholic upbringing, and the force of Conway's preaching cemented his new allegiance. He looked upon Moncure as an older brother, called him his "torchbearer," regarded himself as Conway's "pupil." Later he would go to Harvard Divinity School and study in Germany, and Conway's tragically fateful influence on him would not stop there. But during that first year in Washington, when the future was happily unknown to these four friends, they socialized constantly and joyfully, talked for hours at downtown cafes, danced into the night at "hops" at Willard's and the National. Whirling across the floor with Emily or Charlotte Taylor, Moncure gleefully stomped his old Methodist horror of dancing into unmourned and irretrievable oblivion.[12]

Conway's fondness for stimulating female company found another outlet in a housewife nineteen months his senior who attended his church with her husband, Lieutenant Edward Hunt. Helen Hunt was an educated, witty young woman who loved her husband but found him incapable of sharing her passion for books. One of those "scientific men . . . who want telescopes brought to bear on all nebulae," he reacted to Browning by commenting, "if the man has got anything to say which is *worth* saying, it is worth while to say it so clearly that it can be understood without groping after." Thus stymied, Mrs. Hunt turned to Conway for intellectual and spiritual comradeship. She discussed poetry, Hawthorne, and Emerson with him, and found in him a man who thought women not only capable of ideas but actually more exciting if they had them. They would remain friendly for thirty years. Conway's respect and affection were constant, as much when she was an obscure housewife as when, as "H. H." and Helen Hunt Jackson, she was a nationally known novelist, poet, and the foremost symbol of the liberal crusade for justice for the American Indian.[13]

His confidence boosted by developing friendships and success in the pulpit (where he had yet to push the slavery issue), Conway began his summer vacation in 1855 in high spirits. He took the waters at Saratoga, spent a weekend in Montreal, traveled in northern New England, visited acquaintances in Boston. Late in August he was in Newport. There he discovered the glories of sea-bathing and, noted the vacationing Henry Wadsworth Longfellow, "preached a striking sermon on 'Skeptics,' in which he said a good word for doubters and the much abused free-thinkers." After a brief trip to Concord, where he spent a day with Emerson, Conway returned to Washington and on September 9 began a new season in his pulpit.[14]

On his way back he stopped in Brooklyn, determined to visit a writer whose shocking new book was being much talked about by literary people in New England. Emerson had told Conway about Walt Whitman when the young minister visited Concord. His curiosity aroused, Conway bought a copy of *Leaves of Grass* and read it aboard the steamship *Metropolis* which carried him from Boston to New York. He was thrilled by the original, grand, and sweeping style which resembled nothing so much as the best of the Persian poetry he had recently discovered. If the earthiness of the work bothered him, he left no evidence of it. Thomas Wentworth Higginson, who read it on his way back from the Azores, claimed that it blended well with his seasickness; Charles Eliot Norton said he "would be sorry to know that any woman had looked into it past the title-page." But Conway suffered no seasickness on the *Metropolis*, read parts of *Leaves* to his sister Mildred (who was in New York with him at the time), and in the next decade would cite the work's sexual candor as a main reason for his attraction to it. In any case, by the time the *Metropolis* docked in New York he knew he had to see this self-styled "rough" who wrote the most powerful verse he had ever seen by an American.[15]

On the day of his arrival Conway rode the Fulton Street ferry to Brooklyn and made his way to Rome's Printing Office at Fulton and Cranberry streets. He found the gray-bearded, thirty-six-year-old Whitman, dressed in a simple open-necked blue-striped shirt, absorbed in the revision of proofs. The poet was both surprised and flattered by his visitor, the first person to come to him from any distance because of his book. After listening with amusement to Conway's anecdotes of stuffy New Englanders unable to read the work aloud, Whitman offered to take his new friend for a walk. Down to the ferry and then through the streets of Manhattan the two strolled, Conway visibly impressed by his companion's reciprocated familiarity with omnibus drivers, fruit vendors, news dealers, and other ordinary types. "He says he is one of that class by choice," Conway reported, "that he is personally dear to some thousands of such in New York, who 'love him but cannot make head or tail of his book.' "[16]

The upper-class young man was both fascinated by and envious of Whitman's apparent rapport with these common citizens. He had always longed for such rapport, but could never quite attain it, despite his gradual but genuine liberation from snobbery. Now this longing to commune with working people drew him even closer to Whitman—this desire to gain the confidence of the masses so that one might guide or inspire them, even while sharing in the reflected glow of their simplicity. He did not realize at the time the extent to which Whitman was really separated from the masses, discovering only later that the poet "knew as little of the working class practically as I did. He had gone about among them in the disguise of their own dress, and was perfectly honest in his supposition that he had entered into their inmost nature. . . . It was so [also] in the case of Thomas Paine, who wrote transcendental politics and labelled it 'Common Sense.' " But this insight was for a much later time, after Conway's fascination with Whitman in the 1850s and his service to him in the 1860s had given way to an imperfectly healed breach between the two in the 1870s. For now, as after a second visit in 1857, Conway pronounced himself "delighted with him." "His eye can kindle strangely," he gushed in a letter to Emerson, "and his words are ruddy with health. He is clearly his Book."[17]

Fresh from his sojourn with Whitman, Conway arrived back in Washington eager to do service on behalf of another admired poet. At Newport, Longfellow had told him about an epic poem he had just completed, *The Song of Hiawatha*, which drew on the Indian legends described by ethnologist Henry R. Schoolcraft. Conway eagerly volunteered to review the book in the *National Intelligencer*, whose pages were open to him through his acquaintance with its editors, his parishioners Gales and Seaton. Accordingly, he was one of the first people to get a copy of the book. His review appeared in November, two weeks after *Hiawatha's* publication.[18]

Conway was generous in his praise of *Hiawatha*. Grateful to Longfellow for "the rescue of our highly poetic Indian legends" from literary obscurity, he regarded the result as "a noble American Poem, with as few faults as any other of our times." His review focused on a thought that kept occurring to him as he read the poem: the oneness of mankind in its basic urges, aspirations, and needs. "How remarkable is the unity of Man in the midst of his so great differences! There is not one of these Indian legends which is not native to every race of men, only differing as the fox or deer here might differ from the same in Europe or Asia." At a time of rapid change, when the fabric of American society seemed to be splitting, many Americans were searching for common ground where they could overcome popular differences. In these Indian legends Conway pointed to a heritage that all Americans shared. (He neglected to mention that all white Americans also shared a heritage of exterminating the legends' creators.) But for Conway, this poetic rendering of the old myths was more than an exercise in cultural nationalism. On its deepest level, this Indian folklore expressed a set of human concerns which bridged the gaps between races and nations. "Who is Hiawatha," he wrote, "but Siegfried of the Norsemen, Hercules of the Greeks, Moses of the Jews, Haroun Al Raschid of the Arabs?" The vision of a common human family so dear to the hearts of many reformers found few more ready enthusiasts than Conway, suffering the pain of personal homelessness and exile.[19]

Conway was careful, in the beginning, not to do anything to disrupt the niche he was developing for himself in Washington. For more than a year after his engagement he refrained from agitating the slavery question, or from making it the central topic of a sermon. He confined his preaching largely to general moral and inspirational subjects, or to points of Unitarian theology. His sermons always took their departure from a biblical text, were intelligent, painstakingly constructed, and essentially conventional in their ultimate message.

But what was conventional in some quarters was heretical in others. Conway's family, reading weekly summaries of his sermons in the *National Intelligencer*, heatedly disapproved of his religious teachings. Even his mother was moved to nag him about what she viewed as his dangerous departure from the truth, telling him there was "but *one* way in which intellect can be preserved from wafting or drifting off into atheism, and that is by steering with the rudder of *faith* in the belief that in *Him* (that is Christ) 'dwelleth all the fullness of the Godhead bodily.'" When her son responded angrily she simply redoubled her attack, telling him she had plenty of company in thinking him guilty of "impiety." A childhood friend of his had told her, "Monk is making a model of Theodore Parker in his preaching."[20]

Conservative Protestants were not the only people listening to Conway and seeing the specter of wild Theodore Parker and his bloodcurdling heresies. George Burnap, now having second thoughts about the youth he had helped into Unitarianism, warned Conway early in 1855 that he "ought to take some measures to disabuse those who may have misjudged you, of their impressions as to your want of faith in *historical Christianity*. I know that it was our mutual friend Peabody's impression, that you had hardly *faith enough* to preach. I throw out this as merely a friendly hint."[21]

The reactions of Burnap and Peabody to Conway's preaching illustrate how defensive the Unitarian establishment had become by the 1850s, for in substance the young minister was preaching orthodox Unitarian doctrine. He called "Unitarian Christianity . . . a theory adapted to human conditions and wants," a religion which emphasized the cultivation of man's moral sense. He called himself a Christian and judged nearly everything by Christ's standards. Embracing the Unitarian paradox fully, he "affirmed that Unitarians believe in Christ as divine, making a distinction between his deity and divinity." Jesus was a divinely inspired teacher, more perfect than any other person before or since, "a mediator in his showing the possible exaltation of our nature into communion with God and all virtue." Like all Unitarians, Conway stressed the essential goodness of man, "the difference between him [Jesus] and us being that the divinity is the fact of his life, but only the possibility of ours." And he approached the Bible in the spirit of Unitarian scholarship which had long probed it to discredit its morally or intellectually unappealing components while leaving its basic sacredness intact. In one sermon, "the infallibility of the Bible was considered [and rejected] in reference to the moral bearings of the deluge, where a world was destroyed, young children and animals, because of the wickedness of some." In another he contended with circuitous logic that "if the Bible were scientifically correct it would smack of a Council of Bishops; as it is, it is a revelation of man, with all his imperfections; and, as man is of God, a revelation of Him."[22]

Although parts of Conway's preaching could be construed as reaching beyond Unitarianism toward the airier reaches of transcendentalism, there was really very little in the theological sermons he gave at Washington directly in conflict with established Unitarian belief. The contradictions, loose ends, and inconsistencies in his sermons were the property of his denomination. What troubled Burnap and other leading conservatives was that the rising left wing was pushing certain elements within that established belief too hard, at the expense of other, more piously conventional elements, and with potentially dangerous consequences. In particular, radical Unitarians had begun to dissect the Bible without always retaining an overriding confidence in its sacred character. And they sometimes stressed the subordination of Jesus to God so much that they no longer had proper reverence for their Redeemer. In consequence, conservatives hunkered down in their scriptural bunkers and worshiped their Bibles with unprecedented passion, treating Jesus almost as though he were, after all, God. Certain things could be said in 1840 which seemed heretical in 1855. A counterrevolution was brewing.[23]

One cause for alarm which Conway gave theologically conservative Unitarians was his tone, his enthusiasm for sanctioning doubt. If he did not personally challenge specific Unitarian tenets, he seemed to excuse those who did. What sparked Burnap's "friendly hint" may have been Conway's first published sermon, "The Old and the New," delivered on December 31, 1854. In this he had sung the virtues of combining conservatism with progress and change, but had seemed more attracted to the latter. He congratulated the congregation "on your freedom from that spirit of Reactionism which has disgraced Unitarianism in some quarters," and reminded it "that we cannot expect or wish uniformity of creed among ourselves, more than of mind or feature. . . . We utter

again and again our detestation of creeds and tests, orthodox or liberal—
each saying, with Paul, I AM FREEBORN." Such relativism must have
worried the stalwarts, for fear of where it might lead. And Conway's
sermon on "Skeptics," preached in Washington and Newport in April
and August 1855 and eventually published, was likewise no treat for
conservative minds. It insisted that "every question [is] an open one"
and boldly asserted that "Jesus was the model free thinker."[24]

Shortly after returning from his summer vacation in 1855 Conway
had an opportunity to demonstrate his ministerial independence, in a
way, however, that was compatible with Unitarian doctrine. A yellow
fever epidemic was ravaging Norfolk, Virginia, and the District of
Columbia board of aldermen had set aside a certain weekday for fasting
and prayer. Citizens were asked to repair to their churches on that day
and petition God to relieve Norfolk and spare Washington. Conway
regarded this move as a political gesture that would needlessly rob
people of a day's wages, and also thought it presumptuous to petition
a benevolent God to change His own policy. Since entering Unitarianism,
Conway had believed with increasing conviction that evil was merely
good in the making. In this instance he believed God was using the
plague not to punish but to educate. The epidemic, he argued, was part
of God's plan, enlightening people about the need for sanitation reform
and making them realize that "the rich and educated cannot afford, any
more than the poor, that there should be any class so poor as to be
squalid or unhealthy." For all those reasons, he announced he would
not open the Unitarian church on the appointed fast day.[25]

"The most important result of this incident," Conway wrote later,
"was its revelation that my congregation was essentially rationalistic, and
that leading citizens of Washington by no means shared the vulgar
superstitions." His parishioners supported his action, raised eighty-nine
dollars (at their regular Sunday service) for relief of the Virginia
sufferers, and sponsored the publication of two of his sermons justifying
the church's course. In the current phase of their minister's religious
development, it now seemed unlikely that he could say or do anything
that would alienate them. If some fellow ministers found him theologically unsafe, his congregation evidently did not. Realization of this
reinforced Conway's confidence and strengthened the sense of security
he felt in this precarious clerical post.[26]

Security, however, was something the Unitarian minister in Washington was not adept at handling. It was a two-edged sword. While it gave
him confidence to be bolder, it also made him uncomfortable and fearful
he would lapse into complacency. The viper of conservatism was ever
alert to wrap its coils about the careless. By the beginning of 1856
Moncure Conway could hear it hissing.

For some people there was a mutually reinforcing connection, however
muddled and oblique, between religious radicalism on the one hand,

and social and political radicalism on the other. Orthodox Protestantism, for all the reformist rhetoric of its evangelical sects, was essentially a religion of worldly compromise, emphasizing personal salvation at the expense of broader social regeneration. The sins of individuals were matters for concern, but social ills were endemic, to be erased only at the millennium. Liberal religion, however, constituted a shift of emphasis momentous in its potential consequences. The less one emphasized dogma, the more one stressed freedom of action. The less faith one had in a future life, the more weight one gave to the present. The less one worshiped Jesus as a God, the more one respected him as a human iconoclast with a social mission. The less one looked above, the more one looked about. Thus many Unitarian radicals grew tired of the hypocrisy of worshiping a man they were never expected to treat as God, and came to view Jesus as a person whose timeless importance lay in his ability to arouse men and women to a sense of their responsibilities. They wearied of defending the essential sacredness of a book whose component parts they were always taught to question, and rejected the infallibility of all beliefs based on events they could never prove, in eras they could never reconstruct, in worlds they could never really know. And they carried that spirit of uncompromised independence with them into the pulpit, to confront the problems and issues of their own world, the one world they did know. "When I escaped from the dogmatic burden," wrote Conway, "and took the pleasant rationalistic Christ on my shoulder . . . the new Christ became Jesus, was human, and all humanity came with him,—the world-woe, the temporal evil and wrong. . . . Jesus was no sacrifice, but an exemplar of self-sacrifice."[27]

Mainstream Unitarians like George Burnap and Orville Dewey, able to live with the contradictions of their own creed and often unwilling to pursue the implications of their own theological teachings, looked with growing alarm at the radicals in their midst. They were upset by what seemed to them impiety, but they were equally alarmed by the tendency of that radical minority to enter the arena of lay reform. "The Unitarians as a body dealt with the question of slavery in any but an impartial, courageous, and Christian way," lamented Unitarian abolitionist Samuel J. May. "They, of all other sects, ought to have spoken boldly. But they did not." Unitarianism, for all its potential subversiveness, was in practice an intellectualized religion which accented civility, stability, quiet self-culture, and which usually attracted people who were economically and socially secure. Within this context, social agitation was undignified, un-Christian, either counterproductive or unnecessary, and offensive to conservative citizens of taste, worth and station. Octavius B. Frothingham theorized that Unitarians were suspicious of abolitionists because the latter generally came from a lower social class.[28]

The conservative predilections of the people filling most Unitarian pulpits was mirrored and reinforced by the prejudices of the people in the pews. Unitarian congregations were not hotbeds of radicalism, as many left-wing preachers discovered. Samuel J. May had been dismissed by a congregation in South Scituate, Massachusetts, which accused him of "always preaching for the niggers." Salem parishioners dealt with O. B. Frothingham in similar fashion for a similar offense. Thomas Wentworth Higginson, Samuel Longfellow, Samuel May, Jr., John Pierpont, John Weiss, and many others had fought with their congregations over slavery, usually to their disadvantage. If an antislavery Unitarian minister could expect such resistance in regions where antislavery sentiment was relatively entrenched, he clearly could expect no mercy where slavery was legal and where the congregation was partly composed of politically sensitive officeholders from various parts of the country. What many people told Moncure Conway when he first took the Washington pulpit was true. It was no place to preach abolition.[29]

And so he did not preach it, not for a long time. He was proud of his success at so early an age. He liked his job. He liked the prestige, visibility, and deference that went with it. He did not want to jeopardize it. He liked the friends he was making in this place, the closest thing to home he now had. He did not want to lose them. So on weekdays he worked laboriously on his Sunday sermons, making them thoughtful enough for people to respect him, provocative enough for people to notice him, and diplomatic enough for people to like him. Mainly, he stayed away from the one subject most important to him personally and most dangerous to him professionally. He was free to roam at will as long as he left the forbidden tree intact. The tree stood for over a year, barely scratched. Suddenly, with purposeful violence, he chopped it down.

The re-orientation of political parties spurred by the Kansas-Nebraska Act had proceeded rapidly. By the end of 1855 the new Republican party, pledged to halt slavery's expansion into the territories, was bidding for leadership positions in Washington. When Congress convened in December a furious battle ensued for the House Speakership, lasting several weeks and riveting the country's attention on the capital city.* Among Washington residents few other public issues were discussed. In this climate the Unitarian minister felt his past silence with pain and no little shame. He had truckled to the status quo. As a consequence he was in danger of being fossilized and forgotten, as bolder people carried on the unpopular fight for truth. It would not happen. He decided to assert his own dignity now, to throw all he had gained into the maelstrom and let fate take its course. He would dust off the Framingham persona and place it on a bigger stage for all to see. His congregation would be shocked. Many would hate him. But he would rather be hated by them than by himself. He would be nobody's slave.[30]

* The battle finally ended with the election of Republican moderate Nathaniel P. Banks on February 2, 1856.

It was pure melodrama: revelation, certain reprisal, the chance for an emancipated new life. And the minister had made certain the drama would be noticed. He announced that on January 27, 1856, he would deliver his most important sermon to date, entitled "The One Path." He told Charles Sumner to spread the word in Congress. He notified Horace Greeley, in town to cover the Speakership fight. If Greeley's New York *Tribune*, with its massive circulation throughout the country, reported this event, then for Conway there could be no more opportunity for backsliding, for retreats into comfortable and ambiguous silence. All eyes would be on him, and they would stay on him until the unavoidable clash with his parishioners was finished.

The day was cold and snowy, and many stayed away. But those who counted most were there. A loyal knot of Conway boosters sat in the front pews, reinforced by Sumner himself, to return their pastor's gaze and nod approvingly and cheer him on. Most importantly—for this was a public act—the press was there, the Washington press corps and Horace Greeley, who captured all eyes as he skimmed down the aisle, resplendent in white overcoat and white felt hat, his presence the biggest clue of all that this was, in fact, an Event.[31]

Conway did not keep his audience in suspense. Yes, his sermon was on slavery. No, he would not equivocate. "I shall waste no words on the dogma, that such subjects are not proper to the pulpit. . . . If moral questions should not enter here, what should? And if questions involving the happiness of millions, and the good relations of section with section, and man with man, throughout the land, are not moral, what are?" The problem, the minister continued, was that people were asking him to be silent about slavery on the grounds that politics should not enter the pulpit. But slavery was not a political question. "It is exclusively a moral question, as are all questions affecting humanity." And how should Americans deal with this moral question? By examining their consciences unflinchingly.[32]

Unfortunately, it seemed Southerners had enormous problems doing that. They refused to discuss the matter in their own region, "reminding calm men of those unfortunate persons met with in lunatic asylums, who speak rationally on all topics until you touch that on which they are deranged, when their insanity bursts wildly forth." This being the case, Northerners must act unilaterally and decisively in defense of their own consciences, trusting their Southern neighbors to respect them for their fortitude if not for their convictions. Short of that, Northerners would remain bound to the Southern power structure even as they served as co-conspirators in the enslavement of over three million black human beings, "for whatever the Federal Government sanctions or adopts is of course by complicity of all who are parties to that Federal compact." Only one path was open to Northerners who cared at all about avoiding complicity with slavery: "that of a pure conscience."[33]

How could this be translated into practical action, in particular by those in Washington with power to make or influence policy? "The people of the United States are a firm," Conway argued. "Wherever the firm deals with Slavery, *all* deal with Slavery; and the General Government *has* dealt, and does now deal, with that local institution. I appeal to you, Southern men, is it not the only right thing for those who believe Slavery to be sinful, whether it be really so or not, firmly to declare themselves free from all share in it, if not by your concession, then by whatever means they can, *but certainly to do it?*" Northerners must plant their feet firmly against any further desecration of the flag "by what they believe dishonorable and wrong." That is, they must refuse to return fugitive slaves, fight the expansion of slavery to the territories, oppose it in Washington, D.C., over which Congress was sovereign. "Let every man in the Union only feel assured that he stands beneath the sheltering wing of his country, A PURE MAN."[34]

But was not disunion the only definitive and honorable means of separation from the evil? Not at all. "This proceeds from the assumption that the Union is inextricably involved in the policy which makes all hold slaves. We do not believe that; we think the Union is essentially involved in freedom, and that all its pro-Slavery proclivities are usurpations. We believe, indeed, that it does not interfere with you [Southerners] in your slaveholding . . .; but at the same time we believe our Constitution protects us from compulsory sanction of this, and protects us in our freedom. Thus we cannot enlist against it, but only to redeem it from the distractions resulting from a misinterpretation of our compact. If there is secession, it cannot be on our side." Northern abandonment of its role in slaveholding might cause the South to secede, but it would be up to the South to consider that act and weigh the consequences. The North must do its duty regardless. "A heroic action for virtue, which is such only because imperiling large interests, is a new star lit in the Heavens. . . . If the Union were sundered by such a stand, does it not pay in that it props the whole Earth?" Unlike many of his Garrisonian friends, Conway did not preach disunion; he was explicitly against it. But he was also tired of shrinking before Southern threats of disunion. He did not advocate separation, but he contemplated it without terror.[35]

"Before all, then, let us dismiss fear. Let us, with Montaigne, fear nothing so much as fear." He was into his peroration now, grand and flowery, and he shamelessly made the most of it, savored it like a rich cigar, because he knew he had earned it. He could see success reflected in his friends' faces, in the cluttered notebooks of the reporters. A few stirring words about God and how the Right must always prevail as long as God is on His throne, and it was over. Never before had such a sermon been heard from a white minister in a Washington pulpit. He had done it. He was no slave.[36]

* * *

"This city was thrown into a state of unusual excitement by a sermon from Moncure D. Conway," wrote the reporter for the Washington *Evening Star*, who pronounced the minister's performance "remarkable." He was not alone in his reaction. Conway's friends subsidized the printing of the sermon as a pamphlet, and it was reproduced in full in *The National Era*, *The National Antislavery Standard*, and *The Liberator*. It made a deep impression in abolitionist circles, strengthening Conway's claim to a place there. "I have just read Conway's noble discourse at Washington," wrote John Greenleaf Whittier early in February. "God bless the man for it! Let us not despair of the South when such men are found rising up in her midst."[37] And Greeley provided the hoped-for publicity in the *Tribune*:

> The Rev. M. D. Conway, pastor of the Unitarian Church in this city, today preached a straight-out Anti-Slavery sermon. . . . He urged that the Slavery issue is moral rather than political, and affirmed the right as well as duty of the North to resist the spread of the giant wrong. —As Mr. Conway is a native of Virginia, and has spent nearly all his days in slaveholding communities, it will hardly be pretended that *he* does not know what Slavery is. His discourse was very able as well as fearless, and was heard with profound interest by a most intelligent congregation. Mr. C. expects to lose his pastorship because of it. I have heard him before speak incidentally in the same vein, but never before so clearly and fully.[38]

Not everyone was so pleased. The church's annual report appeared in February, much of it directed at what the executive committee viewed as the minister's sudden display of political partisanship. "Your committee have seen with regret," read the report, "that the pastor has deemed it his duty to discuss in the pulpit a much vexed and angrily contested political question, and this, too, at a season of great political excitement. They have also been deeply chagrined to find that that portion of the press of the country which is devoted to the interests of a particular political faction has not only highly commended the discourse mentioned, and quoted largely from its pages, but has implied, at least, that its sentiments were endorsed by the congregation. . . . Your committee . . . ever have and must continue to disapprove of the use of the pulpit for the discussion of political questions, and . . . they deeply deplore the course taken by the pastor on the occasion referred to."[39]

It could have been much worse. Perhaps the committee felt its minister deserved a second chance, or that this sermon was only an aberration. Perhaps Conway's opponents were not as well organized or even as numerous as he had supposed. No action was taken against him. By early February he could tell Greeley there would be no dismissal.[40] But if his adversaries thought he would be satisfied with one fiery sermon and then lapse into another extended silence, they were wrong. Buoyed by the encouragement of allies and friends, emboldened by the relatively mild reaction of his congregation, Conway returned to the attack. He would answer the committee's report.

His vehicle was *Spiritual Liberty*, delivered on February 17, 1856, and immediately published as a pamphlet. The sermon argued that true Christians, both churchgoers and their ministers, were obligated to attack injustice. "If the souls of men fail to bear their full testimony by word and act against what is wrong, because great interests or powers or laws oppose, that soul is not standing fast in the liberty of Christ, for Christ opposed evil, when fortified by the strongest prejudices of the community, and its interests and its government." The silence which some took for wisdom or good manners was actually a loathsome "servility of spirit. . . . Such sugary names as Patriotism, Harmony, Sacrifice for the country's good, are really deceptive covers for selfish interests and spiritual slavery." And lest anyone miss the pertinence of what he was saying, Conway spelled it out: "Why may the injustice of our ancestors to the Indians be freely denounced in the pulpit, whilst every whisper of injustice to the African must be silenced? . . . The reason the soul is not gagged about the Indian is because we have got all the good we can by injustice to him, and villainy which does not pay is seen to be horrible at once."[41]

Reconciliation with the executive committee and its supporters was not likely after this second act of provocation, although two months of uneasy mutual silence elapsed before the committee formally told its minister to change his course. If he did not, it warned on April 15, "it is respectfully submitted whether it would not be better that our connection should cease at once," lest the "high purposes" of the church be "sacrificed to advance the purposes of this or that political faction."[42]

Before Conway could respond, a development occurred which lent itself to portentous interpretation: the southern wall of the church building cracked and buckled. The minister now had to turn his attention to the required repairs. But since he had alienated many of his wealthiest parishioners, he could not get the needed funds from the congregation. Determined to force the church either to accept or dismiss him, Conway refused to resign, and in May went north searching for money from his antislavery allies.[43]

From May 18 to May 21 Conway was in Chester County, Pennsylvania, attending the Yearly Meeting of the Pennsylvania Progressive Friends. On the last day he spoke briefly. "Manifesting all possible charity toward the slaveholder," wrote a *Tribune* correspondent, "he nevertheless denounced the system, and pledged his endeavor against it in bold and refreshing terms." From there he moved on to Massachusetts. He dined with Longfellow in Cambridge, stayed overnight with Emerson, and spoke at the Concord town hall. On May 27 he was the featured speaker at an afternoon session of the annual New England Anti-Slavery Convention at the Melodeon in Boston.[44]

At the Melodeon he concentrated eloquently on his most common theme. "As long as one man is a slave in this land, we are all slaves, to a certain extent. We are all afraid of something. We are all afraid of some prejudice, some feeling against color, or animosity of some kind. . . . so it is for each man to feel this, that in freeing the slave he is really freeing himself; he is asserting his own individual force, and [can] take things on the same terms with all other men; and not have anything which is selfishly had, and which his brother cannot have." He went on to speak of the practical evils of slavery, and of "a noble woman of Virginia" (his mother, an aunt, a cousin?) who once told him never to "compromise an inch" with it. "She had seen her children, her nephews, grow up in this atmosphere of slavery, with the great power which God has seen fit to make that institution capable of,—warmed out, like a nest of vipers, by this intense heat,—and she would not have me make terms with it. The evil of it! . . . I have never met a man who hated it too much."[45]

Conway's speech was punctuated by cheers and applause, his abolitionist listeners responding to an articulate expression of a theme familiar to all and central to many. For a number of participants, the antislavery movement expressed a whole cast of mind. It reflected an anti-authoritarian ethos which summed up the way they approached their society and its institutional arrangements. Committed to ending both slavery and their complicity in it, many were committed likewise to freeing themselves, as one historian has written, from "submission to worldly discipline of organized governments, political parties, ministers, patriarchal husbands, or [their] own private passions." Thus Conway's deep psychic need for self-emancipation, growing out of his adolescent inability to meet the requirements of the Southern aristocracy, found room for expression and release in this movement. By 1856 his place in it was obvious and secure.[46]

His place was not that of a doctrinally loyal Garrisonian, however (if there ever was such a thing), despite the fact that later in life he would read things back into history and portray himself as having been one. At the Melodeon he went out of his way to challenge a previous speaker, Andrew T. Foss, a Garrisonian who advocated disunion as "now the only practical method for us to adopt." As in his "One Path" sermon, Conway stood by the Constitution as an essentially freedom-buttressing document marred by spurious interpretation. And he reiterated that separating the national government from slavery did not require political disunion. Throughout the antebellum period he would draw a distinction between himself and "the Garrisonian school, with whose views of the Constitution and the Union I do not agree," even though many of his closest abolitionist acquaintances were in that "school." His disagreement, moreover, extended to his attitude toward politics. The political world was shady, but it had a direct bearing on policy and events. Abolitionists, he argued, did little good by staying out of it. Accordingly, he supported the Republican party. And in 1856 he backed John Charles Fremont, its presidential nominee.[47]

Conway extended his stay in the Northeast and arrived back in Washington on June 23, after attending a Fremont rally in Morristown, New Jersey. Tension in the capital city was even greater than when he had left it. In May the violence in Kansas had greatly accelerated, and Charles Sumner had been bludgeoned severely on the Senate floor by an indignant South Carolina congressman. Conway visited the senator at his bedside. The tragic sight made him still more determined to make his pulpit an outpost of abolitionism in the heart of a proslavery city. Soon he would have something to say in that pulpit "about the knocking down of one of my parishioners."[48]

On July 6, 1856, Conway preached the sermon which finished him as pastor of the Washington Unitarian church. The building, recently made safe by preliminary repairs, was crowded. The minister's faithful band of supporters was there, as were additional antislavery camp followers and several reporters. Many of Conway's opponents were also on hand, bracing themselves for one of the last insults they would permit their pastor to throw at them.[49]

Conway spoke of Kansas, Sumner, and his fears of civil war. "This nation is going steadily toward a war, which, should it come, will be the darkest, deadliest, and most awful which ever cursed this planet. All other war yields to civil war in terror." But one might as well "appeal to the fang of the serpent not to strike," as look to slavery's champions and apologists for peace. "No, I make no appeal to slavery to bring us peace; I would be a hypocrite to do so,—and hypocrisy is worse than war; but on you, freemen and friends of Humanity, I call to lend all your efforts for peace."[50]

How could peace be achieved? By the refusal to submit any longer to the grasping demands of slavery. He had said this in January. But since then a political party had nominated a presidential candidate pledged to halt slavery's expansion. The duty of anyone committed to striking a blow for freedom was clear. One must vote. Fremont (his name was never mentioned, but it did not have to be) would resist the South's demands, slavery would recede and shrivel, and true peace would follow. "Brothers, this Union, freighted with so many hopes and joys, is worth another effort to save it. . . . Voting rises to the solemnity and dignity of prayer."[51]

This sermon was more overtly political than any before it, and Conway's enemies were squirming in their seats. He showed them no mercy, at the moment of their greatest discomfort moving to a direct reference to them. "Slavery has a bribe at every pore. . . . I feel the presence of its great, infernal power in this house today. —There lurking amongst you, whispering—'Don't stand such preaching as this: if you do, your friends will turn away from you, and you will be called an abolitionist.' It is up here whispering to me, 'If you do not stop this preaching . . . your friends will be fewer even than they are now.' Get thee behind me, cunning Devil! I will tell on thee."⁵²

"One thing is now forever settled, that the subject is to be definitely dealt with. It is up now, and cannot be put down by any power, nor postponed. . . . Already, oh, my brothers, I hear the flutter of the Angel's wing as he comes to roll away the stone and break the seal of the Slave Power." That was it. Conway turned and signaled the organist to begin playing. But the four parishioners who composed that morning's choir were so upset by the sermon that they could not sing. The organist played the hymn unaccompanied. The congregation sat stunned. The music gave way to a tense silence. Finally the minister gave his benediction. The people filed out, Conway's friends racing to the pulpit to congratulate him. A reporter for the Boston *Traveller* sat enraptured. Noting that "some who listened to his discourse . . . are large slave-owners, and hold offices under the present administration," he considered the sermon "one of the boldest and ablest efforts to which I ever listened." Nobody could contend it was not bold, and everyone knew what it meant. Within days the executive committee spread the word that a meeting would follow the next Sunday service, "to consider the recent course of our pastor."⁵³

Conway's caustic sermon on July 13 was a recapitulation of the church quarrel's history, and a defense of his own role in it. He reminded his parishioners that they had known he was antislavery when they hired him. He repeated the reasons why slavery was a proper subject for a minister. He accused his opponents of hypocrisy and cowardice. And as a shrewd, dramatic, and telling last gesture, he took a pamphlet from his pocket and laid it on the pulpit. A witness reported that he then asked, "Is the real object of this movement to prevent any allusion to political subjects in the pulpit sincere? Or is it because the corruption of certain darling theories are exposed in their naked ugliness?" He knew people thought themselves sincere in their outcries against politics in the pulpit. But "he thought otherwise, and in all kindness should show themselves to themselves." He then waved the pamphlet in front of them.

It was a sermon preached by a Reverend Lunt in the same church in 1851, published by order of the executive committee and approved by the congregation in a general meeting. He read passages from it, an attack on New York's Senator Seward for an antislavery speech that had popularized the phrase, "the higher law." "This sermon Mr. Conway denounced as the vilest and basest attempt on the part of the pulpit to pander to the prejudices of a congregation. . . ." It demonstrated that many parishioners "did not disapprove of the introduction of politics into the pulpit, so long as the minister said smooth things; but when the discussion of measures involved the speaking of right things which were not smooth things, the cry was raised that the pulpit was desecrated."[54]

It is doubtful he changed any minds. At the meeting that followed, the executive committee issued a long report, charging Conway with "converting the pulpit into a political forum, and of having delivered therefrom, on the Sabbath, a discourse better suited to the hustings than the House of God." The meeting's composition was not what the committee had anticipated, however. Conway's allies had turned out in force, and the two sides seemed evenly matched. Fearing the embarrassment of a defeat, those who sided with the committee accepted a suggestion made by the neutral (and absent) William W. Seaton to postpone a vote on Conway's dismissal until October, after the summer recess. Remarkably, Conway was still pastor. "They say I talked awfully," he wrote jubilantly to a young female friend, "never so bad before. 'They wouldn't stand it any longer.' . . . [But] I had more brave friends than they thought. . . . So now I have nothing to do but have a good time until [October]. Hurrah for Freesoil, Free speech, Free pulpit and Fremont!"[55]

These were bracing times for this twenty-four-year-old celebrity. Letters of encouragement had been streaming in, from ordinary citizens and luminaries alike. William Henry Channing congratulated him on his "fidelity under trying circumstances." Wendell Phillips complimented him on his "eloquent and stirring sermon" of July 6. And fellow minister Thomas Wentworth Higginson told him that he expected "more from you than from any of my juniors, among preachers. . . . You have entitled yourself to be tried by the very highest standard, and there are those who will hold you to it. Do not fail us." He would not. He was imbued with his own sense of mission now. He was exhilarated by this assertion of his "own individual force." If there was a shred of justice in his opponents' position, he could not see it. If there was any chance for compromise, he did not want it. He saw himself battling for morality and truth. He would continue to battle, he told his critics, until his "tongue shall turn to dust."[56]

Shortly before he left for a vacation in the White Mountains of New Hampshire, Conway got something less than a fan letter from his mother. The preceding autumn she had determined to stop arguing with him, for to do so was "often too painful for endurance." But now she was in a different mood. She was tired of listening to people she deemed extremists in both sections, and she feared her son was getting carried away by the excitement of the moment. "Something more is necessary to a good end than the mad Hurras! of an excited populace, and the shouting of the watchwords of their leaders; for my own part I can say, they excite *in me,* and such as are of a *conservative spirit,* nothing but intense disgust. . . ." Margaret Conway was as distressed "by hearing a minister of the lord . . . crying 'hurra! for Freedom Free soil Fremont etc. etc.' and declaring their purpose to 'agitate, agitate, continuously' in the hope of producing reform, without regard to its present evil effects on whole communities white and colored, as I am to hear the Governor of old Virginia bodying forth his share of Demagogism, in such terms as 'Gizzard foot,' 'Ebo skins' etc. etc. . . . It is enough to tempt one to become a subject of Queen Victoria."

Unaware of her son's treatment during his last trip to Falmouth, Margaret told Moncure that the neighbors were being kind. They refrained from angry remarks about his course, "which is calculated to interfere with the domestic peace of their village." But then she added something painful, not knowing how little she needed to say it: "I think you had best not come here under the circumstances, as I cannot think you would be welcome to them, and I have no right to complain of it. . . . I think you would risk open insult, which would grieve me." Vexed as she was, she could not close without an expression of the "natural sympathy" which bound her and Moncure together. "I am almost pining to see you, and if I knew how to do it, would see you somewhere, but I see no prospect of it." His father may have cut him off; she had not. To accent the point she ended pathetically with a timeless maternal act: "I will send you some flannel under-drawers before you go on your trip."[57]

Conway may or may not have worn his flannel under-drawers, but he did go to the White Mountains. He stopped first in Boston and Concord, and appeared at the annual First of August Celebration in Abington (commemorating the British West Indian emancipation of August 1, 1834) where he extolled Fremont as "an excellent anti-slavery man" with "some progress in him." Then it was on to New Hampshire, where he clambered over rocks with Gerald Fitzgerald (on vacation from Harvard Divinity School) and splashed in cool mountain pools with twenty-year-old Anna Ricketson, daughter of a New Bedford habolitionist, with whom he flirted shamelessly and with some success.[58]

Finally it was time to start south again. On September 27 Conway was in New York having his head analyzed and his personality assessed by phrenological expert Nelson Sizer. Sizer found his subject to have "a predominance of the motive or billious temperament, tolerably well sustained by the vital or sanguineous." What this amounted to was that Conway was "a very blunt, abrupt man, . . . much more proud than vain, [who] wish [es] to be a leader." Perhaps Sizer revealed his own opinions about the young pastor's recent behavior when he told him he was "more rash than courageous" and "ambitious to be appreciated but not very sensitive" to other people's feelings, due to his "strong love of triumph." The phrenologist suggested that his subject "cultivate a disposition to copy other people and to conform to society," adding that "a little more moral circumspection would also give a higher tone to your character." He also noted that Conway was a man of "strong social dispositions" and "fond of home." "Though there are few men who are more fond of travelling," Sizer prophesied, "yet [you] would carry with you an earnest regard for home wherever you might go."[59]

His congregation sent him packing on October 5. On that day, Conway reported, "the Missourians ecclesiastic of our Church sprung a meeting on our Society and by a small majority were able to vote me no longer their pastor." Conway lost by only five votes, and the closeness of the balloting surprised many people. The minister's allies would try to overturn the vote later. But since they had turned out almost unanimously already, it was doubtful that the outcome could be changed. "He knew our position perfectly well," proclaimed the executive committee, "and gave us to understand that he would have a care for our welfare as a society, by restraining himself. . . . As long as Mr. Conway contented himself with treating the subject in its moral aspect—though we had rather he had let it alone—we gave him a patient hearing; but when . . . he thought proper to bring these party issues into the pulpit, to take partisan ground there, . . . to desecrate the pulpit, as we thought, we dismissed him."[60]

The event's predictability did not cushion the pain felt by Conway's friends. Hudson Taylor, who had supported him throughout, wondered whether fractured friendships were not worse than silence on an important issue. When his niece Charlotte insisted that Moncure had to obey his conscience, Taylor could only cry, "Damn conscience!" Gerald Fitzgerald, who read about the dismissal in the newspapers at Cambridge, was outraged. "Slavery never came so close to me before," he told Conway. "It is awful that the devil should so swagger about in God's world switching his tail and proud of his devilhood. . . . I am the more resolved to devote my life to crushing it out—for weak as I am it *can't crush me* out." He hoped only that when his time came, he might "have the fidelity to stand by my brother's side and do my duty as faithfully as he has done his."[61]

For Conway the dismissal was hurtful. But he regarded the fight as a worthwhile means of airing the issues and strengthening his own self-respect. He thought he could not have acted differently, in any case, for the questions at stake were simple and straightforward. "I have often asked myself, What did they expect?" he wrote the following year. "Did they expect that one believing Slavery a great sin . . . would be silent when he felt that [the] occasion demanded otherwise? . . . I have rather concluded that some supposed they could stand what they found they could not when the trial came; that others believed that a longer acquaintance with the city and the church, a maturer age, would convince me that no good could be accomplished by continuing that style of preaching. Well, I did see more of the city and church, and grew older, and I did not see reason for changing my conviction that the pulpit could not be true to itself without being outspoken on that subject."[62]

The Unitarian congregation in Cincinnati agreed. Their minister, A. A. Livermore, had recently resigned and would soon become editor of the *Christian Inquirer*. Searching for a strong new leader, the parishioners fixed on this gifted young man in Washington who seemed unafraid to tackle hard questions. On October 26 Conway gave his first sermon, on trial, in the Queen City of the West. On November 9 he delivered a fire-and-brimstone antislavery sermon which, to his delight, the congregation both welcomed and published. On November 30 the Washington church turned back a last-ditch effort by Conwayites to restore their pastor. This cleared the way for Conway to accept a permanent appointment in Cincinnati, with an annual salary of two thousand dollars. The circumstances were gratifying. Here was a congregation that wanted him, apparently, precisely because of his refusal to bow and truckle. He viewed the appointment, he told his new parishioners, "as a recognition of the rights of an unshackled ministry."[63] It seemed he would find a home in Cincinnati.

CHAPTER 6

Perhaps English traveler Frances Trollope had reason to scoff at Cincinnati's nickname "Queen City of the West" after her quixotic effort to establish a fancy-goods shop in that frontier town in 1830. But by the 1850s the city had grown into its title. It had mushroomed from a nondescript town of 25,000 in 1830 to a diversified metropolis of 115,000 in 1850 and 161,000 in 1860, gaining not only inhabitants but a cosmopolitan flavor and a rich marbling of sophistication and culture. The city's population in the later 1850s was excitingly diverse: 12 percent Irish (generally less destitute than their brethren on the Eastern seaboard) and nearly one-third German. Cincinnati was the cultural center of the American West, boasting a good symphony orchestra, a fine public library, impressive theaters and galleries, and over fifty journals and newspapers for its literate and information-hungry populace. Isabella Bird, visiting in 1855, spoke exuberantly of "heavily laden drays rumbling along the streets—quays at which steamboats of fairy architecture are ever lying—massive warehouses and rich stores—the side walks a perfect throng of foot-passengers—the roadways crowded with light carriages, horsemen with palmetto hats and high-peaked saddles, galloping about on the magnificent horses of Kentucky—an air of life, wealth, bustle, and progress."[1]

Few Cincinnati institutions illustrated its mid-century level of comfort and sophistication better than the church that hired Moncure Conway in 1856. Although always called the First Congregational Church, it had been Unitarian since its founding in 1830 by emigrés from venerable New England families, including Charles Davis Dana of Massachusetts and William A. Greene of Rhode Island. Occupying a fine site in the heart of the city—on a hill at Fourth and Race streets overlooking the Ohio River and Kentucky shore—the church in the 1850s was patronized by some of Cincinnati's most prominent citizens. Miles Greenwood, employer of five hundred people at the Eagle Iron Works, was known nationally for his sturdy iron housefronts. George Hoadly was city solicitor, a former and future judge of the Ohio Superior Court, and a leading organizer of the state's vibrant Republican party. Robert Hosea, who had made a fortune as a grocer and commission merchant, was a powerful leader in the city's commercial community. John Kebler was a well-known and highly paid attorney whose clients included Horace Mann and Antioch College. A. R. Spofford was a prominent local publisher and future Librarian of Congress. Alphonso Taft was a future cabinet official and diplomat and the father of a future president. William Wiswell, Jr., manufacturer of gilt mirror and picture frames, was renowned as a "liberal patron of the fine arts," whose gallery on West Fourth Street housed "one of the finest collections of works of art by masters in Europe and America."[2]

These men and their Unitarian comrades were accustomed to pastors of equal talent and standing. Since 1850 their minister had been Abiel Abbot Livermore, a rising star in the church, a personable man of intellect and moderation. (After leaving Cincinnati, Livermore turned the *Christian Inquirer* into the liveliest Unitarian publication in America, and ended his career with twenty-seven years as president of the Meadville Theological School.) The loss of Livermore was regretted, but, declared the *Christian Register* in September 1856, Cincinnati was "too important a station to remain long without an able and efficient religious teacher." The parishioners knew what they wanted: a man of national standing and proven energy and talent, still young enough to stay in Cincinnati for some years and enhance his reputation while there. Moncure Conway seemed so ideal a candidate, and fate had so wondrously provided him, that no alternatives were seriously considered. Livermore himself was pleased by the choice. "Conway . . . is a *live* man," he promised, "and will make others live."[3]

Conway accepted the Cincinnati position with something like euphoria, moving from his painful experience in Washington to the joy of an exciting city where a new congregation applauded his boldness and spunk. Despite a few early defections by parishioners unable to stomach his abolitionism, support for his views seemed overwhelming. When the legislature and Governor Salmon P. Chase invited him to address them in March 1857, Conway put politics aside and gave his audience a self-satisfied and didactic talk about "success." It seemed fitting. He viewed his new job as a reward for his previous behavior, and as visible proof that success came to those who stood on principle.[4]

How far Conway's congregation was prepared to go with him became evident in the spring of 1857, when events again impelled him to speak out on slavery. On March 4 James Buchanan, a pro-Southern Democrat sympathetic to a proslavery constitution for Kansas, became president. Only two days later the United States Supreme Court issued the Dred Scott decision, declaring unconstitutional any Congressional limitation on slavery in the territories and barring all blacks, slave or free, from citizenship. The decision staggered all antislavery Americans, but for Conway the blow carried a special sting. One of the justices who had struck down the Missouri Compromise, who had written his own opinion declaring blacks outside "the family of nations" and therefore not entitled to citizenship, was his maternal great-uncle, Peter Vivian Daniel. The Dred Scott decision demanded a public reaction, and in making it Conway would once again be striking at his family.[5]

He chose his forum carefully, desiring maximum visibility and maximum results. On May 13, 1857, the young minister from Cincinnati appeared at the sixth annual Western Unitarian Conference, meeting in Alton, Illinois. The conference had never passed an antislavery resolution. But it had never faced a Dred Scott decision before, nor had it ever before had Moncure Conway in its ranks. Conway went to Alton with one purpose: to put the conference on record in condemnation of both the Supreme Court's action and slavery itself. His resolutions attacked the Court's decision as "one of a series of deliberate assaults on religious and civil freedom in America," and insisted on the "duty of Christians everywhere, in and out of the pulpit, to discuss freely and fully before the people this crime against man, and therefore against God." The resolution did not have an easy time, meeting especially stiff opposition from a large St. Louis delegation led by William Greenleaf Eliot, a well-known conservative who raised the usual arguments about politics in the pulpit, asked Conway to render to Caesar the things that were Caesar's, and remained unmoved by James Freeman Clarke's suggestion that "Caesar has got hold of something which belongs to God, and Caesar ought to give it up." Eliot's intransigence forced the meeting to tone down the resolutions, but still the St. Louis Unitarians withdrew permanently from the conference. Accustomed to defections, Conway did not consider St. Louis a great loss. What mattered was that Western Unitarians had raised their voices on a moral principle, and he had been the catalyst. He returned to Cincinnati in triumph.[6]

Back in Virginia, Conway's mother reflected on the irony of her position. She was tending a dozen cases of measles among area slaves, while her uncle was calling them subhuman and her son was engaged in what she feared was incendiary agitation. Moncure seemed "doomed to be in an excitement on the 'peculiar institution,'" while she went quietly about her business of healing, "spend[ing] my life nursing negroes."[7]

By the time of the Alton meeting, Conway had developed an interest in Ellen Dana, twenty-three-year-old daughter of a prominent Cincinnati businessman and officer in the Unitarian church. Ellen was an intelligent and attractive woman, whose public shyness was belied by the strong opinions, agile wit, and acid temper she readily exhibited to close acquaintances. Annie Besant, the English Secularist who later knew her well, said she united "the most thorough boldness and honesty with very perfect and gentle womanliness. I know of no woman who is, at once, so charming a *woman*, and so true, right through." Ellen found in Moncure a young man who shared her religious, political, and cultural tastes, and she admired his readiness to advance unpopular sentiments. His commiseration with her after her sister's death in November 1857 cemented their relationship. By the following spring they were deliriously entwined.[8]

They exchanged the most mawkish love letters imaginable for an already mawkish genre, turned heads on the street by their "conspicuous" and "remarkable behavior." A playful church member gave the minister a romantic novel with suggestive passages marked; on a train a woman caught him gazing languorously at Ellen's miniature. For her part, Ellen concocted predictably appalling nicknames for her lover. Sometimes Moncure was "Scruffy." Sometimes he was "Beeswax." Always he was madly in love. "Oh for somebody to hold me," he wrote her in March 1858 during a short separation. "I shall die laughing or crying, I don't know which. Darling, . . . I know and feel that you know me altogether—and that knowing me thus you should still love me! Surely I am moved by that."[9]

They married on June 1, 1858, before an overflow crowd at the Unitarian church. Moncure and Ellen stood beneath a bower of white roses as Philadelphia's William Henry Furness performed the ceremony. Cincinnati society turned out in force for the occasion. The city's leading musical society entertained at the evening reception, condemned by one petulant observer for its "criminal extravagance" but considered by most participants as one of the major social events of the year.[10]

Conway had always been fond of female company. But after his infatuation with Kate Emory in 1849 and 1850 there is no evidence that any one woman consumed his emotional energies until his encounter with Ellen Dana. Uprooted and financially insecure after leaving Virginia, for some years he had had little materially to offer a woman looking for a husband. Even in Washington, where he socialized frequently and acquired a taste for dancing, he could save little money and had to spend long hours preparing weekly sermons. But when he moved to Cincinnati he became conspicuously eligible. After two years of experience, writing sermons took far less time. He now had a good salary. National attention had bolstered his self-confidence, as had his new congregation's apparent approval of his politics. And Cincinnati's social life was richer and more exciting than Washington's had been. Thus Ellen, who was informed, well-read, and sophisticated—just the type of woman whose relative rarity he had more than once bemoaned—crossed his path at a propitious time. Eager for a close female companion, Moncure leaped for her with unqualified enthusiasm. He was convinced he had found a perfect match.

He was not far wrong. The marriage blended two strong, autonomous, and tempestuous personalities. If that mix made quarrels inevitable, it facilitated a genuine and lasting mutual respect between two people who prized nothing more than intelligence and strength of conviction. Surely among Ellen's greatest contributions to her marriage and to her husband's growth were her straightforwardness and her impatience with Moncure's tendency toward self-pity and self-dramatization. She had grown up as an antislavery Northern Unitarian, unafraid of spiritual damnation, at peace with dancing, wine, fiction, and the theater, her politics liberal, clear, and uncomplicated. This may have made her a less interesting person than her husband, but sometimes clarity is preferable to fascination. Ellen was sure that Moncure had abandoned a hollow existence in a bankrupt culture and had taken a course promising him maximum happiness. In her view, there was nothing to regret in leaving Virginia and there was no point in self-conscious feelings of martyrdom. If she could sometimes be narrow and callous in not appreciating either the world her husband had lost or his anguish in losing it, she unquestionably served as a buffer between him and morbidity or posturing, while also helping him accept the choices he had made.

Ellen's uncluttered and unpressured background enhanced Moncure's life in another important way. A passionate woman free from inhibitions, Ellen let her husband shed whatever sexual reservations may have pursued him from his own upbringing. As he confided to a journal years later, "my wife revealed to me far beyond her consciousness, the secrets and depths of the human heart, and of my own heart. She enabled me to distinguish between the fictitious 'virtues'—so-called— and real ones,—e.g., between shame at nudity and real modesty." For all his joy in women's company and all the satisfaction he got from the contact involved in dancing, Conway was almost certainly a sexual innocent at the time of his marriage. He was ready for a major sexual involvement, probably longing for one; but it was crucial that Ellen freely and joyfully legitimized and sanctioned his longings. The physical dimension of their relationship remained pronounced for a long time, and probably never disappeared. Their letters are peppered with more than perfunctory kisses and embraces, and with charming suggestions of intimacy: "Had a sweet dream of you all last night"; "Dreamed last night we were cuddled together in an amorous way."[11] After his marriage and after the birth in June 1859 of his son Eustace (named for his Virginia uncle who had died recently at age thirty-seven), Conway began to make male-female relationships a frequent subject of his lecturing and writing. He had always viewed such relationships as important. But now he came to regard them as a major topic for public discussion, and to see sexuality as an inescapable component of that dialogue.

The Conways' honeymoon was less successful than their marriage. It started enjoyably enough, with the couple traveling by steamboat and stagecoach ("This ugly marsupial of locomotion" carrying its "children in its pouch") and ox-drawn wagon to Mammoth Cave. There Ellen donned bloomers and descended into the candle-lit cavern with Moncure and a mulatto slave guide. Thus far all was fun and adventure. Then they went to Virginia.[12]

Conway had not visited his native state since 1855, when he had been run out of Falmouth and had met resistance to religious liberalism in Charlottesville. He had tried to resign himself to exile, but his resignation had never been complete. Shortly before his marriage he had dedicated his first published book, a collection of old sermons, to his parents, thanking them for "the lessons of directness and sincerity which, by word and life, they have ever taught as before all."[13] (The dedication must not have done much to placate his father when Walker saw that the fruits of such "lessons" included noxious productions like "The One Path.") Now, after a three-year separation, Moncure wanted to see his parents again. He had a wife now. He wanted her to know something about his home, and he wanted his parents to know something about her. Surely she would be welcome in Falmouth.

The very silence surrounding this visit says something about the disaster's dimensions. No word of it is spoken in family correspondence until seventeen years later (and then only sparingly), and Conway omits it from his memoirs. There is small wonder in this, for it opened wounds which never healed. Ellen was the most wounded, at least on the surface. Undoubtedly family and neighbors were nervous about Ellen before they saw her. They knew she was a lifelong Unitarian, a Yankee, an abolitionist. That Mildred Conway liked her (she had been a bridesmaid at her brother's wedding) helped little, for Mildred's own allegiances were suspect. When Ellen arrived, the neighbors were alert for offensive or scandalous behavior. They were not disappointed.

Who said what to whom is unfortunately lost, but more than one witness recalled a pivotal episode. Early in their visit Moncure and Ellen went with some neighbors and the slave Dunmore Gwinn to the farm of Anna Dunbar, a widow who had previously owned Gwinn and had been friendly to Moncure in his youth. Dunbar owned four slaves: a man, a woman (Gwinn's sister), and two girls, ages four and one. The older child, whom Gwinn introduced as his niece Evelyn, was sitting on the farmhouse steps as the party arrived. Ellen, delighted by the little girl, spontaneously embraced and kissed her. That was the event which, Conway recalled, "upset the Constitution of the United States" and, Gwinn remembered, "set the magazine on fire."[14]

It was not really so terrible—after the Civil War, Anna Dunbar could admit that she had done such things herself. But for a Godless Yankee abolitionist to impose on their hospitality and then run around publicly kissing slaves seemed to many Falmouth citizens a deliberate and unforgivable insult. Word of the transgression spread rapidly. Ellen, at the very least, was made to feel unwanted. Probably at this point Ellen let some people know just how little she wanted them. Inevitably

Moncure was forced to defend both his wife and himself. During one tense scene he drove his uncle Valentine Conway into a rage by telling him he would be ruined if he continued to support slavery. Mercifully for everyone the trip was cut short. The couple spent the rest of the summer in the Northeast before returning to Cincinnati. For the next seventeen years Moncure's only contact with Virginia was the continuing correspondence of his mother. Ellen went away with a vision of Virginia as the most loathsome place on earth. Moncure did not visit again until 1875. Ellen stayed away forever.[15]

Soon after returning to Cincinnati in the fall of 1858, Conway delivered a series of sermons on the fallibility of the Bible and the impossibility of miracles. It tore his congregation apart. It was a familiar pattern: having enjoyed for two years a comfortable, prestigious, and secure position relatively free from controversy, he now jeopardized it all. His recent experience in Virginia probably revived his combativeness, intensified his own feelings of embattled martyrdom, and reminded him of the necessity of fighting for principles. This latest bitter exposure to his father's world, moreover, was followed quickly by a momentous personal event that bolstered his self-image and heightened his sense of responsibility: early in the autumn of 1858 Ellen became pregnant. Now Moncure would be not merely a son but a father, called upon to present a better world to his own child.

After two comparatively quiet and widely-supported years in Cincinnati, Conway had both the self-assurance to speak out and the anxiety born of a self-perceived passivity. For many months he had felt increasingly dissatisfied with the theological timidity of mainstream Unitarianism. There had been many indications that such timidity was widespread among his parishioners, however willing most of them were to support their minister's advanced political opinions. As he prepared his rationalistic sermons, Conway knew he would alienate a large and powerful segment of the congregation. But it was time to have it out. He would either educate the complacent or break with them completely. Whatever the outcome, he would emancipate himself from the tyranny of their stagnant, propriety-ridden minds. "Hypocrisy is worse than war,"[16] he had said in Washington, and when he began those sermons on miracles he knew he was starting a war. It was a war whose implications far transcended a single congregation in Cincinnati.

The first omen of a Unitarian split in Cincinnati had come early, when Ralph Waldo Emerson accepted Conway's invitation to give four lectures at the church in late January and early February 1857. The pastor had invited his Massachusetts idol without consulting the board of trustees. It may not have occurred to him that Emerson's engagement might encounter resistance. But it did. On January 30 the trustees hastily assembled and considered canceling the lectures. Robert Hosea (president of the board) and John Kebler were especially nauseated at the presence in their pulpit of a man who professed no Christian faith. Finally they permitted the lectures as a matter of good manners. But Conway was warned that henceforth "the church should not be used for any but religious and Church purposes." The warning must have been weakened, however, by the sheer numbers who turned out to hear and applaud the Concord sage. "Mr. Conway has taken a deal of pains for my benefit here and certainly made me up a very respectable class," Emerson told his wife. "I beg you will bear it in mind for his benefit hereafter." Thus if it was clear to Conway that a significant part of his congregation was unwilling to hear departures from mainstream Unitarian theology, it was equally clear that many parishioners were more than ready for them. The factions were there, a confrontation possible whenever a key figure would be willing to force it.[17]

But Conway was neither ready nor eager to precipitate a confrontation in 1857. He was still consolidating his position in his new post and was preoccupied with clarifying the Western Unitarian Conference's stance on slavery. His own religious views were still in flux, evolving quietly under the redoubled influence of German rationalism—a careful and thorough reading of Strauss seems to date from this time—but not yet clear enough to justify comprehensive new pronouncements. So far was he at this time from formally breaking with Unitarian convention that he initially accepted the so-called "Livermore Creed" as his idea of what a church member ought to uphold. Concocted by A. A. Livermore in 1855 to unite the congregation around certain principles, signed by more than two hundred members, the "creed" portrayed its adherents as "believing in One God, our Heavenly Father, in one Lord and Saviour Jesus Christ, in the Revelation contained in the Holy Scriptures, and in the Immortality of the Human Soul, and desiring to unite together for the object of promoting the Christian Faith."[18]

But during the course of 1857 and 1858 Conway moved more deeply into the theological left wing of his denomination. By the middle of 1857 he had ceased to use the Livermore Creed (which had been used in examining prospective members, though nobody was ever required to sign it) and had ceased to administer communion. The latter action was not necessarily heretical—at least one prominent Unitarian conservative, Frederic Henry Hedge, had also abandoned the practice—but usually such a step implied heretical sympathies. By the end of the year Conway was showing more skepticism toward Jesus. He denounced "those dogmas which mystify the nature and office of Christ." He ridiculed the notion that we should revere a man who supposedly "had some secret miraculous aid not afforded to others." By the fall of 1858 his opinions had coalesced sufficiently for him to give the sermons that eventually ended his career as a Unitarian minister.[19]

Conway's sermons do not survive, but an outcry followed them that leaves no doubt about their nature and effect. They were, wrote an impartial observer, "doctrinal sermons, in which he controverted the historical verity of the miracles, assailed the doctrine of the supernatural inspiration of the Bible . . . and derived the proof of the immortality of the soul chiefly from internal or subjective evidences." Not only did he deny the plausibility of miracles, he directed his fire at the very cornerstone of Christianity, the Crucifixion and Resurrection. The Resurrection was preposterous, he said, theorizing that Jesus had merely swooned on the cross and had been laid in the tomb still alive. At some point Conway's enthusiasm for debunking New Testament miracles carried him from the pulpit into the children's Sunday School class. This visit infuriated a number of conservative parents. By December the minister was leading a Bible-conversation class which, he boasted, contained "men and women of all creeds, and no creeds." By early 1859 his actions had spawned a powerful and angry opposition passionately intent on removing him.[20]

The first skirmish was fought in February 1859, out of public view, in the plush surroundings of John Kebler's law office. There Conway faced Kebler, Robert Hosea, and another prominent church member, L. F. Potter. Niceties were not squandered. The trio told their minister that a concerted drive to remove him would begin unless he ceased to repudiate the Bible and to deny the Resurrection. Kebler called attention to Conway's interest in Strauss and then ridiculed the pastor's preaching as a "re-hash of other men's thoughts." Potter said Conway's views on the Bible were "disgusting" and that he "had no business to preach them before women and children." Conway sat back in his armchair, nursed a cigar, and scowled. When his accusers finished, he told them he would continue his present course. Kebler was knotted in rage. Red-faced and trembling, he jumped to his feet. "What do you preach for?" he shouted. Conway stared up at him and answered deliberately, with a mix of calmness and condescension. He spoke as though he were explaining something, as though the question had really been seeking a reply. "Because God wills that I should preach." That day Kebler, Hosea, and Potter drafted a petition for his dismissal.[21]

These men were professional people and solid citizens who required some mental and emotional certainties if they were to proceed efficiently and in peace. As Unitarians, they seemed to need fewer verities than more orthodox neighbors. But precisely because they occupied the fringe of conventional religious belief, because they were almost rebels, they clung to their little collection of truths with particular ardor. Belief in Christ's supernatural attributes and the Bible's supernatural inspiration served as connecting links between themselves and the broader community, while giving them a solid reference point for their own inner, spiritual lives. Their Christianity offered them social legitimacy and also emotional consolation, and it had served them all well. Hosea, for one, had been in the church for twenty years. It was a central institution in his life, a fixed point, and as much an outlet for his needs and a definer of his self as the militia unit he captained and the business community he boosted. Now a twenty-six-year-old upstart wanted to send fixed points spinning. The twenty-six-year-old knew what he was doing. He did not care about fixed points. He preferred the spirit of truth seeking.

Hosea cared. He understood that Conway was striking at the heart of what made Unitarianism a Christian religion. If the minister succeeded in removing Jesus and the Bible from Unitarianism, the religion (even if it kept its title) would cease to be. Conway thought that Jesus had not died on the cross. Hosea branded this as "identical with the views of Strauss, the German rationalist, or infidel, or whatever you call him." In detail Hosea was wrong—Strauss had questioned the Crucifixion's very occurrence, while Conway only interpreted it in an unorthodox way. But in essence Hosea was right. He was fighting to preserve an institution central to his life, just as certainly as if Strauss had been filling the pulpit. "You present to the world the spectacle single of its kind," Hosea's friend Kebler told Conway, "of one keeping his position in a church, a Christian church, to pull it down."[22]

Just as it had made sense for Walker Conway to turn his back on his son, the dissidents' effort to dismiss Conway was the rational act of sensible men. If in the ensuing war they were neither temperate nor consistent nor fair, one should remember that temperateness, consistency, and fairness have limited value in a war for survival.

After several weeks of behind-the-scenes maneuvering, the owners and renters of pews assembled in the church on Monday evening, March 28, 1859, "to consider retaining the services of Rev. Mr. Conway." The minister was absent, but sent a letter which gave no sign of increasing flexibility. "You cannot expel me from the pulpit for preaching my honest views on the subject of miracles," he wrote, "without uprooting the very foundations on which the whole Unitarian Church is laid." That church had originally preached, he believed, "that the human mind should be free, and the right of private judgment . . . should be restored. Now, ere you send me away for speaking from real conviction what I believe concerning certain historical questions of a period nearly two thousand years past, I pray you consider the fetter which you must inevitably bind upon that pulpit." Slavery and superstition were linked in their grasping propensity to shackle freedom of action and freedom of thought. "Whenever my successor ascends that pulpit, you and your children will hear his chains clank at every step he makes." After hearing this letter the assembly debated a resolution approving Conway's conduct. A wrangle ensued over who had a right to vote, and the showdown was postponed until two nights later.[23]

On March 28 the contours of the rift had become clear. The dissidents included at least one-third of the church membership, perhaps closer to one-half; but they did not possess a voting majority. Conway was destined to win a close vote on his removal, but he would lose a very large portion of his parishioners. The split had become so deep that few of the dissenters could ever accept Conway as their minister. Seeing all this and desiring the most amicable and magnanimous solution possible, a group of Conwayites led by George Hoadly forged a substitute resolution. It declared that "this society is so divided in sentiment that the members can no longer work and worship together as one harmonious whole," and proposed creating a committee which would arrange a fair division of church assets between the two groups. With both pro and anti-Conway members supporting this resolution, it carried on March 30 by a three-to-one margin. Soon the resulting committee suggested selling the church building and dividing the proceeds. Before this could happen, however, Conwayite William Wiswell, on his own initiative, took the trustees to court seeking to block any cession of property to the dissident group. Vast new opportunities for acrimonious brawling were thus created. The whole business festered for four years before the Ohio Supreme Court permitted the proposed sale.[24]

Lawsuit or no lawsuit, property or no property, the conservatives formally withdrew from the First Congregational Church in April 1859. They founded their own Society (financed partly by manufacturer Miles Greenwood), the Church of the Redeemer. At first the feuding groups worked out a precarious and increasingly hostile arrangement whereby the Redeemerites used the church building on Sunday evenings. Later in the year, to everyone's relief, they moved into an unused Universalist building on Mound and Sixth streets. In January 1863 they imported as their first settled minister Amory D. Mayo, a conservative who served them for nine years. In their "statement of beliefs," the Redeemerites explained what separated them from their former minister. "We believe in a personal Deity, God, the Creator, supporter and everywhere present Ruler of the Universe, in contradistinction to Emerson's God, Nature, Law pervading matter; we believe in an active, not passive God." They went on to proclaim their belief in "the historical Christ of the New Testament, and not that we have there only an ideal Christ," and to affirm their faith "that the New Testament contains an authentic and substantially true Record of a special Revelation from God to man communicated by Jesus Christ." They believed, too, "that God conferred power upon Jesus Christ to work miracles—and that Christ wrought miracles."[25]

"The cost was all counted beforehand," said Conway, and it probably had been. He knew he would lose many friends and allies, that the bitterness would be extreme, that many who had once welcomed him would no longer acknowledge him on the street. But he had been through all that before. He knew the pain of losing friends was offset by the pleasure of gaining new ones. He knew his self-respect would stay whole. And he knew it would all end in visible proof, to himself and to others, that he was not a stagnant and timid man enslaved by the viper of conservatism. The theme of his first sermon after the

Redeemerites' withdrawal was that orthodoxy of any sort was contrary to the spirit of progress, and without progress all was lost. As it was for the individual, so it was for institutions and for society itself. All must keep moving, or die.[26]

That first sermon (May 1, 1859) contained most of what the dissidents had despised in their minister and confirmed their worst suspicions about his heresy. There was some gloating: "A battle has been fought, and . . . though some have fallen, the standard of our fathers still waves, in God's free air, upon our towers. We celebrate today a victory." There was some backbiting: "Our brethren who left us . . . believe that the Church should be based on the idea of a Redeemer, an idea of the dark ages, which supposed that, as captives in war were either to be slain or redeemed by a ransom paid—so Jesus paid down in so much blood a ransom for captive man." And there was a great deal of blasphemy. The pastor did "not believe that Jesus was born without a human father, that pious insult to the holiest relations of life; that he turned one hundred and fifty gallons of water into so much wine; that he cursed a fig-tree because it had no figs on it, when the time of figs was not yet, and that beneath that imprecation the tree withered away." If there was still any room for doubt about his heresy, Conway obliterated it with one clear and simple sentence: "Your minister is not a believer in what the churches call Christianity."[27]

Time showed that Conway could get along without the Redeemerites. His congregation, down to about two hundred members, began to grow as others got word of this unconventional and provocative preacher. Still technically a Unitarian (although after he left Cincinnati in 1862 he never again used the label), he nevertheless began informally calling his church the "Free Church" (making all pews free as one evidence of the new spirit) and solicited the attendance of anyone who believed in unrestricted freedom of thought. In June 1859 he opened his pulpit to the visiting Hindu Brahmin, Jogarth C. Gangooly. Soon he began an ongoing dialogue with Cincinnati's liberal Jewish community, a development particularly disgusting to John Kebler, observing the continuing degradation of his former church. "I heard . . . that Moses was preached up as equal to Christ," he complained after Conway had preached on "The Glory of Israel"; "that the Jews did not crucify Jesus but the Romans, that the Jews were the germ out of which the flower of the present civilization has sprung etc." Robert Hosea read with a righteous sense of vindication an article in the *Catholic Telegraph*: "An Atheist—yes, an Atheist told us one day last week, that he had taken a one-hundred-dollar pew in Mr. Conway's church, and would take for his friends as many more as he could get." In January 1860 Conway gave a sermon celebrating the birthday of Thomas Paine. Things were getting more and more bizarre, it seemed, in the poor old church at Fourth and Race.[28]

By this point, nothing this minister did could surprise the outraged people who had left him. Not only did they regard him as theologically unsafe, they viewed him as a man whose immoral personal behavior made him unfit for a position of spiritual leadership. Conway was, wrote one Redeemerite, "a frivolous and reckless boy, whose life is a libel upon even the Western standard of clerical propriety. . . ." Many of Conway's supporters believed a difference in cultural style was at the heart of the whole dispute. "There was as much talk about his unclerical conduct," said George Hoadly, "in going to the theaters and dancing, as about his doctrines." Not only did this minister go to dances, he held dancing parties in the church basement, believing that "man, in dancing, does keep time with the music and measure of nature." Not only did he attend the theater, he descended from the dress circle into the pit— "a microcosm of the world," he called it—with flatboatmen and laborers. He forged friendships in the theatrical community, became a sort of unofficial chaplain to the dramatic companies, and both lectured and wrote in the theater's defense.[29]

Conway was not alone among Unitarian preachers in upholding the theater's value. Conservative Edward Everett Hale even believed that government should subsidize dramatic companies in order to give the working class a healthier outlet than bars and brothels.[30] But probably no other contemporary minister combined a comprehensive defense of the theater with such obvious and outspoken personal enthusiasm for it. His defense of the drama, moreover, extended well beyond its supposed usefulness as an agent of moral uplift or social control. "I do not believe that the theatre ever can exist for the purposes of moral or religious or reformatory influence; nor do I desire it." Yet Conway admitted that society benefited by exposing the working class to art. He believed the theater to be "the only form in which Poetry and Art become democratic. Shakespeare comes down from the scholar's shelf. . . . So do the great composers: I heard a newsboy, the other day, whistling on the street a theme from the overture of *Der Freischutz*." Conway saw actors as "the priests and priestesses of a sacred, sensuous civilization," doing "for the neglected senses what some philanthropists are doing for beggar boys and ragamuffins in the streets. They dress up those senses and passions in presentable clothes, and teach them that they are something and have something to do." Beyond its exhibition of art to the masses, the theater gave work to scores of mechanics, painters, and craftsmen, and meant significantly raised incomes for certain local merchants.[31]

But perhaps its greatest social contribution lay in the fact "that it is in the Theatre alone that full justice is done to woman, to both her labor and her intellectual dignity. In the State woman has no existence in her own right; she can not hold property separately, nor vote, nor hold office. In the Church she is a cipher, whilst she is spending her time making ministerial slippers and ottomans. I know of only two places where it is clearly understood that women have souls, to-wit., the Quaker meeting and the Theatre."

> The Theatre not only honors woman, and emancipates her intellect, but it does something more sacred yet by her: it pays her full and solid wages. . . . [T]he respectables and the sternly virtuous accuse the Theatre as the corrupter of feminine purity. So says the pious merchant who gives a woman sixty cents for a shirt which he sells for three dollars. . . . The Theatre, oh, shocking! Just here the theatre comes in and actually saves woman from her most terrible temptation by paying her enough money to support herself. . . . Even the ballet-girls, whose business it is to stand on the stage in those short dresses which so distress the sanctified, thereby get four or five dollars a week, and are left the whole daytime in which to get wages for other work.[32]

Such arguments carried no weight with Conway's critics, who regarded his attitudes as "obnoxious" and "unclerical." Conway, in turn, had no patience with complaints about his personal behavior. He was especially annoyed by what he regarded as his detractors' hypocrisy, for their own behavior was not piously ascetic. John Kebler believed "It was right for the members" to attend the theater, but he "did not consider it right for a clergyman." Robert Hosea had to admit, during the court proceedings, that early in Conway's ministry he had "perhaps been to the theatre with him." Faced with such a situation, sniping at his personal habits only intensified Conway's resolve to continue them.* In his May 1859 sermon inaugurating the "Free Church," he delivered a last swipe at the absent "respectables," reaffirming his fondness for the theater and telling his diminished congregation that its minister was "not clerical. . . . When he becomes so, he will go the whole figure; he will put on surplice, lawn sleeves, white ties, and so forth; he will have little boys to ring bells under his train . . ."[33]

The argument over how a minister should behave involved much more than superficial differences of style. Objections to Conway's dancing and theater-going were not unimportant in themselves, but neither were they the "real" reasons for a church quarrel camouflaged as a doctrinal dispute. Rather, Conway's unorthodox style seemed to the dissidents a predictable symptom and a logical result of his theological bankruptcy. Redeemerites were not surprised that Conway advocated a "sacred, sensuous civilization," for in their view he had, by denying biblical

---

* Conway persisted in his enthusiasm for all varieties of theatrical offerings until the end of his life, and even at the height of his freethought ministry in London was still being criticized for it in some quarters. In 1884 English Theist John Fretwell attacked his fondness for "Saint Rabelais," calling him one "whose altar is the stage, . . . church the theatre and . . . liturgy the filthy trivialities of Parisian playwrights." *The Index*, vol. V, New Series No. 17 (October 23, 1884), 201.

authority, obliterated necessary distinctions between the sacred and sensuous, the holy and profane. To Hosea's horror, Conway relied upon " 'the sacred light which fills each and every soul' rather than upon the truths of God's word and the example and teachings of Christ." For Conway and other radical left-wing Unitarians, this replacement of scriptural tyranny by a celebration of the divine both in people and in Nature meant an exciting enhancement of human dignity and energy. But for traditionalists it meant a collapse of standards without which life was chaos, and a negation of every good reason a church had for its existence.[34]

"I am so disgusted with the actions and looseness in doctrine of many Unitarian ministers and congregations," wrote one preacher commenting on the Cincinnati carnage, "that, were it but possible for me to believe in a Trinity, I would never think of, nor mention the disjointed condition of the Unitarian Church." The problem had been building for some time, but in the opinion of many traditionalists the Cincinnati schism marked the beginning of a crisis. More and more people seemed to be tolerating or agreeing with clerical agitators like Conway, who believed it was "untrue to say that Jesus was personally a full manifestation of the Divine in man," and that Christ was no more entitled to reverence than Confucius, Zoroaster, and "other pure and living guides." "Many are heard to say that they want no Master, no indisputable authority in religious matters," complained A. A. Livermore. To him, such an attitude meant "annihilation of the Christian Church." It was a collision between those who placed internal inspiration above external authority, and those who regarded universal standards and rules as indispensable for societal cohesion. In 1859 the mainstream of America's most liberal Christian sect closed ranks in a mighty effort to uphold Christ's authority against, in the words of the Redeemerites' A. D. Mayo, "self worshippers, who use intuition and literature instead of religion."[35]

The universally acknowledged leader of this mainstream Unitarian counterrevolution was Henry Whitney Bellows, pastor of the Church of All Souls in New York City. Bellows had graduated from Harvard Divinity School in 1837, one year before Emerson's iconoclastic address there, at a time when William Ellery Channing's miracle-accepting notions about "supernatural rationalism" found virtually no opposition within the denomination. But signs of change came rapidly. In 1838 Emerson shocked the Divinity School. In the 1840s the work of Strauss reached America and Theodore Parker raised his rebellious banner at Boston's Music Hall. Periodically Bellows spoke out about these heretical threats from his pulpit on Fourth Avenue and in the pages of the *Christian Inquirer*, which he founded in 1847. For twenty years the threats seemed serious but containable. In 1859, however, the danger clearly deepened. It was no surprise that the first national figure to travel to Cincinnati to aid the Church of the Redeemer was Bellows himself, who gave the new Society an inaugural sermon just after its creation in April.* Bellows was happy with his work, reporting that "the people seemed very much pleased, and regarded my visit as quite providential." His cousin William Bellows, a Redeemerite member, assured him that he had "largely contributed to the respectability and strength of *our* position."[36]

Bellows would not have admitted it in 1859, but the present crisis was partly brought on by what he and his traditionalist colleagues had been preaching throughout their careers. "Supernatural rationalism" had always meant allegiance to Christianity, but it had also demanded adherence to toleration and to the spirit of objective investigation. As late as 1856, A. A. Livermore could lament that "we have not kept up with the people and with the age . . . in our theology, which is still semi-orthodox, nor in Reforms where we are still timid and conservative, nor in our Church organization where we adopt exclusive rather than generous views." This sort of formula permitted Unitarianism to make a fair experiment in being a religion tied to the Christian tradition while at the same time committed to freedom of thought. It could look toward certain standards, and still respect the initiative of an individual mind. It could maintain biblical authority, and still be free from morbid guilts and psychically disfiguring fears about eternal torment. But "supernatural rationalism" was a fragile formula. One should be a rationalist, but one had to accept the "*authority* of Jesus" no matter what. "Some things, thank Heaven, wide and free as inquiring may be," contended Livermore, "are settled principles, fixed facts, axioms." For Henry Bellows, doubt was only an aid to more committed belief. "I wish," he declared, "⁹⁹⁄₁₀₀ of all those who stupidly *believe* would only anxiously doubt the future life. It would give us an immense growth of spirituality."[37]

Here was the Unitarian paradox at its most vulnerable point. One should push one's questions hard and far, but at the precipice one must always draw back. One must doubt, challenge, and wonder, but in the very last analysis one must still believe. Otherwise Unitarianism was an attitude, not a religion. To Conway and others like him, this represented both ideological inconsistency (which it may have been) and a failure of nerve (which it was not). When the Unitarian left wing moved to assert what they considered the true spirit of their creed, mainstream Unitarians were forced to abandon "rationalism" altogether in favor of an unprecedentedly wholehearted embrace of the supernatural. "We have men standing in Unitarian pulpits . . . preaching a type of Rationalism so low that Tom Paine would have shouted over it in his most maudlin

---

* A second lecture was given in the Pike Opera House because of its superiority as a hall. There had been some qualms about hiring a theater for the occasion, but the Redeemerites concluded that "your character and reputation were *too real* to be soiled by the associations of the place." William Bellows to Henry Bellows, April 7, 1859, Bellows Papers, Massachusetts Historical Society.

hours," growled George Burnap in April 1859. "I think it is time to make a stand against this tendency of things."[38] The irony was that in making such a stand, mainstream Unitarians would be changing their denomination into something different from what it had been and from what they had cherished. They would be changing it into a Christian sect momentarily more militant, single-minded, intellectually timid, and less appreciative of ambiguity than it had ever been before.

The first stand was made at the annual meeting of Harvard Divinity School alumni, following that school's morning commencement exercises, on the afternoon of July 19, 1859.* A major address by Bellows, tentatively titled "A New Catholic Church," was scheduled for four o'clock. It was understood by everyone to be a sizzling repudiation of the left wing and a detailed call for a return to specific rules and standards. But before Bellows could be heard, the alumni business meeting had to deal with a resolution moved by the Cincinnati firebrand who had done much to spark the present crisis. By the end of the day, the Divinity School had reverberated with controversy unmatched since Emerson had rocked it twenty-one years before.[39]

In January, Theodore Parker had left the country for health reasons, suffering from an illness generally understood to be grave. (He would never return to America, dying in Florence in May 1860.) Conway, an admirer of Parker since 1853 and in certain ways his disciple, wished the alumni to express sympathy with him in his illness. His resolution, however, was not simply a straightforward personal gesture of good manners. It was a shrewd political maneuver, designed to put the Alumni Association (comprising almost all major Unitarian ministers) on record in support of Parker's ministerial legitimacy—and by implication, the legitimacy of any others who shared his views:

> *Resolved*, that the Association has heard with deep regret of the failure, during the past year, of the health of Rev. Theodore Parker; and we hereby extend to him our heartfelt sympathy, and express our earnest hope and prayer for his return with renewed strength, and heart unabated, to the post of duty which he has so long filled with ability and zeal.[40]

Conway knew he had no hope of getting the alumni to approve his own course in Cincinnati or to sanction explicitly the right of a Unitarian preacher to reject Christian authority. But unlike anything less oblique,

---

* The commencement exercises themselves were orchestrated with special care. "All the conspicuous parts," wrote one observer, "were strongly marked by the Christian idea of the Word, as indwelling in man, and brought to consciousness in the Church—a doctrine marvellously removed from the Emersonian individualism that has been the pride and infatuation of so many aspiring young minds . . . by leading them to set the fragmentary private soul above integrated humanity, and so cut man off from the True Vine." *Christian Inquirer*, July 20, 1859.

this resolution would be guaranteed at least a full debate, putting the state of the Unitarian leadership on record. If it were defeated, the establishment's objections to the theologically unsafe in their midst would be exhibited in the most graceless way possible. Conway would show that mainstream spokesmen had become so immobile and intolerant that, rather than give even a hint of positive recognition to their critics, they would withhold sympathy from a dying man.

James Freeman Clarke seconded the resolution, a plus for Conway since Clarke was a theological moderate whose primary motive was simple compassion. "It would be manifesting the spirit of Christianity toward Mr. Parker to bless him," he said, believing also that Parker's inflexibility might be softened by an expression of "kindly sentiments." But the chairman, Reverend Newell of Cambridge, was unimpressed by Clarke's arguments. He proceeded to recognize a succession of conservative leaders. Ezra Stiles Gannett, the titan of conservative Unitarianism in Boston, objected that such a resolution was unprecedented. More to the point, it "would be a virtual endorsement of Mr. Parker's position as a preacher." Burnap followed, "urging that the preaching of Mr. Parker was hostile to faith in the Bible." Osgood of New York said he would vote for the first clause but not for the second, since Parker "had in some respect come short, not only of the truth of Christianity, but also of the Christian consciousness and spirit."[41]

Thus far each speaker had expressed compassion for Parker's condition, while refusing to do anything which implied support for heresy. None had mentioned Conway. None had suggested that Conway was engaged in a deliberate political maneuver. None had articulated the resentment which many felt toward him for trying (as Bellows would say later) "to force them to endorse his own policy under cover of sympathizing with his prototype." But that silence could not last. George Ellis of Boston's Charlestown section broke it. He complained "that the object of the mover was not fully expressed." Conway jumped to his feet. He "had no intention of committing the association to the theology of Mr. Parker," he insisted, with some disingenuousness. A resolution "sympathizing with brethren removed by sickness from their field of labor" might be unprecedented, but it was a good custom, and ought to begin now. "If the Association felt the sympathy for Mr. Parker which they expressed, let them say so by their vote." He would not withdraw or alter his resolution.[42]

Someone made a motion to adjourn. This offended Clarke, who was embarrassed that his colleagues could show so little magnanimity for a sick man. Did they want Parker to get well or not? If they did, they should say so. If they did not, they should say that too. Now Burnap was up again, shouting, at the end of his patience. This was his last hurrah; he would die within two months, ruing the day in 1852 when he had met a confused young Methodist circuit rider looking for a spiritual home. He had been instrumental in directing Conway into the

Unitarian church. In a fatherly spirit he had helped subsidize his protégé during those lean months at the Divinity School. Now this same young man, having denounced and ridiculed ideas to which Burnap had devoted his life, sat in the same room with him and asked him to acquiesce in his own spiritual assassination. Whether Parker was sick or well did not matter. What mattered was that he was an "enemy to the Bible," and a hypocrite for preaching from it while denying its "Divine origin." Burnap bellowed out "an elaborate argument" showing how Parker and his followers blasphemed the word of God, going on so long that even his allies were irritated. Finally someone interrupted him, calling again for adjournment. A cacophony now erupted, so unseemly that the secretary asked all observers to leave, "especially reporters." This caused another row. The reporters were finally allowed to remain, in the hope "that they knew well enough what to report and what not to."[43]

It was four o'clock. In a nearby building Henry Bellows was about to begin his speech. Was this another part of Conway's ploy, to keep the alumni in session so long that they and many members of the press would fail to hear this critical oration? Some thought so, and increased their clamor for adjournment. But Gannett wanted a vote taken on Conway's motion, prizing "honor more than the pleasure of listening to the address of Brother Bellows." Enough agreed with him that the meeting dragged on.[44]

Conway rose again. He had put the leaders of his church collectively on record at their embattled and embittered worst.* Now, for the first time, he was willing to change his resolution. He would remove the part "supposed to endorse Parker's Theology," leaving the resolution as "simply one of sympathy with him in his affliction." This was what Osgood had suggested, fruitlessly, some two hours before. It is doubtful that even this new, more innocuous proposition would have passed earlier. But it had no chance after the long acrimonious debate, since Conway's adversaries were sure now that he had been toying with them all along. Frederic Henry Hedge, a mild man with friendships in the transcendentalist camp, rebuked Conway and called his actions "an imposition." There was little left to say. Conway's seemingly overdue concession had taken the wind out of the debate. Many now felt that honor did not demand a fight over the watered-down resolution. A motion to adjourn carried by two to one, without a vote on Conway's proposal. The chapel quickly emptied as the ministers rushed off to hear Bellows.[45]

The "New Catholic Church" speech both summed up and transcended the Unitarian schism, demonstrating its links to much broader divisions

---

* "A Layman" wrote to the *Christian Inquirer* (August 20): "Dr. Bellows, in his Address, spoke hopefully of the spread of Unitarianism. But if this is a fair example of the spirit of exclusiveness and bigotry it is to carry with it, though I have been brought up a Unitarian, I hope, as I hope for truth and moral progress, that it will never spread."

in antebellum American society. The Unitarian rift, said Bellows, illustrated the ways in which Americans had become "forgetful and reckless of the dependence of society on organization." "In his individual capacity as an inorganic, unrelated, independent being," he continued, "a man has not, and cannot have, the affections, internal experiences and dispositions, or the powers and blessings which he can, and may, and will receive in his corporate capacity—in either or any of the great departments of his humanity, the Family, the State, the Church." What was needed, Bellows concluded, was a return to "*the doctrine of institutions*, the only instruments, except literature and the blood, by which the riches of ages, the experience and wisdom of humanity, are handed down." He criticized people in and out of the church whose atomistic individualism led them to proclaim their own values and opinions superior to the inherited wisdom of generations, and to overthrow or subvert the institutions which had long held society together.[46]

Believing in the primacy of tradition and order, Bellows had little sympathy for reformist agitators who seemed not to understand that society required rules for its survival. Any minister, in particular, who presumed to have such a higher sense of morality than his fellows that he entered the arena of social reform, was deserting his pastoral responsibilities to congregation and community. The church needed to be "content with its *religious* function and office," and could not be a "guide and critic of . . . social progress." It was quite understandable that such an egotistical preacher would have the bad taste to "dance in a church [a reference to Conway] or worship in a theatre [a reference to Parker]," for having lost all allegiance to institutions, he would also have lost any reliable guide to proper and responsible behavior. "The Transcendental philosophy . . . delights in making the secular and the sacred, the right and the wrong, the grave and the gay, the male and the female, the world and the church, the human and the divine, the natural and the supernatural, the one and the same." If those who sought to blur such distinctions and obliterate externally imposed standards were given free rein by any institution, then that institution was doomed. And what was true of each institution was true also of society itself.[47]

Bellows anticipated by one hundred years the well-known lament of a noted historian that "the closest thing to an [antebellum] intellectual community in the United States consisted of men . . . who had no close commitment to any of society's institutions," and that the irresponsible atomism of reformers helped only to destroy societal cohesion and bring on civil war. Surely Bellows was not attacking a mirage. Institutions, from slavery to the nuclear family, were being criticized more widely than ever before. Intellectual currents legitimized individual thought, while industrialization made reform both more necessary and (through advances in transportation, communication, and printing) more possible. In politics, the Whigs were gone, the Republicans sectional, and the

Democrats fragmented. In religion, the Baptists and Methodists had split in two. Emerson and his sympathizers were saying that people required no institutional mediator between themselves and God. Thoreau had declared that it was "time to look after the *res-privata*—the private state." And Wendell Phillips had proclaimed that "the difficulty of the present day and with us is, we are bullied by institutions."[48]

But Bellows was only half right. Certainly institutions were under attack, but in his defensiveness he grossly exaggerated the extent to which "the dependence of society on organization" was really being questioned. Antebellum reformers frequently channeled their energies into efforts to create the right sort of institutional arrangements for society. Some, for example, devoted their attention to building appropriate prisons for criminals and asylums for the insane. By the 1850s the temperance movement was turning away from moral appeals to the drunkard and toward prohibition by the state (the first ironclad prohibition law was passed in Maine in 1851). Many abolitionists had enough faith in the political system to join third-party movements in the 1840s, and many supported Republicans in the 1850s. Even those who remained outside the system nevertheless sought to influence it. Departures from traditional family patterns (and communitarian experiments were actually much on the wane by the time Bellows spoke) sought not to destroy the family but to modify its arrangements. Finally, religious radicals sought not to destroy organized religion but to alter its theoretical base; sought not to destroy the church's role in people's lives but to make its posture less coercive, dictatorial, and judgmental.

Moncure Conway, drastically uprooted from home and family because they seemed excessively authoritarian, had to oppose any institution he found similarly objectionable. When he challenged the Christian tenets of Unitarianism, his opponents were justified in fighting him; his success would spell the end of the church as they knew it, by either devaluing or discarding the beliefs they most cherished. But from his standpoint, Conway did not wish to destroy Unitarianism as an institution, if he could help it. He wished only to broaden and humanize it. Far from making him simply a restless iconoclast unappreciative of institutions, Conway's homelessness attached him to all institutions capable of providing a sense of home and community. But unlike the Virginia community he had rejected (or had it rejected him?), any new community must be one where camaraderie and mutual support existed concurrently with humane toleration and individual autonomy. That is where Unitarianism had failed him. He had embraced it believing it would offer him both freedom and a congenial spiritual home within a community of kindred spirits. But Unitarians had more sacred cows than he had bargained for, and they clung to them so ferociously, he later said, that "Unitarians who believed in miracles seemed to hate me more than the orthodox did when I left them." He would not submit to religious authoritarianism, Methodist or Unitarian. "If the Unitarian movement had any meaning at all," he wrote in 1859, "it was to satisfy the *skeptical* class. It was not for the orthodox or the indifferent; it was for those who were alienated, by the unreasonable dogmas of the Church, from . . . spiritual fellowship. . . . But in these days the Unitarians ignore the very class their body was formed to nourish; the mother casts away her own children from her breast." Now he intended to show that one could belong to a community without being coerced or throttled. One could have genuine, stable "fellowship" without the necessity of "dogma."[49]

In her gigantic *The Progress of Religious Ideas Through Successive Ages* (1855), Lydia Maria Child said the most important lesson to be gained from religious history was that "religion" was something quite different from and superior to "theology." Conway agreed. After the split in his church he was determined to make it the chief principle upon which his "Free Church" stood. Henry Bellows had scoffed at this notion, complaining that Conway and his ilk wanted "not so much a religion as an honest and sublime aspiration." But Bellows underestimated the profundity of what inhered in a "sublime aspiration." People's search for life's meaning was a religious search. It involved their deepest fears and needs. And it required, at times, the supportive company of others. Among this particular company of searchers in Cincinnati, there would be no tests of theological orthodoxy. Those who stayed with Conway (and a majority did stay) ranged from rationalists like George Hoadly (a future vice-president of the Free Religious Association and the man to whom Conway's *Life of Paine* would be dedicated) to those who still considered themselves Christian but found their minister likeable and stimulating even when they differed from him. "I fear we are more Conwayites," wrote one such person, "than liberals."[50]

None of this implied that Conway lacked specific opinions. At this point he was a believer, much in the manner of Parker, in "the eternal determination of brain and heart in the direction of Theism. Our impregnable position is that fin implies water, wing necessitates air, eye light, ear sound; and that the aspiration within, which has made every God from a grinning ape to the Father of Jesus, is as definite a reality as fin, wing, eye, or ear, and implies the yet unconceived, unnamed, *but not unfelt* Being who is its proper object." He believed in a benevolent universe in which everything happened for an ultimate good. "It is a metaphysical impossibility," he insisted, "to conceive of the existence of an absolute evil intelligence anywhere; for that would imply the eternity of evil in the universe, and affirm the existence of some portion of his creation where God is forever dethroned and powerless." He still prayed. He still believed in a "God," at times (especially of personal stress) in a quite dynamic and personal God capable of responding to an individual's need. Certainly he preferred parishioners who, out of conviction, agreed with him in these positions. But it was more important that the members adopt the habit of questioning; more important that they think for themselves. The formula whereby an institution could present both a stable religious organization and a forum for genuine free thought, and whereby the minister could combine specific beliefs with considered toleration of other beliefs, would be realized most consciously, coherently, and successfully during Conway's long London ministry. But its beginnings lay here, in his last years in Cincinnati.[51]

The Cincinnati schism revealed a great deal about Moncure Conway, not least his ability to garner a loyal and enthusiastic following. George Hoadly told a public meeting that while he "did not perhaps agree with everything that fell from the lips of Mr. Conway, . . . he nevertheless considered him head and shoulders above any other preacher he had ever heard." Although often accused of undermining religion, Conway was in fact responsible for salvaging the religious faith of some people who had almost given it up. "For me," confided one woman in his congregation, "you have opened broader higher views of humanity— brought to life the dead Christ—and inspired me with a faith that I feel would sustain me through severest trials." That this minister was able to keep a majority of his congregation despite all the recrimination, and was able then to increase their numbers from a variety of sources in the community, says a great deal about his ability to attract.[52]

The other side of this was his pronounced ability to repel, especially to repel those people who were sincerely and devotedly attached to a settled system of belief or a fixed code of behavior. If he was convinced that someone was violating the sanctity of his free and independent personality by making him bow to that system or code, he was apt to respond vitriolically, ruthlessly, and self-righteously. This was not entirely counterproductive, for his style focused attention on his cause. But the vigor of his personal attacks, and the obvious enjoyment he sometimes took in cleverly ridiculing people's most sacred beliefs, unnecessarily alienated large numbers and made real and lasting enemies. Thomas Hill, the president of financially troubled Antioch College, was so disturbed by Conway personally that he could not bring himself to accept money from his congregation, could not "accept gratefully what aid he does give men." During the summer of 1859 readers of the *Christian Inquirer* were exposed to a ghastly exchange of name-calling between a "dyspeptic" Robert Hosea and a "sophomoric" Conway, each of whom seemed to delight in exhibiting intemperateness. "Poor Cincinnati!" wrote Unitarian minister Thomas Starr King, watching the early stages of the controversy from Boston. "Conway is simply crazy,— pure hearted and cracked. It is too bad that our societies in responsible places should be fiddled on by such lunatics." It was Conway's tendency toward impulsiveness and excess, and his talent for alienating people, which led fellow radical David Wasson to dub him "a man with his feet in a large number of quicksands."[53]

When Conway left Cincinnati in 1862 he was succeeded by Charles

Gordon Ames, who shared his religious orientation while having none of his flair for controversy. Ames's mild temperament and dislike of the spotlight guaranteed that his place in history would be obscure and that his influence on free religion would be nil. The compensation lay in a well-developed power of observation and a keen facility for analyzing celebrities who crossed his path. His assessment of Moncure Conway at this stage in that radical minister's life, made in a letter to feminist writer Caroline Dall in March 1863, was fair and insightful:

> Mr. Conway is a man of remarkable powers and weaknesses: brilliant, but not well balanced;—conscientious and with a prophetic soul, of clear intuitions in some directions; but not full-orbed and complete, as we crave our prophets shall be; having a certain unhealthy, feverish flush about his earnestness. It does me good to hear people who have listened to him for years speak his praises and tell of the grace, mercy and peace brought to them by his golden words; and yet I know he has left behind him a bequest of social antagonisms and animosities which came not from his fidelity to truth so much as from those glorious onesidednesses of his character for which a certain class of minds could never make charitable allowance. He is a true man; but can never be a safe guide. He has been grievously wronged; but I do not wonder at it, as men of his stamp compel people to misunderstand them.[54]

By the end of 1859 Moncure Conway was probably the most notoriously outspoken member of the Unitarian left wing. He was, in fact, well positioned to become a primary leader of a broad free-religious movement. But he knew that if he were to assume such a role, and if such a movement were to succeed, agitation would have to yield to consolidation. Like minds would have to communicate, formulate programs, consider organizational arrangements. Even though "our Individualism is the fulcrum of our lever," Conway acknowledged that the heretofore uncoordinated utterances of religious radicals must somehow be concentrated.[55]

His vehicle for concentrating radical energies was *The Dial*, published in Cincinnati under his editorship. It was a "monthly magazine for literature, philosophy, and religion," like the transcendentalist journal of the 1840s from which it took its name. This "new avatar of an ancient Spirit" first appeared in January 1860. Its editor proclaimed it "a legitimation of the Spirit of the Age, which aspires to be free: free in thought, doubt, utterance, love and knowledge." *The Dial* would be a free-religious journal in the broad sense by which Conway understood the term: "When we say 'for Religion'—'for Theology' is not meant." It would publish poetry, fiction, literary criticism, articles on social policy, politics, and world religion. A "catholic chapter," descended from the "Ethical Scripture" section of the old *Dial*, printed reflections on life taken from sources ancient and modern, Western and non-Western, including excerpts from the sacred works of India and Persia.[56]

The first issue, however, did not succeed in being a magazine of variety and scope. Conway was forced to write most of it himself under great time pressures, and it had, by his own admission, too much of a "theological character." Conway was learning the hard way that much of an editor's job consists of prying words out of people who would rather not write them, or who would rather write them at some other (usually distant) time. Both Thoreau and Samuel Longfellow disappointed him by declining to contribute. The noted radical minister of Lynn, Samuel Johnson, refused to acknowledge his increasingly irritated pleas for articles. Even Emerson was dilatory, not offering an essay until June, when he submitted an old lyceum lecture, "Domestic Life." It was evident early that Conway would have to write a great deal for the magazine himself, and would have to cast his net widely for additional contributors.[57]

Despite the difficulties, *The Dial* did evolve during its twelve-month life into a journal of interest, substance, and vitality. Its second issue was an advance over the first. It included a feisty article (with which Conway disagreed) by an obscure Ohio farmer ridiculing the idea of prayer, poetry by Conway's old Harvard friend Frank Sanborn, "Quatrains" by Emerson, and the second installment of a thoughtful serial, "The Christianity of Christ," by Octavius Brooks Frothingham, who ranked with Conway as a leading radical Unitarian spokesman. This February issue got a glowing review from the struggling young poet-journalist William Dean Howells in the Columbus *Ohio State Journal*, which naturally caught Conway's eye and brought the two men together. In March Conway gave Howells's recently published first book, *Poems of Two Friends* (co-authored with Louisville journalist J. J. Piatt), a generally favorable review. Before long Howells had contributed four poems to *The Dial*. Thus began a friendship that would last, with varying degrees of intimacy, for almost fifty years.[58]

Of some two hundred articles in *The Dial*, Conway wrote at least thirty. (Initially articles were unsigned, and the authorship of some is impossible to fix with certainty.) The liveliest were on social issues, especially woman's rights, on which Conway was becoming steadily more outspoken. Ellen Conway's influence was probably one factor behind his intensifying interest, as was his reading of Caroline Dall's *Woman's Right to Labor* (1860). Conway successfully solicited an article from Dall, and her book prompted him to investigate "female employment and its underpayment" in Cincinnati. In *The Dial* he applauded the theater for its equitable employment of women. In an article on prostitution he criticized society for forcing women into that trade by undervaluing their labor in other occupations. "Society has built the brothels," he proclaimed. "Few employments are open to women: those few furnish so little and so precarious pay, that the loss of body's life or soul's life are often the horrid alternatives." He went on to advocate careful consideration of European-style licensing systems for brothels (actually tried in several Midwestern cities in the 1870s) and to support the building of lying-in and foundling hospitals. He also championed secular and non-judgmental homes for ex-prostitutes, in contrast to existing homes, "those sunless religious caverns . . . where penances are assigned . . . and they are treated as subjects for hell-fires, instead of being regarded as deeply wronged martyrs of an unformed social state."[59]

Conway also poured his opinions into the seventy book reviews he wrote during the course of the year. Darwin's *Origin of Species*, which he had welcomed in a December 1859 sermon as a breakthrough destined to topple "all temples not founded on the rock of natural science," was of special interest to him. He had fought with Christian traditionalists before the book appeared, and now regarded it as a further vindication of his position. Darwin's ideas were not completely new; the notion of evolution had been in the air for some time. Now the naturalist came forward with scientific evidence for opinions previously supported only by reason and common sense. "Owing to the theological exigency," Conway wrote in his review, ". . . naturalists have been intimidated and the people befogged on the question of their own origin. . . . Where Reason had passed long since . . . , lagging Science is now beginning to come."[60]*

The Dial also gave Conway a chance to boost an old literary hero, in an adulatory review of the third edition of *Leaves of Grass*. "We confidently announce that Walt Whitman has set the pulses of America to music." The editor would not apologize for Whitman's earthy language or imagery. "The writer does not hesitate to bring the slop-bucket into the parlor to show you that therein also the chemic laws are at work. . . . This Poet, though 'one of the roughs,' . . . is never frivolous, his profanity is reverently meant, and he speaks what is unspeakable with the simple unreserve of a child." Finally, Conway could not resist another blow in his bout with mainstream Unitarians, needling the stodgy *Christian Examiner* for its violent denunciation of Whitman, made "with the unctuous air of one who has just read without blinking the accounts of Joseph and Potiphar, Judah and Tamar."[61]

Conway was less profusely approving of the latest book of another noted writer, whose work he had been reading since 1850. In his mixed review of *The Marble Faun*, the editor revealed his wariness of Nathaniel Hawthorne, who always attracted his interest but seldom—at this stage of life—satisfied it. He was justifiably unnerved by the implausible contrivances of the plot (especially involving the treacly Hilda and her doves), which made his theatrically-oriented mind imagine "men and boys behind there, in their shirt-sleeves, tugging at cranks and pulleys." But his problem with Hawthorne ran deeper. The author, Conway

---

* "It was to be twenty-five years," Conway wrote in his memoirs, "before I discovered . . . that it was possible for man to develop himself and his world downward." AME, I, 283.

believed, did not understand that the spirit of the age was progress. Surely his obsession with tragedy and humanity's darker side grated against that spirit. Not that Hawthorne was all gloom; he felt that depth and strength could come from understanding absolute evil. The problem, Conway contended, was that there *was* no absolute evil. Evil was only good in the making. He did see in this work "a struggling into sunshine not to be found in *The Scarlet Letter* or *Blithedale Romance*," but still the book was of an essentially " 'tragical' nature." "Is it not time," Conway asked, "that we recovered from the dyspeptic idea of tragedy?"[62]

Conway got his first close look at Hawthorne in July 1860. It was during a three-week summer vacation, when he attended a dinner at the Boston Literary Club welcoming the writer home after a six-year tour as consul to Liverpool—Hawthorne's reward for writing a campaign biography of his old Bowdoin friend, Franklin Pierce. Separated by many guests at a long table, they did not speak to each other. The young minister stared down at the older man with a look of fascination and puzzlement. In many ways he did not approve of Hawthorne, this seemingly morbid and unprogressive Massachusetts enigma so admired and accepted by many of the Virginians Conway had left. He knew, however, that Hawthorne was a man to take seriously, to reckon with. He did not yet know what that reckoning would involve. Nor did it yet seem urgent or vital. Three decades later it would be, when Conway rediscovered the reality of tragedy and confronted the reality of evil. Then he would read Hawthorne with new eyes and become one of the novelist's more sensitive biographers. But for now, he was content to steal glances down the long table during lulls in the conversation with other men, men he knew and liked and understood.[63]

The Hawthorne dinner was part of a brief summer sojourn in the Northeast that offered Conway further proof of his rising status and popularity in reformist circles. Parker's old congregation invited him to preach at the Music Hall on two successive Sundays. He accepted eagerly, feeling himself a fit inheritor of Parker's mantle. At Newport his wit and sociability made a major hit with the annual colony of vacationing reformers. Marianna Mott went on a day-long sailing party with him and was enchanted. "Mr. Conway . . . talked and read to us the whole time and made us indifferent to the swell of the sea," she reported to Ellen Garrison (wife of William Lloyd, Jr.). "Have you ever seen Mr. Conway? I am sure you will rave about him if you have—he is so charming and so true—and such a sermon as he gave us this morning—It was fire from heaven."[64]

Unfortunately none of these gifts was of much service in saving *The Dial*, which expired with the December issue. It had been financially anemic since its inception, and neither editor nor contributors had ever received a penny for their labors. The subscription list had grown slowly, and by the end of the year it was clear that the monthly could not be sustained. A plan to continue the venture as a quarterly was stillborn.[65] By February 1861 all hope of continuing the Cincinnati *Dial* was abandoned.

Though short-lived, *The Dial* had served Conway well. Beyond helping to fulfill his early and ongoing desire to be a man of letters, it had kept him in the spotlight as one of the most outspoken Unitarian radicals and a prime candidate for leadership of any organized revolt. *The Dial* showed that Conway not only could agitate but could also work hard, reflect, and cooperate. It was, in part, a vehicle for Conway's desire to organize Unitarian left-wingers with himself as a leading spokesman. In a revealing article in June, "The Nemesis of Unitarianism," Conway sketched the contours of the developing church schism. "The reigns of reptilian ceremonies, of Saurian Sabbaths and miracles, pass away before the reign of the Spiritual Man." He then spoke directly to the religious " 'left wing' " that composed much of his readership. "The warning comes to us, 'Enlarge the place of thy tent.' For this, we must have more communion and cooperation." Prepared to shed a community which had failed him by crushing his autonomy, he was eager to forge a new community that would comfort him by celebrating the very independence of its members. "Individuality is never to be lost, even to a hairs breadth: but there is a sphere as well as an atom. . . . We must bear witness to one another."[66]

Henry Bellows knew also that a break was coming. He, too, welcomed it, as a method of purification and a test of strength he was confident that supernatural Christianity would win. During 1860 he and Conway sparred in various ways. In February the young radical had a good time reviewing Bellows's *Re-Statements of Christian Doctrine*, a collection of sermons showing a redoubled reverence for Christ's special nature. The work was "the result of a common sense and good-hearted man's effort to be clerical and mystic," Conway gibed. "Reading it we seem to be listening to the affectations of some French musician, who, having taken a true theme, forgets it in the evolutions of himself, until that over which Beethoven wept in silence and secrecy is exposed to the *bravos* and noisy uproar of a saloon." During the summer and fall they even engaged in a bizarre dispute (joined by others) about the state of the late Theodore Parker's soul. A formal break in Unitarian ranks was brewing. It could well have taken place in 1861, with Bellows leading the conservatives and Conway the radicals. But it did not happen that way.[67]

The climax did not come until April 1865 when, at Bellows's call, delegates from across the country met at his New York church to organize a disciplined and centralized National Conference of Unitarian Churches. Central to the proceedings, wrote Sidney Morse, was the question of "what to do with Christ."[68] With Bellows, Edward Everett Hale, and Cincinnati's A. D. Mayo playing leading roles, a constitution was adopted pledging allegiance to the "Lord Jesus Christ" and upholding the reality of the Resurrection. O. B. Frothingham, watching in disgust from the balcony, walked out and abandoned the name Unitarian. Bellows was gleeful, gloating that Unitarians had finally "finished naturalism and transcendentalism and Parkerism."[69] After two years of consultation and debate, left-wing Unitarians joined with other sympathetic radicals in 1867 to form their own organization under Frothingham's presidency, the Free Religious Association.*

What changed the chronology and perhaps the substance of the Unitarian schism was, of course, the Civil War. The war prompted a temporary truce in the Unitarian conflict by channeling the combatants' energies into one form or another of patriotic endeavor. Bellows organized and directed the United States Sanitary Commission, a civilian group that improved the flow of supplies to the front and bettered the medical care, such as it was, available to soldiers. Conway dropped all concern for religious controversy and threw himself into the cause of emancipation. Far from helping precipitate the breakup of orthodox Unitarianism by diminishing religious faith, the Civil War retarded that breakup by arresting a trend already approaching its climax.

Although it is a matter of speculation, the Civil War might have greatly affected the nature of the Free Religious Association by paving the way for Frothingham's leadership. For all his scholarly ability and capacity for insight, Frothingham was temperamentally conservative and became notoriously erratic and equivocal theologically. Francis Ellingwood Abbot, founder in 1870 of a free-religious organ, *The Index*, was constantly irritated by Frothingham's social passivity (his refusal, for example, to criticize obscenity laws) and by his "neo-Christian" straddling of doctrinal issues.[70] Under Frothingham, the FRA remained a staid, exclusive, rather inbred New England–dominated club, lacking a real sense of purpose or a will to involve itself in public issues. Abbot wanted to see an organization in America that was genuinely free, religious, thoughtful, active, and bold. He was disappointed in the FRA.

Moncure Conway sympathized with Abbot.[71] Conway was probably the most radical man both willing and able to vie with Frothingham for leadership. He was far more willing to speak out on social issues and far less fuzzy in his own religious positions. He was a Southerner with an important Western pulpit, and had a vision that Frothingham lacked of a national organization. Surely Abbot and a number of others would have preferred him. But Conway's opportunity never came. Not only

---

* The secession of the radicals (many but not all of whom joined the FRA) took much of the vitality out of Unitarianism. Deprived of its most vibrant group, outflanked and overrun by intellectual forces affecting both its own members and the broader population, the Unitarian National Conference finally abandoned all authoritative tests of allegiance in 1882—the year of Bellows's death. The FRA, having witnessed the evolution of the Unitarians into the all-encompassing sect familiar in the later twentieth century, became moribund by 1910 and formally expired in 1938.

was he no leader of the FRA, he was not even a member. The Civil War had done more than change the chronology of the Unitarian schism foreshadowed by the events of 1859. It had also eliminated the leading radical participant in those events by pushing him to a personal crisis and then catapulting him from the country.

PART THREE / WAR AND EXPATRIATION

CHAPTER 7

Radical abolitionists had long been walking a tightrope. Seeking to balance extreme resistance to slavery with nonviolent moral suasion, they had hoped to have it both ways by inwardly regenerating the slaveholder and his sympathizers. But after a generation of agitation, almost no slaveholders had been regenerated. Only Northern public opinion was becoming more hostile to slavery. Credit for that went less to abolitionists than to victories slavery itself seemed to be winning: the Fugitive Slave Law, the Kansas-Nebraska Act, Dred Scott. Slavery seemed more entrenched and powerful than ever. As the years passed, many antislavery people found their faith in moral suasion crumbling. By the end of the 1850s the abolitionist tightrope was perilously frayed. On the night of October 16, 1859, John Brown led his men into Harper's Ferry, Virginia, and all but slashed it in two.

Brown was no stranger to abolitionists. He had been a leading antislavery warrior in the Kansas civil war—and the most skilled at self-promotion, at romanticizing his exploits and obscuring his darker deeds. He was not precisely insane, as he has so often been described, but he did give meaning to the term "religious fanatic." Patterning himself after Gideon of the Old Testament, he once told Emerson, in utter seriousness, that it was "better that a whole generation of men, women and children should pass away by a violent death than that a word of either [the Bible or the Declaration of Independence] should be violated in this country." Beginning in 1857 he dazzled antislavery people with public lectures and spellbinding private performances throughout the Northeast, arousing in them the usual feelings of envy, admiration, and guilt a fearless man of action evokes in sympathizers whose work is done in safer havens. In 1858 certain abolitionists—Thomas Wentworth Higginson, Samuel Gridley Howe, Theodore Parker, Frank Sanborn, Gerrit Smith, and George Stearns—learned of Brown's secret plan to lead a guerrilla force into the Appalachians, establish a stronghold there, and encourage slaves to rebel, run away, and join him. The so-called "Secret Six" gave Brown moral and material support, and were not completely surprised (though some recoiled at the violent details) when the blow finally fell.[1]

If less informed abolitionists were stunned by the raid on Harper's Ferry, they quickly recovered and fell into line. Brown had been imprisoned by Virginia authorities along with most of his surviving followers. He had neither ransacked the town's arsenal, nor fomented a slave revolt, nor fled into the mountains—if he still had any of this in mind by the time of the attack. But he turned his tactical defeat into a brilliant strategic victory. He believed, as he wrote on the December day he hanged, "that the crimes of this *guilty land* will never be purged away but with Blood"—and both his raid and its aftermath brought civil war palpably closer. The raid drew many Southerners, periodically troubled by the nightmare of servile insurrection, a little nearer to belief that there was no security within a Union where antislavery radicals supported such a man with impunity. Brown's dignified behavior during his imprisonment, trial, and execution jarred many Northern consciences while bringing abolitionists closer than ever to sanctioning violence. William Lloyd Garrison insisted that he had not abandoned nonviolence, but he cited the American Revolution and "the right of the slaves to imitate the example of our fathers." Wendell Phillips (who gave the eulogy at Brown's burial) called Brown "a Lord High Admiral of the Almighty." Even Emerson, after some hesitation, termed Brown "a new saint" who "will make the gallows glorious like the cross." "We were all Brown's victims," wrote Moncure Conway in 1904, "—even we antislavery men, pledged to the methods of peace."[2]

Conway faced the same dilemma Brown posed for other abolitionists, and ultimately succumbed to the same sort of adulatory rhetoric. His approval of Brown came after some hesitation, however, for there was a special obstacle in his path. He was a Virginian, with loved ones in Virginia. It was one thing to advocate emancipation. It was quite another to flirt with insurrection schemes which might kill people he cared about or knew to be decent. His origins, plus his deep-seated abhorrence of violence, prompted a relatively cautious initial response to Harper's Ferry. On October 23 he lamented from his Cincinnati pulpit that Brown's "healthy feeling for human rights became a morbid monomania, which saw in every slaveholder a border ruffian," and announced his belief that abolitionists would "denounce the method" of Brown. But his disapproval was not complete. Brown had been willing to pay the ultimate price for his moral beliefs, and homage had to be paid him for that. Conway paid it: "I thank God that in this diluvial period of materialism one man is found who can go crazy for an idea,—one who can rave like a half-clad John in the desert for the path of God to be made straight, and declare the axe laid to the root of the tree!" The real criminal in this case was the national government, for coddling the Slave Power.[3]

In ensuing months, first as Brown exploited his new role as heroic martyr and then as the sectional conflict reached its extremity in a milestone election year, Conway's approval of Brown overwhelmed his reservations. In March 1860 he could still warn that Brown's motives and beliefs "must not justify to us Gideon and Samuel and the other model barbarians, whom we venerate at a distance of five thousand years, but would imprison for life in any civilized community." But by June, reviewing an anthology of tributes to Brown, he left all caveats behind. "Every nation must write its own Bible," and Brown had begun America's Book of Exodus. "We think of this brave old man, over-riding all rational methods, with nothing right in his plan, except his perfect truth."[4]

The following month Conway was deeply disillusioned by a remark of New York's Senator William Henry Seward that Brown had been "justly punished." The Cincinnati minister had supported Seward (whose quotable speeches had brought him an undeserved reputation for radicalism) for the Republican presidential nomination. Now he thought it just as well that Seward had lost. Conway was so hurt that he wrote the senator a scolding, verbose, and pompous letter detailing his pain. "We all know that such a deed could not be rightly inaugurated as a normal method of dealing with Slavery," he admitted. "But that does not affect the fact that this old man, with all his imperfection, was living out the idea of right which the Universe had graven on his brain." "Oh, what did you do!" he moaned. "There is no mere earthly possession that I now have, that I would not freely give to have that sentence of yours unsaid. It has filled me with shame and grief. . . . if it had been only that Brown was 'legally' punished, but *justly*—Good God, what does that mean! Is there then no room on earth for heroes, any more?"[5]

Seward was not alone in thinking Brown no hero. Margaret Conway— whose own opposition to Southern extremism made her and her family no less vulnerable during a slave insurrection—agreed. Even after the Civil War began and she had moved North, she and her son were still arguing. "There is no use in our discussing old John Brown," Moncure told his mother in December 1861, "who to you is a wicked man, to me a wild John, forerunner of a Messianic Epoch to this country. Perhaps if Mildred, Richard, Peter and myself had been on auction-blocks at Harper's Ferry instead of negroes, you would have gone to bathe John Brown's feet with your tears and wipe them with the hairs of your head. . . . Herodias (Slavery) demanded his head . . . and got it; but swift thereafter comes the Baptism of the Holy Ghost and of fire."[6]

Conway's decision that Brown was a hero did not really extinguish his reservations about the morality of violent action, nor did it enhance his psychic ability to accept bloodshed. In the wake of Brown's execution he channeled his complex feelings into a children's story, "Excalibur," which first appeared in *The Dial* in January 1860. The story attempted to praise Brown's actions while preaching against any future violence. Conway traced the journey of the mythical sword Excalibur from King Arthur's court all the way to Harper's Ferry, claiming Brown had used it in the raid. The sword had done its work well against slavery, "piercing beneath the scales of the Dragon; and that wound can never be healed." Such a glorious result justified even the drastic means of achieving it. But no further violence was needed to kill a monster now dying of its wounds. "EXCALIBUR still waits the hand of its next true king, who will be he that can conquer without it." The way was now paved for those "who know the power of the Sword of the Spirit, the LOVE which never faileth." Brown's deed was magnificent, not least because it had been done so effectively that it need never be repeated.[7]

The problem was that sanctioning one act of violence in the name of a cause made it more difficult to denounce future violence which might advance the same cause. The dragon of slavery—itself the epitome of violence—might be mortally wounded. But what if it took generations to die? If more violence might kill it quickly and save future generations from bondage, then was not more violence as justifiable as the attack on Harper's Ferry? Which was worse—the deaths of some people now, bringing with them the death of slavery, or the continuing enslavement of millions for unknown years to come? These were questions that "Excalibur" evaded. Conway would have to confront them much sooner than he knew.

When Senator Seward said that John Brown was "justly punished," he was stating a Republican axiom. Although organized for little more than half a decade, Republicans knew that 1860 was their year. They needed only to maintain an air of responsible moderation, remain firm on slavery extension while distancing themselves from radical abolitionists, and the presidency would be theirs. Pledged to block slavery's expansion, they would have no Southern electoral votes, but they would not need them. By the time their presidential convention met in Chicago in May, their primary opposition had disintegrated.

The Democrats had met in Charleston in April, with many Southern delegates demanding outright federal protection for slavery throughout the territories. Unwilling to abandon popular sovereignty for so drastic a pro-Southern measure, Northern Democrats refused to yield to such demands. A number of proslavery delegates walked out, and the convention broke up without choosing a nominee. Democrats would try again six weeks later in Baltimore, but again they would splinter; ultimately the Northern and Southern wings ran separate nominees. With their opponents split in two, Republicans knew they had a victory if they did not blunder. Accordingly, the Chicago delegates rejected Seward and all other candidates whose images might disturb potential voters. Their third-ballot choice was a principled man unburdened by a radical reputation, the eloquent Illinois lawyer, Abraham Lincoln.[8]

Conway first saw Lincoln in September 1859 in Cincinnati. Lincoln was stumping Ohio; by accident, Conway stumbled onto one of his outdoor rallies. At first barely interested in the proceedings, Conway snapped to attention when he heard the speaker describe slavery as a moral wrong—an impressive comment coming from a mainstream politician with high ambitions, made in a city only a stone's throw from a slave state. Although Lincoln was not everything the Cincinnati minister might have wished, the Republicans' refusal to advocate total abolition had never prevented Conway from supporting them, especially over opponents who showed little awareness that slavery was a moral issue at all. As he had supported Fremont in 1856, so he supported Lincoln now. In July 1860 he wrote that a Republican victory would mean "the whole *animus* of the country would be for freedom; the tide of official and popular influence would set that way." He noted the nominee's belief in the moral equality of black people, contending that the inauguration of such a president was "surely . . . something to look forward to." That fall, in the only presidential election (and perhaps the only election) in which he ever voted,* he cast his ballot for Lincoln.[9]

The 1860 election led inexorably to civil war. To many influential Southerners, Lincoln's victory marked a shift of power fatal to slavery and seemed both to ratify and aggravate their region's minority status. Unable to accept this, the South Carolina legislature immediately authorized the governor to call a special secession convention. That state left the Union on December 20, followed in the next six weeks by Alabama, Mississippi, Florida, Louisiana, Georgia, and Texas. On February 4, 1861, delegates from these states met in Montgomery, Alabama and established a provisional government for the Confederate States of America.

As yet there had been no fighting, no killing, no war; and many people wanted it to stay that way. President Buchanan, unwilling to foreclose his successor's options and disinclined to coerce the South anyway, remained passive during the secession winter. Meanwhile, in an effort to mollify the upper South and bring the lower South back into the Union, a substantial minority of Republicans in the House and Senate joined their Democratic colleagues in pushing through a constitutional amendment, sending it to the states for ratification. It guaranteed slavery in states where it already existed. (Subsequent events made the amendment a dead letter, and it was never ratified.) For three weeks beginning on February 4, a well-publicized convention of compromise-minded delegates from twenty-one states met in Washington and

---

* In 1856 Conway would have voted for Fremont if permitted. But he had not yet fulfilled the residency requirements in Ohio, and had had no vote as a resident of the District of Columbia.

fashioned proposals which both guaranteed slavery and permitted its limited expansion. For a time it seemed one of two things would happen: a war of coercion, or drastic concessions to the South in an attempt to save the Union and keep the peace.[10]

If war was abhorrent to antislavery Northerners, sweeping concessions to an ugly and menacing "Slave Power" seemed even more unthinkable. Wishing to avoid either path, many antislavery activists hammered away at an old Garrisonian plank: peaceful disunion. Let the seceding states go, then watch slavery wither, once deprived of the shelter of the United States government. Eventually the wayward recalcitrants would come crawling back. Even if they did not, the country would be rid of their threats and their bullying, and would be a proud nation free from the political control of slaveholders. "Constitution or no Constitution," exulted Wendell Phillips in January, " . . . the Southern states, so long as they be slave states, shall be shovelled out of this Union." Horace Greeley, calmer in language but just as fearful of concessions, editorialized only three days after Lincoln's election that "if the cotton states shall become satisfied that they can do better out of the Union than in it, we insist on letting them go in peace."[11]

From his Cincinnati pulpit Moncure Conway embraced the same theme. He argued that "amputation" of the South might be necessary to save both sections. "Not one step can be taken toward conciliation," he insisted, "until we have prostrated ourselves into the dust before slavery. . . . Even the states which have not gone, but hesitate, hesitate only to make their bribe effectual; only to jingle in our ears the thirty pieces of silver, for which we are called on to betray the innocent again."[12]

As was the case with many of his colleagues, Conway's worst fear was that the federal government and Northern people would slide into the old pattern of submitting to Southern threats. He did not want a war, and (unlike, perhaps, Greeley) preferred disunion to violent conflict. But he preferred anything to more compromise. He and his abolitionist associates were certain of one thing: the crisis had arrived, when the South's aggression would either win total victory or be checked forever. "For myself," wrote abolitionist Sarah Pugh to an English friend, "the feeling is that anything is better than the past, that a tempest is better than stagnation. . . ."[13]

Stagnation seemed much less likely once a Republican president took office on March 4. Throughout the crisis Lincoln had emphasized that no concession was possible on the matter of slavery expansion, although he was willing to guarantee the institution in the Southern states. In his inaugural address he repeated this immovable Republican principle, and added that in his judgment "the Union of these states is perpetual." Secession, he said, was "illegal" and "insurrectionary," and disunion was something a president could never permit. He would take no immediate coercive action against seceded states, hoping that cooler heads would prevail there. But he intended to "hold, occupy and possess" Florida's Fort Pickens and South Carolina's Fort Sumter, which had not surrendered to the rebel government.

For another six weeks an uneasy stalemate persisted, until dwindling provisions at Sumter made further stalemate impossible. Lincoln's decision to resupply the fort led the Confederate government to order its bombardment on April 12. The following day the garrison surrendered. On April 15 Lincoln issued a call for volunteers. Unwilling to fight against fellow Southerners and considering secession a natural right of revolution, Virginia seceded on April 17. By June the Union also had lost North Carolina, Arkansas, and Tennessee. The sides had formed. The war had begun.[14]

Abolitionists now had to come to terms with war. At least the major compromises they had feared had become unlikely. At issue now was whether a conflict to restore the Union could be turned into a crusade for emancipation. "The war plays the deuce with peace principles," wrote William Henry Furness in May, marveling at the rapidity with which he and antislavery colleagues had come to support the violent subjugation of the South. By backing the war, abolitionists might be able to influence its character. Thus, within a month after the fall of Fort Sumter, Garrison, Phillips, and their peers fell into line in support of the war, adding their insistence that it must become explicitly antislavery to be fully justifiable or successful.[15]

Moncure Conway was no exception. After John Brown's raid he had hoped no more violence would be necessary. He had not anticipated, however, that so momentous an opportunity would come so soon. Anyway, war was now a *fait accompli*. It was no longer a question of embracing it or rejecting it, but rather how to direct it toward the noblest possible ends. On the Sunday after the fall of Sumter, Conway announced his support of the president's actions. His congregation sang "The Star-Spangled Banner." On May 5 he elaborated on his position. "Every society is a foe to war," he proclaimed, "but in diseased bodies the wise physician prefers the fever to typhoid." At the end, his congregation applauded. The title of his discourse was "The Horrors of Peace."[16]

The men of Stafford County were quick to rally to the cause of their new country. One hundred and forty-four of them were mustered into the Ninth Virginia Cavalry at Stafford Court House in April, and that was just the beginning. The county was in an exposed position, midway between Washington and the soon-to-be Southern capital at Richmond. Almost certainly the region would become a battleground. In serving the Confederacy, Stafford's citizens would literally be defending their own homes and families. Among those who could be counted on were Peter and Richard Conway, eager to join the army, and their father, who was sure to contribute in whatever way he could.[17]

One Conway still in Falmouth was not so reliable. Margaret Conway had watched the slide toward secession with increasing alarm and disgust, complaining in February to her son Moncure about "this unholy excitement" surrounding her. Once Virginia left the Union in April, Margaret began to think seriously about leaving Virginia. Her husband was prepared to withdraw to Richmond if Falmouth and Fredericksburg were taken by Union forces. She was not prepared to join him, since she was completely out of sympathy with the Confederate cause. In the meantime, her outspoken views were making it difficult to stay in Falmouth under any circumstances. Finally she decided to join her daughter and son-in-law in Easton, Pennsylvania. Her son Peter escorted her there in the early summer. After a brief visit with his sister, Peter returned to Virginia and joined his brother Richard in the Southern army.[18]

In Easton, Margaret's hatred of the Southern cause intensified. By the fall of 1862 she regarded emancipation as such a *"godsend"* that she was calling Mildred and her husband "old fogies" for their occasional flashes of caution on the issue. Her opinions, however, had no bearing on her personal feelings toward the Confederates in her family. She and her husband infrequently found ways of exchanging loving and heartbreaking letters, longing for the day when the war would end and they would be reunited. "My heart is drawn out towards you as it never was before, even in the days of our youth," Walker wrote his wife in March 1862, only a few weeks before he made his proposed removal to Richmond. "If God in His merciful Providence and Grace permits us to come together again I will spend and be spent most gladly in ministering to your happiness. I trust it may be so, but if not I endeavor from my Heart to say 'Thy will be done'. . . . How I am to come out of these times, God knows. I am sure I don't; I am only careful to do right and act according to the best lights I have." Separation was hard for all the family, even for the son who had been away the longest, the son who lamented from Cincinnati in December 1861 that his "dear Father" was "farther off than if he were in China."[19]

If Moncure miscalculated the distance between himself and his father, he did so by making it too short. Walker Conway refused to mention his heretical son's name during the war, and alluded to him only once: ". . . if you go to Cincinnati, I would not advise a long visit," he told his wife in 1862, "but you must judge in all these matters." This son was a humiliation, a disgrace to kinsmen who had patriotism and courage enough to stand and defend their native soil. The Moncures had six or seven men in one company alone. Richard Conway was growing up fast and finally learning responsibility. Early distinguishing himself in battle, he had given up (temporarily) the drinking habits which had always embarrassed his parents, giving his father "hopes of that dear boy which I never could indulge before." And Peter—dashing, intelligent, dependable, the sort of son Walker had always wanted—gave his father "unspeakable pleasure" by returning so expeditiously from Easton to do his duty. Next to them, the less said about the other son, the better. Walker could excuse his wife and daughter: they were women, and ought to be away from the fighting anyway. But his oldest son was not excusable. His oldest son was a traitor.[20]

"Having been born in Stafford Co.,Va.," Moncure wrote to President Lincoln on May 7, 1861, "I am minutely acquainted with the topography of that and a very large part of Eastern Va. . . . If the War Department needed a question concerning such minutiae answered, I could do it . . . to help my country in this her solemn but ever-glorious emergency." The War Department declined Conway's offer, but it did not matter. He had plenty to do. Public opinion must be guided, and emancipation must be championed through whatever means lay open. "We are in grand times my friend," said his Chicago colleague Robert Collyer, "and we shall need all our power to keep right on fearlessly telling the truth, especially after our men at the North begin to fight for the fight more than for the principle."[21]

Conway lost no time in his campaign to make this a war of principle. In June he closed his church for the summer and embarked on an extended speaking tour of the Northeast. He stopped first in Easton to visit his mother and catch up on the latest family news. Then he pushed on to Philadelphia and New York where he began lecturing. July 8 found him in Boston, from which he journeyed by train to Providence with a nervous and haggard Horace Greeley, still "harrassed with fear of a compromise." In Providence, Conway faced his first significant opposition, encountering hisses from "a strong old fogy element" and watching disgustedly as a number of people filed out "during my antislavery touches, evidently from disapproval." Luckily he was able to withdraw to Newport for a few days, where he splashed in the ocean by day and dashed off impassioned letters to the *Tribune* by night, all the time luxuriating in the hospitality of a radical hotel-owner (formerly of Parker's congregation) who refused to take a penny from him and treated him "as if I had been his uncle just arrived from foreign parts."[22]

During this first tour, in both speeches and letters, Conway hammered at two themes which would remain central to his thinking throughout the war. First, he emphasized that immediate, unconditional emancipation was the only way either to justify or win the war. While this position was shared widely by abolitionists, his second theme was more idiosyncratic. He argued that slavery, not the South, was the only real enemy. The North shared responsibility for this war, for it had coddled slavery, tolerated and even encouraged a system that was destroying and maddening Southern countrymen. The North "might have averted the tumor which now eats into our Southern brother's heart; having instead fostered that tumor until delerium has superseded, it must now rescue that brother, if he can be rescued, by the painful surgical way."

The surgery must be brief and decisive. The pain must be minimized. The spirit must be one of compassion, not hate.[23]

This was an increasingly difficult line of argument to uphold in a war-devoured Union, although Conway never swerved from it. He would fight his own people, his own brothers, his own native land; but he could never hate them. If he could not persuade his Northern peers to feel the same way, it was not for lack of trying. Very early, however, he caught a glimpse of what he was up against. In May an otherwise sympathetic correspondent in Boston challenged his hope for Northern "goodwill" toward its adversary. "The vile conduct of the South is producing its natural result," growled the Bostonian, "and the North will soon feel . . . a contempt and detestation of the South so profound that years will be needed to bring back the least feeling of confidence and respect."[24]

Conway's interest in avoiding either the physical devastation of the South or the rise of ineradicable hatred toward its people propelled him toward a naïve assessment of how much emancipation might achieve. Abolitionists were both shrewd and accurate in believing emancipation a valuable weapon in the Northern arsenal. But Conway went further than most abolitionists in the claims he made for it. Not only was it morally right and militarily advantageous, it actually would end the war almost immediately. Although not central to Conway's thinking until 1862, this image of total emancipation as a sort of magic cure-all was present from the beginning—and he continued to believe in it for the rest of his life. As he wrote later, "I knew slavery and the slaveholders well; if the President and Congress should at once declare every slave in America free, every Southerner would have to stay at home and guard his slaves. There could be no war." The North would win by default, while the South would be rid of its mortal disease with a minimum of bloodshed and disruption.[25]

Conway never fully explained why the Emancipation Proclamation, which freed slaves in rebel-held areas, failed to activate his scenario in those regions; why slaves remained cautious when still far from Northern armies, and why Southern troops were not required to keep them in their places. In the end, such explanations would have been academic. Conway's idea was as much psychological balm as practical program. Requiring both emancipation and a short, relatively painless war, he convinced himself that it was possible to have both, and that one could be the vehicle for the other. If his notion was naïve, its message had value. He was saying that people ought to be thinking about ways to achieve freedom without mass slaughter. And he was hinting that a time might come when the horror of the slaughter outweighed any benefits it could bring.

Conway was in New Bedford when the carnage commenced. Casualties in the Northern setback at Bull Run on July 21 were, compared to what would come later, comparatively light: 3,000 Union, 2,000 Confederate.

But they were bad enough, and the dimensions of the Union rout were big enough to burst many people's illusions about the brevity of the war. To Conway the battle was both "a fearful blow" and an opportunity, "the means of rousing this stupid country to the grandest extent and difficulty of the work it has to do." Now, perhaps, people would realize there could be no victory without emancipation. In any case, all residual thoughts of compromising with the "Slave Power" seemed gone forever. "The die is cast," he wrote to Ellen while news of the battle was still coming in. "The blow that has been struck *must* be followed instantly with a heavier one." But even before he knew the battle had been a defeat, he felt no exhilaration over it. The killing had started, while neither peace nor abolition seemed definitely near. He could not tolerate this forever. "I cannot forget that whichever way the battle turns," he told Ellen, "*I* shall have cause to mourn."[26]

In August a new dilemma added to his burden. While in New York to preach at O. B. Frothingham's church he got a telegram offering him a chaplaincy in the brigade of General Schenck, a former member of his Cincinnati congregation. Schenck, who thought he was doing the minister a service, had bruised Conway in an especially sore spot. Conway was of military age, barely twenty-nine when the war began. He was extremely sensitive to any suggestion that he was somehow malingering, doing less for the cause than many young men of anti-slavery convictions who were entering, or would enter, military service. His ministerial background somewhat justified his remaining behind the lines. But the same background did not prevent Thomas Wentworth Higginson from accepting a colonelcy in 1862, or Conway's young disciple and emulator from his Washington days, Gerald Fitzgerald, from enlisting as a private soldier early in the war. His Southern origins could likewise have excused him to some degree; but some Southerners did fight for the Northern side. Conway's Virginia background and family circumstances were powerful factors in dissuading him from military service, but they were probably not in themselves decisive. Rather, they merged with Conway's long-standing revulsion against violence, bloodshed, and death, and that merger made such service impossible. Schenck was putting him in the worst possible position, offering him a job geared to his talents and not requiring him to fight his countrymen, but still making him part of an invading army, the one who said prayers over its soldiers as they went forth to die and kill.[27]

He could never accept such a role. But guilt prevented him from refusing it without a period of brooding. He wrote to Ellen, first explaining its advantages: "This place is honorable and allows many opportunities for doing service to men and to the country. I would have no fighting to do, but much work for the comfort and welfare of the soldiers. . . . The Chaplain's position is equal to the captain of two companies of cavalry." But he closed the letter with a thought that cast a chill over everything else. "His danger is not quite so great perhaps as that of a soldier; unless his camp is routed and then unless he escapes, he taken prisoner, in which case the Virginians would probably not spare *me*. . . ." Then he left it up to Ellen. "Think of it closely and well, my darling, and say all that comes into your heart."[28]

The Confederate army fought according to standard rules of warfare. There was some posturing, then, in Conway's claim that the enemy would not spare him. Yet it was more than that. It was an escape hatch he desperately needed. He had to refuse the appointment, but did not want to be the first to say no. He wanted Ellen to say it, and needed to give her a significant reason for saying it. Of this Ellen was well aware. She knew her husband well and had seen all this before. Even before their marriage Moncure had approached her in similar fashion, toward the end of a long fight over his smoking. He would surely quit, he told her, for he knew he could do so and knew how much it meant to her. He inserted the catch almost parenthetically. He had started smoking "when not in very good health" at the advice of "a fine physician who thought my habits and temperament needed a narcotic occasionally. . . . Before it I was unhealthy—since it healthy." He had given it up, though, for two weeks now, for her—even though "I have had dyspepsia every day since I did so—which I have not had before for eight years." But he would stay a nonsmoker, yes he would, for her—if she still wanted him to.[29]

Ellen knew her husband. She challenged him on many things, but knew when disagreement was useless, even harmful. If she could give him the answer he was fishing for on a seemingly minor issue like tobacco, she could surely give him the answer he required on an issue which touched his innermost doubts and fears. The answer probably came easily to her. It is unlikely she wanted her husband away in the army anyway. Moncure became no chaplain.

He was still a minister, though, and in the fall he returned to Cincinnati, to his family and his church. His congregation was seeing less of him now, however, for the cause came first. Repeatedly he set out on short speaking tours across Ohio, attempting to rally support for the war effort and emancipation. If one's effectiveness can be judged by the attention received from one's enemies, Conway's efforts had effect. At one public meeting he found none other than Congressman Clement Vallandigham, one of the North's most influential Southern sympathizers, in his audience. With satisfaction Conway read the copperhead's Dayton newspaper for reaction to his speech. "It seems to us that about three months in Fort McHenry," snarled Vallandigham, "would have a tendency to improve the gentleman mentally and, for a while at least, rid the community of a nuisance."[30]

As he crisscrossed Ohio sounding the abolitionist trumpet, Conway felt his emotional commitment to his congregation decline. Never, however, did he feel he was moving away from a religious life. He had long regarded reformist agitation as a logical extension of his ministry, and as an intensification of his commitment to a life dedicated to holy causes. "The anti-Slavery movement in America has been a purely religious one," he wrote in 1864. Abolitionists fought "for a real 'idea,' namely, the right of every man to himself. . . ." They made "the greatest sacrifices for this idea, where its denial pressed upon *a race not their own*." And "they rejected all weapons except the legitimate ones of Civilization and Humanity." In their devotion to a cause, their unselfishness, and their humaneness, abolitionists had turned a reform into a religion—one that worked toward social betterment and met the psychic needs of its members as well as any church ever could.[31]

On September 21, a month after Moncure's return to Cincinnati from his Eastern trip, Ellen bore a second son. They named him Emerson. It seemed fitting, almost inevitable, that Conway should give him the name of his own spiritual father, the father who had given him things more precious, he often thought, than had his biological one. There was no comment from Walker Conway about this birth, but the baby's Concord namesake was pleased. "I shall watch the career of this young American with special interest," he wrote, "born as he is under stars and omens so extraordinary, and opening the gates of a new and fairer age."[32]

Still another Conway child, a literary one, saw daylight in the autumn of 1861. Conway had been working on a wartime antislavery tract since the spring. By September his manuscript had reached the length of a short book and was ready for publication. Charles Sumner enlisted in the search for an Eastern publisher, and managed to interest Boston's Walker, Wise and Company. *The Rejected Stone, by a Native of Virginia* appeared in October. One newspaper called it "the *Common Sense* of the present 'revolution.' "[33]

In some ways it was an apt description. *The Rejected Stone* was a magnificent piece of propaganda, termed by *The Liberator* "the most glowing production that has appeared on the War and Slavery since the rebellion broke out." In framing the Constitution, Conway argued, the founders had been forced to leave out the true "corner-stone of the Republic of Man," the stone representing justice. It was up to the present generation to rectify the omission. With intelligence, force, and simplicity, Conway disputed a variety of objections to emancipation and closed with an open letter, respectful but firm, to Lincoln. Emancipation was legal under the war powers granted the president by the Constitution. It was just, considering the harm done by slavery. It was merciful both to slave and South. It was necessary for military success and diplomatic support. Finally, Conway reminded Lincoln "that the people did not place you in office to preserve the Union merely: *that* they had under Fillmore and Buchanan and Pierce. . . ." Rather, by electing a Republican they had "declared that the Union should be administered in the interest of freedom. . . ."[34]

Running through the book were two significant themes. One involved Conway's very plausible interpretation of the secession crisis and war. This conflict, he insisted, reflected a revolution not by the South but by the North. "In fact as far as the *old* Union is concerned, the only arms now defending it are in the South." The old Union meant moral compromise—"that old serpent ever coiling about the tree of life." To restore that meant to ensure an unending procession of crises in the future. The majority of the Northern people, by electing a Republican president, had announced their unwillingness to continue in that old pattern. Fighting for the Union was now just and patriotic, for both morality and common sense indicated that a new kind of Union was being fought for. "WE ARE THE REVOLUTIONISTS," Conway proclaimed. "It was the revolution of the American nation that made this war necessary. The South stands relatively where it always stood. . . ." The Southern revolt was "not a revolution, but a rebellion against the noblest of revolutions. It is a league of confederates against the peaceful and legal evolution of Liberty on this continent. It is an Insurrection against a Resurrection." It was imperative that Northerners understand the dimensions of the revolution they had already made, and muster the courage to see it through.[35]

The other theme weaving through Conway's book was more unique and personal, reflecting the author's own background and needs. A Southerner, his heart was broken as he fought his own brothers, saw his friends on both sides preparing to kill one another. Only a cause with enormous moral content could induce him to support a war against his native land. That cause existed now, if only government and people could be made to see it. Abolition, or the hope of it, was what cemented Conway to the Union cause—and not just because it would uplift the slaves. Certainly it would do that, and would take a terrible burden from the North and its posterity; "but, more than to these or to all others, a decree of emancipation would be MERCIFUL TO THE SOUTH." Passionately Conway described what slavery, "the demon of the South," had bequeathed his native state: "undrained marshes and swamps," "broad and beautiful plains, worn out and desolate," "young men trained to licentiousness and idleness," "eighty-five thousand white adults in Virginia who cannot read or write." He opposed the Southern cause not only for the sake of the slaves but also out of his own deep love for the South, especially Virginia, "withered and wasted by slavery." And yet the terrible fact was that so far, the side he had chosen was betraying him. "Thus far, we stand fighting for as purely a selfish end as the rebels of the South." Bizarrely, at Bull Run the Southerners, more than the Northerners, *"were fighting for their liberty."* Without emancipation, the implication went, this war would represent precisely what Moncure Conway most detested: the arbitrary imposition of one will on another.[36]

The Rejected Stone was published at a propitious time, for it came immediately in the wake of the most serious blow yet to abolitionist hopes for an emancipationist war policy. On August 30 the commanding general of the Western Department, John Charles Fremont, had proclaimed martial law in Missouri and had declared free every rebel-held slave in the state. Conway, enamored of Fremont since 1856, shared in the abolitionist elation. The celebrating, however, soon ended. President Lincoln was unwilling to let a general make policy. More to the point, he was unwilling to let a general alienate conservative support for the war and drive the border states (especially politically shaky and strategically crucial Kentucky) into the Confederacy. On September 11 he revoked the antislavery part of Fremont's order.[37]

The response from abolitionists and antislavery Republicans was outraged and immediate. Garrison, who had been giving Lincoln the benefit of the doubt, publicly denounced his action as "timid, depressing, suicidal," and privately berated the president as "only a dwarf in mind." Conway was profoundly disillusioned at the administration's "execrable and cowardly" behavior. Lincoln "is not the president of the U.S. but of Kentucky," he complained to Horace Greeley (whom he rebuked for the *Tribune*'s mild reaction), lamenting "that we must all be sacrificed to the wretched attitude of that contemptible state." The manuscript of *The Rejected Stone* had already gone to the publisher; otherwise his open letter to the president would have been much harsher. It was too late to change that book, but not too late to begin another, or to go back to the lecture circuit with a message more urgent than ever.[38]

It was also not too late to think about another option. During the secession crisis Conway had thought about traveling to Europe—the first time the written record discloses any interest on his part in going abroad. He had rejected the idea, feeling he was needed in America, whatever the strain on him might be. (It is doubtful he could have afforded the trip anyway.) Now, in the autumn of 1861, his interest in leaving the country revived. His friend William Dean Howells had just received the consulship in Venice as payment for writing a campaign biography of Lincoln. Suddenly that sort of job appealed to him. On the day Fremont's order was revoked, Conway wrote to Howells, asking him how much it paid.[39]

The Fremont episode indicated that a great deal of work still had to be done before the government awoke to the necessity of emancipation, and before public opinion mobilized sufficiently to compel the government to act. After September 1861 Conway, like other abolitionists, escalated his criticism of the administration and stepped up the pace of his own activities. He laid plans for a second, more biting book, organized more and longer lecture tours. Early in December he made a quick trip to Massachusetts, speaking at the Concord town hall on "The Death and Resurrection of Captain John Brown." In January he set out on a month-long tour, his most grueling and triumphant so far.[40]

Conway's reputation was larger now, his audiences more numerous and attentive. Much of this was due to *The Rejected Stone*. It went through three editions, thousands of copies were sent to soldiers at the front, and Conway found it in demand everywhere. In Philadelphia it was "making a huge noise," while in New York, he reported, copies "are sold out here as fast as they come." People were eager to hear the man who wrote with such cogency and passion, someone made doubly interesting by so exotic a background. In Washington he spoke to a distinguished audience (including the Fremonts) at the Smithsonian, and to an overflow crowd at the same church that had banished him in 1856. In Boston he addressed a large enthusiastic gathering at Tremont Temple and a select group of luminaries at the Parker House. In New York twelve hundred people gave him a rousing reception at the Church of the Puritans. The response fortified his spirits despite his dislike of hotel living and separation from his family. "I feel quite lonely," he wrote Ellen from New York, "and can only console myself for being away these bitter nights by knowing that I am doing some work for a great cause and a fearful emergency. . . ."[41]

Probably few of Conway's listeners came away disappointed. As an orator, he was no Wendell Phillips or Henry Ward Beecher. He was too self-conscious to engage in exaggerated mannerisms, and lacked a sure sense of timing. But he was a speaker of considerable talent. His strength lay not in a spellbinding delivery but in a persuasive air of common sense, a mastery of clear and simple Anglo-Saxon English, and an aptitude for building a sustained argument laced with interesting allusions and anecdotes. He understood that he shone to best advantage by simply getting up and talking, by "not cultivating any manner at all." Although in later years he wrote out his speeches, and had always used a manuscript for his sermons, his platform addresses before and during the Civil War were extemporaneous. He worked with a minimum of notes, blending and bolstering his political arguments with captivating stories about slavery and life in Virginia, usually answering questions afterward. "The character for which Mr. C's lectures are celebrated," said the Cleveland *Leader*, was not a style "abounding in rhetorical figures and finely rounded sentences, but . . . that impressive logic which leaves an irradicable [sic] mark upon the mind of the hearer." "Vigorous in thought, not without grace of style, but far more remarkable for pointed and forcible than polished sentences," wrote the *National Anti-Slavery Standard*, "Mr. Conway as a speaker is interesting and impressive, and has a sure hold on an intelligent audience."[42]

Conway attached special urgency to the message he was giving these audiences early in 1862. As yet there had been comparatively little killing, despite Bull Run and a few other small engagements. But it was a new year now. Vast armies had been building and training. In the spring the bloodletting would resume with greater fury. He wanted to stop this if he could. So he dusted off a theory he had used sporadically and made it the centerpiece of his argument. Emancipation, victory, union, and peace all could be had together, and soon. Free the slaves now—universally, without hedging. Once those in bondage understood that the North was fighting for them, they would refuse to work for their masters. The South would be faced with massive disobedience among its black population, ranging from flight to passive resistance to open rebellion. Soldiers would have to be pulled away from the front to guard their homes. Southern resistance would collapse. But to achieve all this, emancipation must come soon. If the administration waited much longer, the South would be too strong, the slaves too wary of Northern promises. This was the "golden hour," and it would not come again.

Conway first gave his "Golden Hour" speech at the Smithsonian on January 17 and was gratified by the reaction. His confidence in his theory grew stronger a few days later in Philadelphia, when he gave the same talk to a small group at the home of William Henry Furness. "Dr. F. & Mrs. L[ucretia] Mott thought it 'in advance even of *The Rejected Stone*,' " he told Ellen, "and if generally heard would 'revolutionize the war.' " On the same day he alerted Emerson to his "new view of this war and how to end it at once . . . I am in dreadful pain with it because it is not publicly recognized, —and I know it is true." He could convince the converted, but that was not enough. He needed to win the public to his idea, the public or the people in power.[43]

He tried. On the morning of January 17 he visited the White House with William Henry Channing, current pastor of the Washington Unitarian church. It was Conway's first meeting with Lincoln, and he was eager to lay out his "golden hour" theory. But Channing, as the older man, spoke first. What he said nearly knocked Conway out of his chair. When asked how emancipation could best be achieved, Channing launched into a discussion of compensated emancipation and showed sympathy for various gradualist schemes. For this Conway was unprepared. He was willing to support compensation as a last resort, provided emancipation was universal and immediate. But he was not in the president's office to talk about that or any other moderate or halfway measure, or to exchange worldly-wise commonplaces about supposed political realities. He was there to plead for peace and freedom, next to which the wallets of slaveholders, the sensitivities of Kentuckians, and the digestion of Democrats were all inconsequential. But he could not bicker with Channing in the president's presence, and Channing's remarks set the tone for the conversation.[44]

When finally he got his chance, Conway asked Lincoln "whether we might not look to him as the coming Deliverer of the Nation from its one great evil." Lincoln said that perhaps they could in the future; at least he would try to see that slavery was put "on the downhill." Conway argued that one could never be sure slavery was going downhill until it was dead; the founders had thought it was declining, but they had proved bad prophets. Finally the president reminded his young critic that an abolitionist moved in a select circle of approving peers, which tended to distort his vision when it came to gauging public opinion. The chief executive, however, had to deal with everyone. From his experience, he said, "the great masses of this country care comparatively little about the negro, and are anxious only for military successes." Clearly Lincoln took Channing more seriously than Conway, whom he regarded as both too radical and too innocent. "Several times" during the discussion, Conway recalled, Lincoln turned to Channing to resume discussion of the latter's "pet idea" of gradual emancipation. Conway barely got a chance to mention his "golden hour" scenario, and what he said made no impression. "I left the White House with a feeling of depression," he remembered. "It was plain to me that . . . though the President felt that slavery should end, he had no notion of any other means of preserving the Union except military force. The idea that peace could be secured by proclaiming freedom seemed to him, I think, a mere religious faith." It seemed clear that Conway would have to change many minds before he could change the president's.[45]

In Boston he had mixed success. A group of writers, reformers, and radical politicians threw a dinner for him at the Parker House on January 28. The guests included Emerson, Lowell, publisher James T. Fields, and Governor John Andrew. All listened respectfully as he talked about his emancipationist ideas and his impressions of Lincoln, whom he described, wrote one listener, as "honest enough, but simply incompetent and without a plan." Not everyone was favorably impressed. Oliver Wendell Holmes, a little out of place anyway in the company of "various unknown dingy-linened friends of progress," thought Conway a bit weird. He had come out of curiosity to hear this "not unfamous [ex-] Unitarian minister of Washington, Virginia-born, with seventeen secesh cousins, fathers, and other relatives," whose "One Path" sermon had caught his attention back in 1856. But while the speaker "talked with a good deal of spirit," he seemed to Holmes to be out of touch with reality. "Speaking of the communication of knowledge among the slaves, he said if he stood on the upper Mississippi and proclaimed emancipation, it would be told in New Orleans before the *telegraph* would carry the news there!" This young radical may have been worth a dinner, Holmes decided, but ultimately, "I don't know that his opinion is good for much."[46]

Emerson's reaction was quite the opposite. In fact, he was so intrigued by Conway's ideas that an interesting role reversal took place: the sage of Concord became the loyal pupil of his young disciple. Either after the dinner or the following day, Conway and Emerson talked about the "golden hour" in the former's hotel room. On January 31 Emerson incorporated Conway's beliefs into a speech he gave at the Smithsonian. He repeated them, explicitly crediting Conway, in an article for the April *Atlantic Monthly*. Once slavery was definitively abolished, wrote

Moncure's father, Judge Walker Peyton Conway (1805–1884), by most measures the most formidable man in Stafford County, and the epitome of the Southern gentry ideal. Courtesy of Houghton, Mifflin and Company, Autobiography, Memories and Experiences of Moncure Daniel Conway (1904)

Moncure's mother, Margaret Daniel Conway (1807–1891), whose emphasis on compassion and feeling provided a crucial alternative model for her son Moncure. Courtesy of Trustees of Columbia University

Moncure's grandfather, John Moncure Conway (1779–1864), for nearly fifty years the clerk of Stafford County, and long a fixture in local society. Courtesy of Trustees of Columbia University

Moncure's uncle, Judge Eustace Conway (1820–1857), a rising star in the Democratic party when cancer killed him prematurely. Courtesy of Trustees of Columbia University

"View of Fredericksburg," 1856 lithograph. Moncure lived in Falmouth, on the opposite bank of the Rappahannock by the bridge at upper right. He and his family attended the simple Methodist church in Fredericksburg, fourth picture from left. Courtesy of Historic Fredericksburg Foundation

Above, Ralph Waldo Emerson (center), whom Conway considered his "spiritual father," shown with Conway's long-time Unitarian ally and mentor, William Henry Furness (right), and Boston writer Gamaliel Bradford. Courtesy of Trustees of Columbia University

Opposite, Moncure Conway, age 21, when a student at Harvard Divinity School. Courtesy of Dickinson College Special Collections

Below, Theodore Parker, radical Unitarian and abolitionist who provided a model for the sort of ministry to which Conway aspired. Courtesy of Trustees of Boston Public Library

Moncure and Ellen Dana Conway, Cincinnati, 1858. Courtesy of Dickinson College Special Collections

Above left, Eliza and Dunmore Gwinn, de facto leaders of the Conway slaves, soon after Moncure helped them settle in Ohio as free people. Courtesy of Antiochiana Collection, Antioch College, Yellow Springs, Ohio

Above right, Moncure's brother Peter (1842–1924), shown with his family in Fredericksburg in later years. Peter was the kind of son his father had always wanted, embracing the terms of his birth as fully as Moncure rejected them. Courtesy of Dickinson College Special Collections

Bottom, Conway labeled this photograph "Our poor little Emerson Conway," who died in 1864 before reaching his third birthday. Courtesy of Trustees of Columbia University

Moncure Conway during the American Civil War. Courtesy of Dickinson College Special Collections

Emerson, "the slaves near our armies will come to us: those in the interior will know in a week what their rights are, and will, where opportunity offers, prepare to take them. Instantly, the armies that now confront you must run home to protect their estates, and must stay there, and your enemies will disappear."[47]

Emerson's support was heartening to Conway, and undoubtedly cemented his conviction that this "golden hour" idea was both crucially important and manifestly correct. But Emerson had no more luck than he in persuading the administration. Back in Cincinnati in February, Conway grew increasingly morose and apprehensive. Armies would start marching soon, and without emancipation "our army must mark its track in human gore and find ashes where cities stood before." Devastation might be necessary, he admitted from his pulpit on February 23. "But . . . in this age of the world no such devastation of human homes and hearts can be justified unless along with it we bear blessings greater than the devastation is evil. . . . It must be something more than mere power which justifies the slaughter of human beings."[48]

In March he dragged himself onto the Northeastern lecture circuit again, giving an average of six speeches a week, duplicating the regimen back in Ohio in April. In Massachusetts his spirits soared when the prestigious house of Ticknor and Fields agreed to publish a book based on the "Golden Hour" speech, and when Sumner and Emerson told him encouraging things about Lincoln's basic antislavery instincts. Sumner even said the president had read *The Rejected Stone*. In Worcester a young officer told him that a copy of *The Rejected Stone* had saved his life by stopping a bullet headed for his heart. "Somebody asked him if it was not the Bible which saved his life," Conway reported. "He says 'no, the Bible wasn't radical enough for that.'"[49]

The flush of optimism was fleeting. On April 6 a large Confederate force fell upon Grant's army in southern Tennessee, pushing it back until it rallied the following day and fought the rebels to a bloody standstill. During the coming weeks, newspapers bulged with casualty lists. Cincinnati hospitals overflowed with wounded. Before long people knew the dimensions of Shiloh. It was the costliest battle fought in North America up to that time. Combined losses were 25,000.

On April 24 Conway wrote to Sumner asking for help. The grind he had been going through was "beginning to tell upon my nervous system and strength"; he needed a rest from all this lecturing and writing, at least for "a year or so." For reasons he did not explain, he had a particular kind of rest in mind. He needed to withdraw from the ranks of actively agitating abolitionists. He did not want to retire to his ministerial duties in Cincinnati. In fact, he did not want to retire to any duties anywhere in America. He wanted to leave the country.[50]

"I had thought some, if Haiti should be recognized of applying for the diplomatic appointment to that country; thinking that my long acquaintance with blacks in Va. might enable me to do that work properly."* Now even that job probably would be too demanding to "bring me much rest, which I need." By implication he wanted a place still further away from reminders of the war. "Is there not some little consulship which will pay a small family's expenses, to be had somewhere, and which the President would give to an antislavery Virginian? I know German enough and French enough to try one almost anywhere." He did not say why the president should give a job to someone who had been criticizing his policies from platforms throughout the country. The point was that he needed a rest. By "rest" he meant a paying job outside America, and there were few available save political ones. It is not clear whether Sumner did anything about Conway's request. The senator was chairman of the Foreign Relations Committee, but his relationship with the president was too intricate and important to jeopardize by pestering him about a diplomatic post for an aggressive young critic. On April 29, after Sumner had failed to answer promptly or satisfactorily, Conway wrote and reminded him of his wish to go abroad. The next day he reminded him again.[51]

Unable to leave the country, Conway was forced to make the best of life within it. But how long could he go on? How long could he tolerate a war which so far epitomized everything he hated: arbitrary coercion, killing and maiming on an unprecedented scale, violence against old friends, neighbors, and family, all utterly devoid of moral purpose? A holy crusade to free the slaves and save the South from itself he could support; a nihilistic bloodbath he could not.

In the spring of 1862 some halting antislavery steps were taken. Lincoln grudgingly acquiesced in emancipation in the District of Columbia and proposed financial aid to any state wishing to abolish slavery gradually. But events in May seemed to show vividly how little could be expected ultimately from the administration. On May 9 David Hunter, commander of the Department of the South, issued a remarkable order freeing all slaves in his jurisdiction (South Carolina, Georgia, and Florida), whether or not they were owned by active rebels. This extraordinary move was Fremont's action writ large, covering much more territory and many more people, and politically far more sweeping. It was, of course, doomed from the start. On May 19 Lincoln revoked it, causing a new round of grimacing in the abolitionist camp. "Our President has again sorely disappointed the antislavery portion of the country," Samuel May told a British correspondent. " . . . It would seem that our Government is smitten with judicial blindness, and is leading us all astray." Conway was less restrained. In July he condemned "the indecent eagerness with which the President hastened to refasten the gyves upon a million human beings whom the noble Hunter had set

* The Senate voted to recognize Haiti on April 4, 1862. The House soon followed, and the president approved the action on June 5. New Hampshire's Benjamin Whidden assumed the post of consul-general in September. See Ludwell Lee Montague, *Haiti and the United States, 1714–1938* (Durham, N.C.: Duke University Press, 1940), 86–87.

free. . . . A million bloodstains crimson your hands, Mr. President; damned spots, which not all the rivers and lakes in America can wash away. . . ."[52]

Conway's mood was darkening as spring gave way to summer and serious fighting resumed in Virginia. Since Shiloh, Ellen had been devoting whatever time she had to nursing wounded soldiers in the crowded hospitals of Cincinnati. "The strain on her was severe," Moncure recalled, and "I also was beginning to drag my harness." The present was a nightmare and the future was a blank—and still he needed that rest. In June he obtained a leave of absence "for some months" from his church, and looked forward to at least a temporary withdrawal from the public eye. At the Western Unitarian Conference in Detroit on June 21, in what was intended to be his last public speech for some time, he put through a resolution which got little debate and no opposition: "Mercy to the South—Death to Slavery."[53]

Probably few people realized the intensity and sincerity of Conway's feelings about "mercy to the South." If they did not understand, it was not Conway's fault. He had stated his position in many ways, on many occasions. In July 1862 he stated it definitively, at length, in his second wartime book—a clarion call and a warning.

Few listened. *The Golden Hour* was commercially less successful than *The Rejected Stone*, even though the same wit and logic permeated its pages. The problem may have been that all its emancipationist arguments had been heard before, and what was left was a highly personal statement for which there was no audience. The abolitionist fraternity read the book and noticed the argument about "a peaceful victory through emancipation," about freeing the slaves and thus forcing the rebels to fall back and guard their homes. But antislavery reviewers gave little attention to the theme trumpeted most loudly and consistently: without emancipation the war was morally bankrupt and utterly unjustifiable. There was a loyalty, Conway wrote, "higher than the banner of the Union—the banner of Liberty." The country seemed numb to that fact. As the killing intensified, the Union grew into a fetish which would not be relinquished regardless of the ghastly cost. "Slavery," he wrote, "is the imposition of one will on another by physical force." Lacking any moral content, this war was rapidly becoming "but the acute form of the same disease."[54]

"The thirst for Southern blood grows," Conway continued, "and presently the North will be demoralized enough to equal the recklessness and spite of Slavery." It was slavery, after all, that had caused this war. But somehow in the grim intensity, even the monstrous exhilaration of the slaughter, that was forgotten. Conway wanted people to remember, and to remember that while they were ignoring their moral duty they were killing fellow Americans and fellow human beings. More, they were killing his own fellow Southerners; and he scorned "the idea that the sorrows which our victorious advance must bring upon the South can be justified by carrying a piece of bunting down there, or the mere governmental authority it represents." He berated Lincoln for neglecting and obstructing abolition, telling him "you have more right to kill an institution that injures man, than you have to kill a man." He pleaded with the Northern people: "True-hearted Northmen, I implore, ere you go further in this butchery, to try if you cannot SAVE the South. . . . Is there in this noon of the nineteenth century so little power of heart and brain that we must yet adhere to the methods of the savage and the assassin?" His question was not rhetorical.[55]

Only later would people see how literally he meant all this, and how deeply he felt it. But it was all there for them to see as early as July 1862. *The Golden Hour* was the nearest thing to a definitive statement of Moncure Conway's feelings about the Civil War once the mass killing had begun. The strain of supporting that as-yet purposeless slaughter had worn him to a frazzle. By the time the book appeared he wondered if he could go on. What he would do after his "leave of absence" he did not know. For now he would rest. Rest. He needed it.

He did not get it.

"I forgot to answer your questions about the servants," Walker Conway wrote his wife late in March 1862. "Frances and her two youngest children went with Mr and the Miss Eustaces and is very much pleased. . . . Nancy and Alfred still occupy their room in our kitchen. . . . Alfred and James Prior cultivate my gardens.—Nancy and Eliza wash for me. . . . Jas Parker works in Fred'g. . . . My servants give me no trouble. They show every disposition to do what they can;—are orderly and obedient . . ." He was in for a shock.[56]

Falmouth and Fredericksburg were in for several. The area changed hands seven times during the war, making it one of the most hotly contested pieces of real estate in the history of North America. Occupied by Confederate troops early in the war, the two towns first fell to Union forces in April 1862. Walker Conway did not dally amid the invaders. Activating a plan made at the beginning of the war, he retreated to the Confederate capital and set up housekeeping in a Richmond boarding-house.[57]

Not everyone had Walker's mobility. Many staunch Confederates had to stay and endure the occupation. One such person was a Mrs. Lacey, whose husband was a rebel officer and whose splendid house ("Chatham," on the Stafford heights across the river from Fredericksburg) had been turned into Union headquarters. Mrs. Lacey seemed quite unreconstructable, telling a New York *Tribune* reporter "she wished that she had two husbands to give to the Rebel cause, and two plantations." But stern as she was, she had to admit the Yankees were taking good care of her property. It was all "uninjured in the least, save by the unaccountable disappearance of 15 or 20 blacks."[58]

Those blacks had plans of their own—as did thousands of their compatriots up and down the Rappahannock. "The stampede of negroes continues with increased numbers," reported the Fredericksburg *Christian Banner* on April 24. "They are going, going, and will soon all be gone." They did not know where they would go, exactly. But from their first glimpse of a blue uniform they knew they would not stand still. In Stafford the slaves were moving, and in Spotsylvania, Caroline, Louisa. Early in July the *Christian Banner* lamented that "facts which occur every hour in our midst convince all of the utter disloyalty of the slave population of our country." "Loyalty" was in the eye of the beholder. But the Conway slaves, like many others, did not waste time philosophizing about that. They left.[59]

In May, Walker Conway wrote his wife a letter (now lost) which Margaret forwarded to Moncure. It was full of "gloom." The "servants" who had been so "orderly and obedient" several weeks earlier had shown their true colors and scattered. Moncure was jubilant, glorying "in the visible presence of God's angel down there jarring open the prison-doors of those poor blacks. . . . I shall not wonder at seeing them in Cincinnati, where they shall not want a friend." Soon he persuaded an acquaintance, artist Oriel Eaton, to donate some land in Yellow Springs for the use of Conway fugitives. He took up a collection to help pay their transportation. Then all he could do was wait.[60]

He waited for two months, anxiety over the fate of his black companions exacerbating an already darkening mood. In July he took his family to the Eatons' summer cottage at Yellow Springs where their longed-for vacation was to begin. On July 13 he was in the middle of a chess game when a letter came from his sister. "*All* our negroes who are not hired in Richmond have taken to their heels," Mildred reported. "I am glad you seem to know what to do for them. . . . I haven't the faintest idea who to write to in Washington or how to get a message to them,— I suppose most of them will stop there for quite a good while yet. . . ." The news was sketchy, but it was all Conway needed. Interrupting chess game and vacation, he caught the next train east.[61]

For two days he traveled on stifling soldier-packed trains, arriving in Washington at noon on July 15. With the help of William Henry Channing he contacted people in the local black community, and by the end of the day had located Dunmore and Eliza Gwinn. This couple had not, he discovered, "sustained the prophecies of helplessness and suffering so glibly made" about emancipated blacks. They "had set up a small cake-and-candy store, taken in washing, and managed . . . to save up in money more than $60." The Gwinns, however, had always been the cream of the Conway slaves—literate, quick, resourceful. Conway had more cause for concern about the others, and of their whereabouts the Gwinns knew little.[62]

It began to look as though Conway would have to extend his search to Stafford County itself. On July 16, after shuffling from office to office in the dark nooks and crannies of the Washington bureaucracy, he obtained a pass from General James Wadsworth "to go to Falmouth and return on Government Boat and R.R. Train." But that night, as he lay in bed in his room, Conway began to feel edgy about this trip. His pass said nothing about transporting blacks. He lacked evidence that anyone could be found near Falmouth. He probably had no taste for the encounters he might have with pro-Confederate townspeople. Finally, there was still one established freedman in the Washington suburb of Georgetown who might know something, whom Conway had not yet consulted: Benjamin Williams, the fugitive he and Theodore Parker had looked for in Boston in 1853. Williams was active in the underground railroad, and if he did not know where the Conway slaves were, he at least would know others who might. It was late at night and rain was coming down in torrents, as it had been for two days. But suddenly Conway was certain that he must not leave without seeing Williams. He kicked off the covers, threw on his clothes, and walked out into the storm.[63]

It was a five-mile walk. No cab would take him because of the violent weather. For hours he slogged through darkness, wind, mud, flooded streets, his body soaked by the downpour. In the early morning hours he crossed the bridge into Georgetown, following the same roads that once had led him to his Methodist circuit. When he reached the black shantytown he was momentarily stymied by the dark. In one home, though, a light was shining. It seemed to be Williams's house. As Conway drew near he heard singing. He knocked. The singing stopped. An eerie, tense silence. He knocked again. "Who is that?" someone yelled. "A friend!" came the answer, "Moncure Conway." A novelist could not have invented it. The doors flung open. There, whooping and clapping, were Walker Conway's slaves.[64]

Or most of them—a few weeks later Conway said the total was thirty-one. They had been trickling in for the last several days, men, women, and children, a few so recently they were still wet from the storm. They had come fifty or sixty miles through territory unknown to most of them, knowing only that this was the way to freedom. Even James Parker was there, Walker's faithful valet, the man who had made several trips to Baltimore and had always come back, but who would not go back anymore. They would all be free now, by their own decree, even if the president denied it. For now, they huddled in this little house on the edge of the capital, gathering strength from one another and their white Virginia friend. They listened in awe as he told them of their promised land in the West. Together they sat through the stormy night, talking, singing, praying, until dawn.[65]

Conway's troubles were just beginning. He still had to get the slaves to Ohio and he faced all sorts of legal and logistical problems. Technically these people were fugitive slaves. Even if nobody was eager to return them to Virginia, it would still be difficult to transport them all to a free state. The railroads were especially touchy about the whole matter, usually asking $3,000 in security for every black going north lest they be sued some day by an owner for aiding the escape of his property. Even if the railroad cooperated, Baltimore might not, and on the way to Ohio one had to go through that volatile, deeply divided city. Worse, one had to change trains there and travel some distance through city streets to a different station. A Massachusetts regiment had learned about the perils of this journey at the very start of the war. A mob had attacked it on its march from station to station, causing seventeen deaths.

Official Washington was not eager to help. After being stalemated elsewhere (including, apparently, at the White House), Conway appealed to Treasury Secretary Chase, an antislavery sympathizer and former law partner of Conway's friend George Hoadly. Chase could give Conway no authority to take the slaves to Ohio: that would have to be between him and the railroad, perhaps even between him and the ticket agent in Baltimore. Chase did give him a letter to General Wool, the commander at Baltimore's Fort McHenry, authorizing Wool to supply military aid if Conway needed it in transporting "his father's slaves" through the city. It was not clear just how useful the letter was. It applied only if trouble seemed imminent, and Fort McHenry was far from the area Conway was worried about. But it was the best Chase could do.[66]

Charles Sumner called a meeting of sympathizers to discuss ways of getting the slaves safely west. There might be problems with the railroad, and nobody had any sure means of solving them. The more dangerous problem was Baltimore. After much inconclusive talk, one man made the innovative suggestion that Conway pose as a slaveholder. "You buy fifty feet of rope," he said, "and tie every buggar's hands behind him, and all Baltimore will bow down to you. They will be sure you are a big slaveholder, taking your slaves through Baltimore into Harford County, to keep them from being freed in Washington." Evidently Conway considered the suggestion, finally rejecting it as too bold to carry off. No, they would walk through Baltimore unbowed.[67]

Late in July, nearly two weeks after his arrival in the capital, Conway set out from Washington with his entourage. Before long they were plunked down in the streets of Baltimore, laden with baggage, the perilous cross-city trek ahead of them. As expected, they could get no omnibus to take them to the other station. They would get no favors. They would have to walk. They began. An angry crowd gathered, although not the sort of crowd they expected. It was a crowd of blacks, angry because they thought their fellows were being taken from Washington to a place where slavery was still safe: the thought expressed by the man in Sumner's room had been borne out in an unforeseen way, without benefit of the fifty feet of rope. For a brief moment black onlookers menaced and sneered. Suddenly the mood changed. Conway slaves whispered to the crowd. Sneers turned to shouts of joy. Baltimore blacks hurriedly produced wagons for Conway's group. Within minutes they were moving across the city in a massive, gleeful, triumphant procession.

It backfired. The procession drew more attention to Conway and his charges. Now another crowd began forming, bigger, uglier, whiter. By the time they reached the station, three hours before the train was to leave, the Conwayites and their escort confronted a hostile mob of whites easily capable of overwhelming them.

Immediately Conway took the slaves into the waiting room. A furious clerk chased them out. Conway asked for any room at all. He offered to pay. He asked if they could wait in the railroad car. It was all useless. They had to stand in the street. But there was precious little street left to stand in. The mob grew thicker and bolder. It pressed forward until it had pinned Conway and the slaves in a little semicircle against the wall of the station. Policemen stood around, doing nothing. The taunts intensified. Conway concentrated on keeping frustrated black men from retaliating. Finally he remembered the letter to General Wool. It could do them no good if the mob really wanted to demolish them. Wool was in Fort McHenry. They and his letter were here in the street with the mob. Still, it couldn't hurt. Theatrically he took it from his pocket and waved it at the crowd. He was determined to take these people through, he shouted, "though it should bring the guns of Fort McHenry upon the city." It worked. Impressed by the little document, the mob's ringleaders moved their people back. But nobody left the scene. Everyone stayed, less menacing but just as abusive, keeping up their taunts and obscenities, waiting to see what happened next.[68]

It was the ticket agent's turn. This poor functionary had been watching the proceedings and undoubtedly would have loved to have been somewhere else. But he had a job to do, so he opened his window for business. His first customer was the man he was afraid it would be, asking what he was afraid he would ask. He wanted passage to Cincinnati for himself and over thirty blacks. "I can't let those negroes go on this road at any price," the ticket agent snapped. Conway produced the letter to General Wool and confidently laid it on the counter. It didn't seem to have very much to do with the railroad, but Conway acted as if it did. The agent read it carefully. Something besides the threat of military force impressed him. "The paper says these are your father's slaves," he said incredulously. "They are," Conway replied. The agent looked at him as though he were from Mars. He asked him, "Don't you know you could sell them in Baltimore for a lot of money?" "Possibly." The agent had seen enough. He was no friend to abolitionists, but he knew a brave and honest man when he saw one. "By God, you shall have every car on this road, if you want it." The agent sold Conway the tickets and personally escorted the whole group to a car they would have to themselves. Then he returned to his ticket window, content in having rewarded someone for making a great financial sacrifice.[69]

For over an hour they sat in the car with the blinds drawn. Outside the crowd dispersed. Darkness gathered. At dusk the train moved out. The slaves did not speak. Only children slept. They were getting closer, closer. But they were not yet safe. This was still a slave state. At every little stop, fists clenched and hearts pounded. Would they be ordered off? Would they fail when they were so close? The night deepened. Hours passed. Still the only sounds were the whistling and belching and lurching of the train. Another stop. The slaves peered into windows. Most saw only mocking reflections in the glass. One caught the name of the place. It was just a tiny wooding-up station. Conway had never heard of it. But when the name was spoken the freedmen began to shout and clap and leap from their seats. They knew this place. It was their business to know. This was Ohio. They were free.

The resettling of the freedmen had a startling and drastic effect on Conway's flagging spirits. The episode could not have been better timed. At the point when he was feeling most ineffectual and helpless, Conway found a means of accomplishing something concrete for the antislavery cause: he could not save four million slaves, but he could save thirty-three. More than that, the perilous journey through Baltimore must have served to assuage any lingering suspicions Conway (or anyone else) might have had about the connection between his noncombatant status and his courage. In June a beaten man, in August he was a crusader reborn.

Leaving the freedmen in Yellow Springs, Conway went to Boston to tell his story at the abolitionists' annual First of August celebration. His performance was breathtaking, making the most of the drama intrinsic to his story. New England abolitionists do not seem to have been aware of the extent of Conway's earlier depression. They knew only that he was a talented, deeply committed young man with a flair for plain speaking and a unique set of credentials. *The Rejected Stone* and *The Golden Hour* had deepened their respect for him. The freedmen episode cemented it. After the First of August festivities they offered him a job.[70]

The job was co-editor of a new antislavery weekly to be published in Boston. Conway accepted enthusiastically and at once. Here was an opportunity to share his message with a wide audience on a regular basis. More, it was a chance to be close to the Boston and Concord people he loved and to dabble in literature again. By the end of August, arrangements were set. George Stearns would put up the money. Frank Sanborn, Conway's old Harvard acquaintance and fellow disciple of Emerson, would be his co-editor. Everything was sealed at a jovial dinner at the Revere House on August 28, "where we had Sumner, [Senator Henry] Wilson, Gov. Andrew and champagne." He told Ellen that the paper would start immediately. The family would resettle at once. "Paper's name *The Commonwealth*."[71]

CHAPTER 8

In September 1862 the Conways settled in Concord, Massachusetts. Moncure would have to commute daily to the Bromfield Street offices of the Boston *Commonwealth*, but it did not matter. It was worth any inconvenience to make his home among the Concord sages, depleted now by the recent death of Thoreau, yet still distinguished enough to cause Moncure to revel in his good fortune. Having sunk to their lowest ebb in midsummer, his spirits had been rising ever since. Now occupying a position of influence amid a large circle of congenial friends and colleagues, Conway began to feel that he could get through this war and perform some real service in the process. If anything could lift him out of his depression and restore his sense of usefulness, it was work in Boston and residence in Concord.

His more hopeful state of mind was clear from a purchase he made as soon as his family moved east: the Barzillai Frost house, a large two-story, four-thousand-dollar home (now 235 Main Street) near the Concord railroad depot. He had first arrived at that depot less than a decade before, a confused and restless young student on a nervous pilgrimage to his spiritual father. His pilgrimage had taken him far since that day, but Concord had stayed remarkably the same. It was as though this special little village had been biding its time, waiting patiently for Conway to come to it, as it knew he eventually must. The house in Concord was the first Conway ever owned. He was there to stay. He felt confident he would be happy there among the Peabodys, Ripleys, Channings, Thoreaus (minus Henry), Sanborns. Emerson was just a short walk away, as close to him now as his biological father was distant. It all looked very promising. Concord would be home.[1]

Home did not mean peace and quiet. There was work to do. Twenty thousand copies of *The Commonwealth*'s first issue rolled off the presses on September 6, followed on September 13 by fifty thousand copies of the second. It was an impressive paper. Professional and literate, *The*

Commonwealth immediately established itself as a leading independent voice for the antislavery cause. The first issue contained speeches by Sumner and Fremont, extracts from the British press, and the famous August exchange between Lincoln and Greeley in which the president said his actions for or against slavery would be determined solely by their effectiveness in saving the Union. The lead editorial pushed for immediate emancipation and the raising of black troops, contending "a black patriot is better than a white traitor." It proclaimed the paper's loyalty to the Union cause, but warned, "loyalty does not mean to encourage fatuity and wrong in the government we would preserve."[2]

Although Sanborn's contribution was not unimportant, in its early stages *The Commonwealth* was primarily Conway's paper. Briefly his name even appeared as sole editor, a circumstance which may have been less inadvertent than it later was announced to have been. Free copies of *The Rejected Stone* and *The Golden Hour* went to anyone buying a two-year subscription. Conway's rhetoric ran unmistakably through most of the political articles—causing an editor of the New York *Independent* to complain of the new weekly's "tendency to use allusions or illustrations too trivial or humorous, and thus to jangle." Conway's interest in the paper's more literary side was also manifest from the start. George Stearns's son later credited Conway (whom he disliked) with giving "a finer literary quality to *The Commonwealth* than any other journal in Boston could brag of." By April 1863 the paper had printed contributions by, among others, Harriet Beecher Stowe, O. B. Frothingham, Lydia Maria Child, Julia Ward Howe, David Wasson, Elizabeth Peabody, Bronson Alcott, and Louisa May Alcott ("Hospital Sketches," her first significant publication).[3]

Conway's stamp was on *The Commonwealth* in yet another way. The paper consistently advocated sympathy and understanding for the Southern people. "We shall advocate mercy to the misguided South," wrote Conway on September 6, "chiefly the mercy which will relieve them forever from that which has maddened them, whilst it has corrupted thousands of hearts in the North—American Slavery. . . ." Northerners must not hate the South, Conway kept insisting; they must not lose perspective and grow hungry for Southern blood. If Northerners judged the South "by the violence and deadly hate of its men and women for Yankees," he wrote in late October, "let them think how we should feel if an armed soldiery stood in Boston or New York. . . ." And again, as always, he returned to his old theme: "Our conviction is, that so soon as the Northern people withdrew all their hatred from the people of the South, adding what they withdraw to their hatred of the infernal institution which has barbarized and maddened the South, so soon will their real foe appear. It is Slavery and Slavery alone. . . ."[4]

"*The Commonwealth* is full of life and power," wrote Robert Collyer justly, and what was true of the newspaper was true of its editor. Conway was buoyed by this new post. He was in the thick of things now, laboring for the cause on a daily basis. For the first time his antislavery work did not take him away from his family for long periods. He still lectured, but usually just in the surrounding region. On the lecture platform, too, he seemed to have regained the old energy. He spoke with power he had lost only a few months earlier. One person who heard him in New Bedford in November was thrilled by the performance, pronouncing it "grand and electric—and universally liked." Not only were Conway's spirits higher, his audiences were warmer. The country seemed more and more ready for emancipation.[5]

The times seemed to be changing. Surely the most dramatic sign was Lincoln's promulgation of the preliminary Emancipation Proclamation on September 22, only two weeks after the birth of *The Commonwealth*. Since July the president privately had been convinced that emancipation was necessary to save the Union. He waited for a Northern victory before announcing the policy, lest abolition be interpreted as an act of desperation taken from a position of weakness. The battle of Antietam (September 17) gave him the occasion he needed. Under the terms of the Proclamation, all slaves in areas still in rebellion as of January 1, 1863, would be "then, thenceforward and forever free."

The Proclamation was not everything abolitionists wanted. It did not address the issue of slavery in the border states, and exempted certain areas already under Northern occupation. It left the door open to slavery's continuance in any state which ceased rebellion before January 1, and in its pragmatism failed to stress the moral question involved in emancipation. Finally, it applied largely to those areas over which the Northern government still had no control, no power to make the Proclamation stick. Although these objections later would seem increasingly important to many abolitionists, immediately after the September announcement their rejoicing was general. Most noteworthy was not what the administration had refused to do, but rather what it had done. It had taken a bold, undebatably major step toward ending slavery in America. If it was less than what abolitionists favored, it was far more than what most had been expecting. *The Commonwealth* shared the widespread euphoria when it praised "this noble voice of your President." Its headline hailed the "Great Victory at Washington; 1863 the year of Jubilee!"[6]

There was much for Conway to be happy about: fulfilling and exciting work, a more stable home life, the company of friends, the sight of the government moving toward emancipation. Still, his happiness was never quite complete. There was still one problem. The war was still on. The killing continued, escalating to more grisly and unforeseen heights. Antietam was the worst yet, worse even than Shiloh. Conway's friend William Henry Furness visited the battlefield soon after the fight and decided to write a piece for *The Commonwealth* about what he had seen. What started as a descriptive article for public consumption quickly evolved into a personal letter to Conway, a passionate antiwar statement written to one person Furness knew would understand:

> . . . Hundreds of dead rebels still remained unburied. In their blackened and swollen forms, not the mother that bore them could recognize a familiar lineament. But for their clothes, we could scarcely have admitted the disgusting objects to be human beings. —I looked up to the mountains, which have always inspired me with feelings akin to their own lofty magnificence, and experienced a keen sense of shame that I belonged to a race which had thus abused its maker's gifts. The horrors of an actual battlefield, the still more moving scenes of the hospitals, have intensified my detestation of war, to such a degree that I admit no evil comparable to it.[7]

Furness could have found no person more sympathetic to his feelings than the editor of *The Commonwealth*. To Conway the carnage seldom had been tolerable, justifiable only if it paved the way for total emancipation. At least Antietam had enabled Lincoln to issue the preliminary Proclamation. The battle then had some meaning. The butchery had some shred of moral content. Now, as the casualties mounted astronomically, it was important there be no backsliding, no stalling. The movement toward abolition must proceed quickly and steadily. There must be no more idle, meaningless slaughter. After the events of September, Conway seems to have been persuaded that the worst might be over. The administration might really be moving toward making emancipation its central war aim. The killing might be minimized, the war somehow cut short. For two months his hopes outweighed his fears. Until Fredericksburg.

During the late summer and early autumn, Fredericksburg enjoyed a respite from the maddening presence of the Union army. Lee's invasion of Maryland had forced the occupying troops to pull back to protect Washington. The reprieve was brief. After Antietam the armies moved back into Virginia. The region around Stafford County braced itself for more trouble. It got it. On November 17 General Ambrose Burnside and the Army of the Potomac appeared on Stafford Heights and occupied Falmouth. The other side of the Rappahannock, however, would not be so easily taken this time. There, on Marye's Heights just behind Fredericksburg, was Lee.

After nearly a month of uneasy confrontation, Burnside began to act. On December 11 he ordered Fredericksburg flattened by a cannonade. The town had been evacuated, but a few lingering civilians were killed anyway. To some terrified slaves the bombardment and resulting fires seemed to mean "the judgment day had come." In their fright, they told Moncure Conway soon afterward, "they almost prayed for the rocks and mountains to fall upon them." To an enraged John Moncure Daniel, watching the spectacle from Lee's headquarters, "it was a 'symphony of hell,'" reminding him of "the pictures of Moscow burning." The next day gave him more cause for fury. Northern troops moved across pontoon bridges into the town and savagely vandalized what was left of it.[8]

If Burnside had been ordered to stage a nihilistic, meaningless bloodbath, he could not have done better than what he did next. On the freezing cold morning of December 13 he put the bulk of his attacking force on a bare, six-hundred-yard-long plain between the town and the formidable Confederate fortifications on Marye's Heights. Then he sent it on a suicidal frontal assault. The troops formed in columns of four and moved out elbow-to-elbow across the open ground, drums beating, flags waving. Cannon ripped into them first. Then rifle fire. Six times the Yankees came on and six times they were butchered. Lee's position was impregnable and the attackers never came close. Most of them probably either fell or retreated without ever having fired a shot. The Union army suffered 12,000 casualties that day, the Confederates less than half that number—and most of the latter were lost in a secondary action downstream. The ignominious history of warfare records few more idiotic wastes of human life.

Two days after the battle the Union troops abandoned Fredericksburg and moved back across the Rappahannock to Falmouth and the Stafford Heights. Conway House became a field hospital. The house was almost bare. Soldiers had made short work of whatever the family had not removed. Now in place of furniture lay a carpet of wounded and dying men. Walt Whitman came down from New York and went through the house searching for his wounded brother. He did not find him. What he did find was grisly, so macabre a contrast to the life the house had previously known as to seem barely plausible. The yard where Moncure had played was covered with rows of corpses and piles of amputated limbs. The room where Moncure had slept was filled with the smell of gore and the strangled cries of dying soldiers.[9]

The army did not leave Stafford County for another six months. During its stay it did not behave graciously. The civilized and generous spirit of the earlier occupation was gone, a shift symbolized by the burning and looting of Fredericksburg. As one historian has written: "The war was changing. . . . It had reached a point now where the fighting of it was turning loose some unpleasant emotional drives. . . . The people here in Virginia had become aliens, and their land was strange and foreign, and therefore subject to hate." The hate was reciprocated. From his Richmond refuge Walker Conway looked with deepening bitterness on the "merciless and infidel invaders." "The Yankee is an outrage on humanity—a crime against civilization," wrote another Stafford native. "The war he wages is a sin against God as well as a tyranny to man."[10]

The battle of Fredericksburg and its aftermath meant many things to Moncure Conway. It meant the intersectional hatred he had hoped to forestall could not be held back. It meant the mindless killing was going forward on its own momentum, unconnected to any deeper moral purpose. It brought the war's brutality home to him as probably nothing else could, by turning his picturesque boyhood haunts into a vast slaughterhouse and by making refugees of many old friends and neighbors. It renewed his old fears about being able to carry on his work, continue to stomach the carnage and support the war against his homeland to its conclusion. We know few details about Conway's life during the two months after Fredericksburg, for during that period he wrote comparatively little, publicly or privately. Increasingly *The Commonwealth* bore Sanborn's stamp. Perhaps Conway wrote little because he could not write much: the fight had gone out of him again. We know one thing for certain. Fredericksburg ended Conway's five-month respite from depression. After Fredericksburg, he changed.

His melancholy and nervousness increased as the casualty figures came steadily in. On December 21 he visited publisher James T. Fields, where he found Oliver Wendell Holmes and the elder Henry James. Holmes was "unusually pleasant," for he had just learned his son had gone through the battle unharmed. Conway could not share his relief. As he discussed the fighting with these men he could feel nothing but emptiness and hurt. He went home to bed, but had trouble sleeping. When he finally did sleep, he was haunted by violent dreams. In one, Senator Wilson of Massachusetts fought a duel with a shadowy, unnamed Kentuckian—a man from a border slave state which had supplied many men to both sides. The combatants paced off the distance between them, turned and fired. They killed each other.[11]

With this disturbed state of mind Conway greeted the first day of 1863, when the Emancipation Proclamation took effect. Even in his depression, he knew that this occasion, however incomplete, was worth celebrating. He chose to mark it with the black people of Boston. Late on December 31 he walked to the African meetinghouse on Joy Street on the back side of Beacon Hill. The eighteen-year-old daughter of William Lloyd Garrison was with him. The church was packed, mostly with blacks keeping a vigil until midnight. "Some say the President will back down from his Proclamation," roared the preacher, "but brethren and sisters, we've come here to watch and see that he don't back down." He continued for a long time, with rising emotion, his words punctuated by fervent "Amens" and ecstatic cries of "Glory!" "The Old Serpent is abroad tonight, with all his emissaries," he warned. "His wrath is great, because he knows his hour is near. He will be in this church this evening. . . . But, brethren and sisters, don't be alarmed. Our prayers will prevail. His head will be bruised. His back will be broken. He will go raging to hell, and God Almighty's New Year will make the United States a true land of freedom." As midnight approached, Conway knelt with the rest of the congregation and experienced a scene he was likely never to forget.[12]

A few minutes before twelve, he heard a hiss at the back of the church. Barely audible at first, it grew louder and more insistent. Other congregants took it up until it filled the building with "hisses so entirely like those of huge serpents that the strongest nerves were shaken." "He's here!" people cried. "He's here!" It was the devil, raging and roaring, wrestling with freedom to the end. He lost. The hisses had their way only until the stroke of twelve. Then they mingled with bells tolling from nearby steeples. Everyone strained to listen. Suddenly the devil was gone. People could hear only the bells. The jubilant congregation erupted in a chorus of "Blow ye the trumpet, Blow." "Fanny G. and I were moved enough to cry and joined hands," Conway wrote just afterward, "singing at [the] top of our voices."[13]

It was a night of triumph. But whose? The black people at the Joy Street church knew who the devil was and what he was up to. Their own duties and choices were equally clear. It had seemed that way for Conway too, at the start of the war. The war—by now longer and costlier than anyone had anticipated—had changed that. It had brought him face to face with the reality of his own conflicting loyalties. It had presented him with a choice between the things which most appalled and terrified him. He had spent nearly the last decade opposing slavery, the arbitrary imposition of one will on another. When the war started he embraced it as a means of putting a stop to that atrocity against human autonomy. Yet the war had not been a quick, clean moral crusade. It had turned into a bloody, protracted war of reconquest, a quarrel over a flag, a struggle against a people's autonomy. He had repudiated the Southern social system but had never ceased to love the place and its people. That love often had been submerged. It had a way of surfacing now, as he watched the breakup of his family, the impoverishment of old neighbors, the devastation of his native ground. On top of all that, this war which had so betrayed its promise had killed many thousands on both sides. If there was anything that horrified Conway more than psychological and moral domination, it was physical violence and bloodshed. There had been so much of the latter that it was getting harder and harder to justify it under any circumstances. Such were his thoughts in the days after he left Joy Street. It had been simple once, and for some it still was. For Conway it was not simple anymore.

Soon *The Commonwealth* was reflecting his doubts. The government was attacking slavery with a rifle butt, he argued on January 10. "Without lacking faith in the butt of the gun, one can't help wishing the sure thing—a minie bullet from the front end." The Proclamation did not go far enough. It was morally suspect for leaving slavery intact in the border states. The government had yet to prove it had the will to enforce it whenever the rebel states were subdued. This war could only be justified as an antislavery crusade. The Proclamation was a first, hesitant step. "But the true fight is only begun."[14]

Increasingly *The Commonwealth* was diverging from the more venerable antislavery weekly published a few blocks away. *The Liberator* was becoming downright patriotic. Garrison had gloried in the gore of Fredericksburg with a gusto which must have made Conway wince. "Never was death more nobly laughed to scorn—never did patriots shed their blood more lavishly in defense of their country's integrity and perpetuity." As for the Proclamation, it was all *The Liberator*'s editor needed to think slavery defeated and Lincoln a savior. "The Proclamation is as life from the dead," wrote Garrison. "True, the work is not ended. The War of Independence had not ceased when Independence was declared. But it seems impossible now that any other result should happen than the extinction of the slaveholding class, and the elevation of black and white to one level and one destiny." "You will see by the papers how we accept 'the Proclamation,' " abolitionist Sarah Pugh told two English friends, "that is variously, depending on the temperament as well as on the principles of the individual."[15]

In late January a group of abolitionists whose temperaments clashed with Garrison's enthusiasm visited Washington. Among them were Wendell Phillips, George Stearns, Elizur Wright, and Moncure Conway. On the morning of January 25 Conway addressed "a large assembly" of legislators and their guests in the Senate chamber. He told his audience the war had gone wrong. God had a plan, he said, and the country was abusing it. The war was meant to end slavery totally and immediately, but somehow not enough people understood. "It is a terrible error when men have one idea about that which they are doing, while God has another. So long as there is that discrepancy between the workman and the builder, the workman will be cutting his hands with his own tools, as this nation has been doing for two years." Slavery must end now. The war must be directed wholly toward that goal. Otherwise it was a travesty of God's intentions and a disgrace to those waging it, for "no result less grand than that freed deliverance would be worth one-millionth of the cost and dreadful outlay we have already paid for it."[16]

In the evening the delegation visited the White House, ushered into the president's office by a weary clerk who muttered something about "that Boston set." The group quickly discovered that Lincoln was tired of the "Boston set" too. Phillips expressed doubts that the Proclamation was being enforced rigorously. The president retorted that all their lives abolitionists had been "working in minorities, and may have got into a habit of being dissatisfied." When the delegation showed its unanimous resentment of this remark Lincoln added testily, "At any rate it has been rare that an opportunity of 'running' this Administration has been lost." Phillips restored some civility to the exchange by telling Lincoln that abolitionists would help "run" him into another term in office if they were sure of his commitment to rid the whole country of slavery. "Mr. Phillips," came the response, "I have ceased to have any personal feeling or expectation in that matter.—I do not say I never had any—so abused and borne upon as I have been."[17]

Talk moved to specifics. Some in the delegation urged appointment of antislavery generals to key positions. Lincoln argued it was more important for men in such positions to know how to win battles. They asked him to reinstate Fremont, who had no command. He firmly refused. Conway (George Stearns soon told Emerson) suggested to the president "that the morality, intelligence and patriotism of New England now sustained his administration, and would continue to give him its support, only as long as it had confidence in the vigor of the Govt." It was a more pragmatic argument than the "golden hour" scenario he had tried to get across to Lincoln a year earlier. Conway knew better now what sort of line was likely to be taken seriously. Besides, the golden hour was long gone now, dead as corpses on the plain of Fredericksburg. But Lincoln was no more impressed with Conway's thoughts than he had been the year before. When the meeting ended Conway was sure the president, however personally antislavery he might be, would move further against the institution only grudgingly and when forced to do so. He went back to Boston, he recalled, "with a conviction that the practical success of the Emancipation Proclamation was by no means certain in the hands of its author."[18]

Shortly after the Washington trip—perhaps on the journey home— Conway spoke to Phillips and Stearns about leaving the country. The Washington visit marked the measure of his powerlessness, the depth of his disillusion, the limit of his capacity to bear it all. He had had enough. Yet he did not put it this way to his colleagues. He would go to England, he told them, and spend some months working to rally British public opinion to the antislavery cause. As a Virginian he could do valuable work there, where so many labored under illusions about the benevolence of the Southern social system. In fact he could serve the cause well there and fully intended to do so. But it was not the whole story. He had had similar urges at other moments of depression over the war: the squelching of Fremont's proclamation, the battle at Shiloh. But now his depression had reached a new dimension, with the increased savagery of the fighting and the end of his hopes for an outright moral crusade. So, with heightened determination and unflagging persistence, he revived his old idea about going abroad. He would not degrade himself this time in the futile quest for a diplomatic post. He would leave as an abolitionist with a mission, subsidized by his friends. Both Phillips and Stearns liked his proposal. He got one hundred dollars from each.[19]

During the next two months Conway solicited aid from a number of friends and colleagues, in person and by letter. By the middle of March he had raised enough money that his trip seemed assured. He told Emerson privately he intended to sell his house. What Ellen and the children would do was not clear; presumably they would move in with friends or relatives if the house were sold before Moncure's return. To Emerson and others, Conway's plans seemed a trifle precipitous and mysterious. Some questioned, Sanborn conceded, "the expediency of Mr. Conway's going abroad at this juncture, maintaining that his labors are needed at home more than there." But Conway's determination was clear, his zeal unquestioned, and for the most part his acquaintances supported his plans.[20]

The whiff of mystery some detected was not imaginary. For one thing, the need for such a mission seemed less urgent than Conway's own desire to go. Anglo-American relations had been strained early in the war, first by the Northern blockade, then (May 1861) by Britain's recognition of the South's belligerent status. In December a real war scare erupted when a Northern naval vessel stopped a British mail steamer in the Caribbean and removed two civilian passengers: James Murray Mason and John Slidell, Confederate emissaries bound for London and Paris, respectively, to plead for recognition of their government. (Ultimately the Lincoln administration gave in to British protests and sent the Southerners on their way.) The situation had remained tense through much of 1862. Confederate victories made British recognition a real possibility, while Washington's slowness in moving against slavery made it hard for antislavery Britons to view the contest as a fight between right and wrong. The serious threat of British intervention had palpably faded, however, after the Southern reverse at Antietam and the North's issuance of the Emancipation Proclamation. In November 1862 Palmerston's cabinet rejected Confederate recognition. "The United States affair," wrote Gladstone, "has ended."[21]

To be sure, British public opinion was still divided and British antislavery groups were clamoring for a lecture tour by an American abolitionist. But they were not asking for Conway, who was little known outside the United States. They wanted a long-established leader in the movement, preferably Wendell Phillips. Even as Conway's plans coalesced and became widely known, abolitionists on both sides of the Atlantic viewed his trip as a side event, in no way fulfilling the long-standing wish to have a major American antislavery activist abroad. In March 1863 Garrison was still trying in vain to persuade the Anglophobic Phillips to go, and was urging Theodore Tilton, G. W. Smalley, and Sidney Howard Gay to bring their "influence to bear upon his mind." Garrison told Oliver Johnson that if Phillips refused, the equally reluctant Gerrit Smith should be urged to make the trip. "Use all power of persuasion with Phillips to go," he wrote, "and I will do all I can to get Smith to change his mind." Only as an afterthought did he add, "Moncure D. Conway is endeavoring to raise the means to go to England. . . ."[22]

Just who sent Conway to England would later become a point of controversy. Conway would contend he was sent by leading figures in the antislavery movement, and probably came to believe honestly that he was. He was not. Conway sent himself to England. His motives for going were so complex and emotionally charged that he simply had to believe otherwise. Even in his letters soliciting funds, he used (perhaps unconsciously) rhetorical obfuscation to make it seem the initiative for his trip came from others. To Gerrit Smith in February he spoke of "the movement that [George Stearns] and Mr. Phillips have united with me in thinking well of—to wit, that I should visit England at this juncture. . . ." Later he learned the usefulness of the passive voice. "It has been agreed," he told Henry Wadsworth Longfellow in March, "between certain friends of Liberty and Union here and in England that if, just at this juncture, an antislavery Virginian (like myself) should appear at some of their meetings in England . . . it would have a good effect." The request for an abolitionist speaker, he told Israel Washburn in April, "has been responded to by some gentlemen over here who have given something toward paying my expenses. . . ." By this time perhaps he believed it himself.[23]

What passed between Moncure and Ellen during this period is a mystery. Since they were together, there are no letters to assist in assembling the puzzle. But their correspondence after Conway reached England indicates a private dialogue about leaving the country permanently had begun before he left. It suggests also that Ellen was not easily persuaded.

Moncure had difficulties of another sort concerning his Virginia family. He was concerned about what would be left to them after the war. He seems to have had some qualms about not being able to help them, especially from far away. In March he wrote to Secretary Chase, asking for assistance in seeing to their needs. He reminded Chase that "my mother, sister and myself have always been loyal, and antislavery," and hoped his father's land in Stafford County would not be confiscated. "It seems hard that my mother should have nothing." The letter bears the imprint of one settling his affairs, tending to important matters while there is still time. Soon he would be leaving. Perhaps he would not be back.[24]

In mid-April Peter Conway visited his father at the Richmond boardinghouse. For two days father and son were constant companions. They shared the same food, slept in the same bed. Then "dear Peter" went back to the army. Walker was bursting with pride. Peter had "improved in health, looks and character," he rejoiced, "if the latter admitted of improvement." No father could ask for a finer son. He knew his place. He did his duty.[25]

At about the same time, on April 11, 1863, Moncure Conway boarded the *City of Washington* in New York harbor, and left the country.

"I have always been healthy and happy at sea," wrote Conway in 1906, with two dozen ocean voyages behind him. None had been more pleasant or stimulating than the first. The *City of Washington* ran into rough weather on the second day, and almost all the passengers suffered from seasickness. Conway was unperturbed, amazing the crew with his steady stomach and soaring spirits. For three days he scurried about below deck tending the sick with homeopathic treatments his mother had taught him. "I have also cured 1 lady of pleurisy," he reported, "2 gentlemen of sore throat, 1 lady of constipation, 1 child of toothache, several of headache. Also last night I by request gave the company a scientific lecture." He was always happy at sea.[26]

On the night of April 22 the *City of Washington* docked at Queenstown. Soon Conway was in London, the houseguest of Peter Alfred Taylor, M.P. Taylor (b. 1819) was a wealthy silk manufacturer elected to the House of Commons from Leicester in 1862 despite extremely radical opinions and what one sympathizer described as an "entire absence of all tact." Taylor would stay in Parliament for many years, winning a reputation as "the champion of forgotten rights, the redresser of unheeded wrongs, . . . in a sense, a 'survival' from the great era of the Commonwealth." Conway later remembered him as "the only thorough republican of high position and wealth I ever knew in England." Taylor was generous in his moral and pecuniary support for liberal causes both at home and abroad. In England he publicly questioned the idea of monarchy, led agitation against the Sabbath laws, and was a prominent lifelong supporter of London's most radical religious institution, South Place Chapel. He corresponded with Polish rebels, helped bankroll Mazzini, and in many ways assisted American abolitionists. To a reformer making his first visit to England, he was just the man to see.[27]

By prearrangement, Taylor's luxurious Camden Hill mansion, Aubrey House, was Conway's residence during his first two months in London. No environment could better have provided the combination of rest and stimulation he needed. Peter and Mentia Taylor made their home a crossroads for reformers, writers, and artists. Thanks to the salon atmosphere of Aubrey House, Conway's acquaintances multiplied. His social life burgeoned. A ceaseless procession of fascinating and sympathetic people crossed his path and dazzled him. At Aubrey House he learned billiards, which became a lasting enthusiasm. He got more dinner invitations than he could handle; in his first two weeks he spent only fifty cents for food. He breakfasted with Richard Cobden, lunched with John Bright, dined with Robert Browning. (The latter was "all that I imagined he would be, . . . worthy to be the author of Pippa.") "I am in such a continuous round of company and agreeable friends," he admitted to Ellen on April 30, "that I have scarcely time to be out and out homesick."[28]

Only Thomas Carlyle, whom Conway visited for tea on May 1, threatened to dampen his pleasure. The sage of Chelsea had come far from the transcendental enthusiasms of his youth. Lately his work had been politically reactionary, and most recently quite nakedly racist. Somehow the liberal fraternity always forgave him, as they forgave Hawthorne in America. "There has been a disposition to pardon . . . Carlyle," wrote Conway. "The man with all these faults does stand so grandly alone, in such absolute sincerity, in such sadness. He gains no princely chaplaincies or professorships by opposing us. . . . So the best young men here still love him."

Carlyle may not have required the love of youthful admirers, but he did not mind their attention. He welcomed a stream of pilgrims to his modest row house, regaling them with the mix of wisdom and abuse he knew they were expecting. By the 1860s he seemed less Carlyle at times than some devilish old character playing the role of Carlyle. During Conway's visit he played it to perfection. He delighted his young guest with historical anecdotes, sketches of famous contemporaries, tales of London. Then he asked about his politics and attacked him for his answers. The world was all wrong, Carlyle thundered. "Our ballot-boxings, our negro emancipation, our cries for liberty, all showed nothing but that the nations were given over to believe a lie and be damned." Conway was overwhelmed and cowed. He said little, finally departing with a sense of "breaking away from a depressing fascination." "Whilst in his presence, I remembered the weird impressions of mingled beauty and awe which I had when journeying through the Mammoth Cave." He would return many times to Cheyne Row in the coming years. Carlyle unnerved him, even repelled him, but Conway always went back. Something inside him kept whispering that Carlyle, as he raged against contemporary notions of "progress," might have something valuable to say.[29]

Except for Carlyle, Conway's first weeks in London were bathed in sunlight. "I am not in such a scolding humor here," he told William Dean Howells, "as I am at home." There were dinners, soirees, outings. There were famous people, and some not so famous but fun. "Ladies more low-necked than in America," he noticed cheerfully, "with finer necks which explain it." He was happy. He had left the torment of the Civil War, crossed an ocean, and found on other shores the joy of a brand-new world. The irony was stunning: an American had left the darkness of his homeland to find beauty, peace, and newness in the Old World. Conway loved London from the start. When not socializing, he explored. He marveled at the grandeur of St. Paul's, the solemn beauty of Westminster Abbey. He sought out the haunts of Dickens characters he had met in his boyhood. "I find a certain new sense of the beautiful born from this immensity," he wrote of the city, "as in the fable Venus arose from the sea."[30]

If only his family were with him. "What do you think now of coming here," he asked Ellen on April 30. Five days later he expanded on the thought. "I hope you will remember that it is best for me to feel my way about the world—for we don't know what it may be best for us to do in future. I already see how we could make a comfortable living here if our Destiny should remove us from the U.S.—I have made many pleasant friends among the best and strongest people." On May 6 he wrote to Howells in Venice, asking about the city and its cost of living. "Perhaps I will send for Mrs. C. and come and reside there. Wouldn't we have times!" With Ellen he was unrelenting. "At this beautiful place [Aubrey House] with its quiet park," he wrote on May 8, "I find that sweet rest that I was so much in need of when I left home. And I only need you at my side, and Eustace and Emerson . . . to make me perfectly happy. Ah, could it only be! Why have fairies, genis, etc., gone out of fashion?"[31]

Ellen's response to all this is not quite clear. Certainly she wanted to leave Concord, having found the community unexpectedly insular and antisocial. "I see nobody," she wrote on May 15. "I find I must be near someone who loves me. . . . I could not live among such cold people as they are here." But there is no evidence she wished to become an expatriate. Her letters remain silent on the subject for a long time. Moncure's remarks suggest such a move had been discussed between them inconclusively, before his departure. His persistence indicates his wife still needed convincing. Ellen's letter of May 15 encouraged him. Quickly he pounced and pressed his advantage.[32]

"After reading your letter I sat meditating, 'If the good Father will only restore her to me again never shall any sea roll between us again, I vow.' . . . O Ellen I love you above all things—I can scarcely sleep because I cannot clasp you to my heart, and I have nobody to thank for it but myself. . . . I am almost crazy to have you come." He meant this. He loved Ellen, and by this time (May 29) missed her fiercely. He was determined they would reunite on his side of the Atlantic.

I expect to go to Venice about the middle of June and if it is a *very* cheap place to live, and if you can sell the house what *do* you think of spending the money in your coming over? I would have to give up The Commonwealth—we should have to live on little. I would write something for English magazines etc., which pay twice as well as American ones. Meanwhile I would be able to write a work or two which I have long desired to write, but cannot amid the multiplicity of engagements etc. in America. Is all this a dream? Is it foolish and impossible? You can tell if it is so. But just now money seems to me of very little importance, and wife and children of a vast deal. —I have not half seen England yet, and people here say it will be impossible to do much here in the way of lecturing etc. in the short time I have proposed to be absent. —I shall have little or no time to see Paris or Rome, none to see Germany, if I return in Sept., and yet if you shall decide against coming I will be on my way early in Sept. (Ah, how I dread the voyage.)[33]

What Conway was doing was not uplifting. It smacked of the sort of mental and moral coercion he despised. He was, in effect, forcing his wife to leave her country regardless of her wishes. In the process he was whining about making a voyage which he was then asking his wife and two small children to make—and which he had, in fact, thoroughly enjoyed. The whole situation involved motives and sensitivities he could not face directly. Ellen probably understood this. She had seen it before. He had acted this way when she wanted him to quit smoking, and again, more seriously, when offered the job as army chaplain. He would not return, but could not face the reasons. So he wrote to Ellen and spoke of options. He said he would come back, as planned, in September. It would mean sacrifices and lost opportunities. It would be terribly grueling for him. Despite that he would return—if she wanted him to. Ellen must have known what he was pressing her to say. She must decide for the two of them, for reasons unspoken. The decision needed to be the one her husband had made long ago without ever saying it out loud. She had seen it all before.

She did not give her husband the answer he wanted. She must have known how much this meant to him and how strongly he felt. But expatriation was not something one embraced until the last extremity. For her, that moment had not yet come. Perhaps events would change her husband's mind and bring him back. Her reply said nothing about leaving America. In fact, her opinion of Concord had seemingly changed overnight. "I am having the nicest time and quite enjoying Concord. . . . I think I have rather got into the good graces of everybody but Mrs. Sanborn and Edith Emerson—they are awfully stiff." It is hard to account for this sudden fondness. Bronson Alcott remembered the Conways finding Concord "a dull exclusive place." Sophia Thoreau later wrote Ellen, "I think with shame of your cold reception in Concord." Ellen had been saying herself that she hated the place. But now she liked it fine. She did not want to leave America.[34]

Conway's letters reveal him to have been guilty not only of coerciveness but also of deception. It is hard to consider all the facts without concluding he had left America intending to stay away. He had not said this to anyone. He had solicited funds from friends and colleagues who thought they were sending him on an antislavery speaking tour, after which he would return to responsibilities in Boston. Just after his arrival in London, before he had done a thing for the abolitionist cause in England, he was searching for ways to stay abroad. Probably nobody who gave him money ever knew this. But they were not the only ones being deluded. Moncure's letters to Ellen imply he was fooling himself almost as much. His deception of the others shows how badly he needed to get away from the Civil War. His deception of himself shows just how hard that was to admit.

He had not forgotten his mission. After a few weeks the sympathetic London *Daily News* and *Morning Star* began to run his letters, and on May 6 he made his debut before an English audience. The occasion was an emancipation meeting at South Place Chapel, probably instigated by Conway's host, Peter Taylor. The chapel was jammed with a standing-room crowd of well over a thousand. Conway gave a vigorous and well-received performance. He told his audience he was a Southerner who had left his native land, having "recoiled from the bad motto 'our country right or wrong.' " He would not hesitate to repudiate the North also, if he were convinced the Northern cause was not that of freedom. "I will not today adhere to the Union or any other cause except as far as I believe it to be that of the Right. Certainly no banner, however much I may love it, shall consecrate for me mere bloodshed." But he went on to defend abolitionists for supporting the war. "It has been alleged that the antislavery men who have been for so many years opposed to the Union because it did not mean justice, are now supporting it because they are overborne by a popular demon. Such a statement is utterly unfounded. They now support the Union freely and cordially, because it is identified with all for which they have been these many years striving. . . ."[35]

Conway was papering over differences he and other abolitionists still had with the administration's war policy. At such a distance, such a strategy was justifiable. Most sympathetic or undecided Englishmen were unlikely to be concerned about particular abolitionist grievances. What mattered was the big picture. Was the North earnestly moving to end slavery? Was the Union cause identified with that goal? Conway's affirmative answers, his insistence in this speech and others during the next few weeks "that our cause is that of Humanity and Justice," were far more emphatic and unequivocal than what he had been saying in America. This was due partly to the fact that he was speaking to a foreign audience. He also may have been saying these things because the more he said them, the more likely he was to believe them himself.[36]

Soon it was not easy. Conway's state of exhilaration could not last forever. In the middle of May news from America ended it. Fighting had started again in Virginia. Once again Fredericksburg was a battle-ground. "The armies on the Rappahannock are sharply engaged," noted Charles Francis Adams, the American minister to London, on May 16, "and God only knows the result, at least on this side of the Atlantic." News was slow in coming. (The transatlantic cable was not laid until after the war.) By May 21 even the unflappable Adams was getting disturbed. "No news from America," he wrote, "and the speculations upon it and greedy anticipations of evil to us swarming more thickly than ever. The pain of this suspense is growing severe. My thought could with difficulty be diverted from the banks of the Rappahannock. . . ."[37]

Adams was not alone. Conway was a nervous wreck as news and rumors dribbled in. At the same time, he got an ecstatic letter from Howells, gurgling with delight at Conway's thought about coming, perhaps moving, to Venice. "You in England? By Heaven! Pan is not dead! . . . Come and dwell with us. . . . You shall live upon green peas, young beets, strawberries and ice cream as we do now. Yes Venice is cheap—but you'll find that out and Mrs. Conway will be the natural consequence or there's no such thing as logic." Venice sounded awfully good, especially as Conway got word of more deaths on the Rappahannock. "I want to start off tomorrow," he wrote Howells on May 16. "How I shall enjoy a little rest . . . I need it. I am weary, faint, almost old from the terrible pressure on heart and nerves. . . ." But he could not rest yet. The war was pressing in on him again and he had to keep lecturing for the cause. More, he had to maintain his painful vigil as information came in from Virginia. "Tonight especially," he told Howells, "the wild and fierce clarions of battle come over the ocean, and I give the first watch to the red planet which hovers over America."[38]

The news was bad. During the first five days of May a terrible battle had raged at Chancellorsville, slightly west of Falmouth and Fredericksburg. The latter town had also seen fierce fighting. At great cost to both sides, Union troops had successfully stormed Marye's Heights, less well fortified than the preceding December. "The slaughter of the enemy [i.e., Southerners] in this action," reported the *Morning Star* on May 19, "is without parallel in the history of warfare, considering the number of men engaged." At Chancellorsville, however, the main Union force had been routed. Fredericksburg was soon abandoned again by the Northerners. "All day yesterday the city was full of rumors," wrote Conway on May 22. "This morning dawns upon our feverish nerves with the tidings which whilst showing that things are not so bad, show also that our position on the Rappahannock is very critical." The nightmare had been repeated: as in December, fearful butchery had taken place around Fredericksburg, resulting in both defeat for the Union army and the further devastation of Conway's native place.[39]

For Conway there was an extra dimension of tragedy to this latest round of fighting. Gerald Fitzgerald, his old friend from Washington days, had been killed. Fitzgerald, a sensitive and intelligent young man, had idolized Conway and had gone to Harvard Divinity School in conscious emulation of him. Conway had aroused in him a hatred of slavery. When the Civil War broke out he had enlisted as a private, believing the fight a holy war between freedom and enslavement. He was last seen leaning against a tree near the river, dying. We do not know precisely when Conway learned of his friend's death, but we know he suffered pangs of guilt he never quite shook off.[40]

Depressed by Chancellorsville and second Fredericksburg, Conway intensified his efforts to move his family abroad. On May 29 he wrote the long disingenuous letter to Ellen which asked her to ratify the decision he had apparently made but not acknowledged. On June 1, their fifth wedding anniversary, he wrote her six stanzas of ponderous but poignant poetry. He missed her. He needed her. He was not sure she would come, and it wore him to a frazzle. "Her coming is not so probable as I could wish it," he reported on May 16, "though quite possible." On June 10 he was still guessing: ". . . her movements are not yet decided." Ellen's reluctance to move aggravated a mood already made taut by the fighting and Moncure's need to escape it. During June Conway's nervousness increased, not eased by a nearly continuous two-week onslaught of rain. This uneasiness and uncertainty could not be permitted to last. He had come to England to escape the brutality and moral ambiguity of the war. Now the war was pursuing him across the ocean, and his wife's passive resistance to his pleas was threatening him with the prospect of returning to it all. Something had to break soon.[41]

There was one small consolation for Conway during these weeks. Confederate emissary James Murray Mason seemed no happier than he. The two did not meet, but Conway heard gossip that the Confederate was, "I rejoice to know, miserable." Mason had not been received by government officials, an event becoming very unlikely as the chances of diplomatic recognition faded. He had to settle for gathering public support for the Southern cause, support which seems to have peaked by this point. Conway was especially pleased by Mason's discomfort because he despised him so much. In 1850, at their only meeting, Mason had disparaged Conway's ideas about free schools. A former senator from Virginia, Mason had authored the Fugitive Slave Law and had been one of the most inflammatory of Southern politicians. After John Brown's raid he had headed a Senate committee that threatened Frank Sanborn with arrest and menaced abolitionists generally. To Conway he epitomized Virginia gone wrong. Thus the younger Virginian took special pleasure in telling readers of *The Commonwealth*, "Mason finds his mission a great bore. Sensitive, proud, and habituated to active political life, he finds nothing to do here. . . ." Before long Conway would give him something to do.[42]

What came to be known as the Conway-Mason affair (or simply the Mason affair) was a milestone in Conway's life. It sealed his expatriation and gave it an aura of exile. It sparked his wife's decision to join him abroad. It opened an increasingly bitter rift between him and many abolitionists in America. In the process it showed graphically just how much the war had changed the antislavery movement. In the coming months and years nobody with a stake in the matter would look at it dispassionately or objectively. Former allies would point to it and rush at one another with self-serving pettiness and a footloose disregard of facts. Before plunging into this tawdry but revealing maze of recrimination, it is well to start slowly and see, step by step, just what the shouting was about.

On June 10, 1863, Conway sent Mason a letter. He had, he told the Confederate agent, "authority . . . on behalf of the leading antislavery men of America, who have sent me to this country," to make a proposition. "If the States calling themselves 'The Confederate States of America' will consent to emancipate the negro slaves in those States, such emancipation to be guaranteed by a liberal European commission, the emancipation to be inaugurated at once and such time to be allowed for its completion as the commission shall adjudge to be necessary and just, and such emancipation once made to be irrevocable—then the abolitionists and antislavery leaders of the Northern States shall immediately oppose the further prosecution of the war on the part of the United States government, and, since they hold the balance of power, will certainly cause the war to cease by the immediate withdrawal of every kind of support from it." Conway wanted to know, in short, whether Mason would work with him in obtaining "a restoration of peace and the independence of the South upon the simple basis of the emancipation of the slaves."[43]

Mason was quick to respond. Conway's offer was "worthy of the gravest consideration," he wrote on June 11, but he could not speak to it without knowing "who those are, on whose behalf and authority you make the proposition referred to." His reply would be forthcoming, but its substance "must depend on what I may learn of your authority. . . ."[44]

Three days passed before Conway wrote again. When he did (June 14) he was far less sure of himself than when he initiated the exchange. "I could easily give you the evidence that I am sent here by leading abolitionists in America," he proclaimed in a draft of his letter. Something about this bothered him. He crossed it out. "I could easily give you the evidence that I represent the views of the leading abolitionists in America. . . ." That was better, at least safer, although it meant retreat. "My second letter to Mason was a virtual admission that I had made a mistake in writing the first," Conway later acknowledged. He had lacked authority to make his proposal. He now could not even bring himself to repeat the claim of having been "sent" to England by the abolitionists. He could not squirm out of his predicament. "I have concluded," he told Mason, "that it was best to write out to America and obtain the evidence of my right to make [the proposal], in a form which will preclude any doubt as to its sufficiency. I shall, then, address you again on the subject." There is no indication he wrote to America for evidence, but his statement, at least, bought time.[45]

Not much. Conway now had more than the war to be nervous about. He had greatly exceeded his authority in making his proposal to Mason, and knew it. Now his recklessness was becoming exposed, and he was at Mason's mercy. On June 15 he awoke early, thinking about his family and weeping. "I have felt blue all day," he told Ellen. The next day he appeared at what seemed to be a triumphant emancipation meeting at the London Tavern. He shared the platform with John Bright, who delivered a powerful speech and gave him a rousing introduction. The hall was so packed that a supplementary meeting was held simultaneously in Sussex Hall to handle the overflow. Newspapers covered the event extensively. It was the biggest, most successful event of Conway's trip thus far. But behind the scenes were intimations of trouble. News of the Mason correspondence was leaking out. Rumors were circulating: this man has blundered. He sensed people thinking: this Conway is a fool.[46]

Mason was sure of it. After Conway's second letter the Confederate knew he had his opponent on the defensive. After the London Tavern meeting he decided to put him on the run. Evidence conflicts as to what Mason knew of Conway, but when he read reports from the London Tavern he concluded the man was important enough to merit more attention. On June 17 the older Virginian sent the younger one reeling. "Our correspondence closes with this reply—it was your pleasure to commence it—it is mine to terminate it." Then came an arrogant and telling cascade of vitriol and ridicule. "This correspondence shall go to the public," Mason menaced. "It will, perhaps, interest the government, and the *soi-disant* 'loyal men' there to know . . . that the 'leading antislavery men in America' are prepared to negotiate with the authorities of the Confederate States for a restoration of peace and the independence of the South. . . ." Here, in Mason's view, was his most damaging blow. As he explained to the Confederate secretary of state, "I thought his proposition to negotiate . . . the independence of the Southern States . . . afforded an opportunity to expose the duplicity of that party [i.e., abolitionists] to their own people, not to be omitted."[47]

Mason did not stop there. In a last haughty flourish he taunted his adversary with a zest once familiar to his long-suffering senatorial opponents. "As some reward . . . for this interesting disclosure, your inquiry whether the Confederate States will consent to emancipation, on the terms stated, shall not go wholly unanswered. You may be assured, then, and perhaps it may be of value to your constituents to assure them, that the Northern States will never be in relations to put this question to the South, nor will the Southern States ever be in a position requiring them to give an answer." Satisfied with his work, the would-be ambassador assembled the correspondence and strolled to the offices of the rabidly pro-Southern *Times*. On June 18 the paper published the whole sorry mess.[48]

* * *

"I am greatly pleased with the correspondence in the *Times*," wrote wealthy Liverpool merchant James Spence, Mason's most valued English collaborator. "I think that nigger worshipper must feel as if he had put his head between the jaws of a vise." Indeed. Conway had managed to commit a number of transgressions at once. He had approached the agent of an illegitimate and unrecognized regime. He had portrayed himself as having authority he did not possess. He had shown himself willing to accept Southern independence, a point setting him apart from virtually all others on the Northern side. Conway's action was a severe embarrassment to abolitionists on both sides of the Atlantic, who scrambled either to repudiate it or explain it away.[49]

Initially Conway was of little help in providing explanations. He spent the next few days moping about Aubrey House before leaving for speeches in Manchester (June 21) and Leicester. For several days he refused to speak publicly about the correspondence. The initiative thus fell to his London host, Peter Taylor. On the evening of June 18 Taylor met with John Bright and editor Samuel Lucas in the offices of the latter's *Morning Star*. There they hammered out a rather clever explanation which appeared in that paper on June 19.[50]

The three men could not deny the rashness of Conway's act, and conceded due embarrassment. But they lunged at Mason's last vindictive paragraph to salvage something for their side. Mason had, in fact, overreached. In his zeal to demolish his hapless adversary, he had virtually admitted the Confederacy would not free its slaves even if independence were offered. The admission could be used as ammunition for those insisting upon the evil of the Confederacy, and so it was used by the *Star*. In the wake of the correspondence, said the newspaper, "it is impossible to pretend that the South cares for independence except as a means of perpetuating slavery." Mason should now consider whether "Mr. Conway may have been baiting a trap for *him*," whether the purpose of the whole crafty correspondence may have been to extract from the Confederate agent a public statement declaring the moral bankruptcy of his cause.[51]

The explanation seemed so plausible it was immediately picked up by others. Even the normally lukewarm *Spectator* wrote on June 20 that the "effect, on the whole—perhaps the carefully calculated effect—of Mr. Conway's measure" would be "to convince Englishmen of the utter futility of their hopes for a Confederate emancipation." The argument then figured prominently in Conway's own explanation of his conduct, which finally appeared in the *Times* and *Daily News* on June 23 and the *Star* on June 24. Conway insisted he had accurately depicted the abolitionist position as "unwillingness to prosecute this terrible war for any less important aim than the complete wiping out of their country's crime and shame." But he had, he knew, erred in making a specific proposal on the abolitionists' behalf, while "inexperience in diplomatic and political affairs" accounted for his decision to deal with Mason personally. He had, however, done the cause a service, as some in the press now realized. (He did not say whether the service had been premeditated.) He had gotten Mason to admit the South was married to slavery, "that every gateway to liberation except that of war is closed." In a dispatch to *The Commonwealth* written on June 23 he expanded the ways he had benefited the Northern cause. John Arthur Roebuck, an idiosyncratic radical M.P. from Sheffield, was about to introduce a resolution in Parliament calling for recognition of the Confederacy. The Mason correspondence, Conway implied, was timed to coincide with Roebuck's effort, and therefore intended to discredit the South at a critical time. It had, he claimed, done so. "Mason has been startled into dropping his mask," and unmasked, he had damaged Roebuck's chances for success.[52]

Maybe Conway believed this. Certainly he did forty years later when writing his autobiography. "Of course my letter to Mason was strategical," he explained. The proposal "I knew would be refused," adding that it was "partly inspired" by Roebuck's upcoming motion. Yet this version of the affair is unconvincing. Roebuck's motion was never given the great chance for success Conway later portrayed it as having. Roebuck himself, whom Cobden called "a moral and physical wreck" and Henry Adams termed "more than three-quarters mad," was taken seriously by few. His resolution was introduced June 30, ran into widespread opposition, and was withdrawn two weeks later without a vote. There is no prior evidence that Conway was really concerned at this point about the actions of Parliament or Palmerston's ministry; he told Howells in May he was "satisfied that England will preserve her neutrality." If he were really anxious about the possibility of Confederate recognition, why give the unreceived Confederate agent heightened status by writing to him? Finally, Conway had withheld his explanation of the matter for days. His account of his "strategy" came only after his friends had created the excuse for him and it had gathered credibility in the press.[53]

Conway's private statements and actions revealed a much more troubled state of mind. On June 25 he visited Minister Adams and apologized profusely. He was so frightened and meek that Adams pitied him, told him to write in like vein to Secretary of State Seward, and then forget the matter. Conway's letter to Seward oozed with penitence and patriotism. "I beg leave to say, Sir, that though an humble and unofficial individual, it is of the greatest importance to me to stand personally well with the Government to which I was never so proud to belong as now, and to serve which I came to England. . . . I have made my explanation to Mr. Adams, who . . . said, to my inquiry, that he believed you would kindly receive a similar apology. . . . I need not say how gratefully I would receive an assurance that my mistake in this matter will be overlooked and pardoned by the government I meant to serve."[54]

Conway had never before expressed such enthusiasm for the national government. Fear, it seems, was acting as a powerful stimulant to his allegiance. He was very apprehensive that the State Department would not "overlook" and "pardon" his blunder. He kept checking with Adams to see if all was forgiven. Finally, in September, the minister called him in and told him Seward had "no disposition to pursue the matter. He [Conway] seemed greatly relieved." What did he fear? Although it was unlikely that much would or could be done to him, one terrifying thing was possible. The State Department had the power to revoke his passport and order him home.[55]

"Oh if I could see you!" he moaned to Ellen shortly after the Mason affair broke. If Adams, Seward, and the abolitionists were ignorant of Conway's intention to stay abroad, Ellen assuredly was not. For weeks she had been resisting his pleas to join him in de facto expatriation. Now she would be pressured more intensely. The Mason affair became a trump card in the half-poignant, half-shoddy campaign Conway was waging against his wife's reluctance to move abroad, and he played it to the hilt. He had already seen the *Star* article; some Englishmen had reacted well to the correspondence; he knew something could be salvaged from it. But the picture he painted for Ellen was unrelievedly bleak. He told her he expected a uniformly hostile reaction in America, so bad he might have to stay away. "If things go on in America so that you think it would be unpleasant for me to be there you must find out and let me know." As usual, he wanted it to seem as if she were making the decision. "I shall expect you to advise me in all matters and shall obey you." On June 23 he was less gloomy, but kept up the pressure. "There is no doubt we could spend a winter over here comfortably and then next summer go on the Continent. . . . I can scarcely think of you and our darlings without a hearty cry."[56]

On June 26, having "gone through just as much excitement as I can stand,"[57] Conway left for a vacation in Venice. He arrived late on the night of July 6 and was greeted warmly by his friend Howells and his wife of six months, Elinor Mead. These friends and this city were exactly what he needed. The Italians cared nothing about the Mason affair. His hosts did not criticize or judge him. In their pleasant apartment overlooking the Grand Canal, he found peace.

For two weeks he kept a schedule. He rose early and had coffee with Howells in the Piazza San Marco. Then the two briefly explored Venetian crannies before returning to breakfast with Elinor. After breakfast Howells went to the consulate and Elinor served as Moncure's guide to the galleries and churches. In the evening the three discussed art and literature, or Howells read aloud what he had managed to write that day in his spare moments. To Conway, everything about this place seemed fine. He liked it so much he went house-hunting in a serious way. "The largest sum we can spend in Venice for the year is $1000," he told Ellen. "We should have these dear friends near us—who *really do love* us." Still it was up to Ellen. "I shall rely upon your judgment in this matter. . . ."[58]

Conway might find peace in Venice, but he could not escape reality. The latter began to burst upon him on July 13. He received, via letters from Sanborn and Phillips, intimations of "the shrill blast of surprise and indignation" which had greeted the Mason correspondence in America. "It seems to me certain that my public life there will now end by an utter loss of influence," he told Ellen. Somehow this did not bother him much. "Whether this be in itself a thing to grieve over I very much doubt." It seemed, in fact, so much a blessing as to have been planned—if not by him, by God. "At times lately it has flitted across my mind that some Higher Power had something to do with my blunder; and that I must accept this as a chance for getting more entirely out of party politics, and dedicating myself more entirely to literature. . . ." He was not simply resigned; he was relieved. He would go quietly, without a fight, and be glad. He told Ellen he could still return to America. "But I do not feel like it." He enclosed a note resigning the editorship of *The Commonwealth*, and told his wife what books he wanted her to bring when she left America. Ellen still had not said she would go (as far as Moncure knew), and the fiction of her having a choice was halfheartedly maintained. Yet Conway had made up his mind, and was saying so more forthrightly than ever. The Mason episode, he said, made it virtually impossible for him to return. What is striking is that he declared his preference for exile before the full force of the criticism reached him, without making a concerted effort to justify himself, and in a happier state of mind than he had known for months.[59]

Ellen had already acted. When she received Moncure's first depressed letters after the affair broke, she knew she could resist him no longer. Nor, amid the criticism he was getting, did she wish to. Her momentous letter caught up with Conway in Milan on July 22, as he was returning to England. Moncure's reply was quick and ecstatic. "Dearest come without delay!" Having sold the house in Concord, Ellen and her two small sons boarded the *Arabia* on August 19 and sailed for England.[60]

It had not been easy for Ellen. She was visiting Moncure's mother and sister in Easton when rumors of the Mason affair began to circulate. Her first news of it came via an anxious letter from Sanborn, along with the latest issue of *The Commonwealth*, disowning Conway's actions if the rumors proved accurate. Moncure's mother was indignant, regarding the whole story as "a downright falsehood." Ellen knew at once it was true. "I am a good deal worried by this move of yours," she told Moncure, "though sure your feeling is right, but equally sure, at present you will have no support in it." As the criticism mounted she stood as one with her husband. "I think you would find it worse than a church quarrel just now," she told him on June 30. The next day she returned to Massachusetts, where she could better defend her husband's interests.[61]

Once in Concord, Ellen had more than harsh words to confront. Just at that moment Moncure was drafted. The move probably was politically motivated. Certainly the timing was suspicious, and the local draft commissioners, whom Sanborn thought "behaved shabbily," informed the press with unseemly enthusiasm. "It is to be hoped he will come home and shoulder a musket," gloated a Salem, Massachusetts newspaper. "It is very evident he can do the country no honor with his pen at home or abroad, but he may be as good as any other man with a musket." Ellen did not wait for instructions from her husband. She paid a three-hundred-dollar commutation fee, even though the house had not been sold and the payment entailed a real financial sacrifice. In mid-August the London *Morning Star* printed an explanation from Conway that was picked up by papers in America. He said he had paid the commutation fee. Then he found it necessary to add, "I am not able to go to the war, on account of an injury to my right eye sustained some years ago." The excuse seemed lame, and was. Conway did have occasional eye trouble during his life, but suffered from nothing serious enough to exempt him from a hungry army increasingly unselective about whom it devoured. He simply could never kill people, especially Southern soldiers. His public rationalization only gave more ammunition to his enemies. An Illinois paper not only attacked him as an "ass" but ridiculed him as "a sore-eyed hero" whose patriotism was "all in his eye." Generally abolitionists and Republicans did not mention the conscription problem, but it bothered Conway enough to give a sharper edge to his misery.[62]

Meanwhile, all during July abolitionists were falling over each other in their haste to denounce the proposal to Mason. Wendell Phillips, always fond of Conway, was relatively lenient: he was willing to believe the correspondence a ploy, "only . . . a means of cornering Mason." Still he could not refrain from repudiating it. He could never "trust such a scheme to the Rebels," or "enter into any conference with them." Others were not so gentle. Charles Eliot Norton called the proposition "wild," betraying Conway's "extraordinary misconception of the real state of affairs." Samuel J. May, Jr., pronounced himself "astonished and disgusted" by the episode. "It will kill Conway here as a trustworthy man or a friend of his country. . . . It is insufferable that at this juncture the Anti-Slavery cause should have to bear the burden of such transparent stupidity and conceit."[63]

Complaints by individuals quickly yielded to more official expressions. In *The Liberator* of July 3, Garrison described himself as "surprised and perplexed" by Conway's move. He insisted that Conway, whatever he might say to the contrary, was "in England on his own responsibility alone." He objected to the substance of Conway's proposal on three grounds. The rebels could not be trusted; the proposition robbed the

North of its self-respect; and the national government, which had already freed the slaves in rebel states, deserved every patriot's support. If anyone still thought Conway spoke for the abolitionist movement, he said, they could go to the annual July Fourth celebration at Framingham, where the matter would be loudly, definitively disposed of.[64]

They had not had much practice, but some abolitionists were quick studies when it came to waving the flag. The Framingham rally, the biggest abolitionist gathering since the Emancipation Proclamation, little resembled earlier meetings where participants had bemoaned the corruption of the times and vented their spleens on the political system and the people in it. Abolitionists had emerged from the wilderness. They were discovering what it was like to be considered respectable, even venerable—and many of them loved it. They were also finding it pleasant to be able to support a government, as many were coming to do with increasing zest. The 1863 Framingham meeting was two things: a strenuous display of nationalistic fervor and a vocal show of disdain for Moncure Conway, a fellow warrior run amok.

It was just as well for Conway that he was far away. They were not gentle at Framingham. First Garrison read a letter from Senator Wilson denouncing the Mason correspondence as "foolish" and "wicked." Then the correspondence itself was read before a jeering crowd of thousands. Garrison stepped forward to assail it, reported *The Liberator*, as "absurd, visionary, unnecessary, unwarrantable. We are for the Government, (great applause) because the Government is in the right as against the rebellion, and we are not disposed to interfere to give a triumph to the wrong side. . . . Abolitionists are incapable of doing a dishonorable act, even to forward the antislavery cause, to any extent. (applause). . . . " Phillips managed to put in a good word for Conway while attacking his actions, and Sanborn pathetically pleaded that his old colleague be given more time to explain himself. Most people were not interested. Far warmer was their response to Samuel May, Jr., who lacerated Conway and introduced two stinging resolutions. The first insisted Conway "entirely misunderstands and misrepresents the Anti-Slavery people and sentiment of America." The second expressed the hope "our Government will never stoop" to deal with the Confederates "in any other character than that of Rebels, Traitors, and Murderers." Both resolutions passed by stentorian voice vote, without a dissenting murmur. Amid it all people drank toasts to the Union, waved flags, shouted three cheers for Lincoln, thanked God for battlefield victories, and sang "Rally round the flag, boys" and "The Star-Spangled Banner."[65]

Exactly nine years earlier Moncure Conway had made his antislavery debut at Framingham. He had then looked on with some discomfort as William Lloyd Garrison burned the Constitution.

News of the Framingham meeting reached Conway when he was returning to London from Venice. He had been braced for massive criticism, since he knew he had erred in noticing Mason and in presuming to act for the movement. Nevertheless he was stunned. The burden of the Framingham criticism surprised and angered him. The speeches were those of people who seemed to be glorying in the fighting. They seemed incapable of separating the issues of abolition and Union, even if by doing so they might both free the slaves and save some lives. They seemed oblivious to the bloodbath, as much a moral issue to Conway as slavery itself. They attacked him for being disloyal, for lacking faith in the government, for considering a deal with the enemy. They were not interested in trying to free the slaves while ending the killing, but in trying to free the slaves while conquering the South. At least on a conscious level, he had not expected this. It shocked him. "It entered into my mind . . . that I had made a mistake in making my proposition to Mason," he wrote Ellen, "but it never entered my mind that any leading antislavery man would question the principle involved—would in any way support the war simply for conquest or Union whether Liberty were or were not involved. The wholesale slaughter of men is vile enough anyway, but to slaughter them except for the holiest cause is worse than Treason to any Govt that does it. I for one wash my hands of it forever!"[66]

Conway was unfair when he accused abolitionists of caring for conquest "whether Liberty were or were not involved." Abolitionists who supported Lincoln did so only after concluding the president was working, however haltingly, toward full emancipation. Others who, like Phillips, remained critical of Lincoln, still were determined to defeat the South and reunite the country, as the only sure means both of getting and guaranteeing abolition. "Union without liberty I spit upon," said Phillips at Framingham, hastening to add his opinion that "disunion with liberty is an impossibility." But if Conway was unfair in one respect, he was accurate in detecting a profound difference between his attitude toward the war and that of most other abolitionists. The difference had caused his departure from the country, although he had not been able to acknowledge it, to himself or them, at the time. The others had not seen their homes wasted and their families divided. They might have similar attitudes toward arbitrary power, but they were not prepared to associate that offense with what the North was doing to the South. Many probably felt none of the psychic horror that violence and death bred in Conway and, unlike him, were now prepared to accept almost any amount of bloodshed for a free, united country. Much was involved, but what it came down to was this: they could stand the killing and Conway could not. They thought reunion with emancipation now justified almost any number of deaths, and Conway did not.[67]

Forever after, Conway would believe he suffered "virtual outlawry" in the wake of the Mason affair, when his effort for peace was struck down so cruelly by "militant America" that he "could not return with any hope of usefulness." This version, though not wholly untrue, is flawed. However hurtful the rebukes, there was no "outlawry ." Unqualified public repudiation was deemed necessary by abolitionists, but afterward they showed a sincere desire to accept their errant brother back into the fold. "We have tried to deal with poor Conway as tenderly as possible," Garrison told Oliver Johnson. "He certainly meant well. . . ." George Stearns wrote Moncure soothingly, reminding him that Mason had made "an *in turn* blunder on his part." In August, Sanborn assured him that Garrison had "expressed the kindest feeling for you," and that the "controversy has been allowed to drop." There might still be angry people about, "but you must not exaggerate this state of feeling." The following spring, people were still reassuring him, mistakenly believing reassurance could bring him home. "Oh we do so miss you here," wrote Phillips, "just *you* whose peculiar place no one can supply—As to your Mason matter, it will never do you the least harm."[68]

The American press was no harsher. The Mason affair was widely noticed, and no paper approved of it. Predictably, Democratic organs exploited it gleefully and used it to portray abolitionists as traitors. Otherwise, however, reaction was relatively mild and short-lived. The Boston *Transcript* dismissed the affair as a mere display of "antagonistic idiosyncracies" by two "bogus ambassadors." The New York *Tribune* treated it lightly, appraising Conway with a touch of affection as a "very green diplomatist" and the whole episode as "little more than a demonstration that the old Virginian is a little craftier than the young one." *Harper's Weekly* actually had a compliment for Conway, pointing out that he had "done us all and the English people a signal service by showing that the rebel agent will not agree to emancipation as the condition of separation and peace." In *The Commonwealth*, Sanborn admitted Conway's indiscretion but vigorously defended his integrity. And whatever disposal there might have been on the part of some papers to make more of Conway's error, it was quickly dissolved by the tide of events. Early in July, Gettysburg and the capture of Vicksburg pushed the Mason affair out of the papers and made it seem a small matter. There was no outlawry.[69]

Conway distorted matters, too, when he said he had stayed away solely because of the abolitionists' display of patriotic militance, which made it seem they were fighting as much for "mere power" as for emancipation. He had left America without really intending to return. The Mason affair did induce him to state his decision forthrightly, and it determined the timing of his resignation from the co-editorship of *The Commonwealth*. But the latter watershed was reached in Venice, before the *nature* of the criticism became clear. When the abolitionists' psychic investment in winning the war became evident, Conway's indignation erupted, and his philosophical differences with many of his old allies became more overt. But that development occurred after he had opted for exile. Conway's expatriation, in short, was sealed but not caused by the Mason affair. What caused it was the anguish felt by a nonviolent Southerner who had taken the Northern side in what proved a long and bloody civil war.

We come back to the questions of what the Mason correspondence really meant, and why Conway began it. It helps to remember the context. His spirits had always been affected by the course of the fighting. For the second time in six months, the fighting in and near Fredericksburg had been brutal. The long wait for news, and the uncertainty that news was accurate, worsened the strain. His friend Gerald Fitzgerald died in this fighting, and perhaps Conway heard of it. In addition, Ellen was resisting his clear desire that she and the children join him, seemingly refusing to understand both his need to stay away and his plea for her to say his need was honorable. The war was pursuing him like a serpent extending its body across the ocean, threatening to trap him in its coils and drag him back into its midst. He could not go back. By his own admission he was physically exhausted and emotionally drained. The weeks of steady rain could not have helped. For several days in June he lapsed into silence, writing nothing, making no speeches. Then he wrote to Mason.

Did he expect Mason to entertain his proposal? Did he think it might succeed? Perhaps he did. He must have known it was unlikely, but if there were the slightest chance, it was worth the effort. He had reached the point when he could no longer support the slaughter. If he could end the war he would do it. His obligation to abolitionists, he believed, would be upheld as long as emancipation were secured.

If, as he subsequently insisted, he knew Mason would reject his offer, what then? We are left with what the proposition meant for Conway personally. It may or may not have been a legitimate, if desperate, effort to end the war. It certainly was a personal catharsis for the man who made it. He was saying, I can no longer let things go on as they are. Slavery must end and the killing must end, and we must try to find a way to end both together. In his "golden hour" plan he had tried to sell the idea to the North. Now he would talk to the South.

Did he really think abolitionists supported his notion that Southern independence was acceptable as long as the slaves were freed? On a conscious level, yes. His indignation when abolitionists denounced this idea was genuine. On a deeper level, though, he knew he was not one of them, knew they could stomach what he could not. Otherwise, why did he have to leave them, his motives camouflaged, his intentions unspoken? Why could he not go back and work with them again? Why did he not consult other abolitionists before he made his proposal to Mason? Because he was sure they would support it, or because he harbored fears they would not? In any case, if abolitionists now closed ranks with him they would give him the reassurance he desperately needed. If, as it happened, they did not, at least he would have gotten things out in the open honorably and would have salvaged his self-respect. (He would also have an honorable reason not to return to America.) It would not be the first time he was repudiated by a community for speaking out against its complacent allegiance to a destructive status quo. The Mason proposal, whatever came of it, was an assertion of his own dignity and independence. Either way, it would be cathartic for him.

The Mason episode is enormously complex, involving psychic impulses too elusive to be caged. It was not simply a strategic ploy, not just an innocent blunder, not merely a poignant effort to stop the war. Conway was trying to find a way, consistent with his antislavery principles, of distancing himself from anyone unwilling to make a meaningful stand against the bloodshed. He wanted to end the killing honorably or stay away from it honorably. That he was unaware of some of the implications of his action does not matter. As he wrote soon afterward in a moment of candor, the episode "will perhaps always seem inexplicable to my friends and (to some extent) to myself."[70]

CHAPTER 9

The Mason affair marked the end of Conway's full-time involvement, physical and psychological, in the American Civil War. In September 1863 he and his family settled in a modest apartment near the zoological gardens, where he threw himself into a blossoming career as a free-lance journalist. Another career revived early in 1864, when he became minister at South Place Chapel. After the summer of 1863, Conway's life began to diverge from American affairs.[1]

His expatriation, nevertheless, was always limited. Part of Conway's journalistic marketability lay in his first-hand knowledge of American issues and public figures. Much of his output for English journals in the next few years dealt with American affairs, in a tone often but not always critical of national policy. And he never abandoned the antislavery cause. He continued to appear on abolitionist platforms in 1864 and 1865 and after the war he supported the Freedmen's Aid Society and wrote in favor of Radical Reconstruction. Probably his greatest contribution to the cause while in England was his third wartime book, *Testimonies Concerning Slavery*, published in London in the summer of 1864.[2]

Testimonies Concerning Slavery was a superb little book, dramatically written and cogently argued. The pro-Northern press responded warmly. The London *Morning Star* said it was "pregnant with truth" and "glowing with eloquence." The *Westminster Review* called it "unanswerable. . . . In so small a compass we do not know where so effective an argument is to be found." In the book Conway recalled growing up amid slavery and offered some personal observations about slavery's impact on Southern society. One chapter vigorously defended American abolitionists, carefully avoiding any mention of the Mason affair or broader abolitionist infighting. The last chapter advised the British people to support the North, even though no "clean and complete reform" ever could be won by the sword. After the war, Conway continued, Britain must pressure America to make abolition meaningful by extending equal rights to the freedmen. He added that the British themselves could still learn some things about the destructiveness of racial prejudice.[3]

The worst illness from which America suffered, Conway had written in *The Golden Hour*, was "prejudice against the Negro,—a disease which always has called for fearful cauterization." When he came to England, he believed, he was coming to a country less beset by that disease. In 1863 he joined the London Anthropological Society, a new organization dedicated to "promoting the study of Anthropology in a strictly scientific manner." Here, Conway believed, he could discuss racial matters more dispassionately than was possible in America. He was soon disappointed. Quickly he concluded that the Society was "led by a few ingenious gentlemen whose chief interest was to foster contempt of the negro."[4]

This assessment was correct. Under the leadership of its founder and president, Dr. James Hunt, the Anthropological Society threw itself into a host of political questions, always on the side of those who argued for black people's innate, irremediable inferiority. Hunt himself published a widely noticed pamphlet, *The Negro's Place in Nature*, in which he argued the polygenist belief that blacks were a separate and lowly subspecies. The Anthropological Society revealed to Conway the depth of racial bigotry in Britain, and was the primary catalyst for *Testimonies Concerning Slavery*.[5]

A substantial portion of *Testimonies* was devoted to vindicating the black race's abilities. Conway quarreled with Hunt and the Anthropological Society by name, hammering them with intelligence and wit. Then he moved from rebuttal to his own brief for racial equality. No portion of that brief, or of the book as a whole, has received more attention from historians than his spirited advocacy of miscegenation.[6]

"In the human world," wrote Conway, "each race is stronger in some direction than all others." This certainly seemed true of whites and blacks. "With regard to the mental characteristics of the Negroes in the Southern States, I have to say, that they seem to me to be weaker in the direction of the understanding, strictly speaking, but to have strength and elegance of imagination and expression." The black person, moreover, was "morally very much superior to the whites of any country in which I have observed whites. . . . He will suffer for those whom he loves. His affections are strong and steadfast; and he lacks selfishness to a degree that has been his undoing." Such traits might brand blacks as inferior in the eyes of most whites, accustomed to judge people by the standards of conventional intellect and brute force. "But, after all, there is, as the world gets older, a growing appreciation of simple goodness, kindliness and affectionateness. Intellect is the captain among the spiritual forces; it is brilliant, aggressive, immediately available; but there are quiet things, seemingly without force, which revolutionise the world as much in the end." Whites could profit by acquiring a deeper appreciation of these "quiet things." One way to do that was racial intermarriage. "I, for one, am firmly persuaded that the mixture of the blacks and whites is good. . . . Under the best circumstances, I believe that such a combination would evolve a more complete character than the unmitigated Anglo-Saxon. . . . We have not yet begun those higher combinations out of which the world's nobler offspring is to come."[7]

At first glance, Conway's assumptions about the emotional and moral superiority of blacks seem to peg him as a racial determinist no less than the Anthropological Society clique he opposed—and as a dreamy romantic to boot. A closer look tells a different story. As noted earlier, Conway's estimate of blacks bore a striking similarity to his assessment of women. Both seemed more emotional, more gentle, more aesthetically sensitive than white men. There was some romanticism in this, and some wishful thinking too. Prizing the emotional life and preferring sensitivity to force, Conway wanted to believe that the gentler qualities were upheld by a significant part of the human race. Yet Conway's view of blacks, like his view of women, was not plucked out of the air. As a boy he had witnessed countless examples of self-sacrifice by black victims of the arbitrary power of whites. He had seen enough of slave culture to know it was both rich and substantively different from that of his own master class. Denied literacy, slaves evolved a culture exploiting the aesthetic versatility of the spoken word and the power of visual evocation. Few modern scholars would quarrel with Conway's statement that "Negro sermons, fables, and descriptions are in the highest degree pictorial, abounding in mystic interpretations which would delight a German transcendentalist."[8]

A scholarly contortionist could take certain Conway statements about blacks and women and present him as believing that their aesthetic sensitivity and "moral superiority" were biologically ordained. Certainly his contention that miscegenation would constructively "soften" the aggressive white race points to this conclusion. The conclusion is wrong. Conway was not an academic but a reformer, seeking to change the world in certain ways. When he spoke of the "moral superiority" of blacks and women he was doing two things: asserting the worth of two oppressed groups, and stating his belief that humanity's preference for violence over gentleness was folly. His most fundamental reformist aim was to purge society of the sort of violent impulses that made human domination a virtue. If miscegenation might help—and current anthropology was sufficiently primitive to offer no clear answer—then he would advocate miscegenation. But he would campaign on other fronts too. The humanizing of society need not depend on biological evolution. It could begin now, by exposing white males, the group which held power and would do so for the foreseeable future, to an alternative set of values. One way to do this was to bring the groups which epitomized those alternate values into the mainstream of political and professional life. "Strike out the word *white* and the word *male* from our laws,"

Conway wrote in 1865, "and we shall reach the noblest transformation."[9]

If individual whites could be improved, so could blacks. When Conway described blacks as generally deficient in the traditional white male virtues of intellect and aggressiveness, he was not saying that this condition was grounded in their genes. When he advocated miscegenation, he was not suggesting that only an infusion of white blood could make black people the intellectual equals of whites. Surely many people believed this, ranging from reactionaries like Hunt to reformers like Harriet Beecher Stowe, in whose fiction mulattoes are smarter and bolder than blacks. But Conway explicitly denounced the notion. "There are, on the contrary," he wrote in *Testimonies*, "many instances of pure Negroes, and those in whom the Negro blood largely predominated, who have been eminent for their attainments." Among these he mentioned abolitionists Charles Remond, Sojourner Truth, and Harriet Tubman, along with scientist Benjamin Banneker, about whom Conway had written a valuable and much-reprinted article. "These . . . indicate sufficiently where, if ordinary fair play were allowed it, the black race might at length come to stand."[10]

Conway was far more likely to caution against racial (and sexual) stereotypes than engage in them himself. In *Testimonies* he warned his readers against accepting the implication of Negrophobes that Africans were a people of "uniform characteristics." He knew that generalizations about blacks, whether Africans or Americans, were usually self-serving and derogatory. There were stereotypes suited to all tastes. "Is your pet horror idleness? The negro will not accept a shilling unless you put it in his pocket for him. Are you a Quaker? The negro cares only for fine dress. Are you prudish? The negro goes naked."[11]

Racial equality, like gender equality, was indispensable to Conway's dream of a world free from the domination of some people by others. He longed for a society that epitomized the oneness of people, the brotherhood and sisterhood of humankind, where there would yet be full scope for the free expression of individual personality: a real community permitting real freedom. Not even the horror of the Civil War had destroyed his faith that human beings could achieve this. In the years ahead his faith would waver. He would begin to doubt whether a noncoercive community was possible. Yet he would never cease to seek it. The less possible it seemed, the more essential it was.

Written explicitly for a British audience, *Testimonies Concerning Slavery* was not published in America.[12] Conway's name remained prominent in the antislavery press during 1864, however, for he took an active part in the abolitionist quarrel over Lincoln's re-election. During that quarrel the opposing faction exhumed the Mason affair and hurled it at Conway, who responded in kind. As usually happened when abolitionists fought each other, arguments on both sides were often peevish, puerile, and petty. Yet something more came out of them. Conway, more self-confident and secure than a year earlier, was able to move the debate to a serious philosophical plane. In doing so he posed, perhaps more explicitly and pointedly than any other antislavery American, one of the most compelling questions the Civil War produced.

Since the war began, abolitionists had argued among themselves over how much to trust Lincoln and how much to push him. By 1863 those who trusted him could point to substantial accomplishments, notably the Emancipation Proclamation and the recruitment of black soldiers. To Lincoln's critics, these gains were less important than the government's tardiness and halfheartedness in achieving them. Such a government, they contended, could never be counted on to make black freedom meaningful. In December 1863, when the president unveiled his preliminary plan for Reconstruction, they became more sure of this than ever.

Under Lincoln's plan virtually all Confederates who pledged future loyalty would be pardoned. When 10 percent of those who had voted in 1860 took this oath, they could establish a new state government. These state governments could handle their black populations as they chose, as long as they recognized emancipation. Presumably this meant that civil and political inferiority would be acceptable, as would a labor system that tied blacks to the land in a serflike way. (In 1864 such a system of peonage went forward in occupied Louisiana under orders of the military commander there, with Lincoln's blessing.) Garrison was willing to stand by the president, grateful for what progress had been made and hopeful that more might follow. But for others the Reconstruction plan was too much. Sanborn lambasted it in *The Commonwealth*. Phillips took to the lecture circuit, denouncing the president to all who would listen.[13]

Many did. A slim majority of abolitionists seems to have lost enough patience with Lincoln by this point to wish him defeated,[14] and in this they found many allies of less radical persuasion. There was no shortage of alternative candidates acceptable to abolitionists: Salmon P. Chase, John C. Fremont, John Andrew, Benjamin Butler, perhaps even Ulysses S. Grant. By spring it was Fremont, popular among German-Americans and a hero to many abolitionists for his 1861 antislavery order, who had emerged from the pack. On May 31 a peculiar coalition of Democrats and disgruntled abolitionists convened and made the ex-general their presidential nominee.

Through all this, Conway's main sources of inside information were Phillips and Sanborn. Conway's long-time disenchantment with Lincoln found considerable reinforcement from both correspondents. He agreed with Phillips's judgment that the president was "no believer in *the negro*— as a citizen," and that "the mind that looks at the question thro' such an atmosphere is not fit to settle it." He also shared Phillips's enthusiasm for Fremont, despite misgivings about the convention which had nominated him. Sanborn was less sanguine about Fremont, as was *The Commonwealth*'s main financial backer, George Stearns, and that paper refused to endorse him. Yet Sanborn's anti-Lincoln bias was no less decided for that. During 1864 *The Commonwealth* solidified its reputation as the antislavery newspaper most critical of the president. Even when it became probable that Lincoln would be renominated at the June Republican convention, *The Commonwealth*'s editor still hoped enough pressure could force the president to step aside after the convention in favor of a candidate more committed to black equality. To achieve this, criticism had to be maintained at fever pitch. Lincoln's inadequacies had to be demonstrated in as many ways and from as many sources as possible. In May 1864, Sanborn turned to Conway for help.[15]

Although Conway had ceased to be co-editor of *The Commonwealth*, he had remained an occasional foreign correspondent. Now Sanborn sought to use his talents in the anti-Lincoln crusade. "One great source of Lincoln's strength," he explained, "is the belief that he is very popular in England and in Europe. . . ." If it turned out there was "a growing feeling, there as well as here, that we have had about enough of him, you ought to know it, and proclaim it in your letters to the *Com*." If the English really liked Lincoln, Sanborn wanted to know that "privately." In any case, he wanted Conway to criticize Lincoln "without scruple" in public letters.[16]

Conway was not reluctant to enter the fray, for at that moment he received infuriating news from America. In Jacksonville, Florida, a black sergeant had ordered his men to refuse duty until the army paid them the same wages white soldiers received. For this Sergeant William Walker was shot for mutiny. Conway discovered his anger at the execution was shared by many English friends. He thought he might help Sanborn's cause by conveying this to readers of *The Commonwealth*. So he wrote a long harangue against the government in general and the president in particular, expressing the "indignation and horror" felt by Englishmen at the "murder" of this "heroic" soldier. He went on to criticize Garrison strongly for declining to condemn the execution. In so doing, Conway not only stepped up his participation in the anti-Lincoln campaign, but also threw himself openly into the abolitionist schism the campaign had spawned.[17]

The first word of rebuttal came not from Garrison, but from Garrison's ally Oliver Johnson, editor of the *National Anti-Slavery Standard*. Late in June, Johnson printed excerpts from Conway's *Commonwealth* letter, branding it as "colored by the extravagance which usually mars the productions of the writer." Johnson's remarks were wholly personal, and did not mention the issues Conway, however provocatively, had raised. After some additional unflattering comments, Johnson closed by attacking at the sorest and most vulnerable point: "The recollection of his correspondence with the Confederate envoy, Mason, should teach

Mr. Conway to be modest in his judgments and sparing in his rebukes of other Abolitionists, especially of so old and tried a soldier of freedom as Mr. Garrison."[18]

The "soldier of freedom," meanwhile, was enjoying some of his greatest triumphs. Early in June, Garrison attended the Republican convention in Baltimore, where he saw much "to gladden my heart, and almost make me fear that I am at home dreaming. . . ." He watched with satisfaction as Lincoln won unanimous renomination, and as the delegates endorsed a constitutional amendment abolishing slavery throughout the country. On June 10 he and Theodore Tilton spent an hour with the president at the White House. "There is no mistake about it," he wrote the next day, "in regard to Mr. Lincoln's desire to do all that he can . . . to uproot slavery, and give fair play to the emancipated. I was much pleased with his spirit, and the familiar and candid way in which he unbosomed himself." For so many years an outcast who equated government with corruption, Garrison was now a respected celebrity, a valued and devoted booster of the president, and a political pragmatist. In July he even suggested that it might be wise to move slowly on black suffrage.[19]

For a number of abolitionists it was a shoddy spectacle. One man cancelled his thirty-year-long subscription to *The Liberator*, labeling Garrison's present posture "a recantation of your whole public labors." He was not alone. Many believed Garrison had "abandoned his tradition, resigned his call—left his post." *The Liberator* suffered enough defections that it almost went bankrupt. But the truth was not all on one side. The arguments of those who stood by Garrison had much to recommend them. Doubtless Phillips and his followers overestimated their ability to control events if they succeeded somehow in removing Lincoln, and overestimated the extent of pro-black sentiment among the Northern white population. Samuel May, Jr., correctly observed that "Lincoln has been as much *too slow* for Mr. Conway, . . . Wendell Phillips, etc. as he has been *too fast* for a very great body of Northern 'Democrats,' and— to their shame be it spoken—many Republicans also." If Lincoln had stepped down or been defeated, it was very possible that his replacement would have been far less committed to black rights than he. Only when the Democratic party nominated Negrophobe George McClellan for president in late August did many abolitionists see the danger and temper their criticism. The fact was that much *had* been gained, however slowly and grudgingly, and Lincoln *had* demonstrated a capacity for "growth" on racial issues. Garrison may have forsaken intellectual consistency and reformist purity in standing by the president, but he believed he did so in a way which served his principles. By conventional political terms he was right.[20]

A word should be said about Garrison personally. He had grown up a poor boy, largely self-educated, abandoned by his father. For most of his adult career he had been socially unrespectable, even reviled. He had worked tirelessly for a cause, sometimes at personal risk, for over thirty years. Now, at age sixty, for the first time in his life, he had prestige. It would have been strange had he not enjoyed it and tried to keep it, and it is a bit ungenerous to blame him. A comparison with his arch-rival Phillips is instructive. Phillips had grown up a rich boy, educated at Harvard, his father a mayor of Boston. Phillips could never be tempted by prestige because, in his mind, he never lacked it. It was his by breeding, something he could never lose, no matter how many conservative yahoos (and Brahmins) snubbed him. Ironically, this upper-class security enabled him to pursue with remarkable consistency a life "defined . . . by his radical commitments." The similarity to Conway is striking. One begins to see why the two liked each other so much.[21]

Phillips was quick to commiserate with Conway when Johnson shel-lacked him in the *Standard*. "My dear fellow I feel very keenly for you under these taunts." Yet what he had to say about American affairs was not designed to get Conway out of the feud. Lincoln was on the ropes, he said, and some more pummeling could bring him down. "You must [not] *print* this nor say it *in public* but Sumner is just as thoroughly disgusted with Lincoln as I am—Andrew is very much incensed with him—so others— . . . Party considerations keep them all silent. . . . During my whole winter's travel and lecturing seeing all classes I have never yet met one man who avowed a simple preference for Lincoln or wish on *his account* for his re-election."[22]

Conway needed no encouragement. He got the *Standard* about the same time he got Phillips's letter, and on July 26 sat down in fighting spirit to answer Johnson's attack. His letter was unapologetic, aggressive, sometimes ugly. He again brought up Sergeant Walker's execution and demanded that Johnson take a position on it. He called the inequity in black soldiers' wages a "robbery." "It is very plain that Walker sacrificed his life for a principle as much as John Brown did." His execution was "murder" and Lincoln was "his murderer." (The president had to approve personally all military executions.) Conway went on to char-acterize Lincoln as "an irredeemable Kentuckian and an impossible American," suffering from "an utter lack of culture" and "brutally ignorant of history and of his own age."[23]*

Conway freely acknowledged that Southern-sympathizing "copper-heads" were active in the Fremont movement. "If any Copperhead stands by my side for the abolition of slavery, the equality of the negro

---

* Conway's opinion of Lincoln did not mellow much with age. "While recognizing Abraham Lincoln's strong personality and high good qualities," he wrote in his autobiography, "I cannot participate in his canonization. . . . Abraham Lincoln decided that the fate of his country should be determined by powder and shot. In the canonization of Lincoln there lurks a consecration of the sword." Hamlin Garland, who discussed Lincoln with Conway during their one meeting, came away thinking Conway "a harsh, unlovely person." The *Literary Digest* (February 11, 1905) called Conway's estimate of Lincoln "the harshest note in his life's story." *AME*, II, 94; Garland, *Companions on the Trail* (New York, 1931), 277.

before the law, and the decapitation of an imbecile President, I will embrace that kind of Copperhead with my whole heart, and pray that the land may swarm with such! . . . Until Fremont yields to the Democrats the anti-slavery plank in his platform, I am with him heart and soul." True, many pro-Fremont Democrats did not look well on the war effort, and some even called for a negotiated settlement with the South. This did not seem to bother Conway as long as they could be induced to support emancipation and the genuine equality needed to make black freedom meaningful. This, after all, was what the war was about, wasn't it?[24]

In this context Conway met Johnson's Mason taunt head-on. A year earlier, Conway had had much to answer for. He had addressed an unrecognized Confederate official. He had made a concrete proposal without consulting anyone. He had presumed to speak for the whole abolitionist movement. Much of the ensuing fury had clouded the main issue and had revolved around these secondary blunders. This time Conway went straight to the heart of the matter. Whatever his indiscretion in writing to Mason and making an unauthorized proposition, the central question was this: did abolitionists support the Civil War for the sake of emancipation, or did they support the Union for its own sake? Would they sanction the carnage even if slavery were no longer an issue? Was this a war for principle or for power?

"Whilst I very soon found out that it was a mistake to write *to him* [Mason] at all," Conway wrote, "it never occurred to me before that I had given the Abolitionists too high credit in saying that . . . should the issue of freedom to the slave be out of the way, they would oppose the slaughter of thousands of human beings for a question of empire." Recent events were revealing the reality. "I am no longer so sure as I was that the pure and simple interest in which the Abolitionists are supporting this slaughter is the welfare and freedom of the slave." If abolitionists had altered their priorities, if they had lost their hatred of war, he wanted them to say so. "Please tell me whether, were the slaves all free and equal before the law, you would sanction the present bloodshed to recover the Union you so long denounced and sought to sunder in the interest of such negro freedom?"[25]

Conway challenged Oliver Johnson from the seaside town of Brighton, where his family had gone for the health of his younger son, Emerson. This child, not quite three years old, had always been sickly. From the spring of 1864 his condition had been deteriorating steadily and drastically. Measles gave way to a mysterious disorder diagnosed as hydrocephalus. In May the Conways moved to Wimbledon to take advantage of the country air.

Emerson seemed to improve. But in July a military review began at Wimbledon. As Moncure and Ellen tried to nurse their desperately ill son, soldiers drilled within earshot. Emerson sank again as rifles crackled and artillery roared. The Conways had never hated anything so much as they hated all armies now. In a final effort to save their child they moved again, to Brighton.[26]

The sea air did not help. Neither did a local homeopathic doctor. The Conways later discovered to their horror that this physician consulted "spirits" about the boy's treatment. Soon Emerson could not walk, to his own puzzlement and frustration. He knew he was very ill. He craved his parents' attention. He became terrified if one of them was not with him. Moncure and Ellen took turns at his bedside. They held his hand. They paced the room with him in their arms. They heeded his pitiful cries to "kiss me again." On August 4 he died.[27]

They buried him on a hill overlooking the sea, his grave marked by an ivy-covered cross. The cross was an odd touch, perhaps, for people who had broken with Christianity. But they needed healing, and consistency often is cruel. "I seem to myself to have absolutely known *nothing* of what real grief is hitherto," Conway told William Dean Howells. "I think at least I shall hereafter have a clearer eye to recognize the angels God sends to me." In mid-August, physically exhausted and shattered by grief, Moncure and Ellen, with five-year-old Eustace, left to find rest on the Continent.[28]

At Heilbrönn, Conway met David Friedrich Strauss, whose *Life of Jesus* had made such trouble for American Unitarians. Strauss was just returning to theological writing after a twenty-year absence, in 1864 publishing a popularized version of his work on Jesus. Conway called on him with a letter of introduction. The two walked for some time along the banks of the Neckar. The conversation was slow, for Strauss's English was no better than Conway's German. Somehow they managed. They talked about freedom, and about control. Conway later paraphrased Strauss's remarks. The German said that his own religious writings were meant to strike "at the root of the whole tree of political and social degradation," by validating the questioning spirit. "The man who gives up the whole of his moral nature to an unquestioned authority," Strauss claimed, "suffers a paralysis of his mind, and all the changes of outward circumstance in the world cannot make him a free man." Conway had found a kindred soul.[29]

In one respect Conway did not get the comfort from Strauss he wanted. He was searching for some meaning in Emerson's death, some way of taking solace from it. Evidently without telling Strauss of his recent tragedy, he asked him if there was anything worth reading about immortality. Strauss thought for a time. Then he answered "No."[30]

In September Moncure and Ellen stopped at Ostend on the Belgian coast. There they found a trace of the relief they had been seeking. Beautiful little Ostend endeared itself to them as no other place had. They, and later Moncure alone, would return many times. Watching promenaders on the Digue, men and women splashing in the waves, children playing on the shore, they began to find hope for the future and courage to face it. At Ostend they repledged their love for one another, and found it strong enough to transcend, if not conquer, disaster. Nine months later Ellen bore another son, Dana.[31]

In mid-September they were back in London, where Moncure resumed his duties at South Place Chapel. Their old apartment had too many reminders of their dead son—Moncure never liked to be reminded of death—so they moved to new lodgings at 28 Notting Hill Square, near Aubrey House. Economist John Elliot Cairnes, author of the influential book *The Slave Power* (1862), was a neighbor in the same building. Through him the Conways met John Stuart Mill and his circle. Thus new surroundings and new friends joined with the therapy of work and the comfort of a new child to ease the pain the Conways had suffered.[32]

As one wound was healing, another was opening wider. Garrison's followers had been angered by Conway's July letter to the *Anti-Slavery Standard*. On August 27 Oliver Johnson printed the letter and responded, heatedly and without restraint. Conway, he charged, was "narrow, censorious, intolerant and divisive," and his assertions were "ridiculous." Sergeant Walker had indeed been guilty of "mutiny," and had been justly shot. Abolitionists' support of Lincoln, who had done so much to help the slaves and was the best candidate one could hope to get, was simply "common sense applied to public affairs." Johnson went on to describe himself as "disgusted" by Conway's nonchalance at keeping spiritual company with antiwar Democrats, and implied he was guilty of treason. At the least, Conway was politically stupid and morally defective. Johnson quoted from the Mason correspondence, calling the episode "a mistake which should make its author forever distrustful of his own unaided judgment in practical affairs." In that correspondence, he alleged, Conway had mangled the simple truth on at least two counts: he had not been sent to England by the abolitionists, and they had given him no authority to do anything. Such a man should not now be trusted and should "for the rest of his life, be slow to impeach the sagacity and fidelity of others." Conway's question to him—whether abolitionists would support more slaughter if slavery were no longer at issue—Johnson parried with a haughty evasion: "At present, we choose to devote ourselves to the discussion of practical rather than hypothetical questions."[33]

By the time this reply reached Conway, the president's re-election had become assured. McClellan's nomination in late August made many anti-Lincoln abolitionists nervous, less inclined to take votes away from Lincoln by sticking with Fremont. The decisive event, however, was the capture of Atlanta on September 2. By making military victory probable in the foreseeable future, Sherman's progress in Georgia dissipated Northern war-weariness and guaranteed Lincoln's success. Fremont dropped out of the race in mid-September. In November the president handily defeated McClellan.

If the election campaign had incited Conway's renewed and heightened warfare with pro-Garrison abolitionists, its resolution did nothing to calm the antislavery combatants. The feud had taken on a life of its own. In mid-October Conway wrote to the *Standard* again. He admitted the election was a dead issue, but insisted on getting some things straight. First, Johnson was wrong in saying the abolitionists had not sent him abroad. "The leading anti-slavery men of America *did* send me to England, paying my expenses hither and giving me such introductions as would secure my representing the American cause before English audiences. Wendell Phillips first proposed the trip to me, and Mr. Garrison at once sanctioned it. . . ."[34]

Far more important, though, was the question of authorization. Conway admitted that he had not been authorized to speak to Mason, a mistake he regretted. But he still contended that he had "authority," as one who had known leading abolitionists for some years, to state their principles. A central principle, he believed, was that violence was not justified merely to save the Union. "I asked you," Conway told Johnson, "if you would support this carnage for a less principle: you refused to reply, calling it 'hypothetical.' It is not hypothetical to me. . . . You are bound to reply, or else retract the charge that I made an unauthorized statement of the motives of Abolitionists in sustaining this war."[35]

Conway refused to let what he viewed as the primary issue die. If they believed it, then Garrison and his cronies must say it out loud, explicitly, nakedly: we are fighting for national consolidation now. We will do so even if slavery is not involved. It is a question of power. And it is worth the deaths of all these men.

His stubbornness was winning him allies. "What is Mr. Conway's offence with your public?" asked English writer F. W. Newman. "Precisely what Mr. Garrison for 30 years was chargeable with: viz. the feeling the negro question so exclusively, as to have no care whatever for patriotism." Cracks were even appearing in the Garrisonian ranks. After Conway's October letter appeared in the *Standard* on November 19, New Bedford abolitionist Daniel Ricketson wrote to *The Liberator* (November 25) and announced "my change of opinion in his [Conway's] favor." Until now Garrison himself had stayed out of the fight. Now, with Conway gaining sympathy, he could remain aloof no longer. At the end of Ricketson's letter he announced he would answer Conway the following week.[36]

He did not. Garrison's remarks on December 2 begged Conway's central question and revolved instead around the factual point on which the younger man was most vulnerable. "He 'sent' himself to England," concluded Garrison, "and made personal appeals far and near to procure the means to defray his expenses—and that is the whole of it." To pound the point home, Garrison printed a letter from an unnamed Philadelphia abolitionist who claimed cryptically, "Mr. Conway's *mission*—rhetorically so called—has a private as well as a public history. . . . I therefore say to Mr. Conway and his friends, the less said on the point of being *'sent,'* the better."[37]

The fight over the issue of Conway's sponsorship dragged on long enough that Conway's friends had to ask him privately to desist. "I cannot agree that you were in any sense *'sent'* by the Abolitionists," wrote Phillips. "That phrase was unhappily chosen." George Stearns thought Conway's case a bit stronger, but could not remember "whether we proposed it or you did." The truth was that on this matter Conway was wrong. Garrison was right. The English trip had been Conway's idea from the start. Nobody else had sent him. He had needed to escape the war but could not fully admit it. Thus he had to believe that his trip had been clamored for by others. Doubtless he firmly believed that now and perhaps always had. It was not objectively true. The Philadelphian was right. There was a private history to Conway's mission.[38]

Conway's myopia on that point, however, did not diminish the significance of his main question. A number of people now wanted that one answered. "Mr. Conway has put a very important question as to the real policy of the Anti-Slavery party in connection with the war," wrote antislavery Englishman G. Julian Harney in *The Liberator* of December 9. "I beg to submit that that question is not answered by discussing whether Mr. Conway was 'sent' to England, or went there on his own inspiration. . . ." The issue would not down. The question would keep coming up. If Conway did not ask it, others now would. After Harney's letter, Garrison bit the bullet and answered it.[39]

In doing so he could not resist another swipe at the "untruthfulness" of Conway, who had sent himself abroad and "begged the needed funds." But in the end he spoke to Conway's challenge. "It is no part of the moral philosophy of Abolitionists to do evil that good may come." Presumably the loss of the South would be an intolerable evil under any circumstances. "The rebellious South being wholly without excuse for her course, and the Government entirely in the right, neither as Americans nor as philanthropists could the Abolitionists with honor or propriety pledge themselves to endeavor to force the Government to recognize the independence of the Southern Confederacy, even to secure so great a boon as the abolition of slavery." It would have been hard to put it more baldly.[40]

But not impossible. Oliver Johnson had relented to Conway's badgering three weeks earlier. "The Abolitionists, as we understand them, hold, not that the abolition of slavery is the end of the war, but a necessary and therefore rightful *means* to that end. And we do not hesitate to say that, if war is ever justifiable, it is so in this case on the part of the North, and would be even if the rebels should abolish slavery."[41]

Conway's bitter feud with Garrison and his followers illustrated how drastically many abolitionists had altered their political and moral priorities, and induced them to admit it as directly as possible. Doubtless Conway deluded himself in evidently thinking that the anti-Garrison wing of the movement fully supported his own position. Hardly any abolitionists, whatever they thought of Garrison's flirtation with political pragmatism, would have been willing now to let the South go under any circumstances. Probably because of Conway's identification with this idea, Phillips shrewdly declined to defend him publicly—he told Conway "it would . . . show us radicals 'quarreling' as they say among ourselves"— while at the same time he privately urged Conway on. He understood that Conway's emphasis on the wastefulness of the fighting, plus his lack of enthusiasm for a prospective military victory, made him a dangerous ally. He also knew that Conway, in attacking Garrison, could do him a great service.[42]

What Phillips and Conway shared was a fear that abolitionism was losing its soul. Garrison, by collaborating with and apologizing for the administration, was compromising the movement's ability to act as an independent voice of conscience, a definer of the ideal. Garrison had a strong case in supporting Lincoln, and in no way did he regard himself as changing his principles, which he believed had substantially triumphed. But as time went on, disaffected activists had more and more reason to be disturbed by some of their colleagues' breezy willingness to follow Republican leadership. There *was* still much to be done to guarantee black rights and to assure that the freedmen did not fall back into de facto slavery, and the administration *did* seem reluctant to move decisively or expeditiously on these points. By 1865 Garrison wanted to dissolve the American Anti-Slavery Society on the grounds that there was nothing more for it to do. (In May the Society voted to remain active. It persisted, under Phillips's leadership, until ratification of the Fifteenth Amendment in 1870.) Many believed, with Sanborn, that by a policy "of excuse and palliation" for the "short-comings" of the government, Garrison and his remaining disciples were "risking the value of a life-long instruction." However uncharitable or unreasonable Phillips sometimes could be, he was not wrong in saying there was still work to do, that the country had not lost its need for prophets.[43]

Conway's antislavery work from 1864 into Reconstruction was essentially part of Phillips's effort to keep the uncompromising spirit of the abolitionists alive. He did not, as one historian has written, "retain a sterile kind of purity by withdrawing all support from the war." On the contrary, he never ceased to believe (and say) that as long as the war had to go on, the North was more worthy of support than its opponent. This was inherent in his journalism and in *Testimonies Concerning Slavery*. But, like Phillips, he made more of his opposition than his support. His criticism, moreover, was very useful to Phillips, who encouraged it and also profited from it. Conway was valuable to Phillips because he was expendable. He was out of the country, and had developed a reputation for idiosyncrasy. If in his attacks on Lincoln or Garrison he went too far, pro-Phillips abolitionists could easily distance themselves from him. At the same time, they could capitalize on any rhetorical victories he might win in his fracas with the Garrison wing. If he drew the other side out, if he helped expose the extent of Garrison's fall from grace— and the quarrels which spun off from Conway's controversy indicated that he succeeded in this—so much the better. Conway had physically escaped the war, as he had needed to do. Yet he had not ceased to care who won, if there had to be a military victor. In the meantime he was interested, like the Phillips faction, in seeing that the victor came out of the war as morally responsible as possible.[44]

There was one respect, however, in which he did differ from almost all the others. Since the start of the war he had been hit especially hard by the killing. His Southern blood contributed to his reaction, as did his deep-seated horror and hatred of violence. Always he had cherished two objectives: to end slavery and stop the bloodshed. If one could do both only by sacrificing national re-unification, then he was quite willing to pay that price. He had said so in the Mason episode, and was still suggesting the idea in print as late as January 1865.[45] By then he knew such a solution would never be considered as a matter of practical policy. Yet he still held high the principles involved. National consolidation, if it mattered at all, should be only a vehicle for emancipation— not the other way around. Killing should be seen as a great moral wrong, equal to slavery, and far worse than the mere breakup of national power.

One has an inevitable impulse to see Conway as a bit quixotic and maladjusted. Quixotic because the proposal embodied in the Mason affair was never practically possible, maladjusted because he was psychically unable to come to terms with the war's violence. But something in his complex, lonely, poignant stance demands that he not be dismissed.

Conway offered an alternate vision. Surely he was unrealistic whenever he believed his views were widely shared, and in 1863 if he thought he would have support for his concrete proposal. But he was never a policy maker. His lack of conventional realism matters less than the value of his vision. He reminded anyone who would listen that both liberty and life are sacred, and that respect for one involves respect for the other. He stood with Phillips in insisting that when Garrison and his colleagues called emancipation merely a means to a greater end, they had lost their moral compass. Almost alone, he went beyond this charge to demand that all abolitionists, if they still cared about upholding first principles, take a stand against "all lust of empire," for peace as well as liberty.[46] It was in keeping with his lifelong dream of a society that was both truly civilized and truly free.

The post-war world was neither. The promise of early Reconstruction gave way to Southern white resistance and national fatigue. At century's end Southern blacks were still largely a class of poor, disfranchised, intimidated, segregated peons. Conway, who never ceased to advocate black equality, regarded the situation as evidence that the Civil War had been an unrelieved disaster, a "damnable double-tongued war that lured the best youth to their graves with promises now broken." Americans had undervalued liberty. The result was a new form of racial domination. They had undervalued peace. The result was 620,000 deaths—2 percent of the 1860 national population—plus the further glorification and sanctioning of violence and war. In the end even abolitionists had lost their way, succumbing to the attractions of "mere power." When that is the main concern, he had warned, the result can be neither liberty nor peace.[47]

"It were idle to say," wrote Conway in January 1865, "that the victories of the Union are now the victories of emancipation. Sherman's progress through Georgia is traceable in burning towns but not, so far as the world learns, in broken fetters. Few are the cries of joy from liberated slaves that mingle with the wailings of those whose homes are desolated. Are these the fine issues to which the spirits of American reformers have been finely touched?"[48]

Moncure Conway was quixotic, maladjusted, unrealistic—and disturbingly prophetic. He has not lost the power to haunt.

After the war the Virginia Conways straggled home and returned to the business of life. Richard moved to a farm in a nearby county where he eked out a hardscrabble existence for his growing family. Peter, heir apparent to his father, stayed in town. The war had been hard on him, dealing him a nearly fatal bout with typhoid plus a leg shattered by an artillery shell. But he had survived, and now wore his wound as a badge of honor. The community welcomed him back as a hero, a bright and honorable young man with a golden future. His father could not have been prouder.[49]

Walker was back too. He had resisted the Yankees to the end. When Richmond fell he had retreated west to Charlottesville. There he made plans to move to whatever Confederate enclave still held out in the West. Only when it became clear that the war was really over did he admit defeat. In June the Fredericksburg *Ledger* happily announced his return to the area, calling him "too valuable a business man to remain long unemployed." The war had changed both the size and character of his fortune, but Walker Conway was still an important man on the Rappahannock. Having lost his slave labor, he elected to abandon farming for a full-time career in banking. He sold the house in Falmouth and much of his Stafford County land, and moved with his wife and Peter to Fredericksburg. There he helped found the banking house of Conway, Gordon and Garnet, and became a respected figure in local government. He did not lose his place.[50]

Margaret Conway had preceded her husband home, thanks to money sent her by their exiled son. Moncure, who had not been able to reconcile North and South, could at least bring together the war-scattered members of his own family. In a symbolically charged gesture near the end of the war, he sent his mother fifty dollars and asked that she use it to reunite the family. She never "allowed the family to forget that 'Moncure's money brought us all home again.' "[51]

Conway's gesture did not mean that he had forgotten his political differences with the other men in his family. The estrangement those differences had caused would never cease to hurt. For a time he harbored the hope that with the war over his father's views would change. Yet Moncure's continued inability to write to him betrayed his pessimism. Knowing his father would not acknowledge him, Moncure confided to his mother his hope that Walker would resist Southern white efforts to keep the freedmen in submission. "Do they think that God can be cheated? Do they not see that the negro must have all of his civil and political rights? . . . How do I hope and pray that pa will take the true, brave, human and democratic side on this question. . . . The weak, the short-sighted and selfish may misunderstand him, but he will crown a useful life—always leaning toward the just side with a most important service to mankind as well as his state." It was, of course, a vain plea. Walker Conway was not about to take advice from a son no longer his. He would fight for what was left of his old world. He served on the Fredericksburg city council as a loyal Democrat, opposed Radical Reconstruction, and never lost his commitment to the racial status quo.[52]*

Moncure's support for Reconstruction was not limited to family exhortations. Among Americans living abroad, he was one of the leading proponents of the radical position, and a number of Englishmen, prominent and obscure, consulted him for information and advice. He barraged *The Commonwealth* with letters supporting black suffrage and denouncing President Johnson's encouragement of Southern white intransigence. Most importantly, he offered the English public some of the clearest, most sober and responsible expositions of the radical program—including, ultimately, the attempted removal of Johnson—to appear in the English press.[53]

American affairs, however, were no longer Conway's primary concern. By the late 1860s he was established as a leading radical minister in London, developing a reputation for himself in England that was quite detached from his former American career. If he was genuinely concerned about political events in the United States, his articles about

---

* In 1869 Moncure was still trying to explain himself (indirectly) to his father. "I can only trust that when the time comes—as however late, it must—that my father shall apply to the subject his good sense and his honest heart, it may seem to him better on the whole that his son should have followed what he believed the truth, than to have purchased the smiles of relatives by hypocrisy and suppression of his convictions." MC to Margaret Daniel Conway, August 26, 1869, CU.

them were part of a much more varied new career as a free-lance journalist. Conway had left America to escape something, without much thought to what he would find in his transatlantic refuge. He was lucky. What he found was nothing less than the chance for a full new life, the chance for happiness and usefulness on the other side of the sea. He would not spurn it. He would stay.

There always had been a tension in Conway between his drive for independence and his need for interdependence, a compulsion to confront and a craving to reconcile, an impulse toward conflict and a longing for peace. For much of his life he had kept these competing needs balanced, though uneasily. The Civil War had disrupted the balance and forced him to take sides actively in the bloodiest conflict in American history. It had burdened him with the most macabre of ironies, compelling him to fight the violent subjugation of one people by violently subjugating another—his own people. Ultimately, it was an irony he could not accept.

Conway emerged from this chastening experience with a renewed commitment to reconciliation. He had not lost his talent for polemics, but to some extent he had lost his taste for them. He would still take unpopular stands on hard issues. He would still worry about submitting to authority. He would still confront the complacent. But increasingly his emphasis would be on community more than conflict. As a writer, he could interpret America for Europe and Europe for America, while helping to strengthen a transatlantic community of writers and thinkers. From his highly visible position of responsibility at South Place Chapel he could speak and write about his dreams of human unity. At the intellectual crossroads which South Place was, he could fulfill his longing to serve as mediator.

"London had cordially offered me," he said later, "what my native country had not—a field for the exercise of the ministry for which my strange pilgrimage from slaveholding Virginia and Methodism to freedom and rationalism had trained me."[54] As minister at a chapel dedicated to freedom of thought, he would have his first sustained opportunity for the sort of life he had so long craved, a life as a respected leader in a genuine community of men and women who would never bind him to a creed.

POSTSCRIPT

Conway's years in London were his happiest. His family life was full and contented, made richer by the birth of a daughter, Mildred, in 1868. His living was ample, thanks to the steady stream of articles that poured from his pen. He developed a transatlantic reputation through his journalism and the visibility of South Place, the liveliest center for free thought in Britain. His distinguished ministry was largely unencumbered by the internal feuds his ministries had known in America. He had time to give to real scholarship, producing a series of books that included, most notably, *Demonology and Devil-Lore* (1879), one of the best works on that subject until well into the twentieth century.

He even made a sort of peace with Virginia. In 1875–76 he went on a lecture tour in America—his first visit since his departure in 1863—during which he visited Fredericksburg and had a poignant reconciliation with his father. The spirit carried over to Cincinnati, where he was present at the reuniting of the two church factions that had split so bitterly in 1859.

Reconciliation now seemed at the heart of both his life and his work. He spoke and wrote passionately about the need for reciprocal understanding and support on the part of nations, races, and sexes. He tried to bridge the gap between continents through his own literary work and through his services as agent for authors on both sides of the Atlantic. "There is a feeling of sadness," he wrote in 1876, "that I cannot reduce the Atlantic to a little stream, that we may . . . bind the free progressive minds of England and America into one great fraternity."[1]

Beneath the surface, all was not quite so placid. Conway never fully freed himself—and Ellen less so—from the feeling of being an outsider in London, and as time went by they were increasingly ready to try America again. In 1885 they did.

They settled in New York City, where Moncure devoted himself to

221

literary work, producing two forgettable novels and several scholarly books, the best of which were a sensitive biography of Hawthorne (1890) and an excellent *Life of Thomas Paine* (1892). If Moncure was back in America, however, he still was not of it. The temper of the times distressed him, especially a growing militarism and a worsening racial climate. The death of his brilliant twenty-one-year-old son Dana in 1886 darkened his mood and dampened his faith in "progress."

By 1897, at the end of a four-year return engagement at South Place, Conway's philosophy had undergone a striking change from what it had looked like at the end of the American years. Much of his adult career had been spent proclaiming the Emersonian creed that evil is only "good in the making," that the direction of the world was inexorably toward the better, that "progress" could never long be retarded. That faith had supported his break with Virginia. It also had helped provoke his departure from war-torn America and the lessons the war might otherwise have taught, when he abandoned the darkening, guilty New World to find innocence and sunlight in the Old. During his first South Place ministry he had always proclaimed the glory of evolution, ever onward and upward, and the illusory nature of evil, wrong, and pain— things that only "helped" us by alerting us to what was good. Personal and political events in the 1880s made that increasingly hard to believe. By 1897 it was impossible. That year Ellen died.

It was partly the way she died. Her cancer was detected in 1896. The operation made things worse. She wanted to die at home—wherever that was. In the summer of 1897 they left South Place forever and moved in with their daughter and son-in-law in New York. Ellen suffered terribly. Moncure did too. He sat with her through long hours, until she urged him to go out. He walked the streets as a ghost, stopped in at theaters and music halls, but did not see or hear. He visited Elizabeth Stanton, who tried fruitlessly to soothe him. He could not live without his wife. He would have to. She died on Christmas day.

It seemed the gods were mocking him. Ellen's death was not enough. The next spring America went to war with Spain, in what Conway considered the blatant rape of a weaker nation. The enthusiasm for the war, even by freethinkers (though many would join him in denouncing the subsequent colonial war against the Filipinos), disgusted him. In May he lambasted the members of the Free Religious Association, in a defiant speech at their convention, for their complacency in the face of evil. It existed. Pain was real, wrong was real, inevitable progress was illusion. "All our Ethical Culture movements and free religion are sadly in need of a devil," he told them. "Satan is gone, Antichrist has gone, our pulpit-devil is no devil at all, merely a man of straw. . . ." But there was a devil in the world. There was irremissible evil. He knew it now. On that score, Emerson had been wrong. Now, in 1898, the "devil is the murder which is labelled with the divine name . . . and sometimes masquerading as civilization, and humanity—the real devil is *War*." The

Free Religionists did not like his speech. They more warmly applauded later speakers who sang praises to this new violent crusade for freedom. Within a month Conway left the country.[2]

He settled this time in Paris, which he thought the most civilized city in the world. His faith in France was soon reinforced as he watched intellectuals and artists defeat the forces of militarism during the Dreyfus affair. For the next nine years he spent most of his time in Paris, visiting New York in the warmer months to see friends, children, and grandchildren. In Paris he became the oldest member of a fascinating circle of artists and writers. He worked on some scholarly projects, and on the monumental memoir that appeared in 1904. To French friends, his American past was little known. He was to them simply "a writer of trained critical methods and a lucid style, who knew all the details of their own Revolution, and who had always manifested his warm sympathy for their country."[3]

In 1903 came the Emerson centennial. Concord celebrated. Conway was invited. He was in New York at the time and could have gone. He did not. He sent a letter, he wrote a few appreciative articles, but Emerson was no longer his guiding star. "Emerson had not dealt with evil in nature," had not seen the world as it was. "The high hopes and visions he inspired of a fairer world," Conway wrote in a public letter, "seem steadily turning to illusions." Evil was not good in the making. Evil was evil.[4]

In 1904 came the Hawthorne centennial. Concord celebrated. Conway was invited. He went. He spoke on the Hawthorne he had known, and failed to know. "When the anti-slavery agitation was going on Hawthorne did not unite in it, because he did not see with us the millennial America which was to blossom like a rose so soon as slavery was cleared away." Conway had avoided Hawthorne during that war, though for a time they lived in the same town. He regretted that now, for Hawthorne had had much to tell him. "The world set in Hawthorne's heart was the world as it existed—a world all-inclusive, with heights and depths." Hawthorne's was not a cranky or "dyspeptic" vision, as Conway had called it in 1860. It was a vision that could better appreciate the nobility of the heights for knowing the terrible reality of the depths.[5]

As a youth in Virginia, Conway had read Hawthorne and admired him. His cousin's Richmond *Examiner* had sung the novelist's praises. But on leaving Virginia, Conway had decided Hawthorne had nothing to say to him. In 1853 he had visited Concord for the first time, to see only Emerson. The sage pointed the way to a bright new world, and Conway spent decades in his quest for it. Now, fifty-one years later, he was back in Concord. For the last time. For Hawthorne.

He was not rejecting everything that Emerson had meant for him. In fact, part of Emerson's legacy seemed more important than ever. In an age of growing pressure to conform, individuality was all the more essential, the "torpor of tradition" was still an enemy. Arbitrary power, domination by the will of others, was still a scourge, especially in an age of imperialism and national chauvinism when peoples, as well as people, were dominated. "This going through the world with the idea that we are to Americanize or to Anglicize all people and nations of the world is a horrible effort to destroy the variety and freedom of nature. I make the same warning against it that Emerson makes about children, when he says to the parent: 'Get off that child! You are trying to make that man another You: one is enough.' "[6]

Yet Conway now combined this Emersonian respect for individuality and freedom with a Hawthornesque knowledge—rejected long ago when he left Virginia—that no amount of fearless individuality and untrammeled freedom would usher in a perfect world. He still worked for causes; they still mattered. But he had no illusions about what those causes would achieve. The best anyone could hope for was to make one's own life a thing to be proud of, to make others happy, to live truly, to know and give love.

He did that. In his last years, the dual lessons of his American years, the lessons of Emerson and Hawthorne, of Concord sunlight and Virginia shade, came together. The result was a life of wisdom and dignity and measured purposefulness. The little knot of Paris Bohemians loved him as one loves a very special man.

He loved them too, and their children. The children were important to him—he saw his own grandchildren so seldom. Always the teacher, he encouraged them to care, to love, to ask questions. As his mother had taught him when a boy in Virginia, he encouraged them to be themselves, to be dissatisfied with convention, to always ask why.

Photographer Edward Steichen, watching his daughter Mary play with this Jehovah-like sage, thought he had a real genius for communicating with children. Surely Mary Steichen, whom Conway taught to be bold and free-spirited, learned her lessons well. As Mary Steichen Calderone, she would become an internationally known spokeswoman for sexual sanity and knowledge, always confronting the conventional, always asking why. Moncure Conway would have been proud.[7]

"My little Mary and he were such good friends," wrote Steichen, "and when I told her he was dead she said, 'Pourquoi?' "

NOTES

ABBREVIATIONS

MC   Moncure Conway

EDC   Ellen Dana Conway

CU   Columbia University (unless otherwise noted, the Conway Papers)

DC   Dickinson College (unless otherwise noted, the Conway Papers)

HU   Houghton Library, Harvard University

AME   Moncure Conway, *Autobiography, Memories, and Experiences*, 2 vols. (Boston and New York: Houghton Mifflin, 1904)

INTRODUCTION

1. My account of the Conway memorial service derives from Frances Garrison Villard diary, December 14, 16, 1907, HU; Anonymous account of the service by a former member of his Cincinnati congregation, Biography File, Cincinnati Historical Society; *South Place Magazine*, Vol. XIII, No. 6 (February 1908), 91.

2. Anonymous account of Conway memorial service of December 14, 1907, Biography File, Cincinnati Historical Society.

3. Article by Andrew Carnegie in *New York Times* [c. January 1908], newspaper scrapbook, CU.

4. Edward Steichen to Eustace Conway [November 1907], DC; Circular and list of subscribers to Conway memorial fund, South Place Ethical Society, London; Peter McGwinn to Peter V.D. Conway, December 19, 1907, CU.

5. Higginson's remarks introducing MC, in *The Free Religious Association: Proceedings at the Thirty-first Annual Meeting* (Boston: The Free Religious Association, 1898), 14.

6. Peter Walker, *Moral Choices: Memory, Desire, and Imagination in Nineteenth-*

Century American Abolition (Baton Rouge: Louisiana State University Press, 1978), 34.

7. *AME*, I, 371–373; MC diary, December 31, 1862, CU.

CHAPTER 1

1. Margaret Daniel Conway to Eustace Conway, June 4, 1879, CU.

2. MC to EDC, March 2 [1876], CU.

3. Information on Conway's ancestry can be found in genealogical notes in the Conway Papers, CU, in the Richmond *Times-Dispatch*, January 10, 1904, and in *AME*, I, 1–6.

4. There is no adequate history of Stafford County, but John T. Goolrick, *The Story of Stafford: A Narrative History of Stafford County, Virginia* (Fredericksburg, Va.: The Fredericksburg Press, 1976) can be helpful if read with care.

5. The indispensable source for biographical information on most old Virginia families is Horace Edwin Hayden, *Virginia Genealogies* (Wilkes-Barre, Pa.: E. B. Yordy, 1891). For the Daniels see Hayden, 306–317. For Peter Vivian Daniel see John P. Frank, *Justice Daniel Dissenting: A Biography of Peter V. Daniel, 1784–1860* (Cambridge, Mass.: Harvard University Press, 1964). For editor John Moncure Daniel see Frederick S. Daniel, *The Richmond Examiner During the War; or, the Writings of John M. Daniel, With a Memoir of his Life* (New York: Printed for the Author, 1868).

6. For John Moncure Conway see Hayden, 278, and *AME*, I, 6, 18. For Eustace Conway see Hayden, 288–289. Today at the Stafford County courthouse the entrance is flanked by portraits of Walker and Eustace Conway, while a portrait of Richard Moncure hangs over the bench and a portrait of John Moncure Conway hangs nearby.

7. For Walker Conway see Hayden, 284, 285.

8. MC to EDC, September 10, 1875, CU.

9. Land tax records, Stafford County, 1832–1840, Virginia State Library.

10. The Falmouth Manufacturing Company, known also as the Falmouth Cotton Factory, first appears in 1840 in Stafford County land tax records, Virginia State Library. Its assessed value of $23,635.45 remains constant through 1851. An advertisement for the factory's products signed by W. P. Conway and J. W. Slaughter appears in the Fredericksburg *Weekly Recorder*, August 17, 1844. For information on the Southern cotton textile industry see Clement Eaton, *The Growth of Southern Civilization, 1790–1860* (New York: Harper and Row, 1961), 228–229; and Robert S. Starobin, *Industrial Slavery in the Old South* (New York: Oxford University Press, 1970), 12–13 and *passim*. Walker Conway's election as president of the Bank of Virginia is announced in the Fredericksburg *Weekly Advertiser*, March 7, 1857.

11. *AME*, I, 15–17.

12. *Ibid.*

13. Margaret Daniel Conway to MC, March 10, 1880, CU ("*drugging* ordeal"); Margaret Daniel Conway to MC, June 2, 1857, CU ("the only person"); MC to EDC, September 14 [1875], CU ("larger than"); Margaret Daniel Conway to EDC, June 2, 1874, CU ("such constant demand"). The standard work on homeopathy is Martin Kaufman, *Homeopathy in America* (Baltimore: Johns Hopkins University Press, 1971).

14. Notes for Reminiscences, CU. The quotation is from MC's novel, *Prisons of Air* (New York: Lovell, 1891), 203, and relates to Edmond Elder, his autobiographical protagonist: "In Edmond there had been a nature inherited from his father, but it was never strong . . . that having passed away, his maternal inheritance . . . rose full-grown in him."

15. *AME*, I, 30, 32–33.

16. *Ibid.*, I, 15, 26; Dickinson Copy-Book (MC's journal), March 31, 1848, CU, records a day of hunting, during which he also took the time to read *Much Ado About Nothing*. In several different places Conway reports that he never hunted again after 1850. The quotation ("I set my mother . . .") is in *AME*, I, 46. The one schoolyard fight in which Conway could recall having participated was the result of his defending a female friend, Mary Eliza Jett, who was being taunted by children "superior to her in position but not in intelligence." Moncure "plunged in among them with a stick striking right and left with my eyes shut tight—crying, 'Mind, I don't see anybody.' " Mary Eliza died young, but her mother never forgot Moncure's championship of her, and reminded him of it many years later. MC to EDC, September 22, 1875, CU.

17. *AME*, I, 12; Hayden, 286.

18. *AME*, I, 23–24; MC, *Demonology and Devil-Lore*, 2 vols. (New York: Henry Holt and Company, 1879), I, 326–327. *Demonology* was also published in London, by Chatto and Windus.

19. *AME*, I, 33.

20. *AME*, I, 10 ("Come, Monc"); Maria is listed in the Fredericksburg Methodist Church records, Fredericksburg, Va., as being in the "colored" Sunday school class in 1843, and her death is recorded in 1845. Peter Humstead's reading lessons are mentioned in *AME*, I, 21. Willie Lee Rose has pointed out that Conway was technically incorrect in his adult assertion that it was illegal to teach slaves to read. Rather, Virginia law "forbade general meetings of classes and accepting *money* for teaching slaves to read." But Rose realizes that Conway was "only slightly" wrong, for these laws both reflected and spurred a general disapproval of teaching literacy to slaves under any circumstances. See Rose, ed., *A Documentary History of Slavery in North America* (New York: Oxford University Press, 1976), 406. There is correspondence from Dunmore Gwinn, Eliza Gwinn, and James Parker to MC at CU. Parker's trips to Baltimore are mentioned in MC, *Testimonies Concerning Slavery* (London: Chapman and Hall, 1864), 71.

21. Stafford County slave schedules, 1850 and 1860; MC, *Testimonies*, 1–2; John Moncure Conway's will is in Will Book R, Stafford County courthouse.

22. The most thorough account of the Nat Turner uprising is Henry Irving Tragle, *The Southampton Slave Revolt of 1831* (Amherst: University of Massachusetts Press, 1971; New York: Vintage Books, 1973). William Styron's novel, *The Confessions of Nat Turner* (New York: Random House, 1967), a self-styled "meditation on history," is powerful and enduring, and has withstood criticism from those who desire a more unambiguous and politically conscious protagonist. Re Turner and the ensuing slavery debates, see Joseph Clarke Robert, *The Road from Monticello: A Study of the Virginia Slavery Debate of 1832* (Durham, N.C.: Duke University Press, 1941), Alison Goodyear Freehling, *Drift Toward Dissolution: The Virginia Slavery Debate of 1831–1832* (Baton Rouge: Louisiana State University Press, 1982), and Carl Degler, *The Other South: Southern Dissenters in the Nineteenth Century* (New York: Harper and Row, 1974), 13–17. For Dew's argument see Thomas R. Dew, *Review of the Debate of the Virginia*

Legislature of 1831 and 1832 (Richmond: T. W. White, 1832) and Dew, "Professor Dew on Slavery," *The Pro-Slavery Argument* (Charleston: Walker and Co., 1852; Philadelphia: Lippincott, 1853). William Sumner Jenkins, *Pro-Slavery Thought in the Old South* (Chapel Hill: University of North Carolina Press, 1935) is a standard work.

23. Notes for Reminiscences, CU ("colored associates"); MC, *Testimonies*, 27 ("I had no means of knowing").

24. MC, *Testimonies*, 103 ("warm advocate"); *AME*, I, 72 ("doomed institution"). Material on Eustace Conway can be found in his obituary in the Fredericksburg *Weekly Advertiser*, May 23, 1857. George Fitzhugh's fame rests primarily on two books, *Sociology for the South* (Richmond: A. Morris, 1854) and *Cannibals All!* (Richmond: A. Morris, 1857).

25. MC, *Pine and Palm* (New York: Henry Holt and Co., 1887), 293. Also published in London by Chatto and Windus.

26. *Ibid.*, 293–294. Richard Conway's copy of the book is at DC.

27. The connection between Fanny Moncure and Gisela Stirling is made in *AME*, I, 128. This cousin and her husband lived at Inglewood, which had been MC's early home. On a visit there late in 1852, shortly before he left Virginia permanently, MC was, as he noted in his journal (DC), "laughed at and persecuted about my radicalisms and scepticisms." But he found sympathy from Fanny, who, Conway's autobiography states, "confessed that she could not see the justice of slavery."

28. Maria Weston Chapman, ed., *Harriet Martineau's Autobiography*, 2 vols. (Boston: Houghton Mifflin and Co., 1885; first published in 1877), I, 344; L. Minor Blackford, *Mine Eyes Have Seen the Glory: The story of a Virginia Lady Mary Berkeley Minor Blackford 1802–1896 Who taught her sons to hate Slavery and to love the Union* (Cambridge: Harvard University Press, 1954), 42 and *passim*; Charles Eliot Norton to James Russell Lowell, April 6, 1855, in Sara Norton and Mark de Wolfe Howe, eds., *Letters of Charles Eliot Norton with Biographical Comment*, 2 vols. (Boston and New York: Houghton Mifflin, 1913), I, 124–127. See Anne Firor Scott, *The Southern Lady: From Pedestal to Politics, 1830–1930* (Chicago and London: University of Chicago Press, 1970), 4–79; and Scott, "Women's Perspective on the Patriarchy in the 1850's," *Journal of American History*, Vol. LXI, No. 1 (June 1974), 52–64. Catherine Clinton, *The Plantation Mistress: Women's World in the Old South* (New York: Pantheon Books, 1982), though marred by a polemical tone, contains much useful information.

29. Scott, *Southern Lady*, chaps. 2 and 3. Susan Dabney Smedes, who lived on a Mississippi plantation, wrote, "It was a saying that the mistress of a plantation was the most complete slave on it." Smedes, *Memorials of a Southern Planter* (Baltimore: Cushings and Bailey, 1887), 179.

30. Blackford, 44; Mary Boykin Chesnut in her diary, March 18, 1861, in C. Vann Woodward, ed., *Mary Chesnut's Civil War* (New Haven and London: Yale University Press, 1981), 29, 31; James Hugo Johnston, *Race Relations in Virginia and Miscegenation in the South, 1776–1860* (Amherst: University of Massachusetts Press, 1970), 237–249; MC, *Testimonies*, 3. The special burdens which black American women historically have shouldered are sensitively explored in Jacqueline Jones, *Labor of Love, Labor of Sorrow: Black Women, Work, and the Family from Slavery to the Present* (New York: Basic Books, 1985).

31. MC, *Testimonies*, 44.

32. Margaret Daniel Conway to MC, November 6, 1856, CU.

33. *Ibid.*; Dunmore Gwinn to MC, November 10, 1891, CU; Eliza Gwinn to MC, May 17, 1881, CU; Churchill Taylor to MC (in Moncure Taylor's handwriting), June 3, 1879, CU.

34. *AME*, I, 332–333 ("taken up such strong opinions"); Margaret Daniel Conway to MC, September 30, 1862, CU. In 1855 Mildred sarcastically assailed a neighbor, John Scott, who had "returned from Kansas to spend the winter, instead of staying out there to fight the abolitionists with true patriotism." Mildred Conway to MC, December 15, 1855, CU. Scott later joined the Confederate army and died in battle.

35. John Moncure Conway's will, Will Book R, Stafford County courthouse.

36. Later correspondence hints of Jane and Margaret's close relationship to Walker Conway's family, and the 1840 census lists two young adult white women of their age living with the family. For the Washington Unitarian church case, see below, Chapter Five.

37. Margaret Daniel Conway to MC, October 10, 1855, CU.

38. Degler, 90. Re Clay and Helper see David L. Smiley, *The Lion of Whitehall: The Life of Cassius M. Clay* (Madison: University of Wisconsin Press, 1962), Hugh C. Bailey, *Hinton Rowan Helper, Abolitionist Racist* (University: University of Alabama Press, 1965), and Joaquin José Cardoso, "Hinton Rowan Helper: A Nineteenth Century Pilgrimage," Ph.D. diss., University of Wisconsin, 1967. Helper's classic work, grounded in a statistical comparison of North and South, is *The Impending Crisis of the South: How to Meet It* (New York: A. B. Burdick, 1857). Goodloe's arguments are summarized in his pamphlet, *Inquiry into the Causes Which Have Retarded the Accumulation of Wealth and Increase of Population in the Southern States* (Washington, D.C., 1846).

39. Re the Grimkés, see Gerda Lerner, *The Grimke Sisters from South Carolina: Rebels against Slavery* (Boston: Houghton Mifflin, 1967) and Katharine Dupre Lumpkin, *The Emancipation of Angelina Grimke* (Chapel Hill: University of North Carolina Press, 1974). The standard work on Birney is Betty Fladeland, *James Gillespie Birney: Slaveholder to Abolitionist* (Ithaca, N.Y.: Cornell University Press, 1955). There is no modern work on Fee, but information can be gleaned from *Autobiography of John G. Fee, Berea, Kentucky* (Chicago: National Christian Association, 1891). Fee's antislavery position is well outlined in his book, *An Anti-Slavery Manual, Being an Examination in the Light of the Bible, and of Facts, into the Moral and Social Wrongs of American Slavery, with a Remedy for the Evil* (Maysville, Ky.: printed at the Herald Office, 1848). Samuel Janney of Loudoun County in extreme northern Virginia also opposed slavery, and in 1850 was tried (and acquitted) for the "crime" of denying in a Leesburg newspaper that "owners had right of property in their slaves." For the most part, however, this Hicksite Quaker remained in his own community and devoted himself to religious affairs. Generally discreet in his public social and political criticisms, as were most Southern Quakers, Janney was on the periphery of the Virginia social system and posed no serious threat to it. See Janney, *Memoirs* (Philadelphia: Friends' Book Association, 1881), 97–106 and *passim*. See also Patricia Hickin, "Gentle Agitator: Samuel M. Janney and the Antislavery Movement in Virginia, 1842–1851," *Journal of Southern History*, XXXVII (May 1971), 159–190.

40. Degler, *The Other South*, 59.

41. George Fitzhugh, *Cannibals All! or, Slaves Without Masters* (Cambridge: The Belknap Press of Harvard University Press, 1960; first published in 1857), 25; see also Fitzhugh, *Sociology For the South* (Richmond: A. Morris, 1854), 214–

215. William H. Chafe has made a significant contribution toward eliciting clear thinking on the analogy between women and blacks. See his *Women and Equality* (New York: Oxford University Press, 1977), 45–113. Since girls generally had no money during the time of his boyhood, young Moncure would include his sister in the gift when buying a present for his mother. MC recalled this in a letter to his daughter Mildred, September 9, 1891, CU.

42. John Stuart Mill, *The Subjection of Women* (London: Longmans, Green, Reader, and Dyer, 1869), 55; Elizabeth Cady Stanton to Gerrit Smith, January 3, 1856, in Theodore Stanton and Harriot Stanton Blatch, eds., *Elizabeth Cady Stanton As Revealed in Her Letters, Diary and Reminiscences*, 2 vols. (New York: Harper and Brothers, 1922), II, 64; Woodward, ed., *Mary Chesnut's Civil War*, 15.

43. Lydia Maria Child and Theodore Tilton are quoted in Ronald G. Walters, *The Antislavery Appeal* (Baltimore: The Johns Hopkins University Press, 1976), 105. Tilton's comment was made in an 1863 published oration, "The Negro: A Speech," readily accessible in Donald G. Mathews, ed., *Agitation for Freedom: The Abolitionist Movement* (New York: John Wiley and Sons, 1972), 161–174. Conway's statement "strike out the word . . ." appears in *The Commonwealth* (Boston), April 22, 1865. His advocacy of interracial marriage is in MC, *Testimonies*, 75–77. For a general discussion of the romanticized view of racial differences held by many antislavery Northerners, see George M. Fredrickson, *The Black Image in the White Mind: The Debate on Afro-American Character and Destiny, 1817–1914* (New York: Harper and Row, 1971), 97–129.

44. MC to EDC, September 19, 1875, DC. The 1860 Stafford County slave schedule lists George Conway's four "slaves": a thirty-one-year-old mulatto woman, a nine-year-old mulatto girl, an eight-year-old mulatto boy, and a seventy-year-old black woman.

45. MC, *Testimonies*, 15–18; *AME*, I, 29.

46. MC, *Testimonies*, 11–13, 52–53; *AME*, I, 28.

47. MC, *Testimonies*, 4–6; MC, "The Negro As Artist," *The Radical*, Vol. II (September 1866), 39. See also *AME*, I, 12–13.

48. MC, *Testimonies*, 6; Mildred Conway March to MC, August 3, 1897, CU. Mildred (b. 1837) was quite young when Charles was sold, and had little if any personal contact with him. Thus her remembrance of him was based purely on reputation. Many historians of slavery have pointed to deceit and petty larceny as common forms of slave self-assertion, while stammering in the presence of whites was not uncommon among slaves who felt their constraints most keenly. See, for example, Kenneth M. Stampp, *The Peculiar Institution: Slavery in the Ante-Bellum South* (New York: Vintage Books, 1956), chap. 3; and Eugene D. Genovese, *Roll, Jordan, Roll: The World the Slaves Made* (New York: Pantheon Books, 1974), 646–647. Re Charles see also MC's letter in the *New York Times*, November 23, 1900. In Conway's novel *Pine and Palm* (1887), chap. 10, a character patterned after Charles Humstead meets a better fate, purchase by a sympathetic antislavery man.

49. *AME*, I, 12 ("Advancing ahead of us . . ."), 22.

50. *AME*, I, 32; MC journal entry in Dickinson copy-book, July 4, 1848, CU.

51. London *Daily News*, August 22, 1870; MC, *Pine and Palm*, 266; MC, "Faith," ms discourse, October 20, 1872, CU.

52. *AME*, I, 22, 32.

53. Notes for Reminiscences, CU; MC, "Apologia," *Farewell Discourses* (London: E. W. Allen, 1884), 162 ("treadmill of services," "to this day"). A slightly revised version of the "Apologia" was printed in *The Index*, October 2, 1884.

54. Elmer T. Clark, ed., *The Journal and Letters of Francis Asbury* (Nashville: Abingdon Press, 1958), I, 596. John Janney Johnson, *A History of the Fredericksburg United Methodist Church, 1802–1975* (Fredericksburg, Va.: United Methodist Church, 1975) is readable, reliable, and informative. The indispensable book on the debate over slavery within the Methodist Church is Donald G. Mathews, *Slavery and Methodism: A Chapter in American Morality, 1780–1845* (Princeton: Princeton University Press, 1965). "With the meeting of 1820," Mathews writes (p. 51), "slavery ceased to be a major item of business in the General Conference."

55. *AME*, I, 44–46.

56. *AME*, I, 19–20. Information on the Sunday class meetings is in a ms book entitled "List of Church Officials," United Methodist Church, Fredericksburg, Va.

57. Obituary of Eustace Conway, Fredericksburg *Weekly Advertiser*, May 23, 1857; Ms book, "List of Church Officials," United Methodist Church, Fredericksburg, Va.

58. Mathews, *Slavery and Methodism*, 264.

59. Johnson, 28–35; MC, "Fredericksburg First and Last," *Magazine of American History*, Vol. XVII, No. 6 (June 1887), 451–452. In 1866 the Baltimore Conference voted to join the Methodist Episcopal Church South, and the two Fredericksburg congregations reunited.

60. *AME*, II, 304 (James Parker); MC, *Testimonies*, 4 ("These humble and ignorant souls"); MC, "An Exhumed Sketch by Nathaniel Hawthorne and Some Reflections Thereon," *The Open Court*, December 5, 1889 ("literal and primitive Christians"). See also *AME*, I, 27–28. Genovese, *Roll, Jordan, Roll*, 161–284, is excellent on slave religion in general, as is Donald G. Mathews, *Religion in the Old South* (Chicago: University of Chicago Press, 1978) on slave evangelicalism in particular.

61. Walker Conway to Robert Emory, January 14, 1847; Conway to Emory, March 4, 1847 (quoted), Dickinson College Archives, DC.

CHAPTER 2

1. The definitive work on Dickinson College is Charles Coleman Sellers, *Dickinson College: A History* (Middletown, Conn.: Wesleyan University Press, 1973). Walker Conway was a trustee of Dickinson from 1848 until the Civil War. Carlisle, like Fredericksburg, was in the Baltimore Conference; it opted for the Central Pennsylvania Conference in 1868.

2. Sellers, chap. 9. See also Frederick E. Maser, *Methodism in Central Pennsylvania, 1771–1969* (Lebanon, Pa., 1971), 92–94.

3. *AME*, I, 47. The Dickinson Catalogue for 1847–48 lists 43 freshmen, 39 sophomores, 31 juniors, 29 seniors, and a total enrollment (counting preparatory and law students) of 189.

4. *AME*, I, 49–50.

5. Sellers, 205–209; *AME*, I, 47–50. Re McClintock see George R. Crooks, *Life and Letters of the Rev. John McClintock* (New York: Nelson and Phillips, 1876).

6. The quotation is from McClintock's suppressed article written for the *Christian Advocate* and dated April 29, 1847, summarizing the points made in the preceding articles. McClintock Papers, Emory University, photostat at DC.

7. Much of my information on the McClintock riot derives from Martha Slotten, "The McClintock slave riot of 1847," unpublished paper, DC. Re Carlisle and McKim's abolitionism see William Cohen, "James Miller McKim: Pennsylvania Abolitionist," Ph.D. diss., New York University, 1968, 52–60 and 60n.

8. Slotten, *op. cit.*; Sellers, 225–226; AME, I, 50–51; trial testimony printed in the Carlisle *American Volunteer*, September 2, 1847.

9. Carlisle *Herald*, June 9, 1847. The *Herald* expressed satisfaction that it was only the town's "negroes" and not the town's "citizens" who had rioted, noting that "our citizens generally made no interference."

10. Slotten, *op. cit.*; McClintock diary, June 2, 1847, McClintock Papers, Emory University, photostat at DC. MC's account in *AME*, I, 51–52, repeated in Sellers, 226, places McClintock's appearance before the students on June 3, but McClintock's diary indicates he spoke to them on the night of the riot. Perhaps he made two appearances. McClintock wrote in his diary on June 2: "The truth of the case was that my human and Christian sympathies were openly exhibited on the side of the poor blacks—and this gave mortal offence to the slaveholders and their *confreres* in the town. The sentiment of the *aristocracy* of the town . . . is all proslavery: and in this they are hand and glove with the lowest rabble."

11. Carlisle *Herald*, June 16, 1847. The list of signers included over fifty students from the border slave state of Maryland, and twenty-one from Virginia. McClintock's statement is in his diary, June 8, 1847, McClintock Papers, Emory University, photostat at DC.

12. Slotten, *op. cit.*; McClintock diary, August 30, 1847, in McClintock Papers, Emory University, photostat at DC. McClintock initiated an appeal on behalf of the convicted blacks, and nearly a year later the state supreme court unanimously ruled their sentences unjust and ordered their release. The Carlisle *American Volunteer* (September 2, 1847), in particular, was upset by the acquittals of McClintock and many of the blacks. Many witnesses had testified, as did one Mr. McFarlan, that "Mr. McClintock was as bad as any of the niggers."

13. John McClintock to his father, November 28, 1847, McClintock Papers, Emory University, photostat at DC.

14. McClintock's description of the Dickinson regimen is quoted in Sellers, 210.

15. John McClintock to Stephen Olin, October 1848, in Crooks, *Life and Letters*, 201. McClintock by this time was editor of the *Methodist Quarterly Review*.

16. The quotation is from MC, *Revivalism* (pamphlet; London, 1875), 13. Re the Methodist stress on the revival see Theodore L. Agnew *et al.*, *History of American Methodism*, 2 vols. (New York and Nashville: Abingdon Press, 1964), I, 514–515. A good discussion of the adolescent conversion experience is in Joseph F. Kett, *Rites of Passage: Adolescence in America, 1790 to the Present* (New York: Basic Books, 1977), 62–85.

17. *Christian Advocate and Journal*, July 28, 1847. MC, "Dura Studentis, by a Peripatician," ms sketch in Dickinson copy-book, CU. Internal evidence dates this at three weeks into the fall term. The sketch was a contribution to a college "periodical" not printed but only read in the chapel. The wording differs slightly from the excerpt published in *AME*, I, 53.

18. Carlisle *Herald*, January 12, 1848; MC journal entry for January 7, 1848 in Dickinson copy-book, CU. On January 19 the *Herald* reported that the "revival of religion in the Methodist Church, of this borough, still progresses, with unabated interest. As the result of it we learn that forty-one persons were on Sunday last admitted on probation to the communion of that church."

19. MC journal entries, January 8–9, 1848 in Dickinson copy-book, CU. The weather is reported in the Carlisle *Herald*, January 12, 1848.

20. MC journal entries, January 10–16, 1848 in Dickinson copy-book, CU.

21. MC journal, January–March 1848; quotation, March 5, 1848, Dickinson copy-book, CU.

22. MC journal, March 19–21, 1848, Dickinson copy-book, CU.

23. MC journal, April 6, 10, 27, 1848, in Dickinson copy-book, CU; *AME*, I, 39–41, 62.

24. MC journal, May 10, [June] 23, 1848, Dickinson copy-book, CU.

25. MC journal, May 1848, in Dickinson copy-book, CU; Douglas Southall Freeman, *Lee's Lieutenants*, 3 vols. (New York: Charles Scribner's Sons, 1942–44), I, 664. Re John Moncure Daniel see Frederick S. Daniel, *The Richmond Examiner During the War; or, the Writings of John M. Daniel, with a Memoir of his Life* (New York: Printed for the Author, 1868); MC, "Fredericksburg First and Last," *Magazine of American History*, Vol. XVII, No. 6 (June 1887), 450–451; Lyon Gardiner Tyler, ed., *Encyclopedia of Virginia Biography* (New York: Lewis Historical Publishing Company, 1915), III, 153–154; Hamson A. Trexler, "The Davis Administration and the Richmond Press, 1861–1865," *Journal of Southern History*, Vol. XVI, No. 2 (May 1950), 177–195. Re Daniel and MC in 1848 see *AME*, I, 60–61.

26. MC journal, July 10, 30, August 7, 1848, in Dickinson copy-book, CU. On August 3 Conway wrote, "I went over to Uncle Es to hear him speak to the Dem. Association at night it was the ablest speech I've heard this year."

27. MC journal, April 21, 1848, in Dickinson copy-book, CU; *AME*, I, 62–63. Unfortunately there is no complete run of the Fredericksburg *Democratic Recorder* extant, and almost all of Conway's articles are lost.

28. MC came upon the manuscript of *The Flute Player* while going through old papers in 1897, and threw it away. "Your mother is abusing me for tearing it up before she read it," he told his daughter, "and says she hasn't the least doubt it is better than anything I've written since." MC to Mildred Conway Sawyer, April 16, 1897, CU.

29. *AME*, I, 65; Richmond *Examiner*, December 15, 1848.

30. Richmond *Examiner*, January 12, 1849.

31. "Methodist Quarterly Review for January, 1849," *The Collegian*, No. 1 (March 1849), 16–17. The article on Channing may have been written by John McClintock, who became editor of the *Methodist Quarterly Review* in 1848.

32. *AME*, I, 68.

33. *Ibid.*, 65–67.

34. "Love in a College," *The Collegian*, No. 1 (March 1849), 6. The style and vocabulary of this article stamp it unquestionably as MC's, as does an extended reference to novelist George Lippard, whose romances Conway was disdainfully devouring at the time. Re Kate Emory see *AME*, I, 69–70.

35. Circular, "Annual Commencement, Dickinson College," Dickinson College Archives, DC; Carlisle *Herald*, July 18, 1849. The commencement speech was not quite MC's first public address. On July 4 he had had better success,

without completely conquering his nervousness, with a lighthearted talk given at the sixtieth anniversary of the Union Philosophical Society (one of Dickinson's two literary societies), to which he belonged. That speech, said a reporter in the Carlisle *American Volunteer* (July 12, 1849), "was a rich treat to the laughing public. It was really a fine piece of comic composition, and was spoken in a style admirably suited to the sentiment; the slight embarrassment under which he seemed to labor only increased the effect."

36. "Editor's Table," *The Collegian*, No. 4 (June 1849), 94.

37. *AME*, I, 70–73.

38. *Ibid.*, I, 72.

39. *Ibid.*, I, 73–75. The journal Conway kept between the time of his graduation and the end of 1850 evidently does not survive, although Conway used it when writing his memoirs.

40. *Ibid.*, I, 75–76; Richmond *Examiner*, April 2, 1850.

41. *AME*, I, 75–77. Conway's review of Poe, now in the Library of Congress, was intended for the Washington *Union*, edited by Thomas Ritchie and Edmund Burke, but was apparently not published. See Richard Beale Davis, "Moncure D. Conway Looks At Edgar Poe—Through Dr. Griswold," *Mississippi Quarterly*, Vol. XVIII, No. 1 (Winter 1964–65), 12–18.

42. The quotation is in *AME*, I, 77.

43. Immediate documentation for this episode is lacking—Conway's journal for this period has not survived—but the frequency with which he alluded to it in later years, plus the solid evidence of Emerson's impact on him during subsequent months, lend it credibility. Conway first mentioned it in print in "The Transcendentalists of Concord," *Fraser's Magazine*, Vol. LXX, No. CCCCXVI (August 1864), 245–264. His last account of it is in *AME*, I, 77–79. See also MC, *Emerson At Home And Abroad* (Boston: J. R. Osgood and Co., 1882), 3–7; and MC, "Emerson: The Teacher and The Man," *The Critic*, Vol. XLII, No. 5 (May 1903), 404–405. The quotation is from the *Fraser* article, 255.

44. "Emerson," *Blackwood's Edinburgh Magazine*, Vol. LXII, No. CCCLXXXVI (December 1847), 643–657.

45. MC, *Emerson At Home And Abroad*, 3–4.

46. MC to Sarah Brooke Farquhar, January 17, 1854, photostat, DC.

47. *AME*, I, 81–84; Kate Emory to MC, August 15 [1850], CU. Re MC's Washington visit, see the Richmond *Examiner*, May 24, 1850; and MC, "Washington," *Fraser's Magazine*, Vol. LXXIV, No. CCCCLXI (September 1866), 338.

CHAPTER 3

1. MC, *Free-Schools in Virginia: A Plea of Education, Virtue and Thrift, vs. Ignorance, Vice and Poverty* (Fredericksburg, Va.: printed at the *Recorder* office, 1850). The earliest evidence of Conway's research on this pamphlet is MC to Conway Robinson, August 24, 1850, DC. On April 9, 1852, *The Liberator* reported that eighty thousand white adults in Virginia were listed as illiterate by the latest census, ten thousand more than in 1840, and linked this illiteracy to the effects of slavery.

2. MC, *Free-Schools*, 13–15.

3. *Ibid.*, 17–18.

4. *Ibid.*, 18; MC, *Testimonies Concerning Slavery* (London: Chapman and

Hall, 1864), 32–33. Virginia did not establish a public school system until 1869.

5. The quotation is in *Free-Schools*, 32.

6. Louis Agassiz, "The Diversity of Origin of Human Races," *Christian Examiner*, XLIX (July 1850), 110–145; *AME*, I, 89–90; MC, *Testimonies*, 28–30. The quotation from John Daniel is in *Testimonies*, 29. Re polygenesis see also William Stanton, *The Leopard's Spots: Scientific Attitudes Toward Race in America, 1815–59* (Chicago: University of Chicago Press, 1960), 100–112; and George M. Fredrickson, *The Black Image in the White Mind: The Debate on Afro-American Character and Destiny, 1817–1914* (New York: Harper and Row, 1971), 71–96.

7. MC, "Diversity of Origin of Races—Slavery," unpublished ms, dated Warrenton, Va., December 1850, CU.

8. *AME*, I, 90. Obviously, it would be preferable to have direct contemporary evidence for Conway's reaction to his article than to rely on his autobiography. But there is no such evidence either to confirm or refute his turn-of-the-century recollection. Conway's letters from this period do not exist, nor has any journal been found, though I strongly suspect he kept one. His journal which begins in January 1851, however, contains no racist references and early displays a growing antipathy both to slavery and racism. The sudden contrast between this journal and the article on polygenesis is so striking that the autobiographical account rings true. Since circumstantial evidence supports that account and no evidence, circumstantial or otherwise, refutes it, I accept it.

9. *Ibid.*, I, 90–91.

10. The quotation is from MC to Sarah Brooke Farquhar, January 17, 1854, photostat, DC, original at University of Texas, Austin. On linkages between Emerson and evangelicalism see *AME*, I, 91; MC, "Emerson: The Teacher and the Man," *The Critic*, Vol. XLII No. 5 (May 1903), 405; Theodore L. Agnew *et al.*, *History of American Methodism*, 2 vols. (New York and Nashville: Abingdon Press, 1964), II, 610.

11. The quotation is in *AME*, I, 85–86. See also MC, *Testimonies*, 34.

12. Kate Emory to MC, November 21 [1850], CU; MC journal entries, January 20, 21, 1851 in ms journal (January 1851–June 1853), DC. Although Conway drew somewhat on this revealing journal when writing his autobiography, its whereabouts were unknown to scholars until 1977, when I discovered it in private hands. Much of it is reproduced here for the first time.

13. Entries of February 1851, MC journal, DC; *AME*, I, 92–93.

14. Entries of March, April 1, 1851, MC journal, DC; *AME*, I, 93–94.

15. Entries of April 7, 16, 18, September 12, 1851, MC journal, DC.

16. Entries of April 6, 1851; April 24, 1852; May 13, 1851, MC journal, DC; *AME*, I, 96.

17. Entries of April 21, August 15, 31, 28, September 9, 10, 1851, MC journal, DC.

18. Entries of May 2 (smoking), 16, 7, 8, 11, 1851, MC journal, DC.

19. MC, "Books that Have Helped Me," *The Forum*, Vol. VI (January 1888), 539; *AME*, I, 101. MC's journal for this period records frequently what he was reading.

20. *AME*, I, 101. The image of Conway reading Emerson in the saddle while riding between ministerial engagements was not a journalistic device created by him later. His journal entries of April 11 and September 15, 1851, corroborate it.

21. *AME*, I, 102.

22. *Ibid.*, I, 103. For information on this Quaker community, see William Henry Farquhar, *Annals of Sandy Spring, or, Twenty Years History of a Rural Community in Maryland* (Baltimore: Cushings and Bailey, 1884). Warren Sylvester Smith's article, "The Imperceptible Arrows of Quakerism: Moncure Conway at Sandy Spring," *Quaker History*, Vol. 52, No. 1 (Spring 1963), 19–26, derives largely from Conway's autobiography.

23. Entries of July 31, August 11, 1851, MC journal, DC.

24. On the Hicksite Quakers, see Robert W. Doherty, *The Hicksite Separation: A Sociological Analysis of Religious Schism in Early Nineteenth Century America* (New Brunswick, N.J.: Rutgers University Press, 1967).

25. Entry of September 27, 1851, MC journal, DC; William Henry Farquhar to MC, May 3, 1868, CU.

26. Entry of February 7, 1852 ("too much a Rationalist"), MC journal, DC; fragment of a letter, MC to ? ("donning broadbrim and drab"), CU. This letter was written in Washington, perhaps during Conway's Unitarian ministry there, 1854–1856. On the Quakers and slavery, see MC, *Testimonies*, 36–39; *AME*, I, 105–106; and MC, "The Quakers and Their Triumph," ms sermon, January 13, 1867, CU.

27. *AME*, I, 98–99 (question on resurrection), 117 ("not beloved"). Susan Budd, examining the "conversion experiences" of one hundred fifty British Secularists in detail and another two hundred more cursorily, concludes that conversion to unbelief was usually rooted in moral alienation more than in intellectual skepticism. See Budd, "The Loss of Faith in England, 1850–1950," *Past and Present*, No. 36 (April 1967), 106–125; and Budd, *Varieties of Unbelief: Atheists and Agnostics in English Society, 1850–1960* (London: Heinemann, 1977), 104–123.

28. MC to Ralph Waldo Emerson, November 4, 1851, published in *AME*, I, 109.

29. Ralph Waldo Emerson to MC, November 13, 1851, published in *AME*, I, 109–110. The original is in the Berg Collection, New York Public Library.

30. MC to Ralph Waldo Emerson, December 12, 1851, CU.

31. Entry of October 2, 1851, MC journal, DC.

32. Entries of March 5, 8, 1852, MC journal, DC.

33. Entry of March 14, 1852, MC journal, DC. Peyton died of typhoid fever.

34. *AME*, I, 30 (duckling); Mildred Conway to MC, July 19, 1856, CU; Entries of September 23, March 14, 1852, MC journal, DC.

35. Entry of March 15, 1852, MC journal, DC.

36. Entry of March 25, 1852, MC journal, DC.

37. Entry of April 28, 1852, MC journal, DC.

38. Entries of April 28, 29, 30, 1852, MC journal, DC. Sarah Farquhar's comment is recalled in an entry of May 4, 1852.

39. Entry of March 26, 1852, MC journal, DC. Smith's lectures to his senior class were published as *Lectures on the Philosophy and Practice of Slavery* (Nashville: Stevenson and Evans, 1856).

40. *AME*, I, 114–115; Entries of May 6 (Margaret Fuller), May 1, (hummingbird), 1852, MC journal, DC.

41. *AME*, I, 117–118; Entries of July 1852, MC journal, DC. To his annoyance, the list of M.A. recipients in the next Dickinson catalogue omitted

Conway's name. J. A. McCauley (president of Dickinson) to MC, August 31, 1877, CU, confirms that Conway did receive the degree. The perfunctory M.A. was not unusual at nineteenth-century American colleges; Harvard's requirements for it were the same as Dickinson's.

42. Entries of July 25, August 4, October 14, 1852, MC journal, DC.

43. Entries of October–November 1852, MC journal, DC.

44. Entry of November 15, 1852 (Becky's funeral), MC journal, DC; *AME*, I, 122.

45. Entry of November 15, 1852, MC journal, DC; MC to the Bishop and members of the Baltimore Annual Conference, February 1853, Lovely Lane Methodist Church, Baltimore.

46. Entries of December 8 (*"made-up"*), 15 ("home"), 25 (Christmas), 19 ("These two months"), MC journal, DC.

47. The Fredericksburg *Herald* is excerpted in *The Liberator*, October 8, 1852; Entries of December 19 (Eustace), 31 (chess club), 1852; January 1, 1853 (Marye, "peculiar views," slave-hiring), MC journal, DC.

48. Entries of January 1 ("my dear relations"), 3 (Fanny Moncure), 1853, MC journal, DC. Re Fanny Moncure see also *AME*, I, 127–128. MC's recollection of his mother's support is in *Testimonies Concerning Slavery*, 40–41. The argument about the intuitions vs. Reason is described in MC's journal, December 30, 1852.

49. Entries of February 12, 14, 1853, MC journal, DC; *AME*, I, 128–129.

50. *AME*, I, 38–39.

51. W. B. Cairns mentions the accusations of "tuft-hunting" in his piece on Conway in the *Dictionary of American Biography*, II, 365. Douglas Stange repeats the charge that Conway was "an inveterate name-dropper" in his book *British Unitarians against American Slavery, 1833–1865* (Cranbury, N.J.: Associated University Presses, 1984), 201.

52. MC to Ralph Waldo Emerson, December 12, 1851, CU.

53. MC, "Letter From Virginia," ms intended to be read at South Place Chapel, October 1875, CU.

54. Entries of December 13, 1852 and February 1, 1853, MC journal, DC.

55. Entries of January 1, 1853 and May 6, 1852, MC journal, DC; MC, *Testimonies*, 45.

56. MC to Sarah Brooke Farquhar, January 17, 1854, photostat, DC, original at University of Texas, Austin.

57. In her widely noticed book, *The Feminization of American Culture* (New York: Knopf, 1977), Ann Douglas contends that members of the nineteenth-century liberal (especially Unitarian) clergy joined forces with middle-class literary-minded women, whose peripheral status in society they shared. She argues that together, in a successful bid for higher status, these groups made a central contribution to the sentimentalization (or trivialization) of American culture and the enervation of previously more rigorous American thought. For Douglas, the emphasis on feelings and emotions represented a repudiation of hard-headed rational inquiry and a "failed political consciousness." She does not explain, however, how so insidious a set of attitudes could have helped propel an unprecedented number of men and women into reform activity (activity she ignores) often directly beneficial to women, in part precisely because slavery, alcoholism, male legal hegemony, and other social conditions offended emotionally based sensitivities which contemporaries had begun to value. Some in Douglas's own sample, including Lydia Maria Child, Dorothea Dix, Harriet

Beecher Stowe, William Ellery Channing, and Theodore Parker, made significant contributions to the amelioration of social abuses. They were not, moreover, intellectual lightweights, as anyone familiar with Parker knows. He, for one, may have engaged in fewer intellectualized theological contortions than the seventeenth-century Puritans whom Douglas admires, and he surely prized "sentiment" where they had scorned it. If this constituted "failed political consciousness" by the standards of certain twentieth-century feminists, it also meant toleration of free thought to a degree undreamed of by Puritans, and an attempted legitimization for men of a side of life long closed to them. Douglas's choice of villains also seems bizarre on other grounds: in a world in which male-female friendships based on any sort of equality were difficult to find, these groups forged such friendships.

CHAPTER 4

1. MC journal, Feb. 26, 1853, DC; MC to Sarah Brooke Farquhar, March 2, 1853, photostat, DC. Original at University of Texas, Austin.

2. MC journal, February 27, 1853, DC. The quotation is in MC to Sarah Brooke Farquhar, March 2, 1853, photostat, DC.

3. *AME*, I, 152 (Alcott), 158–159 (Lowell).

4. *AME*, I, 156–158 (Longfellow), 155 (Sparks); MC journal, March 13 (Longfellow), April 13 (opera), March 6 ("my passion for music"), 1853, DC; MC, "Longfellow," *The Melbourne Review* No. 33 (January 1884), 5. Conway's reaction to *Don Giovanni* was probably similar to that of the autobiographical protagonist in his 1891 novel, *Prisons of Air* (p. 196): "Edmond . . . felt a little surprise at one or two of the scenes, but he was no prude and the music charmed him."

5. *AME*, I, 133–134; MC, "The Transient and The Permanent in Theodore Parker," June 13, 1889; *A Catalogue of the Officers and Students of Harvard College, for the Academical Year 1852–53, Second Term* (Cambridge, 1853).

6. MC to Sarah Brooke Farquhar, March 2, 1853, photostat, DC.

7. MC journal, March 27, 1853, DC; Marginal note by MC in his student Bible, CU.

8. George Burnap quoted in the *Christian Inquirer*, January 15, 1859; *The Education of Henry Adams* (Boston, 1918), 34. The most perceptive account of mainstream Unitarianism is Daniel Walker Howe, *The Unitarian Conscience* (Cambridge: Harvard University Press, 1970).

9. *AME*, I, 163–164.

10. See George H. Williams, ed., *The Harvard Divinity School* (Boston: Beacon Press, 1954). Re Norton see Howe, 90–92, 312–313.

11. Stephen E. Whicher, ed., *Selections From Ralph Waldo Emerson* (Cambridge: The Riverside Press, 1957), 106–107; Howe, 76–77.

12. Jerry Wayne Brown, *The Rise of Biblical Criticism in America, 1800–1870. The New England Scholars* (Middletown, Conn.: Wesleyan University Press, 1969), 140–148 and *passim*.

13. There is no book dealing with the left wing of Unitarianism, although Stow Persons, *Free Religion* (New Haven: Yale University Press, 1947) and Sidney Warren, *American Freethought, 1860–1914* (New York: Columbia University Press, 1943) deal with the post–Civil War activities of many radical Unitarians after

they left the church for the Free Religious Association and kindred groups. There are few modern biographies of individual left-wing Unitarians. Tilden G. Edelstein, *Strange Enthusiasm: A Life of Thomas Wentworth Higginson* (New Haven: Yale University Press, 1968) is a noteworthy exception. J. Wade Caruthers, *Octavius Brooks Frothingham, Gentle Radical* (University: University of Alabama Press, 1977) is poor. There is room for a new evaluation of Theodore Parker, although Henry Steele Commager, *Theodore Parker, Yankee Crusader* (Boston: Little, Brown, 1936) is a classic.

14. Brown, 149–152. In addition to Commager, see John White Chadwick, *Theodore Parker: Preacher and Reformer* (Boston: Houghton Mifflin, 1900).

15. MC journal, February 27, 1853, DC; MC to Sarah Brooke Farquhar, March 2, 1853, photostat, DC.

16. *AME,* I, 129, 132–133.

17. MC journal, March 10, 1853, DC; *AME,* I, 133; MC, "The Transcendentalists of Concord," *Fraser's Magazine,* Vol. LXX, No. CCCCXVI (August 1864), 259–260.

18. MC, untitled ms sermon in England on Theodore Parker, CU; MC, "The Transient and the Permanent in Theodore Parker," 3 installments, *The Open Court,* May 23–June 13, 1889 (quotation from 3rd installment).

19. *AME,* I, 163; Frank Sanborn to MC, September 13, 1854, DC.

20. MC to Sarah Brooke Farquhar, March 2, 1853 ("as majestic"), photostat, DC; MC journal, May 3, 1853, DC; MC to Sarah Brooke Farquhar, May 5, 1853, photostat, DC.

21. MC to Sarah Brooke Farquhar, May 5, 1853, photostat, DC. This letter is the only detailed contemporary account of Conway's day in Concord and his first meeting with Emerson.

22. *Ibid.*

23. *Ibid.*; *AME,* I, 144 ("dearly loved a garden"); MC to Ralph Waldo Emerson, November 6, 1854, CU (objections to *Walden*). In *AME,* I, 140–141, Conway's account of his meeting with Thoreau differs in minor detail (and is mistakenly placed in the summer of 1853) but I have relied on his letter to Farquhar, which he lacked when writing his memoirs.

24. *AME,* I, 140–149; MC, "Books That Have Helped Me," *The Forum,* Vol. IV (January 1888), 540; MC journal, June 27, 28, 1853, DC. The quotation is from MC, "Emerson: The Teacher and the Man," *The Critic,* Vol. XLII, No. 5 (May 1903), 407.

25. *AME,* I, 167–169. Longfellow mentions attending the reading in his journal, [April] 27 [1854], in Samuel Longfellow, ed., *Life of Henry Wadsworth Longfellow With Extracts From His Journals and Correspondence,* 2 vols. (Boston: Ticknor and Company, 1886), II, 243. Although Longfellow places the reading in Conway's room, where it had originally been scheduled, it was actually moved to another, more spacious room in Divinity Hall.

26. MC to Ralph Waldo Emerson, March 3, 1854, CU.

27. Text of address given by MC at the Cooper Union on December 10, 1905, commemorating William Lloyd Garrison's centenary, Garrison Family Papers, Smith College; MC journal, March 13, 1853, DC.

28. The most complete account of the Burns affair is still *The Boston Slave Riot, and Trial of Anthony Burns, Containing the Report of the Faneuil Hall Meeting, the Murder of Batchelder; Theodore Parker's Lesson for the Day; Speeches of Counsel on Both Sides, Corrected by Themselves; Verbatim Report of Judge Loring's Decision; and,*

a Detailed Account of the Embarkation (Boston, 1854). The story is well told in Jane H. and William H. Pease's brief book, *The Fugitive Slave Law and Anthony Burns: A Problem in Law Enforcement* (Philadelphia: Lippincott, 1975); in Stanley W. Campbell, *The Slave Catchers: Enforcement of the Fugitive Slave Law, 1850–1860* (New York: Norton, 1972), 124–132; in Edelstein, 155–161; and in Samuel Shapiro, "The Rendition of Anthony Burns," *Journal of Negro History* 44 (January 1959), 34–51. My account draws from all these sources, plus *The Liberator*, June 2, 9, 16, 23, 1854.

29. MC, *Testimonies Concerning Slavery* (London: Chapman and Hall, 1864), 43–45; *AME*, I, 175–177.

30. *AME*, I, 184, 175–177. Conway's recollection of the Burns affair from a distance of fifty years is marred by several minor inaccuracies, and his chronology of events is skewed. His claim not to have attended the Burns hearing is refuted in speeches made by Wendell Phillips and himself a month later at Framingham Grove, published in *The Liberator*, July 7, 14, 1854.

31. Parker's speech is excerpted in Pease and Pease, 82–85. Parker specifically urged "managing this matter without shooting anybody," and evidently had in mind a rescue similar to that of Shadrach in 1851.

32. Charles Eliot Norton to Arthur Hugh Clough, May 30, 1854, in Sara Norton and Mark de Wolfe Howe, eds., *Letters of Charles Eliot Norton with Biographical Comment* (Boston and New York: Houghton Mifflin, 1913), III. Lawrence quoted in Pease and Pease, 43.

33. MC's memory of Hallett's role in preventing a settlement, in *AME*, I, 176, is correct. See Pease and Pease, 39–43.

34. MC recalls the rendition and places himself in Andrew's office in his article, "Mayflowerings," *Fraser's*, Vol. LXXI, No. CCCCXXV (May 1865), 556–557. Burns was kept in irons at the traders' jail in Richmond, then sold to a North Carolinian who sold him in February 1855 to a Massachusetts minister for $1,325 at Barnum's Hotel in Baltimore. On March 7, 1855, he was welcomed back to Boston and feted at Tremont Temple. He subsequently attended Oberlin College and became a Baptist minister. *The Liberator*, March 9, 1855; Edelstein, 173.

35. *The Liberator*, July 7, 14, 1854.

36. *Ibid.*; John L. Thomas, *The Liberator: William Lloyd Garrison* (Boston: Little, Brown, 1963), 387; *AME*, I, 185.

37. *The Liberator*, July 7, 1854. In *AME*, I, 184, Conway says, "My brief speech was a plea for peaceful separation of North and South after the manner of Abraham and Lot." In fact, he was a featured speaker in the afternoon session, and *The Liberator* reports make no mention of any plea for peaceful disunion.

38. *The Liberator*, July 14, 1854.

39. *Ibid.*

40. *AME*, I, 182–183; Faculty Minutes of the Divinity School, July 1, 9, 20, 1854 ms in Harvard Archives, Pusey Library.

41. *AME*, I, 180–181; Faculty Minutes of the Divinity School, June 20, 1854, ms in Harvard Archives, Pusey Library.

42. Richard J. Hinton, *John Brown and His Men* (New York: Funk and Wagnalls, 1894), 535–536; *A Catalogue of the Officers and Students of Harvard College, for the Academical Year 1852–53, Second Term* (Cambridge, 1853). James C. Malin accuses Leeman (as his name is spelled in all accounts of John Brown)

of a desire for plunder in *John Brown and the Legend of Fifty-Six* (Philadelphia: American Philosophical Society, 1942), 697–698. Among those who repeat Hinton's information are Oswald Garrison Villard, *John Brown, 1800–1859. A Biography Fifty Years After* (Boston and New York: Houghton Mifflin, 1911), 685; and Stephen B. Oates, *To Purge This Land With Blood: A Biography of John Brown* (New York: Harper and Row, 1970), 173, 242, 293–295. Oates (p. 281) misdates by almost six weeks "Leeman's" last-minute letter to his mother. In his account of the wine incident (*AME*, I, 180–181), Conway refers to the culprit simply as "X." The faculty minutes name Leaman, however, while the catalogue lists his home as Hallowell, Me., the home of the John Brown raider. To my knowledge, this is the first time the truth about Leaman's past has been pieced together and written.

43. MC to Ralph Waldo Emerson, November 6, 1854, CU.

44. Frank Sanborn to MC, September 13, 1854, DC.

CHAPTER 5

1. William Henry Furness to MC, undated, CU; Notes for Reminiscences, CU. Samuel Longfellow, the most advanced antislavery man to serve thus far in the Washington pulpit, had lasted less than a year there.

2. *AME*, I, 186; letter by MC in the *Christian Inquirer*, March 21, 1857; MC to Ralph Waldo Emerson, November 6, 1854, CU. Channing would be Unitarian minister in Washington during the Civil War, after the composition of the congregation had drastically changed.

3. *National Intelligencer*, March 6, 1855; *Ordination Services of the Rev. M. D. Conway, February 28, 1855* (Washington, 1855); *Christian Inquirer*, March 21, 1857; *AME*, I, 195–196.

4. *AME*, I, 188–191.

5. Walker Peyton Conway to MC, September 18, 1854, CU. Walker quoted Moncure's complaint ("it is strange") verbatim from his son's recent letter to him, now evidently lost.

6. *AME*, I, 189–190; Notes for Reminiscences, CU.

7. *AME*, I, 190–192; Biographical sketch of MC in *The Index*, June 10, 1871.

8. MC, "Then and Now in the Old Dominion," *Atlantic Monthly*, Vol. IX, No. LIV (April 1862), 501; Notes for Reminiscences, CU; MS Lecture on Virginia (probably a sermon given in Cincinnati, 185–), CU.

9. Details of the Fitzhugh trip are to be found in Joseph Sheldon, Jr., to MC, March 5, 1855, and A. Alexander Little to MC, March 11, 1855, CU; in Jay B. Hubbell, *The South in American Literature, 1607–1900* (Durham, N.C.: Duke University Press, 1954), 434–437; and in *AME*, I, 224–225, where Fitzhugh's letter to "G.C.," April 12, 1855, is printed. The original of this letter is at CU.

10. *AME*, I, 248. For a sketchy but helpful history of the Washington church, see Laurence C. Staples, *Washington Unitarianism: A Rich Heritage* (Washington, D.C.: Metcalf Publishing Company, 1970), chap. 4 and *passim*. In a day-long search through rubble in the storerooms and closets of the Washington Unitarian church, I could find no records dating from the period of Conway's ministry.

11. *AME*, I, 200; list of books bought, in Financial Accounts, CU.

12. *AME*, I, 200, 220–222; Charlotte Taylor to MC, March 21, 1857, and Gerald Fitzgerald to MC, June 3, 1858, CU; MS sermon by MC, "Two Years in the District" [Cincinnati, 1856], CU.

13. *AME*, I, 201–203; Helen Hunt to MC, April 6, 1856 (quotations), June 1, 1857 (enthusiasm for Emerson), CU.

14. Notebook of Miscellany, 1854–55, CU; Henry Wadsworth Longfellow journal, August 26 (misprinted as August 16), 1855, in Samuel Longfellow, ed., *Life of Henry Wadsworth Longfellow With Extracts From His Journals and Correspondence*, 2 vols. (Boston: Ticknor, 1886), II, 261.

15. *AME*, I, 215–218; Thomas Wentworth Higginson, *Cheerful Yesterdays* (Boston and New York: Houghton Mifflin, 1898), 230; Charles Eliot Norton to James Russell Lowell, September 23, 1855, in Sara Norton and Mark deWolfe Howe, eds., *Letters of Charles Eliot Norton With Biographical Comment*, 2 vols. (Boston and New York: Houghton Mifflin, 1913), I, 135.

16. The central primary source for this visit is MC to Ralph Waldo Emerson, September 17, 1855, printed in *AME*, I, 215–216. A fragment of this letter is at CU. MC's article, "Walt Whitman," *The Fortnightly Review*, Vol. VI, No. XXXV (October 15, 1866), 538–548, evidently employs journalistic license in compressing his two visits to Whitman (1855 and 1857) into one. His account in *AME* treats the two separately.

17. MC to Ralph Waldo Emerson, September 17, 1855, in *AME*, I, 215–216; *AME*, I, 219.

18. *National Intelligencer*, November 24, 1855.

19. *Ibid.* MC was dragged into an imbroglio which developed when a Pennsylvanian who signed himself "T.C.P." accused Longfellow of stealing the style and many of the events from a Finnish epic, *Kalewala*. Longfellow was indignant at this attack on his integrity, calling it "truly one of the greatest literary outrages I ever heard of." Conway returned to the *Intelligencer* in the poet's defense with, wrote Longfellow, "a very good reply." Henry Schoolcraft wrote to say that he had never heard of *Kalewala* and that all incidents in *Hiawatha* (despite any resemblances to episodes cited by T.C.P.) derived from native Indian lore. This completed Longfellow's public vindication. But there was a bit more to T.C.P.'s charge than Conway ever knew. Longfellow had admitted to familiarity with *Kalewala* while denying its influence. His journal, however, indicates a clear connection between the two epics. On June 5, 1854, the poet noted, "I am reading with great delight the Finnish Epic, *Kalevala*. It is charming." Seventeen days later he wrote, "I have hit at length upon a plan for a poem on the American Indians, which seems to me the right one, and the only, . . . I have hit upon a measure, too, which I think the right and only one for such a theme." The measure was trochaic dimeter, the meter used in *Kalewala*. *National Intelligencer*, Nov. 27, 29, Dec. 11, 1855; Henry Wadsworth Longfellow to Charles Sumner, Dec. 3, 1855, in Samuel Longfellow, ed., *op. cit.*, II, 268; MC to H. W. Longfellow, Nov. 29, Dec. 5, 1855, HU; H. W. Longfellow to MC, Nov. 30, 1855, HU; Dec. 5, 1855, in *AME*, I, 212–213.

20. Margaret Daniel Conway to MC, Feb. 10, October 1855, CU.

21. G. W. Burnap to MC, January 2, 1855, CU. An indication of Burnap's overbearing personality is supplied by the reaction to him of MC's sister, who in 1855 was visiting relatives in Baltimore when the Burnaps invited her to dinner. "Oh! didn't I wish it would rain tho'! But it didn't and I went. . . . I was

however a great deal more pleased with Mrs. Burnap than I had expected to be. . . . But Dr. Burnap—Whew!" Mildred Conway to MC, undated [1855], CU.

22. *National Intelligencer*, June 12 ("a theory adapted"), 19 ("a mediator," "council of bishops"), 5 ("infallibility"), 1855. For a representative explanation of antebellum Unitarianism, including various points which would have been thought suspect by 1855, see Rev. Alvan Lamson, "Unitarian Congregationalists," in I. Daniel Rupp, ed., *An Original History of the Religious Denominations at Present Existing in the United States* (Philadelphia: J. Y. Humpreys, 1844), 703–718.

23. No account of the Unitarian counterrevolution of the 1850s has been written. This will be discussed at greater length in the following chapter.

24. MC, *The Old and the New: A Sermon Containing the History of the First Unitarian Church in Washington City* (Washington, D.C.: Buell and Blanchard, 1855), II. MC's sermon on "Sceptics" is summarized in the *National Intelligencer*, April 24, 1855, and is published in *Tracts for Today* (Cincinnati: Truman and Spofford, 1858).

25. MC, *The True and the False in Prevalent Theories of Divine Dispensations, A Discourse Delivered in the Unitarian Church, Washington City, on Sunday, September 16, 1855, in Behalf of the Norfolk and Portsmouth Sufferers* (Washington, D.C.: Taylor and Maury, 1855), 16–17 and *passim*. Many years later, after his approach to evil had undergone a profound transformation, Conway looked upon this sermon as facile and naïve. "Although I opposed the many pulpit assertions that the plague was a judgment from Heaven, I had nothing much better than commonplace optimism with which to confront such superstition." *AME*, I, 196.

26. *AME*, I, 198; *National Intelligencer*, September 20, 27, 1855. The two sermons were *The True and the False* and *Pharisaism and Fasting, A Discourse Delivered in the Unitarian Church, Washington City, September 30, 1855* (Washington, D.C.: Buell and Blanchard, 1855).

27. *AME*, I, 219.

28. Howe, *The Unitarian Conscience*, chap. X. May is quoted in Douglas C. Stange, *Patterns of Antislavery among American Unitarians, 1831–1860* (Cranbury, N.J.: Associated University Presses, 1977), 180. Octavius B. Frothingham, *Boston Unitarianism, 1820–1850* (New York: G.P. Putnam's Sons, 1890), 196–197.

29. Stange, 180–182 and *passim*.

30. MC's account of the ensuing fight with his congregation over slavery, in *AME*, I, 230–249, portrays himself as considerably less caustic and more conciliatory than he was, and incorrectly paints himself as favoring peaceful disunion.

31. Washington *Evening Star*, undated, newspaper scrapbook, CU. *AME*, I, 231–235. MC says (231) that he had reached "the conclusion that perpetual discord, if not war, could be escaped only by separation of North and South." To bolster this claim, he published a small excerpt from the sermon taken badly out of context. By 1904 Conway had embraced pacifism, and with *fin de siècle* disillusionment looked upon the Civil War as having been a tragic and meaningless slaughter. Accordingly, he was almost pathetically eager to camouflage or overlook the partisanship of his antebellum career.

32. The sermon was published as *The One Path: or, The Duties of The North and South* (Washington, D.C.: Buell and Blanchard, 1856). It is most readily available in MC, *Tracts for Today* (Cincinnati: Truman and Spofford, 1858), 176–194. The quotations are from "The One Path," *Tracts for Today*, 177.

33. *Ibid.*, 180–181.

34. *Ibid.*, 187–188, 191.

35. *Ibid.*, 189, 193.

36. *Ibid.*, 193–194.

37. Washington *Evening Star*, undated, newspaper scrapbook, CU: *National Antislavery Standard*, February 16, 1856, reprints "The One Path" from the *National Era*; *The Liberator*, February 22, 1856; John Greenleaf Whittier to unidentified correspondent, February 2, 1856, in John B. Pickard, ed., *The Letters of John Greenleaf Whittier* (Cambridge: Belknap Press of Harvard University Press, 1975), II, 291.

38. New York *Tribune*, January 29, 1856.

39. Extract from the annual report for 1855, in the *Christian Inquirer*, April 18, 1857.

40. New York *Tribune*, February 9, 1856.

41. MC, *Spiritual Liberty, A Discourse Delivered in the Unitarian Church, Washington, D.C., on Sunday, February 17, 1856* (Washington, D.C.; Buell and Blanchard, 1856), 6.

42. *AME*, I, 236.

43. *Ibid.* On pp. 242–243, MC says that after his dismissal there was concern that the money raised on this trip would be used by a church not, after all, dedicated to antislavery, and that he gave the funds to the church treasurer with instructions that it be used only at his (Conway's) order. Perhaps the money was freed for use during the Civil War, when the congregation (under the ministry of William Henry Channing) was decidedly antislavery.

44. Quotation in the New York *Tribune*, May 29, 1856; see also *The Liberator*, June 25, 1856. H. W. Longfellow journal, May 25 [1856] in Samuel Longfellow, ed., *op. cit.*, II, 280; *AME*, I, 236–237; *The Liberator*, June 6, 1856.

45. *The Liberator*, June 6, 1856.

46. James Brewer Stewart, *Holy Warriors: The Abolitionists and American Slavery* (New York: Hill and Wang, 1976), 91.

47. *Ibid.*; letter from MC in the *Christian Inquirer*, March 21, 1857 ("with whose views"). MC is associated with the Garrisonians, explicitly or by implication, in George Fredrickson, *The Inner Civil War* (New York: Harper and Row, 1965), 126–127; Carleton Mabee, *Black Freedom: The Nonviolent Abolitionists From 1830 Through the Civil War* (New York: Macmillan, 1970), 363–364; Richard H. Sewell, *Ballots for Freedom: Antislavery Politics in the United States, 1837–1860* (New York: Oxford University Press, 1976), 341–342.

48. MC to William Logan Fisher, June 25 [1856], Logan-Fisher-Fox Mss., Historical Society of Pennsylvania; *AME*, I, 238; MC to Anna Ricketson, July 14 [1856] ("the knocking down"), HU.

49. *AME*, I, 239–242.

50. *The Liberator*, July 18, 1856 (reprinted from the Boston *Traveller*).

51. *Ibid.*

52. *Ibid.*

53. *Ibid. AME*, I, 242. *Christian Inquirer*, July 19, 1856.

54. Report in the Boston *Telegraph*, reprinted in *The Liberator*, July 25, 1856.

55. *Ibid.* See also *Christian Inquirer*, July 19, 1856; New York *Daily Tribune*, July 14, 1856. MC to Anna Ricketson, July 14 [1856], HU.

56. William Henry Channing to MC, August 12, 1856, CU; Wendell Phillips to MC, July 12, 1856, McKim-Garrison Papers, New York Public Library;

Thomas Wentworth Higginson to MC, June 5, 1856, CU. See also a letter from eleven citizens of Jefferson, Ohio, August 18, 1856, in *AME*, I, 246–247n. MC is quoted in a letter from the Executive Committee of the Washington Unitarian Church published in the *Christian Inquirer*, April 18, 1857.

57. Margaret Daniel Conway to MC, October 10, 1855 ("too painful," "natural sympathy"), July 5, 1856, CU.

58. *The Liberator*, August 15, 1856; MC to Anna Ricketson, July 30 [1856], HU.

59. Handwritten ms by Nelson Sizer, *Phrenological Character of Rev. M.D. Conway . . .* , rare book room, CU.

60. MC to Ralph Waldo Emerson, October 7 [1856], CU; letter from Washington Unitarian Church Executive Committee in the *Christian Inquirer*, April 18, 1857. On the dismissal see also *The Liberator*, October 10, 1856, and the *Christian Inquirer*, October 11, December 6, 1856.

61. *AME*, I, 249; Gerald Fitzgerald to MC, October 8, 1856, CU.

62. Letter from MC in the *Christian Inquirer*, March 21, 1857.

63. John Kebler to MC, October 13, 1856, CU; MC, *Virtue vs. Defeat* (Cincinnati: Cincinnati *Gazette* Company, 1856); E. S. Stevens to MC, December 1, 1856, CU; *Cincinnati Daily Gazette*, December 15, 1856; Minute Book of the First Congregationalist Church, Cincinnati, October 31, November 10, 18, 1856, Cincinnati Historical Society; MC to Robert Hosea et al., December 10, 1856 (quotation), Cincinnati Historical Society.

CHAPTER 6

1. Isabella Bird is quoted in Paul Angle, "Cities of the Middle Border," *American Heritage*, Vol. VIII, No. 1 (December 1956), 126. For information on Cincinnati I have drawn from the annual *Williams' Cincinnati Directory, City Guide and Business Mirror*, 1855–1862, and Charles Cist, *Sketches and Statistics of Cincinnati in 1859* (Cincinnati, 1859). See also MC, "The Queen of the West," *Fraser's Magazine*, Vol. LXXIII, No. CCCCXXXIII (January 1866), 42–68.

2. Cist, *op. cit.*, 278–282; *The Governors of Ohio* (Columbus: The Ohio Historical Society, 1954; 2ⁿᵈ ed., 1969), 115–119; John Kebler to Henry Bellows, March 19, 1859, Bellows Papers, Massachusetts Historical Society.

3. Record book in MC's hand, October 26, November 18, 1856; First Congregationalist Church (Unitarian) Minute Book, October 31, November 10, 18, 1856, Unitarian Church Records, Cincinnati Historical Society; John Kebler to MC, October 13, 1856, CU; *Christian Register* quoted in *Christian Inquirer*, September 27, 1856; A. A. Livermore to Henry Bellows, November 25, 1856, Bellows Papers, Massachusetts Historical Society.

4. Fredericksburg, Va. *Weekly Advertiser*, March 21, 1857.

5. John P. Frank, *Justice Daniel Dissenting: A Biography of Peter V. Daniel, 1784–1860* (Cambridge: Harvard University Press, 1964), 256–257. The definitive work on the Dred Scott decision is Don E. Fehrenbacher, *The Dred Scott Case: Its Significance in American Law and Politics* (New York: Oxford University Press, 1978).

6. MC to William Greene, May 19 [1857], Greene Papers, Cincinnati Historical Society; Douglas C. Stange, *Patterns of Antislavery among American Unitarians, 1831–1860* (Cranbury, N.J.: Associated University Presses, 1977),

223–225; Church Minute Book, May 3, 1857, Unitarian Church Records, Cincinnati Historical Society.

7. Margaret Daniel Conway to MC, June 2, 1857, CU.

8. MC to William Greene, May 19 [1857], Greene Papers, Cincinnati Historical Society; MC to Ellen Dana, November 19, 1857, CU; Annie Besant to MC [c. January 1898], CU; Annie Besant, *An Autobiography* (London: T. F. Unwin, 1893).

9. MC to Ellen Dana, March 3 [1858], CU.

10. *AME*, I, 287; William Henry Furness to MC, April 12, 1858, CU; Cincinnati *Daily Gazette*, June 2, 1858; *Christian Inquirer*, June 12, 26 ("criminal extravagance"), 1858.

11. MC journal entry in notebook also containing "Notes for Reminiscences," Paris, December 16, 1899, CU; MC to EDC, January 24 [1862], CU.

12. MC, "Down the Ohio to the Underworld," *Fraser's Magazine*, Vol. LXXIV, No. CCCCXLIV (December 1866), 753–770.

13. MC, *Tracts For Today* (Cincinnati: Truman and Spofford, 1857), dedication page.

14. Stafford County slave schedule, United States Census, 1860. This visit is recalled in MC to EDC, September 10, 1875, CU, and September 19, 1875, DC; EDC to MC, September 27, 1875, CU; and Dunmore Gwinn to MC, November 10, 1891, CU. Perhaps Ellen's action bothered people so much because she punctured their preconception of the hypocritical Yankee who claimed to love blacks but could not bear to touch them, a stereotype embodied six years earlier by Miss Ophelia in *Uncle Tom's Cabin*. Ellen was a more honest and consistent abolitionist than Ophelia, and thus, perhaps, less easy for slaveowners to tolerate.

15. MC to EDC, September 10, 1875, CU; September 19, 1875, DC.

16. *The Liberator*, July 18, 1856.

17. Minute Book, January 30, 1857, Unitarian Church Records, Cincinnati Historical Society; Ralph Waldo Emerson to Lidian Emerson, January 29, 31, 1857, in Ralph L. Rusk, ed., *The Letters of Ralph Waldo Emerson* (New York: Columbia University Press, 1939), V, 60–61; Cincinnati *Gazette*, January 27, February 6, 1857.

18. Book containing constitution and bylaws drawn up under Livermore's ministry, July 1855, Unitarian Church Records, Cincinnati Historical Society. Among the 209 signers was Ellen D. Dana.

19. MS sermon, "Socinus," given by MC in Cincinnati, December 27, 1857, CU.

20. Opinion by Judge Collins in *The Unitarian Church Case* (Cincinnati: William Doyle, 1860), 98; Court testimony in Cincinnati *Gazette*, January 21, 1860; Unidentified news clipping, "The Split in the Unitarian Church," newspaper scrapbook, CU; Report on the Cincinnati Church, apparently by MC, in the *Christian Inquirer*, January 15, 1859.

21. *The Unitarian Church Case, op. cit.*, 70, 90–91; Cincinnati *Gazette*, January 24, 1860.

22. John Kebler to MC, June 23, 1859, Unitarian Church Records, Cincinnati Historical Society.

23. Minute Book, entry of March 28, 1859, in which MC's letter is transcribed, Unitarian Church Records, Cincinnati Historical Society.

24. Minute Book, March 30, 1859, Unitarian Church Records, Cincinnati

Historical Society; George Augustine Thayer, *The First Congregational Church of Cincinnati (Unitarian): A History* (Cincinnati: The Ebbert and Richardson Company, 1917), 33–34.

25. Handwritten statement of beliefs, Church of the Redeemer, undated, Unitarian Church Records, Cincinnati Historical Society; *Christian Inquirer*, May 14, 1859.

26. MC, *East and West: An Inaugural Discourse, Delivered in the First Congregational Church, Cincinnati, O., May 1, 1859* (Cincinnati: Truman and Spofford, 1859), 8 and *passim*.

27. *Ibid.*

28. *Christian Inquirer*, June 11, 1859; John Kebler to Henry Bellows, May 9, 1860, Bellows Papers, Massachusetts Historical Society; Letter from Robert Hosea in the *Christian Inquirer*, August 13, 1859; MC, *Thomas Paine: A Celebration Delivered in the First Congregational Church, Cincinnati, Ohio, January 29, 1860* (Cincinnati: Published at the office of *The Dial*, 1860).

29. William Bellows to Henry Bellows, April 6, 1859, Bellows Papers, Massachusetts Historical Society; Cincinnati *Gazette*, January 21, 1860; Sermon by MC, "The Duty of Christians to Attend the Theater," unidentified news clipping, newspaper scrapbook, CU; MC, *The Theater: A Discourse Delivered in the Unitarian Church* (Cincinnati: Truman and Spofford, 1857); MC, "The Citizen and the Drama," lecture delivered before the Phoenix Dramatic Association on October 25, 1860, published in *The Dial*, Vol. I, No. 12 (December 1860), 762–773.

30. Edward Everett Hale, *Public Amusements for the Rich and Poor* (Boston: Phillips, Sampson and Company, 1857). See David Grimsted, *Melodrama Unveiled: American Theater and Culture, 1800–1850* (Chicago: University of Chicago Press, 1968), 22–23.

31. MC, "The Citizen and the Drama," *op. cit.*, 768.

32. *Ibid.*, 771–772.

33. Robert Hosea's court testimony reported in the Cincinnati *Gazette*, January 21, 1860; Kebler's views reported in John G. Anthony's testimony, *ibid.*; MC, *East and West*, 6.

34. Cincinnati *Gazette*, January 21, 1860; Handwritten memorandum on the origin of the split in the Unitarian church, author unknown, Unitarian Church Records, Cincinnati Historical Society.

35. Charles Ritter to Robert Hosea, August 5, 1859, Unitarian Church Records, Cincinnati Historical Society; *Christian Inquirer*, November 12, July 16, 1859; Mayo quoted in Caruthers, *Octavius Brooks Frothingham*, 113.

36. Henry Bellows to his daughter, April 25, 1859, William Bellows to Henry Bellows, May 24, 1859, Bellows Papers, Massachusetts Historical Society; Henry Bellows, *The Importance of a Positive and Distinct Theology* (Cincinnati: Robert Clarke and Company, 1859). Re Bellows see John White Chadwick, *Henry W. Bellows: His Life and Character* (New York: S. W. Green's Sons, 1882). Re mainstream Unitarianism's adherence to "supernatural rationalism" see Howe, *The Unitarian Conscience*, 87–90.

37. A. A. Livermore to Henry Bellows, October 15, 1856, and Henry Bellows to Orville Dewey, July 9, 1856, Bellows Papers, Massachusetts Historical Society; *Christian Inquirer*, July 16, August 20, 1859.

38. George Burnap to Henry Bellows, April 28, 1859, Bellows Papers, Massachusetts Historical Society.

39. John White Chadwick, *Theodore Parker, Preacher and Reformer* (Boston: Houghton Mifflin, 1900), 363–364.

40. *Christian Inquirer*, August 6, 1859.

41. *Ibid.*

42. *Ibid.*; Letter from Bellows, dated August 4, 1859, in the *Christian Inquirer*, August 13, 1859.

43. *Christian Inquirer*, August 6, 1859.

44. *Ibid.*

45. *Christian Inquirer*, September 10, 1859.

46. *Christian Inquirer*, September 3, 1859. Bellows's address was published and widely circulated as *The Suspense of Faith* (New York: C. S. Francis and Company, 1859), and was followed by *A Sequel to "The Suspense of Faith"* (New York: D. Appleton and Company, 1859), which he delivered at his own All Souls Church on September 25.

47. *Christian Inquirer*, September 3, 1859.

48. Stanley M. Elkins, *Slavery: A Problem in American Institutional Life* (Chicago: University of Chicago Press, 1959), 141; Henry David Thoreau, "Life Without Principle," *The Atlantic Monthly* XII (October 1863), 484–495, written as a lyceum lecture in 1854; Wendell Phillips, "Public Opinion," *Speeches, Lectures, and Letters* (Boston: Lee and Shepard, 1892), 46.

49. MC, "Apologia," *Farewell Discourses* (London: E. W. Allen, 1884), 165; *Christian Inquirer*, November 12, 1859.

50. Lydia Maria Child, *The Progress of Religious Ideas Through Successive Ages*, 3 vols. (New York: C. S. Francis and Company, 1855), I, vii–viii; *Christian Inquirer*, August 13, 1859; E. D. Wilder to EDC, April 5, 1864, CU.

51. Editorial note by MC appended to [Orson Murray], "On Prayer," *The Dial*, Vol. I, No. 2 (February 1860), 130; MC, *The Natural History of the Devil* (pamphlet; Albany: Weed, Parsons and Company, 1859), 12.

52. Hoadly quoted in unidentified news clipping [April 1859], newspaper scrapbook, CU; E. D. Wilder to MC [1862], CU.

53. Thomas Hill to Henry Bellows, November 30, 1860, and Thomas Starr King to Henry Bellows, April 9, 1859, Bellows Papers, Massachusetts Historical Society; Wasson quoted in Frank Preston Stearns, *The Life and Public Services of George Luther Stearns* (Philadelphia: Lippincott, 1907), 264.

54. Charles Gordon Ames to Caroline Dall, March 12, 1863, Dall Papers, Massachusetts Historical Society. A biographical sketch of Ames, written by Dall, appears in *The Liberator*, November 18, 1864.

55. MC to [Samuel] Longfellow, November 19, 1859, Barrett Collection, University of Virginia.

56. MC to Henry Wadsworth Longfellow, November 21, 1859, March 20, 1860, Longfellow Papers, HU; *The Dial*, Vol. I, No. 1 (January 1860), 11 ("legitimation"). For more on the Cincinnati *Dial* see Clarence L. F. Gohdes, *The Periodicals of American Transcendentalism* (Durham, N.C.: Duke University Press, 1931), 194–209.

57. MC to Henry Wadsworth Longfellow, March 20, 1860, Longfellow Papers, HU; MC to Henry David Thoreau, November 19, 1859, and Thoreau to MC, November 23, 1859, University of Rochester; MC to Samuel Johnson, March 16, 1860, Essex Institute; MC to Ralph Waldo Emerson, December 18, 1859, Emerson Papers, HU; Emerson to MC, June 6, 1860, in Rusk, ed., *Letters*

of Ralph Waldo Emerson, V, 220–221. Emerson's lecture appeared in the October issue.

58. *AME*, I, 307–310; William Dean Howells, *Years of My Youth* (Bloomington and London: Indiana University Press, 1975; first published in 1916), 152.

59. C. H. Dall, "The Late Lawsuit. Men and Women vs. Custom and Tradition," *The Dial*, Vol. I, No. 5 (May 1860), 286–293; MC to Caroline Dall, February 10, 14, 20, 1860, Dall Papers, Massachusetts Historical Society; *AME*, I, 289–290; [MC], "Prostitution," *The Dial*, Vol. I, No. 11 (November 1860), 673–675.

60. *The Dial*, Vol. I, No. 3 (March 1860), 196–197.

61. *The Dial*, Vol. I, No. 8 (August 1860), 517–519.

62. *The Dial*, Vol. I, No. 4 (April 1860), 262.

63. *AME*, 315–316; MC, *Life of Nathaniel Hawthorne* (New York: A. Lovell and Company, 1890), 198–199. I have discussed Conway's later rediscovery of tragedy in *Moncure Conway, 1832–1907: American Abolitionist, Spiritual Architect of South Place, Author of "The Life of Thomas Paine"* (London: South Place Ethical Society, 1977), 25–29. Conway's failure to appreciate Hawthorne in 1860 is, of course, laced with irony. Of all people, Conway—raised amid slavery, exiled from his home—might have been expected to understand the reality of evil and the ambiguity of "progress." Yet the very extent of his alienation from his father's world, and the compensating fervor with which he embraced Emersonianism, prevented him for a time from doing so.

64. MC to Robert Collyer, October 1, 1860, DC; Marianna Mott to Ellen Wright Garrison, July 27 [1860], Garrison Family Papers, Smith College.

65. MC to Henry David Thoreau, November 26 [1860], Berg Collection, New York Public Library; MC to William Lloyd Garrison, January 9, 1861, Garrison Family Papers, Smith College; MC to Myron B. Benton, January 9, 1861, in *Troutbeck Leaflets*, No. 9 (Amenia, New York: Privately printed, 1925), 7–8.

66. [MC], "The Nemesis of Unitarianism," *The Dial*, Vol. I, No. 6 (June 1860), 364–365.

67. *The Dial*, Vol. I, Nos. 2, 8, and 10 (February, August, October 1860), 136, 469, 646.

68. Sidney H. Morse to MC, undated [1865], CU.

69. Bellows quoted in Conrad Wright, *The Liberal Christians* (Boston: Beacon Press, 1970), 105.

70. Caruthers, *Frothingham*, 115–116.

71. Francis Ellingwood Abbot to MC, November 15, 1869, CU. This letter refers to MC's "kindest of letters, received when I first publicly relinquished the name of Christian." MC to Abbot, December 16, 1869, published in *The Index*, January 15, 1870.

CHAPTER 7

1. Brown is quoted in Stephen B. Oates, *To Purge This Land With Blood: A Biography of John Brown* (New York: Harper and Row, 1970), 197. This is the most balanced modern biography of Brown.

2. Oates, 351, 318; *AME*, I, 303.

3. *AME*, I, 300.

4. *The Dial*, Vol. I, No. 3 (March 1860), 200; Vol. I, No. 6 (June 1860), 390.

5. MC to William Henry Seward, July 17, 1860, Seward Papers, University of Rochester.

6. MC to Margaret Daniel Conway, December 16 [1861], CU.

7. MC, "Excalibur," *The Dial*, Vol. I, No. 1 (January 1860), 38–48 (quotations on 48).

8. David M. Potter, *The Impending Crisis* (New York: Harper and Row, 1976), 405–447. The best modern works on Lincoln are Stephen B. Oates, *With Malice Toward None: The Life of Abraham Lincoln* (New York: Harper and Row, 1977) and Oscar and Lilian Handlin, *Abraham Lincoln and the Union* (Boston: Little, Brown, 1980). Benjamin Thomas, *Abraham Lincoln* (New York: Knopf, 1952) is still useful.

9. *The Dial*, Vol. I, No. 7 (July 1860), 455.

10. Potter, 514–554.

11. Oscar Sherwin, *Prophet of Liberty: The Life and Times of Wendell Phillips* (New York: Bookman Associates, 1958), 431; David M. Potter, "Horace Greeley and Peaceable Secession," in Potter, *The South and the Sectional Conflict* (Baton Rouge: Louisiana State University Press, 1968), 220.

12. MC, "Secession," ms sermon, undated, CU.

13. Miss [Sarah] Pugh to Mrs. Edmondson, February 4, 1861, Estlin Papers, Dr. Williams's Library, London.

14. On the Sumter crisis, see David M. Potter, *Lincoln and his Party in the Secession Crisis* (New Haven: Yale University Press, 1942); Kenneth M. Stampp, *And the War Came* (Baton Rouge: Louisiana State University Press, 1950); Richard Current, *Lincoln and the First Shot* (Philadelphia: Lippincott, 1963); and George H. Knoles, ed., *The Crisis of the Union, 1860–1861* (Baton Rouge: Louisiana State University Press, 1965).

15. William Henry Furness to MC, May 7, 1861, CU.

16. *AME*, I, 324–327; MC, "The Horrors of Peace," discourse given at the Unitarian church in Cincinnati, May 5 [1861], in unidentified news clipping, newspaper scrapbook, CU.

17. *Muster-Roll of Stafford County, Va. In The War In Defense of Virginia, 1861–1865*, ms book, Stafford courthouse.

18. Margaret Daniel Conway to MC, February 13, 1861 ("unholy excitement"); MC to EDC, June 25, 1861; Walker Conway to Margaret Daniel Conway, March 27, 1862, CU.

19. Margaret Daniel Conway to MC, September 30, 1862; Walker Conway to Margaret Daniel Conway, March 27, 1862; MC to Margaret Daniel Conway, December 16 [1861], CU.

20. Walker Conway to Margaret Daniel Conway, March 27, 1862 (quotations); MC to EDC, June 25, 1861, September 14 [1875], CU.

21. MC to Abraham Lincoln, May 7, 1861, Lincoln Papers, Library of Congress; Robert Collyer to MC [May 1861], CU.

22. MC to EDC, June 25, July 16 (written in Providence; "harrassed with fear"), July 16 (written in Newport; "his uncle just arrived"), 1861. On this trip see also MC, "Mannahatta," *Fraser's*, Vol. LXXII, No. CCCCXXIX (September 1865), 283–285.

23. Letter by MC (under the pseudonym "Argos") to the New York *Tribune*, July 23, 1861 (written July 18 at Newport).

24. L. B. Russell to MC, May 4, 1861, CU.

25. *AME*, I, 330.

26. MC to EDC, July 23 [1861], CU.

27. MC to EDC [August 1861], CU. Conway's autobiography (I, 337), which says he spoke at Frothingham's church in August, helps date this letter.

28. MC to EDC [August 1861], CU.

29. MC to EDC, March 3 [1858], CU.

30. *AME*, I, 338–339; *Dayton Express*, November 1861, clipping in newspaper scrapbook, CU.

31. MC, *Testimonies Concerning Slavery* (London: Chapman and Hall, 1864), 79–80.

32. MC to Ralph Waldo Emerson, October 2 [1861], Emerson Papers, HU; Emerson to MC, October 6, 1861, CU.

33. MC to Charles Sumner, August 22, September 23, October 5, 7 [1861], Sumner Papers, HU; Springfield (Ohio) *Republic*, undated clipping, newspaper scrapbook, CU.

34. Undated clipping, newspaper scrapbook, CU; MC, *The Rejected Stone: or Insurrection vs. Resurrection in America* (Boston: Walker, Wise, and Company, 1861), 24–28, 93–112.

35. MC, *The Rejected Stone*, 9, 35, 77–80.

36. *Ibid.*, 95–99, 9, 52, 69.

37. See T. Harry Williams, *Lincoln and his Generals* (New York: Alfred A. Knopf, 1952), 34–41; James M. McPherson, *The Struggle For Equality: Abolitionists and the Negro in the Civil War and Reconstruction* (Princeton: Princeton University Press, 1964), 72–73.

38. *The Liberator*, September 20, 1861; McPherson, *op. cit.*, 73; MC to Horace Greeley, September 18, 1861, Greeley Papers, New York Public Library. Conway wrote in a similar vein to Charles Sumner, September 17 [1861], Sumner Papers, HU. John Charles Fremont to MC, December 25, 1861, CU, thanks Conway for "the cordiality of your letter to me at St. Louis," but I have not located Conway's letter.

39. MC to William Dean Howells, September 11 [1861], Howells Papers, HU.

40. MC to Ralph Waldo Emerson, December 1 [1861], Emerson Papers, HU; MC to Charles Sumner, December 12 [1861], Sumner Papers, HU. Ralph L. Rusk, in *The Letters of Ralph Waldo Emerson*, 6 vols. (New York: Columbia University Press, 1939), V, 259n, misdates the John Brown speech as taking place in late January. Conway's January speech in Concord was "The Golden Hour." MC to Emerson, January 22 [1862], CU; Emerson to MC, undated, Barrett Collection, University of Virginia.

41. MC to EDC, January 24 [1862] ("huge noise," fast as they come"), CU; W. A. Croffut to MC, January 5, 1862, CU; MC letter, dated Boston, January 27, in Cincinatti *Gazette*, newspaper scrapbook, CU; *National Anti-Slavery Standard*, February 8, 1862; MC to EDC, January 15, 16, 21, 22, 24 ("these bitter nights"), 1862, CU.

42. MC to EDC, October 3 [1875], CU; Cleveland *Leader*, undated clipping from either 1861 or 1862, newspaper scrapbook, CU; *National Anti-Slavery Standard*, April 11, 1863.

43. MC to EDC, January 22 [1862], CU; MC to Ralph Waldo Emerson, January 22 [1862], CU.

44. MC to EDC, January 21 [1862], CU.

45. *AME*, I, 345–347.

46. Oliver Wendell Holmes to John Lothrop Motley, February 3, 1862, in John T. Morse, Jr., *Life and Letters of Oliver Wendell Holmes*, 2 vols. (Boston: Houghton Mifflin, 1896), II, 162–163.

47. Edward Waldo Emerson and Waldo Emerson Forbes, eds., *Journals of Ralph Waldo Emerson*, 10 vols. (Boston: Houghton Mifflin, 1913), IX, 373n; [Ralph Waldo Emerson], "American Civilization," *The Atlantic Monthly*, Vol. IX, No. LIV (April 1862), 502–511, quotation on 509.

48. MS sermon, "The Southern Mote and Northern Beam," February 23, 1862, CU.

49. MC to EDC, March 11, 13, 17, 28 ("radical enough") [1862], CU; MC to William Greene, March 24 [1862], Greene Papers, Cincinnati Historical Society.

50. MC to Charles Sumner, April 22 [1862], Sumner Papers, HU.

51. MC to Charles Sumner, April 22, 29, 30 [1862], Sumner Papers, HU. Conway distorted the record when he later wrote (*AME*, I, 353): "I was informed by Sumner that the President would give me a foreign consulate if I desired it—which I did not."

52. Samuel May to Richard Davis Webb, May 27, 1862, in Clare Taylor, ed., *British and American Abolitionists* (Edinburgh: Edinburgh University Press, 1974), 485; MC, *The Golden Hour* (Boston: Ticknor and Fields, 1862), 157–158.

53. *AME*, I, 354–355; *National Anti-Slavery Standard*, July 5, 1862. In *AME*, I, 354, Conway incorrectly states that the Unitarian Conference met in May.

54. MC, *The Golden Hour*, 13, 116–117, 160 ("higher than . . ."), 28 ("slavery is . . ."). For a typical abolitionist reaction to the book, see the *National Anti-Slavery Standard*, July 19, 1862.

55. MC, *The Golden Hour*, 73–74 ("Southern blood"), 85 ("piece of bunting"), 132 ("more right"), 155–156 ("this butchery").

56. Walker Peyton Conway to Margaret Daniel Conway, March 27, 1862, CU.

57. MC, "Fredericksburg First and Last," *Magazine of American History*, Vol. XVII, No. 6 (June 1887), 452–468. Federal troops moved into Falmouth on April 18, into Fredericksburg on April 27.

58. New York *Tribune*, May 12, 1862.

59. Fredericksburg *Christian Banner*, April 24, July 2, 1862.

60. MC to Mildred Conway March, May 14 [1862], CU.

61. Mildred Conway March to MC, July 11, 1862, CU; MC, *Testimonies Concerning Slavery* (London: Chapman and Hall, 1864), 103. The chess game was resumed in 1876, when Conway returned to Yellow Springs on a lecture tour. He won, and the moves were published in the local press. *AME*, I, 355.

62. MC to EDC, July 15, 1862, CU; MC, *Testimonies*, 104.

63. MC, *Testimonies*, 105–106. The pass from General Wadsworth (who was killed in the Wilderness in May 1864) is at CU.

64. *AME*, I, 358–359.

65. MC, *Testimonies*, 106–107. In a letter in the London *Morning Star*, June 2, 1863, MC said he had "recently gone to Washington to discover some forty slaves of my father's. . . ."

66. MC to Salmon P. Chase, March 5, 1863, Chase Papers, Library of Congress; MC, *Testimonies*, 108.

67. MC, *Testimonies*, 109; *AME*, I, 360; MC's speech at the First of August celebration at Abington, 1862, published in the *National Anti-Slavery Standard*, August 9, 1862 ("every buggar's hands").

68. MC, *Testimonies*, 109–110.

69. *Ibid.*, 110–111.

70. *National Anti-Slavery Standard*, August 9, 1862; William Lloyd Garrison to Wendell P. Garrison, August 1, 1862, Garrison Papers, Boston Public Library; New York *Tribune* article dated August 4, newspaper scrapbook, CU.

71. MC to EDC, August 28 [1862], CU.

CHAPTER 8

1. MS material on the "Frost house" at the Concord Free Library, Concord, Mass.; *The Concord Journal*, January 13, 1955.

2. *The Commonwealth*, September 6, 1862.

3. *The Commonwealth*, October 11, December 27, 1862; Frederick Beecher Perkins to MC, September 8, 1862, CU; Frank Preston Stearns, *The Life and Public Services of George Luther Stearns* (Philadelphia: Lippincott, 1907), 263–264.

4. *The Commonwealth*, September 6, October 25, 1862.

5. Robert Collyer to MC, December 26, 1862, CU; Joseph Ricketson to Deborah Wester, November 14, 1862, Boston Public Library.

6. *The Commonwealth*, September 27, 1862.

7. William Henry Furness to MC, undated [September 1862], CU.

8. New York *Tribune*, January 29, 1863; [John M. Daniel], *The Life of Stonewall Jackson. From Official Papers, Contemporary Narratives, and Personal Acquaintance. By a Virginian.* (Richmond: Ayres and Wade, 1863), 227.

9. Whitman wrote in his journal on December 21, 1862, at Falmouth: "Spent a good part of the day in a large brick mansion on the banks of the Rappahannock, used as a hospital since the battle—seems to have receiv'd only the worst cases. Out doors, at the foot of a tree, within ten yards of the front of the house, I notice a heap of amputated feet, legs, arms, hands, etc., a full load for a one-horse cart. Several dead bodies lie near, each cover'd with its brown woolen blanket. . . . The large mansion is quite crowded upstairs and down, everything impromptu, no system, all bad enough, but I have no doubt the best that can be done; all the wounds pretty bad, some frightful, the men in their old clothes, unclean and bloody. Some of the wounded are rebel soldiers and officers, prisoners. . . . I went through the rooms, downstairs and up. Some of the men were dying. . . ." Whitman had met Conway, of course, shortly after publishing *Leaves of Grass*. However, he evidently did not know that this was the Conway family home, where Moncure had spent most of his boyhood and youth. See Floyd Stovall, ed., *Walt Whitman: Prose Works 1892*, 2 vols. (New York: New York University Press, 1963), I, 32–33.

10. Bruce Catton, *Glory Road* (New York: Doubleday, 1952), 67; Walker Conway to Margaret Daniel Conway [fragment, April 1863], CU; letter from a Stafford County native in the Richmond *Daily Dispatch*, June 20, 1863.

11. MC diary, December 21, 1862, CU.

12. This scene is described in three places, with slight variations: MC diary,

December 31, 1862, CU; MC, *Demonology and Devil-Lore*, 2 vols. (London: Chatto and Windus; New York: Henry Holt, 1879), I, 332–333; *AME*, I, 371–373.

13. MC diary, December 31, 1862, CU.

14. *The Commonwealth*, January 10, 1863.

15. *The Liberator*, December 26, 1862, January 9, 1863; Sarah Pugh to Mary and Harriet [Estlin], February 2, 1863, Estlin Papers, Dr. Williams's Library, London.

16. New York *Tribune*, January 29, 1863; MC diary, January 25, 1863.

17. Conway recalled this meeting in the New York *Tribune*, August 30, 1885.

18. *Ibid.*; George Luther Stearns to Ralph Waldo Emerson, February 18, 1863, Emerson Papers, HU.

19. MC to Gerrit Smith, February 27 [1863], Smith Papers, Syracuse University.

20. Ralph Waldo Emerson to William Emerson, March 11, 1863, in Ralph L. Rusk, ed., *The Letters of Ralph Waldo Emerson*, 6 vols. (New York: Columbia University Press, 1939), V, 319–320; *The Commonwealth*, April 17, 1863. Conway's letters of introduction included: Wendell Phillips to Richard Davis Webb, April 7, 1863, CU; Ralph Waldo Emerson to [Alexander] Ireland, April 9, 1863, CU; William Lloyd Garrison to [Mary] Estlin, April 10, 1863, Estlin Papers, Dr. Williams's Library, London; Garrison to Elizabeth Pease Nichol, April 10, 1863, Boston Public Library; Garrison to Andrew Paton, April 10, 1863, DC; Garrison to George Thompson, April 10, 1863, partially published in the London *Morning Star*, June 17, 1863.

21. The standard work on British and American (both Union and Confederate) diplomacy during the Civil War is Ephraim Douglass Adams, *Great Britain and the American Civil War*, 2 vols. (London: Longmans, Green and Co., 1925). A solid work synthesizing modern scholarship is Brian Jenkins, *England and the War for the Union*, 2 vols. (Montreal: McGill-Queen's University Press, 1975, 1980).

22. F. W. Chesson to Oliver Johnson, April 7, 1863, in Taylor, ed., *British and American Abolitionists*, 503; William Lloyd Garrison to Oliver Johnson, March 10, 1863, Boston Public Library.

23. MC to Gerrit Smith, February 27 [1863], Smith Papers, Syracuse University; MC to Henry Wadsworth Longfellow, March 11, 1863, Longfellow Papers, HU; MC to Israel Washburn, April 1863, Washburn Papers, Library of Congress.

24. MC to Salmon P. Chase, March 5, 1863, Chase Papers, Library of Congress. A letter from Conway to Sidney Howard Gay, March 30 [1863], Gay Papers, CU, indicates that his trip originally had been planned for March, but was postponed due to an illness suffered by his son Emerson.

25. Walker Conway to Margaret Daniel Conway [fragment—April 1863], CU.

26. MC, *My Pilgrimage to the Wise Men of the East* (Boston: Houghton Mifflin, 1906), 8; MC to EDC, April 19 [1863], CU.

27. J. Morrison Davidson, *Eminent English Liberals. In and Out of Parliament* (Boston: James R. Osgood, 1880), 25–35; *AME*, II, 57; R. B. Read to George Jacob Holyoake, July 25, 1860, Holyoake Papers, Co-operative Union, Manchester ("entire absence").

28. *AME*, II, 57, 83–84, 339; MC to EDC, April 30, May 4 ("all that I imagined"), 1863, CU.

29. *The Commonwealth*, June 5, 1863.

30. MC to William Dean Howells, May 6 [1863], Howells Papers, HU; MC to EDC, April 30, 1863 ("low-necked"), CU. Conway described his April and May explorations of London in *The Commonwealth*, May 22 ("as in the fable of"), June 19, 1863.

31. MC to EDC, April 30, May 4, May 8, 1863, CU; MC to William Dean Howells, May 6 [1863], Howells Papers, HU.

32. EDC to MC, May 15, 1863, CU.

33. MC to EDC, May 29, 1863, CU.

34. EDC to MC, June 21, 1863, CU; Bronson Alcott to his wife, March 10, 1866, in Richard L. Herrnstadt, ed., *The Letters of A. Bronson Alcott* (Ames: The Iowa State University Press, 1969), 389; Sophia Thoreau to EDC, January 1, 1869, CU.

35. "First Speech at South Place," ms at CU; MC to William Dean Howells, May 6 [1863], Howells Papers, HU; MC to EDC, May 8, 1863, CU; London *Morning Star*, May 4, 7, 1863; *The Commonwealth*, June 5, 1863. Re later meetings see the *Morning Star*, May 4, 1863, and *The Commonwealth*, June 12, 1863.

36. The quotation is from MC to William Dean Howells, May 6 [1863], Howells Papers, HU.

37. C. F. Adams diary, May 16, 21, 1863, Adams Papers, Massachusetts Historical Society.

38. William Dean Howells to MC, May 12 [1863], CU. This is a copy in MC's handwriting. He had sent the original on to Ellen. MC to Howells, May 16 [1863], Howells Papers, HU.

39. London *Morning Star*, May 19, 1863; MC letter in *The Commonwealth*, June 12, 1863.

40. *AME*, I, 221–222.

41. MC to EDC, May 29, 1863, CU; Poem by MC, June 1, 1863, ms, CU; MC to William Dean Howells, May 16, June 10 [1863], Howells Papers, HU; C. F. Adams diary, June 15, 16, 1863 (rain), Massachusetts Historical Society.

42. *The Commonwealth*, June 12, 1863.

43. The Conway-Mason correspondence can be found in *AME*, I, 413–415. It appeared in *The Times* (London) on June 18, 1863.

44. *Ibid.*

45. MC to James Murray Mason (draft, not sent), June 14, 1863, CU; *AME*, I, 417.

46. MC to EDC, June 15, 1863, CU. Re the London Tavern meeting see *The Times* (London), London *Morning Star*, and London *Daily News*, June 17, 1863; London *Daily Telegraph*, June 18, 1863; New York *Herald*, July 1, 1863; *The Liberator*, July 10, 1863. In its account of the meeting, on June 26, 1863, *The Commonwealth* referred with concern to rumors circulating about Conway's proposal to Mason.

47. James Murray Mason to MC, June 17, 1863, in *AME*, I, 415; Mason to Judah P. Benjamin, June 20, 1863 (Diplomatic Dispatch #40), in Dispatch Book, 1862–1865, Mason Papers, Library of Congress. This dispatch is published in full in Virginia Mason, *The Public Life and Diplomatic Correspondence of James M. Mason, With Some Personal History* (New York and Washington: The Neale

Publishing Company, 1906), 416–419. A more accessible collection of Mason's diplomatic correspondence is in the second volume of James D. Richardson, ed., *The Messages and Papers of Jefferson Davis and the Confederacy, Including Diplomatic Correspondence, 1861–1865*, 2 vols. (New York: Chelsea House—Robert Hector, 1966). This collection, however, omits considerable material—including all references to the Conway affair—without informing the reader. For example, it prints Dispatch #40 (510-512), but deletes two paragraphs, including a long one on Conway, without any indication that anything has been left out.

48. James Murray Mason to MC, June 17, 1863, in *AME*, I, 415.

49. James Spence to James Murray Mason, June 19, 1863, Mason Papers, Library of Congress.

50. *AME*, I, 419. Re the Manchester meeting see *The Commonwealth*, July 17, 1863.

51. London *Morning Star*, June 19, 1863.

52. Conway's letter to *The Commonwealth* appeared in the July 10 issue. See also *The Liberator*, July 20, 1863. Newspaper sources differ as to whether Conway's initial explanatory letter was written on June 21 or June 22.

53. *AME*, I, 418, 420, 425; Richard Cobden to John Bright, April 24, 1863, Bright Papers, British Library; Worthington Chauncey Ford, ed., *A Cycle of Adams Letters, 1861–1865*, 2 vols. (Boston: Houghton Mifflin, 1920), II, 40–43; MC to William Dean Howells, May 6 [1863], Howells Papers, HU. Re Roebuck's resolution see Jenkins, *op. cit.*, II, 309–313.

54. Charles Francis Adams to William Henry Seward, June 25, 1863, published in *The Liberator*, February 5, 1864; MC to Seward, June 28, 1863, Seward Papers, University of Rochester.

55. C. F. Adams diary, September 15, 23 (quotation), 1863, Adams Papers, Massachusetts Historical Society; MC diary fragment, September 23, 1863, CU; MC to Frank Sanborn, September 23 [1863], CU.

56. MC to EDC, [June 20 ? 1863], June 23 [1863], CU.

57. MC to EDC, June 23 [1863], CU.

58. MC to EDC, July 6, 1863, CU; *AME*, I, 428–432; Kenneth S. Lynn, *William Dean Howells: An American Life* (New York: Harcourt Brace Jovanovich, 1971), 114–117. Lynn mistakenly makes Ellen present on this trip. Howells wrote to fellow writer Edmund Clarence Stedman: "Conway of the Conway and Mason correspondence spent two weeks with us this summer—a sadder and a wiser man for his essay in diplomacy. I suffered with him, for we were friends in America, and his error seemed more calamitous than it has turned out to be." Howells to Stedman, August 16, 1863, in Mildred Howells, ed., *Life in Letters of William Dean Howells*, 2 vols. (New York: Doubleday, 1928), I, 66.

59. MC to EDC, July 14 [1863], CU.

60. MC to EDC, July 22 [1863], CU; *The Commonwealth*, August 21, 1863. The Concord house sold for $4,200. The Conways had bought it for $4,000 the previous summer. MS material on the "Frost house" at the Concord Free Library, Concord, Mass.

61. Frank Sanborn to EDC, June 27, 1863, DC; *The Commonwealth*, June 26, 1863; EDC to MC, June 30 [1863], CU.

62. Frank Sanborn to MC, July [1863], CU; *The Essex Statesman* (Salem, Mass.), July 15, 1863; London *Morning Star*, August 18, 1863; Undated clipping from an unidentified Alton, Ill. newspaper, in newspaper scrapbook, CU. MC

alludes to his conscription in a letter to William Dean Howells, August 5 [1863], Howells Papers, HU.

63. Wendell Phillips to EDC, July 1, 1863, McKim-Garrison Papers, New York Public Library; Charles Eliot Norton to Charles Sumner, June 30, 1863, in Sumner letter-book, Vol. 64, HU; Samuel J. May, Jr., to Richard Davis Webb, July 1, 1863, May Papers, Boston Public Library. One of Sumner's female constituents did think Conway's plan was "well worthy of consideration by our Government." She suggested that John Greenleaf Whittier might want to serve on a commission to carry it through. Ellie Winslow to Sumner, June 30, 1863, in Sumner letter-book, Vol. 64, HU.

64. *The Liberator*, July 3, 1863.

65. *The Liberator*, July 10, 1863; *The Commonwealth*, July 10, 1863; *National Anti-Slavery Standard*, July 18, 1863.

66. MC to EDC, July 22 [1863], CU.

67. Phillips is quoted in *The Commonwealth*, July 10, 1863.

68. MC, *My Pilgrimage*, 25–26 ("outlawry"); *AME*, II, 45 ("militant America"); MC to William Lloyd Garrison II, July 22, 1899, Garrison Family Papers, Smith College ("usefulness"); William Lloyd Garrison to Oliver Johnson, July 14, 1863, Boston Public Library; George Stearns to MC, July 15, 1863, CU; Frank Sanborn to MC, August 16, 1863, CU; Wendell Phillips to MC, March 16, 1864, CU.

69. Boston *Transcript*, July 2, 1863; New York *Tribune* quoted in *The Liberator*, July 17, 1863; *Harper's Weekly* quoted in *National Anti-Slavery Standard*, August 1, 1863. See also New York *Herald*, July 2, 1863; Chicago *Tribune*, July 3, 1863; Cincinnati *Gazette*, July 2, 1863.

70. *The Commonwealth*, July 10, 1863.

CHAPTER 9

1. South Place Chapel Minute Books, January–February 1864, January 1865, January 1866, South Place Ethical Society, Conway Hall, London; *The Liberator*, February 26, 1884; MC to William Dean Howells, January 10 [1864], HU.

2. MC, *Testimonies Concerning Slavery* (London: Chapman and Hall, 1864). For examples of Conway's continuing antislavery activities, see an account of his speech at a farewell soiree for George Thompson, in *The Liberator*, February 12, 1864, and a flyer publicizing his appearance before the Ladies' Negro's Friend Society, May 12, 1864, bound in a volume entitled *English Papers*, rare book room, CU.

3. *Westminster Review*, Vol. XXVI, New Series No. II (October 1, 1864), 502–503; London *Morning Star* quoted in *The Liberator*, September 23, 1864. See also the *National Anti-Slavery Standard*, October 8, 1864, and Thomas Hughes to MC, October 18, 1864, CU.

4. MC, *The Golden Hour* (Boston: Ticknor and Fields, 1862), 125.

5. Re the Anthropological Society see John W. Burrow, "Evolution and Anthropology in the 1860's: The Anthropological Society of London, 1863–1871," *Victorian Studies* 7 (1963), 137–154; and Ronald Rainger, "Race, Politics,

and Science: The Anthropological Society of London in the 1860's," *Victorian Studies* 22 (1978), 50–70. See also *AME*, II, 1–2.

6. MC, *Testimonies*, 56–77.

7. *Ibid.*, 70–77.

8. *Ibid.*, 71. In an article, "The Negro as Artist," *The Radical*, Vol. II (September 1866), 39–42, Conway called attention to the plight of gifted black American actors, who usually had to go to Europe to find work. His article elicited a poignant letter of thanks from one of the actors described. S. Morgan Smith to MC, October 13, 1866, CU.

9. *The Commonwealth*, April 22, 1865.

10. MC, *Testimonies*, 60–61. See MC, "Benjamin Banneker, The Negro Astronomer," *The Atlantic Monthly*, Vol. XI, No. LXIII (January 1863), 79–84. This was reprinted in England as Tract #9 of the Ladies' Emancipation Society in April 1864. Banneker's best biographer calls it "one of the most substantive" publications about him. Silvio A. Bedini, *The Life of Benjamin Banneker* (New York: Charles Scribner's Sons, 1972), 296.

11. MC, "The Massacre at Jamaica," *The Radical*, Vol. II (December 1866), 200; MC, *Testimonies*, 66–67. See also Conway's South Place address, "On the question of the negro," reported in the *National Anti-Slavery Standard*, December 15, 1866.

12. Mary Elizabeth Burtis has suggested that *Testimonies Concerning Slavery* may have gone unpublished in the United States "because no publisher would have wished to assume responsibility" for a book that sanctioned "interracial relationships." This is unconvincing, since racial intermarriage was already being debated in American books and newspapers. See, for example, an advertisement for a book entitled *Miscegenation* in *The Liberator*, February 12, 1864. Conway's book was specifically designed for a British audience, and there is no evidence he tried to publish it anywhere else. See Burtis, *Moncure Conway, 1832–1907* (New Brunswick, N.J.: Rutgers University Press, 1952), 115.

13. See James M. McPherson, *The Struggle For Equality: Abolitionists and the Negro in the Civil War and Reconstruction* (Princeton: Princeton University Press, 1964), 240–246; *The Commonwealth*, December 25, 1863, January 1, 1864.

14. At the convention of the Massachusetts Anti-Slavery Society in January 1864, a resolution of no-confidence in the administration, moved by Phillips, passed by a small margin. A similar resolution passed by three votes at the American Anti-Slavery Society's national convention in May. McPherson, 260–261, 268.

15. Wendell Phillips to MC, March 16, 1864, CU; MC to William Dean Howells, May 11 [1864], Howells Papers, HU; MC to John Emory McClintock, July 21 [1864], DC; Frank Sanborn to MC, May 3, 1864, CU, and June 3, 1864, DC; McPherson, 267–270.

16. Frank Sanborn to MC, May 3, 1864, CU.

17. Excerpts from Conway's letter were reprinted in the *National Anti-Slavery Standard*, June 25, 1864. By order of the War Department, all black enlisted men—there were no black officers—received $7 a month, compared with a monthly minimum of $13 and maximum of $21 for white enlisted men. The inequity in wages was rectified retroactively in the summer of 1864 for black regiments recruited in the North, and in 1865 for regiments of ex-slaves recruited in the South. See McPherson, *op. cit.*, 217; James M. McPherson, *The*

Negro's Civil War (New York: Vintage, 1967), 201; Dudley Taylor Cornish, *The Sable Arm: Negro Troops in the Union Army, 1861–1865* (New York: Norton, 1956), 181–196.

18. *National Anti-Slavery Standard*, June 25, 1864.

19. William Lloyd Garrison to Helen Garrison, June 8, 11, 1864, in Clare Taylor, ed., *British and American Abolitionists* (Edinburgh: Edinburgh University Press, 1974), 522; McPherson, *Struggle For Equality*, 294–295.

20. Benjamin Emerson, 2d to William Lloyd Garrison, in *The Liberator*, July 29, 1864; Octavius Brooks to Frothingham to MC, January 2, 1865, CU; Samuel May, Jr., to Richard Davis Webb, September 13, 1864, May Papers, Boston Public Library; Frank Sanborn to MC, September 16, 1864, DC.

21. The quotation is from James Brewer Stewart, *Holy Warriors* (New York: Hill and Wang, 1976), 183. Before the abolitionist split in 1864–65, Conway thought Garrison took Phillips for granted. Emerson: "Conway says, that when Phillips speaks, Garrison observes delighted the effect on the audience and seems to see and hear everything except Phillips; is the only one in the audience who does not hear and understand Phillips." It was, in fact, remarkable that Phillips accepted so cheerfully and so long a subordinate role to Garrison in the American Anti-Slavery Society—more remarkable than his ultimate rebellion. Garrison indeed may have taken him for granted, mistaking his voluntary subordination for an acknowledgement of Garrison's superior abilities. Surely Garrison was surprised when Phillips moved against him. I suspect, again, that Phillips's confidence and breeding helped lead Garrison to underestimate him. He had never seriously challenged Garrison before, because the latter was performing well and because his own ego did not require a formal position of leadership. Edward Waldo Emerson and Waldo Emerson Forbes, eds., *Journals of Ralph Waldo Emerson*, 10 vols. (Boston: Houghton Mifflin, 1913), IX, 455.

22. Wendell Phillips to MC, July 16, 1864, McKim-Garrison Papers, New York Public Library.

23. *National Anti-Slavery Standard*, August 27, 1864.

24. *Ibid.*

25. *Ibid.*

26. *AME*, II, 10–13.

27. *Ibid.*

28. *Ibid.*; MC to William Dean Howells, October 18 [1864], Howells Papers, HU.

29. *AME*, II, 13–14. Conway wrote notes on his conversation with Strauss (apparently now lost) shortly after it occurred, and quoted from these in his autobiography.

30. *Ibid.*

31. *AME*, II, 15. Conway paid tribute to Ostend's charms in his novel *Prisons of Air* (New York: John W. Lovell Company, 1891), 201.

32. *AME*, II, 15.

33. *National Anti-Slavery Standard*, August 27, 1864.

34. *National Anti-Slavery Standard*, November 19, 1864.

35. *Ibid.*

36. Francis William Newman to Epes Sargent, September 7, 1864, Boston Public Library; *The Liberator*, November 25, 1864.

37. *The Liberator*, December 2, 1864.

38. *The Liberator*, January 20, 1865; Wendell Phillips to MC, January 18, 1865, McKim-Garrison Papers, New York Public Library; George Stearns to MC, March 13, 1865, CU.

39. *The Liberator*, December 9, 1864.

40. *Ibid.*

41. *National Anti-Slavery Standard*, November 19, 1864.

42. Wendell Phillips to MC, July 16, 1864, McKim-Garrison Papers, New York Public Library.

43. *The Commonwealth*, February 3, 1865.

44. George Fredrickson, *The Inner Civil War: Northern Intellectuals and the Crisis of the Union* (New York: Harper and Row, 1965), 127.

45. MC, "President Lincoln," *Fraser's Magazine*, Vol. LXXI, No. CCCCXXI (January 1865), 20–21. Early in 1865 the Confederacy did, in fact, move toward at least partial, compensated emancipation in a desperate effort to gain moral stature in the North and abroad and thus salvage political independence. But by then the military momentum was so overwhelmingly on the side of the Union that no political or moral gesture, however revolutionary, could end the killing short of total Confederate defeat. See Robert F. Durden, *The Gray and the Black: The Confederate Debate on Emancipation* (Baton Rouge: Louisiana State University Press, 1972), 147–156; Emory M. Thomas, *The Confederate Nation: 1861–1865* (New York: Harper and Row, 1979), 290–294.

46. MC, "President Lincoln," *op. cit.*, 20.

47. *AME*, I, 221.

48. MC, "President Lincoln," *op. cit.*, 20.

49. MC to EDC, September 14 [1875], CU.

50. Margaret Daniel Conway to MC, May 2, 1865, CU; Fredericksburg *Ledger*, June 10, 1865; *AME*, II, 300–301.

51. Margaret Daniel Conway to MC, May 2, 1865; MC to EDC, October 6–7, 1875 (quotation); Peter Conway to MC, March 1884, CU.

52. MC to Margaret Daniel Conway, January 23, 1866, CU.

53. J. A. Froude to MC, June 3 [1866], Huntington Library; October 15, December 20, 26 [1866], CU; John Stuart Mill to MC, August 10, October 23, 1865, CU; F. W. Newman to MC, August 4, 1865, CU; John Bright to MC, September 27, 1866, CU; MC, "The American 'Radicals' and their English Censors," *The Fortnightly Review* 18 (February 1, 1866), 705–720; MC, "The Purpose and the President of the United States," *Fraser's Magazine*, Vol. LXXV, No. CCCCXLV (February 1867), 243–261; MC, "The New Rebellion in America," *Fraser's Magazine*, Vol. LXXVI, No. CCCCLV (November 1867), 622–637; *London Review*, November 30, 1867; MC, "The Internal Conflict of America," *The Fortnightly Review*, Vol. III, New Series No. XV (March 1, 1868), 311–318. For representative Conway letters in *The Commonwealth*, see issues of May 13, 20, June 24, July 8, 22, December 2, 1865.

54. *AME*, II, 45.

POSTSCRIPT

1. MS "Letter from Virginia," October 1876, CU.

2. MS speech before the Free Religious Association, May 1898, CU.

3. *The Times* (London), obituary of MC, November 19, 1907. Conway died on November 15.

4. Journal entry (c. 1900) in notebook also containing "Notes for Reminiscences," CU; MC to Herbert Burrows, May 15, 1903, in *Emerson's Centenary: His Thought and Teaching, A South Place Lecture by Herbert Burrows, With a Letter by Dr. Moncure D. Conway* (London: A. Bonner, 1903), 14. Conway had received an honorary doctorate from Dickinson College in 1892.

5. MC, "The World set in Hawthorne's Heart," in T. W. Higginson, ed., *The Hawthorne Centenary Celebration at the Wayside, Concord, Massachusetts, July 4–7, 1904* (Boston and New York: Houghton Mifflin, 1905), 123; MC's review of *The Marble Faun* in *The Dial*, Vol. I, No. 4 (April 1860), 262.

6. MC to Herbert Burrows, *op. cit.*; MC's speech to the Free Religious Association in *The Free Religious Association: Proceedings at the Thirty-first Annual Meeting* (Boston: the Free Religious Association, 1898), 28.

7. Edward Steichen to Eustace Conway [November 1907], DC.

BIBLIOGRAPHICAL NOTE

The only previous biography of Moncure Conway was written as a dissertation in the English department at Columbia University by Mary Elizabeth Burtis, published as *Moncure Conway, 1832–1907* (New Brunswick, N.J.: Rutgers University Press, 1952). This is a competent book, despite a few minor errors, but it lacks historical context and depth. It is more narrative than analytical, more plodding than creative. Perhaps the worst that can be said of it is that it makes its fascinating subject look dull.

Whatever else Conway was, he was not dull—and lately historians have begun to appreciate both his fascination and his importance. The revival of interest in him by historians dates from George Fredrickson's *The Inner Civil War: Northern Intellectuals and the Crisis of the Union* (New York: Harper and Row, 1965). Fredrickson's thesis is that anti-institutionalist antebellum reformers regained their faith in institutions—even acquired a fondness for them—in the wake of their Civil War experience. Since the Conway-Mason affair compelled many Garrisonian reformers to explicitly repudiate—pleading changed circumstances—their prewar philosophy, that episode, and Conway himself, are important to Fredrickson's book.

In biographical detail Fredrickson is off at times: he implies that Conway had been a prewar Garrisonian, accepts the misconception that Conway truly was sent to England by the abolitionists, and exaggerates the extent of Conway's withdrawal from political activism after 1863. But he is right in contending that Conway's actions in 1863 highlighted an important philosophical shift by many reformers. Fredrickson also performs a signal service by taking Conway seriously, by pointing to Conway's autobiography as a significant book, and by alerting others to the richness of the issues suggested by Conway's life.

Until now the most important book dealing in more detail with Conway's American years has been Peter Walker's *Moral Choices: Memory,*

Desire, and Imagination in Nineteenth-Century American Abolitionism (Baton Rouge: Louisiana State University Press, 1978), 3–86. Walker's objective was to understand why a man of Conway's social background became an abolitionist. (He also examines Jane Swisshelm, Frederick Douglass, Henry C. Wright, Salmon P. Chase, and Thomas M. Cooley.) His sources are primarily the autobiography, *Testimonies Concerning Slavery*, the novel *Pine and Palm*, and Conway's letters from his mother.

To Walker, Conway's need both to consummate and escape his "carnal love for his mother" provides "the core of the elusive *why* of his life." Walker contends (misleadingly, I think) that in his autobiography Conway downplayed his mother's antislavery feelings, for he was still unable to face her central influence on him, or his own feelings for her. In *Pine and Palm*, his semi-autobiographical protagonist's marriage to Gisela Stirling, an antislavery Southerner, safely "allows Conway to express and consummate his love for his mother." A character based more explicitly on Margaret Conway would have been, says Walker, "too frighteningly overwhelming" for Moncure to handle.

Conway's mother, and the demons she supposedly aroused in him, are never far from center stage in Walker's book. In Carlisle, Walker says, Conway was driven to pursue Kate Emory in an effort to "save himself," to transcend and put to rest his carnal Oedipal desire. Kate was "most of all" why he had a conversion experience. The "stunning blow" of the news that she was engaged to another enabled, even in part spurred, Conway to leave Methodism. Walker dismisses Conway's alternate account of these events as "prevarication."

I agree that Margaret Conway was central to Moncure's life, but sharply disagree with Walker's rigidly psychoanalytic interpretation. The latter not only lies far outside the domain of proof, it is also unhelpful, for it trivializes Conway by basing his actions (despite an occasional qualification) in psychic idiosyncrasy rather than in a mix of idiosyncrasy and culture. All social and cultural context is absent from Walker's theorizing: the specifics of the father's world, the role every Conway son was expected to play, the importance of Peyton's death, the numerous other influential women around young Moncure, the women's world and what it represented. Even Ellen Conway is a shadow, given five cursory paragraphs and no real personality. She is but a device supplying her husband (though Walker acknowledges she was "about Conway's own age"—in fact she was fifteen months younger) "with the strengths he had always sought from older women."

Revealingly, Walker uses only Margaret's letters to Moncure, not his to her. A use of the correspondence as a whole would have shown two strong personalities confiding in each other and arguing as mutually respectful equals. In short, it would have shown a man greatly influenced and partly shaped by his mother but in no way dominated or haunted by her. For Margaret most affected Moncure not by dominating him— that came from his father—but by teaching him to resist domination.

She, in common with other women and more than any man until Emerson, encouraged him to find, and be, himself.

Walker's account demonstrates the pitfalls of disembodied psychohistory. An imaginative *tour de force*, it is inadequate as biography or history. It relies, literally, more on Bruno Bettelheim and Erik Erikson than on the people of antebellum Stafford County.

My work constitutes an effort to reconstruct and draw meaning more productively from that life which Fredrickson's book introduced me to as an undergraduate. A companion volume (though intended, as is this one, to stand alone), *The Transatlantic Years*, is in preparation. For now, readers wishing to see more on Conway's later life can ferret out my pamphlet, *Moncure Conway: American Abolitionist, Spiritual Architect of South Place, Author of "The Life of Thomas Paine"* (London: South Place Ethical Society, 1977).

The present work is based heavily upon research in primary sources, the core of which—manuscript collections, documents, newspapers, and magazines—is listed here. Also listed are Conway's books and major pamphlets. Conway was a discursive writer, and even the books he wrote in later life—no matter what the subject—provide both insight into and glimpses of his American years. Other books, and miscellaneous minor sources, are cited in the notes.

SOURCES

MANUSCRIPT COLLECTIONS

Charles Francis Adams Papers, Massachusetts Historical Society, Boston
Henry Bellows Papers, Massachusetts Historical Society
John Bright Papers, British Library, London
Salmon P. Chase Papers, Library of Congress, Washington, D.C.
Moncure Conway Papers, Columbia University, New York
Moncure Conway Papers, Dickinson College, Carlisle, Pennsylvania
Caroline Dall Papers, Massachusetts Historical Society
Dickinson College Archives, Dickinson College
Ralph Waldo Emerson Papers, Houghton Library, Harvard University, Cambridge, Massachusetts
Estlin Family Papers, Dr. Williams's Library, London
Garrison Family Papers, Smith College, Northampton, Massachusetts
William Lloyd Garrison Papers, Boston Public Library
Sidney Howard Gay Papers, Columbia University
Horace Greeley Papers, New York Public Library
William Greene Papers, Cincinnati Historical Society
Harvard University Archives, Pusey Library, Harvard University
Thomas Wentworth Higginson Papers, Houghton Library
George Jacob Holyoake Papers, Co-operative Union, Manchester, England
William Dean Howells Papers, Houghton Library
Oliver Johnson Papers, Boston Public Library
Samuel Johnson Papers, Essex Institute, Salem, Massachusetts
Abraham Lincoln Papers, Library of Congress
Henry Wadsworth Longfellow Papers, Houghton Library
James Murray Mason Papers, Library of Congress
Samuel May, Jr., Papers, Boston Public Library
McKim-Garrison Papers, New York Public Library
Methodist Church Records, United Methodist Church, Fredericksburg, Virginia
Whitelaw Reid Papers, Library of Congress
William Henry Seward Papers, University of Rochester, Rochester, New York
Gerrit Smith Papers, Syracuse University, Syracuse, New York

267

South Place Chapel Records, South Place Ethical Society, Conway Hall, London
Edmund Clarence Stedman Papers, Columbia University
Charles Sumner Papers, Houghton Library
Unitarian Church Records, Cincinnati Historical Society
Israel Washburn Papers, Library of Congress

DOCUMENTS

Civil War Muster Rolls, Stafford County Courthouse, Stafford, Virginia
Stafford County Land Tax Records, Virginia State Library, Richmond
United States Census, Stafford County, Virginia, 1830–1860
Will Books, Stafford County Courthouse, Stafford, Virginia

NEWSPAPERS

Carlisle, Pennsylvania *American Volunteer*
Carlisle, Pennsylvania *Herald*
Christian Examiner (New York)
Christian Inquirer (New York)
Cincinnati *Commercial*
Cincinnati *Gazette*
The Commonwealth (Boston)
Fredericksburg, Virginia *Christian Banner*
Fredericksburg, Virginia *Weekly Advertiser*
Fredericksburg, Virginia *Weekly Recorder*
Harper's Weekly (New York)
The Index
The Liberator (Boston)
London *Daily News*
London *Morning Star*
London *Times*
The Nation (New York)
National Anti-Slavery Standard (New York)
National Intelligencer (Washington, D.C.)
New York Times
New York *Tribune*
Richmond, Virginia *Dispatch*
Richmond, Virginia *Examiner*

MAGAZINES

The Arena
Atlantic Monthly
Blackwood's Edinburgh Magazine
Christian Advocate and Journal
The Collegian (Dickinson College)
The Critic

The Dial (Cincinnati)
The Fortnightly Review
The Forum
Fraser's Magazine
Harper's New Monthly Magazine
Magazine of American History
Methodist Quarterly Review
The Open Court
The Radical
Southern Literary Messenger
Westminster Review

PUBLICATIONS BY MONCURE CONWAY

BOOKS

Addresses and Reprints. Boston and New York: Houghton Mifflin, 1909.

Autobiography, Memories and Experiences. 2 vols. Boston and New York: Houghton Mifflin, 1904.

Barons of the Potomack and Rappahannock. The Grolier Club, 1892.

Centenary History of the South Place Society. London: Williams and Norgate, 1894.

Demonology and Devil-Lore. 2 vols. London: Chatto and Windus, 1879; New York: Henry Holt, 1879.

The Earthward Pilgrimage. London: John Camden Hotten, 1870; New York: Henry Holt, 1874; London: Chatto and Windus, 1876.

Emerson at Home and Abroad. Boston: J. R. Osgood, 1882; London: Trübner, 1883.

Farewell Discourses. London: E. W. Allen, 1884.

George Washington and Mount Vernon. Brooklyn: Long Island Historical Society, 1889.

George Washington's Rules of Civility. New York: United States Book Company, 1890.

The Golden Hour. Boston: Ticknor and Fields, 1862.

Idols and Ideals. New York: Henry Holt, 1877.

Lessons for the Day. London: Watts, 1907.

Life of Nathaniel Hawthorne. New York: A. Lovell, 1890; London: Walter Scott, 1890.

The Life of Thomas Paine. New York and London: G. P. Putnam's Sons, 1892.

My Pilgrimage to the Wise Men of the East. Boston and New York: Houghton Mifflin, 1906.

A Necklace of Stories. London: Chatto and Windus, 1880.

Omitted Chapters of History Disclosed in the Life and Papers of Edmund Randolph. New York and London: G. P. Putnam's Sons, 1888.

Pine and Palm. New York: Henry Holt, 1887; London: Chatto and Windus, 1887.

Prisons of Air. New York: John W. Lovell, 1891.

The Rejected Stone: or, Insurrection vs. Resurrection in America. Boston: Walker, Wise and Company, 1861.

Republican Superstitions as Illustrated in the Political History of America. London: Henry S. King, 1872.

Solomon and Solomonic Literature. Chicago: The Open Court Publishing Company; London: Kegan Paul, Trench, Trübner and Company, 1899.

Testimonies Concerning Slavery. London: Chapman and Hall, 1864.

Thomas Carlyle. London: Chatto and Windus, 1881; New York, Harper and Brothers, 1881.

Thomas Paine et la Revolution dans les Deux Mondes. Paris: Plon Nourrit, 1900.

Tracts for Today. Cincinnati: Truman and Spofford, 1858.

Travels in South Kensington. London: Trübner, 1882; New York: Harper and Brothers, 1882.

The Wandering Jew. London: Chatto and Windus; New York: Henry Holt, 1881.

MAJOR WORKS EDITED AND COMPILED

The Sacred Anthology: A Book of Ethnical Scriptures. London: Trübner, 1874; New York: Henry Holt, 1874.

The Writings of Thomas Paine. 4 vols. New York: G. P. Putnam's Sons, 1894–96.

MAJOR PAMPHLETS

Christianity. London: Trübner, 1876.

Consequences. London: Thomas Scott, 1875.

East and West: An Inaugural Discourse Delivered in the First Congregational Church, Cincinnati, O. Cincinnati: Truman and Spofford, 1859.

The First Love Again: A Discourse Delivered in the Church of the Redeemer, Cincinnati, Ohio, November 28, 1875, on the Occasion of the Reunion of the Two Societies, Which Had Divided Fifteen Years Previously, Chiefly on the Issue of Supernaturalism. London: Waterlow and Sons, 1875.

Free Schools in Virginia: A Plea of Education, Virtue and Thrift, vs. Ignorance, Vice and Poverty. Fredericksburg, Virginia: Office of the *Recorder*, 1850.

Intellectual Suicide. London: Waterlow and Sons, 1875.

A Last Word. Spoken at the Athenaeum on the Closing of Our Services There, June 27th, 1880. London: Waterlow and Sons, 1880.

The Natural History of the Devil. Albany, New York: Ladies' Religious Publication Society, 1859.

The Old and the New. Washington, D.C.: Buell and Blanchard, 1855.

The One Path: or, The Duties of North and South. Washington, D.C.: Buell and Blanchard, 1856.

Our Cause and Its Claims Upon Us. London: G. Levey, 1876.

The Peril of War. London: Waterlow and Sons, 1878.

Pharisaism and Fasting. Washington, D.C.: Buell and Blanchard, 1855.

Revivalism. London: Waterlow and Sons, 1876.

Spiritual Liberty. Washington, D.C.: Buell and Blanchard, 1856.

The Theater. Cincinnati: Truman and Spofford, 1857.

Thomas Paine: A Celebration. Cincinnati: Office of *The Dial,* 1860.
The True and the False in Prevalent Theories of Divine Dispensations. Washington,
    D.C.: Taylor and Maury, 1855.
Unbelief: Its Nature, Cause, and Cure. London: Waterlow and Sons, 1877.
Virtue vs. Defeat. Cincinnati: Cincinnati *Gazette* Company, 1856.

INDEX

Abbot, Francis Ellingwood, 141
Abolitionism: and Civil War, 151, 179,
210, 214–15; and *The Commonwealth*,
172–75; Conway's views of, 17, 81–
87, 199–201, 205–10, 212–15,
259n21; and emancipation, 154, 159,
164–65, 174, 216; and Framingham
rally, 197–98; and interracial marriage, 19–20; and John Brown, 145–
48; and Lincoln, 179–80, 198, 206–9,
212–13, 215; moral aspects of, 17,
145; and religion, 100–101, 157;
Southern women's views of, 15; and
violence, 146–48, 151. *See also* Eman-
cipation; Mason affair; Slavery
Adams, Charles Francis, 187–88, 193–94
Adams, Henry, 73, 193
Alcott, Bronson, 71, 186
Allen, William Henry, 29
Ames, Charles Gordon, 135–36
Andrew, James, 25
Andrew, John, 84, 171, 206
Antietam, battle of, 174–75
Asbury, Francis, 23
Atlanta, battle of, 212
Aylett, Patrick Henry, 91

Baird, Spencer Fullerton, 29
Banneker, Benjamin, 205
Bellows, Henry Whitney, 127–33, 134,
140
Besant, Annie, 66, 115–16
Biddle, William, 31
Birney, James, 17
Blackford, Mary Minor, 13, 14

Blacks: women compared to, 204–5. *See
also* Emancipation; Slavery
Blatch, Harriot Stanton, xi–xii
Brent, William, 90–91
Bright, John, 183, 191, 192
Brooke, Roger, 53–54, 59
Brown, John, 88, 145–48, 159–60
Buchanan, James, 114, 149
Burnap, George: and Conway's atten-
dance at Harvard Divinity School, 71,
72; and Dickinson College, 60; on
evil, 73; as mainstream Unitarian, 97,
98, 100, 128–29, 130–31; personality
of, 242n21
Burns (Anthony) affair, 82–84, 90–91,
240n30, 240n34
Burtis, Mary, 258 n12, 263
Butler, Benjamin, 206

Cairnes, John Elliot, 212
Caldwell, Merritt, 29
Carlyle, Thomas, 52, 184
Chancellorsville, battle of, 188–89
Channing, William Ellery, 39, 127
Channing, William Henry, 90, 109, 161–
62, 167
Chase, Salmon P., 114, 206
Chesnut, Mary Boykin, 12–13, 14, 18
Child, Lydia Maria, 18–19, 74, 134
Christian doctrine, 72–75, 97–101, 105,
119–22, 123, 127–31, 133–35, 140–41
Christian Inquirer. See Bellows, Henry
Whitney
Cincinnati: Conway's ministry in, 112,
113–14, 116, 119–27, 135–36, 156–

275